BṚHADĀRAṆYAKA-UPANIṢAD

BṚHADĀRAṆYAKA-UPANIṢAD

Text in Sanskrit and Translation with Notes in English from the Commentaries of Śaṅkarācārya and the Gloss of Ānandagiri

By

DR. E. ROER

WITH A PREFACE BY

PROF. MANILAL N. DVIVEDI

BKP

BHARATIYA KALA PRAKASHAN
DELHI (INDIA)

First Edition : 2000
Second Edition : 2013

ISBN : 978-81-86050-61-3 (H.B.)
ISBN : 978-81-8090-355-7 (P.B.)

Published by
BHARATIYA KALA PRAKASHAN
3421-A, IInd Floor, Narang Colony,
Tri Nagar, Delhi-110035.
Phone : 27393083, 32967505
Website : www.bkbooks.com
Online Partner : www.booksnyou.com

Laser Typesetting by : **Twinkle Graphics,** Delhi-110(

Printed at : G.S. Offset Printers Delhi

PREFACE

THE chronology of the Old Testament has influenced almost all the speculations of Oriental scholars in regard to the possible date of the *Vedas* and the *Upaniṣads.* It is very difficult to say anything with positive confidence on this subject, but this much is certain, that the Upaniṣads, at least the ten principal ones, are not in any way posterior to the *Vedas.* The argument that a philosophy like that embodied in the Upaniṣads cannot exist side by side with the nature-worship of the *Vedas,* loses its force when the *Suktas* of the *Veda* are regarded as symbolic only of those esoteric truths which were taught through the *Upaniṣads* to the select few. Symbology helps the solution of many a riddle over which philology has either sat in despair or which it has understood only to misunderstand. The history of all the great religions of the world shows, that there is nothing inconsistent in the possible existence of a sublime philosophy with the empty formalities of popular religion. And this circumstance in itself is an indirect argument against the later origin of the *Vedas* and the *Upaniṣads.*

Veda means knowledge, and *Upaniṣad* means both the exoteric philosophy of *Brahman*, the *Advaita*, and sittings for the discussion of that philosophy. The *Upaniṣads* are aptly called the *Vedānta*, the end of the *Veda*, that which is reserved for those who have freed themselves from the useless bonds of formal religion. The *Veda* consists of three parts: *Mantra*, *Brāhmaṇa* and *Upaniṣad*, including the *Āraṇyakas*. The *Mantra* portion contains hymns addressed to various powers, all symbolic of important truths intended, on the one hand, to teach the religion of faith and forms to the ignorant, and the philosophy of sublime unity to the initiated, on the other. The one is the *Karma-mārga*, the religion of *forms*, and the other is the *Jnāna-mārga*, the religion of philosophy or knowledge. There is a way between the two, leading from *Karma* to *Jnāna*, called *Upāsanā*, or the invoking of any particular power of nature. This is different from the general *Karma-mārga*, inasmuch as *Karma* does not mean anything performed with a special aim and for a special purpose. *Karma-mārga* is only the general religion of faith which leads to *Upāsanā* and *Jnāna*. The word *Karma* should in this place not be confounded with that philosophical law of necessity which is called by that name.

The *Upaniṣads* teach the philosophy of absolute unity. By unity is meant the oneness of the subject, all experience of objective existence being regarded as in and of it. Experience implies consciousness, and consciousness, apperception or "pure reason" is the only reliable, self-illumined, absolute factor of our knowledge. All else is but mere representation in and through the mode of this consciousness. The world of being is nothing, considered apart from consciousness which, in its turn, is entirely independent of experience. It cannot in any manner be negatived, for the very negation implies its existence. This is the realm of the absolute, ever-existent, *Brahman*, an abstraction appropriately expressing this idea of unity in duality, being a term expressive of the whole of that which can be none other than a compound of Thought and Being.

This Absolute is not the Unknowable of Agnosticism, nor the inexplicable atom of Materialism. Materialism is in fact out of question, inasmuch as the Absolute of the Upaniṣad is not a result of organisation nor a property of matter. It is something always independent of everything, and self-illumined, self-subsistent. It is everywhere; but for it the world of experience is nowhere. But the Agnostic who stands half-way between Materialism and Transcendentalism identifies the Absolute with the Unknowable and makes it the source of all that translates itself into experience. This doctrine is entirely untenable, for that which is Unknowable is not the Absolute, but that which produces the various modifications and representations of it through experience. That something which IS and is not known *per se* by the very law of consciousness not permitting such knowledge, is the Unknowable *par excellence.* But to describe the fountain of knowledge, absolute consciousness, which is seen in daily individual experience, as the Unknowable or even the unknown would, at least, be a strange perversion of metaphysical language.

The effect of this philosophy on practical ethics is immense. Any system of ethics not based on some clearly demonstrated world-idea falls short of practical use, and is *pro tanto* a deviation from the path of adequately fulfilling the object of existence. The variety of experience is not real, nay even experience itself is nowhere from the point of the Absolute. To lead that life wherein the variety of experience does not affect either for weal or woe is the highest practical rule of conduct in accordance with the proper aim of existence. This does not imply entire inertia as some would understand it. The variety of experience *creates* distinction, and sets up false limits where there exist none. Pain and pleasure, good and evil, virtue and vice, merit and sin, are all conventions based on this variety of experience, and admitted for the sake of that experience. But in the Absolute no such distinctions are possible, and the highest bliss which cannot be described in words other than those implying negation of everything positive known to us, consists in forgetting the source of separateness and realising that unity which is the very being and nature of the cosmos. And more than this philosophy holds that the individual is a copy of the great cosmos and that through the unity of the two in the Absolute there is always possible an easy way from the one to the other. When the sense of separateness is killed out, the Absolute in the individual, and the microcosm is at once understood as the macrocosm. Pain and pleasure, evil and good, are all merged in the unity of the Absolute where all is that indescribable something which is neither pleasure nor pain, but something supremely sublime and happy, so to speak. This process of killing out this idea of separateness is no inertia, so far as ordinary language is understood; and though it may not be that blind submission to the will of an anthropomorphic deity, it is certainly the highest possible activity and energy on a superior plane. It is not neglect of duty nor renunciation of the world either; it is mere forgetting of self and its environments. This is *mokṣa*. *Mokṣa* in the popular sense is a something to be achieved, in the *Upaniṣad* it is already achieved, every being is one with the Absolute, is, in fact the Absolute; what is to be achieved is destruction of the sense of separateness, which being accomplished, *mokṣa* is easily realised. The disregard of this vital difference between the two ideas has led many Orientalists to regard the *mokṣa* of the *Vedānta*, and the *nirvāṇa* of the Buddhists, as something bordering on pure inertia or entire annihilation.

The illusion-theory is another puzzle in the way of many. Some try to set it down to later interpolation. That this is not so, will be evident from the text of the *Upaniṣads*; but a suggestion by the way may be usefully given. Experience is endless, and this endless variety creates distinctions which lead to the sense of separateness. All that is illusion in the phenomenal, is only these distinctions or limitations and the sense of separateness created by them. The basis or substratum of the illusion cannot be said to be nothing nor something. It is as indescribable as the Absolute and is known to BE, though never apart from or outside of the Absolute.

Many students of Indian philosophy enamoured of the idea of *mokṣa* taught by it seek to achieve it by various processes, physical or mental, generally, known as *Yoga*. Those who do so without being fully saturated with the spirit and substance of the *Upaniṣads* merely take a leap in the dark and court certain death, spiritual as well as physical. The first requisite is proper familiarity with the first principles of *Advaita* philosophy (*S'ravaṇa*); and entire love with them (*Manana*). Then follows that sublime state wherein the sense of separateness is being slowly forgotten. But even here nothing but strict practice of the noble virtues and perfect altruism will be necessarily required of the student.

M. N. DVIVEDI

CONTENTS

॥ बृहदारण्यकोपनिषत् ॥

BṚHADĀRAṆYAKA-UPANIṢAD

INTRODUCTION

By S'RĪMAT S'ANKARĀCĀRYA

OM! Salutation to Brahman and the other Brahmarṣis, perfect in the traditional knowledge of Brahman, whose names are enumerated in the lineage from teacher to teacher.[1] Salutation to the religious instructors.[2]

This brief[3] commentary of the Vājasaneyi Brahma Upaniṣad, which commences with the words: "The dawn is the head of the sacrificial horse," is composed for the sake of those who wish to liberate themselves from the world, in order that they may acquire the knowledge, that Brahman[4] and the soul[5] are the same, a knowledge, by which the liberation from the cause of

[1] Brahmarṣis are the sages, who in continuous succession from Brahman, Brahmā, Parameṣthin, etc., taught the knowledge of the universal soul. They are enumerated in the Vaṁs'a Brāhmaṇa, a part of the present Upaniṣad.

[2] The plural is here the plural majestatis, meaning the preceptor of S'aṅkarācārya, whose name was Goviṅda.

[3] Brief it is called, in comparison with the more voluminous commentary, called the Bhartṛprapañcabhāṣya.

[4] Brahman, the universal soul.

[5] The individual soul. According to the Vedantis the soul, independent of the body, is the substance which is pure existence, knowledge and bliss, and which must therefore not be confounded with its faculties, the senses, the mind, intellect, etc.

the world[1] is accomplished. This knowledge of Brahman is called Upaniṣad because it completely annihilates the world, together with its cause (ignorance) in such as possess this knowledge : for this is the meaning of the word Sad,[2] preceded by Upāni.[3] A work which treats on the same knowledge, is also called Upaniṣad. The above-mentioned Upaniṣad, which contains six chapters, is called Āraṇyaka, as being spoken in a desert, and Bṛhad (great) from its extent.[4]

The connexion of this Upaniṣad with the ceremonial part[5] *of the Vedas* will now be mentioned. The whole Veda has the design to explain by what means objects of desire and aversion that cannot be proved by perception or inference, may be obtained or removed; for every man has naturally the wish to obtain objects of desire, and remove objects of aversion. The Veda has not to investigate objects of the senses, because the knowledge of what satisfies desires, or removes objects of aversion, is produced by perception and inference.[6]

[1] The cause of the world is ignorance.

[2] Sad means to destroy, or to go.

[3] Upa means near, Ni expresses certainty.

[4] This Upaniṣad, besides the names of Vājasaneyi-Brahma—Upaniṣad and Bṛhad-Āraṇyaka-Upaniṣad, bears also the denomination of Kāṇva-Upaniṣad.

[5] The Vedas are divided in two parts, the first is the Karmakāṇḍa, the ceremonial part, also Pūrva-kāṇḍa, and treats on ceremonies, the second is the Jñānakāṇḍa, the part which contains knowledge, also named Uttara-kāṇḍa or posterior part and unfolds the knowledge of Brahman or the universal soul.

[6] The Mīmāṁsakas and Vedāntis assert five kinds of evidence, *viz.*, perception, inference, verbal communication, comparison and presumption. Some add also privation. The Cārvākas recognise

Further, unless there is a knowledge of the existence of the soul in another life, there cannot be a wish to obtain or remove objects of desire or aversion in a subsequent life ; this is clear from the conduct of those who [1] do not admit any other desires but those, prompted by one's own nature. In consequence the Vedic science is founded on the *knowledge* of the existence of the soul, relative to a former life, and upon the special means by which objects of desire and aversion in another life may be obtained or removed. The existence of the soul as independent of the body, is evident from positive declarations of the Vedas, as shown by the following passages : " This is the investigation whether after the death of man *the soul exists* ; some assert, the soul exists, the soul does not exist, assert others." This is the commencement of one *Upaniṣad*,[2] and it concludes with the words : it exists.[3]

Another passage says : " Some souls after death are born (again) to obtain a body like animals, others

but one, *viz.*, perception. The followers of Kaṇāda and those of Sugata (Buddha) acknowledge two, perception and inference. The Sāṅkhyas reckon three, including affirmation. The Naiyāyikas, or followers of Gotama, count four, *viz.*, the foregoing together with comparison. The Prābhākaras, as first observed, admit five. And the rest of the Mīmāṁsakas, in both schools, prior and later Mīmāṁsa, enumerate six. Col. M. E., Vol. I, pp. 303, 304. In our passage, perception and inference include the other kinds of evidence.

[1] The Lokāyatikas are here meant according to Ānandagiri. They do not acknowledge the existence of the soul, independent of the body, and accordingly do not perform any actions relative to a future life.

[2] See Kaṭha Upaniṣad, I, 20.

[3] K. U., VI, 13.

are changed into the condition of a trunk, according to their works, according to their knowledge of the Vedas."[1]

Another passage commences: "*It* (the soul) is itself light, its knowledge and ceremonial works follow it (in another life); *man* becomes holy by holy work."

Another passage which commences: "I will declare" concludes with the words: *the soul is* knowledge.

The assertion, that *the existence of the soul as independent of the body,* can be proved by perception, is not correct; for there is contradictory assertion of such who argue the contrary.

For, if from perception a knowledge of the existence of the soul in connexion with another body, could be derived, we should not be opposed to the Lokāyatikas[2] and Bauddhas,[3] who assert that the soul does not exist.

[1] K. U., V, 6—7.

[2] The Cārvākas (or Sūnyavādis) so named from one of their teachers, the Muni Cārvāka. From Bṛhaspati they are called also Bārhaspatyas. The appellation Sūnyavādis, implies the asserter of the unreality and emptiness of the universe, and another designation, Lokāyata, expresses their adoption of the tenet, that this being is the Be-all of existence: they were, in short, the advocates of materialism, and atheism, and have existed from a very remote period, and still exist, as we shall hereafter see. Wilson's Sects of the Hindus, p. 15.

They (the Cārvākas) restrict to perception the only means of proof and source of knowledge. Others, however, admit probability and tradition. Col. M., E. Vol. I, p. 403. Sadānanda in the Vedānta Sāra, calls up for refutation no less than four followers of Cārvāka; one maintaining, that the gross corporeal frame is identical with the soul, another that the corporeal organs constitute the soul, a third affirming that the vital functions do so; a fourth insisting, that the mind and the soul are the same. C. M. E., pp. 403, 404.

[3] Bauddhas. There are four sects among the followers of Buddha: 1. The Mādhyamicas, who maintain, that all is void.

For with regard to objects of the senses, as for instance a pot, no contradiction takes place, as if one would assert the non-existence of a pot, *although it is perceived by the senses.* If you hold, such contradiction may exist by referring to the well-known topic of the trunk and the man, if the same object is taken by some for a trunk, by others for a man, we remind you of the fact, that all dispute ceases, when the nature of the object has been ascertained. For there is no dispute about the nature of an object of the senses, for instance, of a trunk, when it has been ascertained by perception. The Vaināsikas[1] on the other hand, although acknowledging the *I*, yet reject the opinion of the existence of the soul, independent of the internal body. Accordingly, since the soul is different from any

2. The Yogācāras, who assert that, except internal sensation or intelligence (Vijñāna), all else is void. 3. Sautrāntikas. They affirm the actual existence of external objects no less than of internal sensations. The exterior objects to be known by immediate perception. 4. Vaibhāṣikas, who agree with the latter, except that they contend for a mediate apprehension of exterior objects, through images, or resembling forms, represented to the intellect. C. M. E., Vol. I, pp. 390, 391.

[1] Hence these Buddhists (the Sautrāntikas and Vaibhāṣikas, who believe, that objects cease to exist, when no longer perceived, they have but a brief duration, like the flash of lightning, lasting no longer than the perception of them. Their identity is but momentary) are by their adversaries, the orthodox Hindus, designated as Pūrṇa—or Sarva—Vaināsikas arguing total perishableness, while the followers of Kaṇāda, who acknowledge some of their categories to be eternal and invariable, and reckon only others transitory and changeable; and who insist that identity ceases with any variation in the composition of the body, and that a corporeal frame, receiving nutriment and discharging excretions, undergoes continual change, and consequent early loss of identity, are for that particular opinion, called Ardhavaināsikas 'arguing half perishableness.' Col. M. E., Vol. I, pp. 393, 394.

object of the senses, its existence cannot be proved by perception.

Nor can it be proved by inference. If you say, that the S'ṛuti applies arguments in proving the existence of the soul, and that these arguments are based upon perception, we do not admit this on the ground, that there is no perception of the soul, relative to a former birth. When, however, the existence of the soul by the Veda is acknowledged, and also by common arguments, according to the meaning of the Veda, the followers of the Veda, the Mīmāṁsakas and Tārkikas (or logicians), will substitute the fiction, as if the perception of the *I* and the arguments in accordance with the Vedas, were produced by their own intellect, and hence say, that the soul is proved by perception and inference.

The ceremonial part of the Vedas is intended for the special instruction of him, who with certainty knows that the soul exists, subject to transmigration, and who in consequence is anxious to avail himself of special means to obtain and remove objects of desire and aversion in connexion with another body. The ignorance, however, with regard to the soul, which produces the wish to obtain what is desired, and to remove what is not desired, and which by its nature prides itself in the feelings of self, dominion and possession is not annihilated *by ceremonial works*; this can only be effected by the opposite knowledge of the identity of Brahman with the individual soul. For as long as this ignorance is not annihilated, so long the ignorant soul, owing to passion, hatred and other natural faults, resulting from works, and owing to the transgression of commands and prohibitions of the S'āstra continues to accumulate by thoughts, words and by the body, works which are called unholy, and which are the causes of evil concerning events that fall within the senses as well as that which do not fall within them. All this is the result of the greater power of natural faults. Hence *in proportion to the faults*, transmigration *ensues from the highest state downwards* to the lowest state of inanimate matter.

Sometimes the purification by means of the S'āstra has a greater power. Hence the soul acquires by actions of mind, speech and body a state which is called virtue, and which is the cause of good. This virtue is twofold—virtue resulting from knowledge and mere virtue. The reward of the latter is the obtaining of the world of the manes (Pitṛs) and of other like worlds. The reward of virtue, resulting from knowledge, is the obtaining of the world of the Devas, and of other worlds, upwards to the world of Brahman. Thus it is said in the S'āstra : sacrificial works directed to Brahman are preferable to works directed to the Devas. Also the Smṛti [1] teaches: work, according to the Vedas, is twofold, (such as concerns active life, and such as refers to contemplation ; the former satisfies desires, the latter abstains from them through knowledge).

[1] Manu, 12, 88.

If lastly, virtue and vice are equally balanced in a person, he obtains the condition of man. Thus by the power of ignorance and other innate faults, a soul has to transmigrate, in accordance with its virtue or vice, into worldly forms, different in name, shape and works from the state of the world of Brahman downwards to the condition of inanimate matter.

Thus this manifested world, subject to the connexion between cause and effect, was not manifested before its creation. " This world which, like a sprout springs from seed, proceeds from ignorance, which is placed as the result from works, from the performer and effects upon the soul, is without beginning, is without end, is without reality." To remove the ignorance of a person who shows by reflections, as just described, his dissatisfaction with the world, the following Upaniṣad is commenced ; in order that he may obtain the knowledge of Brahman, which is opposite to that ignorance.

The knowledge, however, of the ceremonies regarding the sacrifice of a horse, is required that those who are not fit to perform the horse-sacrifice may obtain by this knowledge the same reward.[1]

If one by such passages from the S'ruti as the following: " By knowledge or by holy actions *the mentioned reward may be obtained*," and " He who

[1] *Viz.*, at the commencement of the Upaniṣad a description of the As'vamedha or horse-sacrifice, which does not properly belong to it, is given for the object, that Brāhmaṇas and others may obtain by knowledge the reward of this sacrifice, which can in reality only be performed by kings.

overcomes even this world," would conclude that the knowledge was only a kind of work; he would be in error, first, because passages as such: "who offers the sacrificial horse," and "who knows[1] him thus," leave it optional to *perform that sacrifice either by knowledge or in reality*; secondly, because it (this knowledge) is also mentioned in the second part of the S'ruti, which treats on knowledge; thirdly, because also by other ceremomies a similar representation is made. Hence it follows, that from knowledge alone the reward of the horse-sacrifice is derived. The chief of all ceremonies, however, is the As'vamedha, because its reward includes the universal and special state of Hiraṇya Garbha.[2]

Further at this commencement of the knowledge of Brahman, the ceremony of the horse-sacrifice is described for the purpose to show the worldly tendency of all sacrifices; for its reward is shown as the devourer which is death.

If it be said that the regular[3] ceremonies have no worldly effect, we deny this on the authority of the S'ruti, which enumerates the effects of all works. For every ceremony requires the assistance of a wife.

[1] That is to say, who knows the sacrifice of the horse to be an emblem of Prajapati.

[2] The universal state is Hiraṇyagarbha as soul of the universe, or Īs'vara, who rules all; the special state is Hiraṇyagarbha as present in every individual. Here the special state means of course the state of a special divinity.

[3] Regular ceremonies are such, which, if not performed, are cause of sin, and if performed, are no cause of merit, ceremonies which every Brāhmaṇa is bound to perform, as for instance the regular ceremonies, called Sandhyavandana. *Vide* Vedāntasāra.

When by such wishes as the following, "may I have a wife," which are based on our very nature, the connection of all ceremonies with objects of desire—moreover, as the reward of the ceremonies to be performed by a son, the world of the Ṛṣis or Devas, have been pointed out, the state of Hiraṇyagarbha will be shown *as reward of the Aśvamedha* at the end of this chapter by the words: "This world is three-fold by name, form and work."

Thus the world is the manifest effect from all actions. These three (names, forms and works) then were before the origin of the world not manifested. Again they become manifest from the effects of the works of all living creatures as a tree spring from seed. This world, which is at the same time manifest and not manifest, the object of ignorance, which is morpheus and amorpheus: is for the sake of the ceremony, the performer and the effect, placed through ignorance upon the soul by its semblance of it. Therefore the soul, although it is separate from the world, although in its nature it is without the distinction of name, form and work, although it is without duality, essentially eternal, pure, intelligent and blissful, is yet manifested by the difference of ceremony, performer, effect, and by other distinctions. Therefore as the erroneous conception of a rope as a snake is removed by a correct apprehension, so the knowledge of Brahman is commenced to annihilate the ignorance, the cause of desire and other faults, and also of works, of a person who is dissatisfied with this *world*, which naturally represents the distinctions of ceremonial act of the performer and of the effect, and which naturally applies causes and effects by such sentences, as: this is so or so. In this, the part commencing with: " The dawn is the head," etc., is designed for the knowledge of the horse-sacrifice. The sacrifice is represented under the emblem of a horse, on account of the eminence of the horse. The eminence again is derived from the sacrifice bearing its name and from its being the representation of Prajāpati.[1]

---

[1] The As'vamedha and Puruṣamedha, celebrated in the manner directed by this Veda (white Yajur Veda) are not really sacrifices of horses and men. In the first mentioned ceremony, six hundred and nine animals of various prescribed kinds, domestic and wild, including birds, fish, and reptiles, are made fast, the tame ones, to twenty-one posts, and the wild, in the intervals between the pillars; and after certain prayers have been recited, the victims are let loose without injury . . . This mode of performing the As'vamedha and Puruṣamedha, as emblematic ceremonies, not as real sacrifices, is taught in this Veda and the interpretation is fully confirmed by the rituals, and by commentators on the Saṁhitā and Brāhmaṇa . . . The horse, which is the subject of the religious ceremony, called As'vamedha, is also avowedly an emblem of Virāj, or the primeval and universal manifested being. Col. M. E., Vol. I, pp. 61, 62.

FIRST CHAPTER

FIRST BRĀHMAṆA

ॐ पूर्णमदः पूर्णमिदं पूर्णात्पूर्णमुदच्यते ।
पूर्णस्य पूर्णमादाय पूर्णमेवावशिष्यते ॥

ॐ शान्तिः शान्तिः शान्तिः ॥

Om ! whole is that, whole (too) is this ; from whole, cometh the whole ; take whole from whole, (yet) whole remains.

Om ! Peace, Peace, Peace, Harih, Om.

---

1. ॐ उषा वा अश्वस्य मेध्यस्य शिरः । सूर्यश्चक्षुर्वातः प्राणो व्यात्त-
मग्निर्वैश्वानरः संवत्सर आत्माश्वस्य मेध्यस्य । द्यौः पृष्ठमन्तरिक्ष-
मुदरं पृथिवी पाजस्यम् । दिशः पार्श्वे अवान्तरदिशः पर्शव
ऋतवोऽङ्गानि मासाश्चार्धमासाश्च पर्वाण्यहोरात्राणि प्रतिष्ठा
नक्षत्राण्यस्थीनि नभो माꣳसानि । ऊवध्यꣳसिकताः सिन्धवो
गुदा यकृच्च क्लोमानश्च पर्वता ओषधयश्च वनस्पतयश्च लोमानि
उद्यन् पूर्वार्धो निम्लोचञ्जघनार्धो तद्विजृम्भते यद्विद्योतते यद्विधूनुते
तत्स्तनयति यन्मेहति तद्वर्षति वागेवास्य वाक् ॥

OM! The dawn in truth is the head of the sacrificial horse. The sun is the eye; the wind the breath; the fire, under the name Vaiśvānara, the open mouth; the year the body of the sacrificial horse. The heaven is the back; the atmosphere the belly; the earth the footstool (hoof); the quarters the sides; the intermediate quarters the bones of the sides; the seasons the members; the months, and the half months, are the joints; day and night the feet; the constellations the bones; the sky the muscles; the half digested food the sand; the rivers arteries and veins; the liver and spleen the mountains; the herbs and trees the various kinds of hair. The sun, as long as he rises, is the fore-part of the body; the sun as long as he descends, is the hind part of the body. The lightning is like yawning; the shaking of the members is like the rolling of the thunder, the passing of urine is like the rain of the clouds: its voice is like speech.

"The dawn is in truth," etc. The dawn means here the hour of Brahman. "In truth." is said for the sake of reminding, and reminds of a well-known time. "Is the head," from its being the principal time; for the head is the principal part of the body. For the object of purifying the animal, representing in its members the various parts of the ceremonies, time and other conditions of the sacrifice are typified by the head and other parts. It is represented as Prajāpati by giving it the emblems of Prajāpati; for the representation of the animal by time, the worlds and the divinities is its representation as Prajāpati, for this is the nature of Prajāpati, as Viṣṇu and other deities are represented under the form of an image. "The sun is the eye," as nearest to the head, and as being the tutelary deity of the eye.[1] "The wind is the breath," from its identity with it. "The mouth is fire, under the name of Vais'vānara"; Vais'vānara is the special name of Agni, meaning, whose mouth is wide open. Agni is also the deity of the mouth. "The year is the body," *viz.*, the year, as containing twelve or thirteen months. The year is the body of the members of time; for the body is in the midst of the members, as the S'ruti says. "Of the sacrificial horse"; this is here repeated for the sake of connection, "The heaven is the back," both being placed alike above. "The atmosphere the belly," both being hollow. The earth the footstool. The quarters, although four, are the two sides, by the similarity of both. This comparison is not improper for the reason, that the number of both is different; for as the two sides of the horse are turned to all quarters, there is no fault in this comparison. "The intermediate quarters," *viz.*, Agneyi (regent of the south-east), etc., the bones of the sides. "The seasons are the members," from the similarity of the parts of the year with the members of the body. "The months and half months the joints," from their similarity. "Days and nights the feet" in plural number from the difference of days, as days of Prajāpati, of the Devas, of the Pitṛs, and of men. "Feet," because they proceed for the time as body proceeds with the days and nights, as with the feet of the horse. "The constellations the bones," from their similar white colour. "The sky," meaning here the clouds of the sky, because the sky was formerly mentioned as the belly, are the muscles, from the similarity of both in oozing either water or blood. "The half digested food the sand," from the similarity of the separate parts. The rivers, "arteries and veins," because both ooze. "The liver and the spleen," the mountains, *viz.*, the two pieces of flesh to the right and left under the heart; they are called "mountains" from their hardness and height. The herbs, small plants, the hair of the body; the "trees," the hair of the head, according to their likeness. The sun rising

[1] As the eye is nearest to the head, so the sun is nearest to the dawn. This is the point of their resemblance.—*Ānandagiri.*

until noon is the forepart of the horse above the navel; the sun, descending from the midst of his course, is the other half, the hips and loins, from their respective similarity. "The lightning is like the yawning," from the likeness of the mouth, when it suddenly opens, with the rending of a cloud. "The shaking of the members is like the rolling of thunder," from the similarity of the sound. "The passing of the urine is like the raining of the clouds—both sprinkle alike. The voice is like the neighing of the horse; in this there is a natural likeness.

2. अहर्वा अश्वं पुरस्तान्महिमान्वजायत तस्य पूर्वे समुद्रे योनी रात्रिरेनं पश्चान्महिमान्वजायत तस्यापरे समुद्रे योनिरेतौ वा अश्वं महिमानावभितः संबभूवतुः । हयो भूत्वा देवानवहद्वाजी गन्धर्वानर्वासुरानश्वो मनुष्यान् समुद्र एवास्य बन्धुः समुद्रो योनिः ॥

The day is the Mahima, placed before the horse; its birth-place is the eastern sea; the night the other Mahima, which is placed behind the horse; its birth-place is the western sea; these Mahimas are placed around the horse. The horse, under the name of Haya, carried the gods, under the name of Vāji the Gandharvas, under the name of Arva, Asuras, under the name of As'va, men. The sea is its companion, the sea its birthplace.

"The day," etc., this is said in illustrations of the golden and silver cups, called Mahima, which are placed before and behind the horse. The day is the golden cup, from the similar splendour of both. How is the day placed as the cup before the horse? By its being an emblem of Prajāpati; for Prajāpati who is represented by Āditya (the sun), etc., is designed by the day. In naming the horse Prajāpati is meant, as the lightning is manifest by manifesting a tree. The birthplace of the golden cup means here the place where it is kept. Thus the night represents the silver cup, from the likeness of the colour, or of the hind-part of the horse. Behind this horse, the cup, by name Mahima, is placed. Its birthplace is the western sea. Mahima means greatness; for it shows the opulence of the horse, that the golden and silver cups are placed on either side. These cups, under the name of Mahima, are placed round the horse. The repetition is here made for the sake of praise, *viz.*, the Mahimas, which have those distinctions, and the horse gifted with greatness. The same praise is intended by the words: "The horse under the name of Haya." *Haya* is derived from the root Hinoti, the action of going, going in an eminent manner, unless it means a peculiar race. "It carries the gods," means either it gained the condition of a god by its being the representation of Prajāpati, or it became the carrier of the gods. But is not the office of carrying a blame? By no means; for carrying is the nature of the horse, and as by this nature it acquires an eminence, as being connected with the gods and other *superior* beings, it is rather a praise. In the same manner the word Vāji and the other terms of the horse denote different races. The horse, under the name of Vāji, carried the Gandharvas under the name of Arva, the Asuras, under the name of As'va men. The sea, which represents here the universal soul, its companion; there is its dwelling-place. The sea, its birth-place, the cause of its production. In this way the purified birth-place, or the purified dwelling-place is praised. In the waters is the birth-place of the horse, says the S'ruti; thus the sea is its well-known origin.

SECOND BRĀHMAṆA

1. नैवेह किंचनाग्र आसीन्मृत्युनैवेदमावृतमासीत् । अशनाययाशनाया हि
मृत्युस्तन्मनोऽकुरुतात्मन्वी स्यामिति सोऽर्चन्नचरत्तस्यार्चत

आपोऽजायन्तार्चते वै मे कमभूदिति तदेवार्कस्यार्कत्वम् कᳲ ह वा अस्मै भवति य एवमेतदर्कस्यार्कत्वं वेद ॥

There was not any thing here before: this was indeed enveloped by death, who is voracity;

For voracity is death. He created this mind, desiring: May I have a soul. He went forth worshipping. From him when worshipping, the waters were produced, He then reflected: To me, when worshipping, water (Ka) was produced. For the same reason fire obtained the name of Arka. Happiness is indeed produced for him, who in this manner knows the nature of Arka.

The origin of the fire, required for the performance of the horse-sacrifice, will now be explained. As it is intended to describe the particulars of the fire *with regard to the horse-sacrifice*, the birth of the fire is here introduced for its praise.

" There was not any thing here before." " Here," in this universe, there was not any thing that could be distinguished by differences of name or shape. " Before," *viz.*, before the creation of the mind and other productions.

'Then was there not the universal void?[1] For this follows from the passage of the S'ruti: " There was not any thing here," which means there was neither an effect nor a cause. It follows also from the idea of production; for suppose a pot be produced, consequently there is no existence of the pot before its production.'

But hence does not follow the non-existence of the cause, as is evident from the lump of earth (from which the

[1] This is the opinion of the Mādhyamicas, one of the four sects of the Bauddhas.

pot is produced); let it be granted, that there is no existence of a thing, that is not perceived;[1] let therefore the effect not exist; this, however, does not affect the existence of the cause, as it can be perceived (before it produces the effect).

'No, before the production there is no perception whatever, either of cause or effect. If then non-perception, which is a negation, is the cause of the whole world, neither cause nor effect can be perceived before its creation; therefore the negation of all (cause and effect) must be admitted.'

We deny this. First, because the S'ruti declares: "By death was this indeed enveloped"; for if there was nothing to envelope, and nothing to be enveloped, the S'ruti could not say, this was indeed enveloped; for there is no such a conception as the son of a barren woman, adorned with a sky-flower. And it is said, by death indeed was this enveloped; therefore, by the evidence of the S'ruti, it follows both, that before the creation of the world there was a cause which was enveloping, and that there was an effect which was enveloped. We deny it secondly, by argument; for we may know by inference the existence of cause and effect before the production; for if a real effect takes place, it must be produced by a real cause, and cannot be produced by an unreal cause.

The existence of a cause of the world before its creation is argued in the same manner as the existence of the cause of a pot and of other productions. If you[2] argue the non-existence of the cause of the pot, etc., from the reason, that the pot could not be produced, unless the lump of earth[3] and other similar things disappear,[4] we cannot

[1] As of an effect, which is not perceived, before it is produced by its cause.

[2] The opponent of course.

[3] From which the pot is produced.

[4] *Viz.*, the opponent reasons in this way: If the effect (for instance, the pot) has no actual existence, the cause (the lump of earth) does also not exist. If the effect has actual existence, the cause (the lump of earth) has disappeared, *i.e.*, exists no more.

agree, since earth and other substance are the *real* causes ; for earth, gold, etc., are the causes in the production of a pot, and not the peculiar shape of the lump, since, if there is not the former, (earth), there is not the latter, (the pot). Namely, even if there is not a peculiar shape of the lump, the production of a pot and similar effects takes place from such substances alone, as earth, gold and similar causes. Therefore not the peculiar shape of the lump is the cause in the production of a pot. On the other hand, if there do not exist earth, gold and similar substances, the production of a pot, etc., does not take place ; consequently, earth, gold, etc., are the causes, not the peculiar shape of the lump ; for every cause, when producing an effect, produces this effect, only by concealing (making disappear) its former effects, because it is impossible that from one and the same cause, at one and the same time, many effects should be derived.[1]

Nor does the cause disappear with its former effect : therefore the production of the pot by the disappearance of the lump, (which you say, is the cause) shows, that the lump is not the cause. If you say, 'that before the production a cause does not exist, because, independent of the lump of earth, earth and other substances have no existence,' we object ; for earth and other substances do not disappear with their former effects, but are yet found in the last productions, as in a pot, etc.

If you maintain, 'that without the lump, the pot, etc., earth and other causes are not perceived,' we deny this also, because, when a pot, etc., is produced, the lump, etc., has disappeared, while the earth and other real causes are there still remaining. If you say, 'that the connection (between cause and effect) depends upon comparison,[2] and

[1] For instance. The shape of a lump of earth, from which a pot is to be made, must disappear in order that the production be possible. This shape, however, is not the cause, but it is merely a former effect of the same cause, earth.

[2] S'aṅkara has omitted to give the argument of the opponent, which is based upon the supposition that the relation of cause and effect can only be apprehended by comparison. Ānandagiri

not upon the permanence of the cause (in the effect)'; we deny this also, for as the parts of earth that compose a lump, are found in a pot by mere perception, there is only a semblance of inference, and therefore comparison and other similar actions do not take place.

Moreover the different mode of operation in perception and in inference is not incompatible, because inference, which is always preceded by perception, would otherwise have nowhere a place to depend upon.

If it be supposed, that 'all has only a momentary existence, and accordingly in a sentence; that is this, both terms refer only to a momentary existence,' it follows that the notion of "that" is dependent on the notion of another "that" which is again dependent on another, so that there is no stability. It further follows, that the notion "that is like this," is also impossible, (the term "this" being dependent on a similar series) hence the conclusion is unavoidable: there is no dependence whatsoever. The connection between the two notions of that and this is also impossible, because there is no subject[1] to perceive them. If you say, 'there is a connection between them by comparison,' we object, because the mutual connection of the notions of that and this cannot be understood. And if there be no connection between one object and another object, the idea of comparison cannot take place.

Granted, that there is no comparison, the notion of that is possible. No, because, like the notion from comparison, the notions of that and this have no reference to any real object. 'Granted that all notions have no real object, what then?' You must then admit that true as well as false notions refer to objects which are objects of nothing.

supplies this as follows: All that exists, is only momentary; but these modes (cause and effect) exist; therefore they are momentary. Is thus the momentary existence of all that exists, has been shown, and the relation of cause and effect depends upon comparison, delusion is unavoidable.

[1] No sentient subject, no reasonable being, because it would be involved in the same eternal change.

If you lastly say, 'this may be so,' we contradict, because, if all notions are without object, you cannot form the idea of a false notion. Hence, your opinion, that the notion of that depends upon comparison, is not true and we therefore conclude, that the real existence of the cause before the production is proved.

This is also true with regard to the effect, on the ground of its manifestation. 'How is the existence of the effect before its production proved on the ground of its manifestation?'[1]

Manifestation is the ground of this (effect)—hence manifestation means a perception dependent on a knowledge which is present; for as in common life a pot and similar things, enveloped by darkness, became an object of knowledge, when the cause of enveloping has been removed by means of light, etc., and do therefore not disapprove their former existence, so also we argue the existence of this world before its production; for unless a pot exists, it cannot be perceived, even if the sun rises.

'It certainly is not perceived by you, unless it exists. For if productions, as a pot, etc., do at any time[2] not exist, they are not perceived by you, if the sun even rises. If the lump of earth is not at hand, and no enveloping cause, as darkness, are present, the effect will not be perceived on the ground that it exists.'

[1] The objection of the opponent, according to Ānandagiri, is as follows; If you say, that an effect is proved by its manifestation, how does the existence of the effect follow from its manifestation, for from the existence of the effect follows also its manifestation, and again you maintain, that the existence of the effect is based upon its manifestation. This is a false circle. The answer of the Vedantis is: The previous existence of an effect, which is not perceived, is proved by its manifestation, which is perceived. There is therefore no false circle. The argument for the previous existence of an effect is based on this premise: All that is manifested, exists before its manifestation, as a pot enveloped by darkness.

[2] Reference is here made to the past and future time; for if, says Ānandagiri, an effect, that is destroyed, or that is to be, did exist like a present effect, it would be also perceived. This, however, is not the case, and therefore the argument is not correct.

We do not admit this, because there is a twofold kind of enveloping; for things that envelop an effect, as a pot, etc., are twofold; first, things which screen, as darkness, etc., when the earth and other substances are already manifested; secondly, the modification of the parts, earth and other substances in the state of another effect as of a lump, etc., before the manifestation of the earth *in the effect of a pot*, etc. Accordingly, the perception of an effect, as a pot, although existing before its production, cannot take place, because it is enveloped (in another effect). The distinction, however, according to the common ideas of destroyed, produced, existing, not existing, is merely the twofold distinction of the ideas of manifestation and disappearance.[1]

This is improper, because the lump, the two halves of the pot,[2] etc., are different from any thing that envelops; for any screen, as darkness, which envelops any production, as a pot, etc., appears something different from the pot and similar things while the lump or the two halves do not appear different from the pot. Therefore your assertion, that a pot, which is in the state of a lump or of the two halves, is not perceived because it is enveloped, is improper, because it is different from the idea of enveloping.'[3]

[1] By the disappearance of the half, a pot is destroyed; by removing the lump and other enveloping things it is manifested; its manifestation by means of a light, etc., is its existence; its disappearance by means of the lump, etc., is its non-existence.

[2] To understand the following, it is necessary to know that the usual way among the Hindus to make a pot is, first to form two separate parts, the Kapālas, the halves of the pot, and to join them afterwards in the middle.

[3] This objection is based upon the supposition, that the thing, which is enveloping, is not identical with the thing that is enveloped by it, as for instance, darkness is not identical with any thing that is enveloped by it. Therefore, the opponent argues, the lump of earth cannot envelop a pot or any other production, because both (the lump and the pot) are identical. The refutation of this is twofold, according to a distinction in the term identical, *viz.*, the assertion that the enveloping thing cannot be identical with the thing enveloped, means either, that it cannot be identical as to its appearance in space, etc., or not identical as to its cause. The first is

We do not agree, for, *on the one hand*, milk and water (when mixed) and similar things, appear in an identical state although the water and similar things are enveloped by milk, etc. *On the other hand*, if you say, that 'there is nothing which envelops, because the parts of a half that is ground to dust are contained in the pot,' etc., we deny this; for if the different parts are in another effect, there is evidently an enveloping. 'There must, however, be an effort to remove what envelops, because the pot and other effects, which are in the state of the lump or of the halves, are not perceived in consequence of their being enveloped, and accordingly a person, who is desirous of any production, as of a pot, must direct his effort to destroy what envelops it, and not to the production of the pot. This, however, does not exist, and it is therefore improper to say, that there is no perception of a thing which exists, because it is enveloped.' We deny this, because it is against the rule in practice; for the manifestation of a pot, etc., does not take place only by an effort to destroy obstacles, as is evident from the effort to produce a light, if a pot and other productions are enveloped in darkness. If you say, 'that this is done to destroy darkness, *viz.*, that the effort made to produce a light, is merely made to let darkness disappear, and if the darkness is destroyed the pot is[1] manifested by itself; for there is nothing (no obstacle to the sight) in the pot,' we do not grant this, because the perception takes place, when the pot is manifested; for as the manifested pot is perceived by means of a light, so it is not before the light is employed. Therefore the light is not for the means to destroy the darkness, but rather for the means of manifesting the pot,

refuted by the fact, that the contrary takes place, for instance: when milk and water are mixed, water, which is enveloped by milk, is perceived as one and the same with the milk, which could not be the case, if the thing that envelops must be different from the thing that is enveloped. The second is refuted on the ground, that different effects in one and the same cause are separated from each other, and do therefore not destroy each other.—Ā. G.

[1] That is to say, when the screen, darkness, is removed, there is no obstacle to its manifestation

because the perception takes place by manifestation. Sometimes there may be an effort also to destroy what envelops, as in the destruction of a screen, etc., but on this account it is not the rule. A person who wishes the manifestation of any thing, must make an effort to destroy all that envelops.

This follows also from the success of a work, if done in accordance with its rule. We said, that an effect, which abides in the cause, is an obstacle to another effect. If then an effort is made to destroy an effect, which was before manifested, for instance, a lump, or the two halves which were *before* concealed by the lump,[1] then is produced an effect which is called splitting or grinding, etc. A pot, which is enveloped by such effects, is not perceived, and requires therefore another effort; hence a person who wishes the manifestation of a pot, can only be successful, if the needful action of producing a pot is used by him. Therefore the effect exists even before its production. —This follows also from the distinction of the ideas of past and future. It is only reasonable, that the ideas of "there was a pot," and "there will be a pot," like the idea of "there is a pot" do not refer to an object that does not exist.—It also follows from the action of any one, who is desirous of a future production; for nobody would act with regard to a desire of things that have no existence.—It follows also from the truth of the knowledge of the Yogis, with regard to past and future *events*. If a future pot were not an existing thing, divine knowledge, from immediate perception with regard to a future pot, would be a false. We do not take notice here of an effect, which is perceived at the present time; for we granted *before* inference for the existence of an effect *which has been, or which is to be.—This also follows* from the impossibility of the country. When potters are engaged in the fabrication of a pot, it is evident by this proof that the pot is to be; for if with any time the future existence of the pot is connected, then to connect with that time,

[1] That is to say, which were before in the state of the lump; for this is a previous effect of the same cause (earth).

a not existing pot, is a contradiction; for a pot, that is to exist, does not exist, means, it is not to exist; it is the same, as if it be said: This pot now before us does not exist.—Further, let potters be engaged in the fabrication of a pot, and let it be said the pot does not exist before its production. If then the meaning of the word *not existing*, is, that the pot does not exist in the same manner, as potters and other artisans, who are engaged in their work, exist, then there is no contradiction. Why not? Because the pot exists in its own form, which is to exist; for neither the existence of the lump, nor of the half, is the existence of the pot. Taken in this view, when potters are engaged *in making a pot*, there is no contradiction in the idea of a pot which does not exist before its production. If you, however, prohibit the idea of the condition of the pot as a future production, there is a contradiction; but you did not prohibit this; for with every action is not only existence or futurity connected (but also the past). Further, among the four privations,[1] the mutual privation with regard to the pot is perceived as something different from the pot, as the negation of the pot may be for example cloth; but it never can become *the negation of* a pot itself; for the negation of a pot, for instance cloth which exists, is never something negative, but something positive. If this is the case, then all the other negations, *viz.*, antecedent negation, destruction and absolute negation, which may take place with regard to the pot, are something positive, different from the pot itself, because they have the same connection with it as the mutual negation. In this manner refer all negations to something positive. If this is the case, antecedent negation of the pot does not mean a negation of the pot itself before its production. Therefore

[1] Negation or privation is of two sorts, universal and mutual. Universal negation comprehends three species antecedent, emergent and absolute. Antecedent privation is present negation of that which at a future time will be. Emergent negation is destruction, or cessation of an effect. Absolute negation extends through all times, past, present and future. Mutual privation is difference. It is reciprocal negation of identity, essence, or respective peculiarity. (Col. M.E., Vol. I, pp. 288, 289.)

if you say, "the antecedent negation of a pot," you must acknowledge the (existence of the) pot itself, or you could not connect it with the genitive case (of the pot). If you say, 'it is connected with it by rhetorical figure, as if one speaks of the *body* of a stone figure,' yet, if you pronounce such a sentence as the negation of a pot, the connection of the rhetorical negation is with the pot, and not with the nature of a pot (then the negation is only artificial negation and not the real negation of the pot). If you say, 'that the negation of a pot is something different from the pot,' then we must refer you to the answer we have given before.

Further, before the production of a pot, there cannot be a connection of the pot which does not exist with its cause which exists, which is as if you would give horns to a hare, because the connection is always mutual. If you say, 'there is no fault in our case, because the connection is only an accidental one,' we object, because even an accidental connection cannot take place for elements, of which the one exists, the other not exists; for with regard to two elements that exist, either the necessary or accidental connection may take place; but it does not take place for elements, of which the one exists, the other does not exist or for elements, of which either does not exist. It is therefore proved that the effect exists before its production. The Upaniṣad now explains the nature of death, by whom this (universe) was enveloped by the words:

"Who is voracity." The desire to devour is voracity—this is death, for voracity is the true definition of death. By death, then, whose nature is voracity, *this universe* was enveloped. How is voracity death? The answer is: "For voracity is death." The meaning of the word "for" is, that the reason is well known; for he who desires to devour, kills according to his voracity the living creatures. Consequently death is represented by voracity; Voracity as a desire is a quality of the soul in its modification as intelligence; therefere this Hiraṇyagarbha, in his modification as intelligence, is called death. By this death was this effect enveloped, as a pot and other productions are enveloped by earth in its modification as a lump. "He created this mind"; the above-mentioned death, by the desire to create the productions, afterwards to be specified, made the so-called mind, capable to reflect on his creation, *viz*., the internal sense which is possessed with the faculty to ascertain knowledge and with other faculties. For what purpose did he create the mind? The answer is: "May I have a soul," may, by the soul, in its modifications as mind, I have mind. Prajāpati, possessed with mind by the manifestation of mind, having adored himself, said: I have succeeded. "From him," from Prajāpati, "when worshipping, the waters," the element whose quality is taste, "were produced," as the embodied parts of his devotion, that is to say, he created the water after the production of the sky and the other two elements,[1] as it accords with the authority of another passage of the S'ruti, and the improbability of a reverse order of the creation. "He then reflected, when worshipping, (Arcate) water (Ka) was produced for me." For the same reason, that death was called Arka, Arka or the fire, in its connection with the sacrifice of As'vamedha, obtained the name of Arka; for the second appellation of fire is Arka. The name of Arka, as derived from Arcana, which means to worship for one's welfare or as derived from its connection with water, denotes a quality of fire. To him who in this manner, as has been mentioned knows the nature of Arka, water, or happiness (the word Ka is used for both) is indeed, of a certainty, produced.

2. आपो वा अर्कस्तद्यदपाꣳ शर आसीत्समहन्यत सा पृथिव्यभवत्तस्याम-
श्राम्यत्तस्य श्रान्तस्य तप्तस्य तेजो रसो निवर्ततताग्निः ॥

Or the waters are Arka. The froth of the waters, which was there, became consistent. This became the earth. On *the creation of* this he became fatigued.

[1] Air and fire.—Taittareya Upaniṣad, I, 2.

The splendour, the exudation of him, when he was fatigued, heated, was poured out as fire.

"Or the waters are Arka." Who is again called Arka? The waters, the embodied parts of the devotion, are Arka, as produced from Arka or fire. As it is said in the S'ruti: And in the waters is placed the fire. But they are not directly called Arka, because this is the proper place to describe the fire, but not the water. And afterwards it is also said: This fire is Arka, "The froth of the waters, which was there," like the cream of curdled milk, "became consistent"; the froth of the waters, heated from within and without by the generative splendour, became consistent, "became the earth". The meaning is, that from these waters the mundane egg sprang forth. "On this," on the production of the earth, "he," death, Prajāpati "became fatigued"; for everybody, after the performance of work, gets fatigued, and it is the great work of Prajāpati to create the earth. What does it mean that he got fatigued? From the body of Prajāpati, when fatigued, heated· distressed, his creative splendour as exudation, his substance was poured out. Which is the fire that was poured out? It is Prajāpati as the Virāj (who is throughout splendour) within the egg, the first-born, containing within himself the whole organism of productions. He is the first embodied soul, as it is said in the Smṛti.

3. स त्रेधात्मानं व्यकुरुतादित्यं तृतीयं वायुं तृतीयꣳ स एष प्राणस्त्रेधा
विहितः । तस्य प्राची दिक्छिरोऽसौ चासौ चेर्मौ । अथास्य
प्रतीची दिक् पुच्छमसौ चासौ च सक्थ्यौ दक्षिणा चोदीची च
पार्श्वे द्यौः पृष्ठमन्तरिक्षमुदरमियमुरः स एषोप्सु प्रतिष्ठितो यत्र क्व
चैति तदेव प्रतितिष्ठत्येवंविद्वान् ॥

He made himself threefold, Āditya as the third, Vāyu as the third. This life parted threefold. His eastern quarter is the head. The quarters on either side are the arms. Then his western quarter is the tail, the quarters on either side are the things, the south and north the flanks, the sky the back, the atmosphere the belly ; this *earth* the breast. This fire is placed in the waters ; for wheresoever one repairs, there he is placed. This results from the knowledge of the wise.

This Prajāpati, when born, divided his own self, the organism of all productions, threefold. How threefold ? Besides Agni and Vāyu, he made Āditya as the third to complete the number of three ; in the same manner, beside Agni and Āditya, Vāyu as the third, and also, beside Vāyu and Āditya, Agni as the third, according to their equal power to fill up the number of three. This Prajāpati, the life of every individual in the world, was divided threefold according to the nature of Agni, Vāyu, and Āditya, especially according to his own nature as death, without giving up the nature of Virāj. This first-born fire, as Arka in its connection with the ceremony of the Aśvamedha, this fire as Virāj, which is purified according to holy rite, is also represented under the symbol of a horse ; for, we said, the whole origin, as above mentioned, is narrated for his praise. Thus is his sacred origin. "His eastern quarter is the head," both being alike by their excellence. "The quarters on either side," *viz.*, the quarters of Īśā and of Āgneyi, "are the arms". "Then the western quarter of the fire is the tail," *viz.*, the part of the hip and loins, as being opposite to the front part. "The quarters on either side," *viz.*, Vāyu and the seasons, "are the thighs," being like to the corners of the back ; "south and north the flanks," being like by their connection with the two former quarters. "The heaven the back, the atmosphere the belly," as in the former description ; "this *earth* is the breast," both being alike by their position downwards. "This fire," being alike Prajāpati, or the fire as the substance of the worlds and of the other created beings, "is placed in the waters". As another passage of the Śruti says: thus are all these worlds within the waters. "For wheresoever anybody repairs, there he is placed" there he gains his abode. Who? He who thus knows the nature of the fire, which in the manner described is placed in the waters; for this is the fruit of his knowledge.

4. सोऽकामयत द्वितीयो म आत्मा जायेतेति स मनसा वाचं मिथुनꣳ
समभवदशनाया मृत्युस्तद्यद्रेत आसीत्स संवत्सरोऽभवत् । न ह
पुरा ततः संवत्सर आस तमेतावन्तं कालमबिभः । यावान्सं-
वत्सरस्तमेतावतः कालस्य परस्तादसृजत तं जातमभिव्याददात्स
भाणकरोत्सैव वागभवत् ॥

He desired: Let a second self of me be produced. By his mind he created speech, created union, *viz.*, the devourer, death. The seed which there sprang forth became the year. For the year was not before him; he was conceived for the space of such time. After the time, which is contained within the space of a year, he created him. When he was born, he opened his mouth against him. He cried. Thus was speech produced.

"He desired." Who? Death. He by himself, according to the successive order of creation of the water and the other elements created himself within the egg, as the Virāj, as Agni containing the organism of all productions. He also made himself threefold, as it was said. How was his activity, while he created? The answer is: "He," death, "desired". What? "Let a second self of me," a body, by which I am possessed with a body, "be produced". Having thus desired, he created, by his before-created mind, speech, *viz.*, speech representing the three Vedas; he created the union of speech with the mind, that is to say, he reflected in his mind on the creation of the three Vedas in their successive order. Who? Death, represented by voracity, as it is said, death is represented by the desire to devour. This is here repeated, in order that it be not connected with another. "The seed," the generative seed both of knowledge and ceremonies, the cause of all productions of Prajāpati, the first embodied soul, which (seed) he perceived by his contemplation of the three Vedas, "which there," in that union, "sprung forth, became" (being conceived in the form of an egg, after he had entered with this generative seed the water, which he had created in accordance with his recollection of its [the water's] production in a former birth) "the year". This means, Prajāpati, the framer of the period, called a year, became the year. "For the year was not before him," before Prajāpati, the framer of the annual period. As long as the duration of a year is, so long a time was Prajāpati, the framer of the annual period, conceived. What did he do after the completion of this time? "He created him"—which means, he broke the egg. When the babe, fire, the first embodied soul, was thus born, death in accordance with his voracity, "opened his mouth against him" to devour him, upon which the babe, according to his natural ignorance, got afraid and cried. "Thus was speech produced" the sound of speech produced.

5. स ऐक्षत यदि वा इममभिमꣳस्ये कनीयोऽन्नं करिष्य इति स तया वाचा तेनात्मनेदꣳ सर्वमसृजत यदिदं किंचर्चो यजूꣳषि सामानि छन्दाꣳसि यज्ञान् प्रजाः पशून् । स यद्यदेवासृजत तत्तदत्तुमध्रियत सर्वं वा अत्तीति तददितेरदितित्वꣳ सर्वस्यैतस्यात्ता भवति सर्वमस्यान्नं भवति य एवमेतददितेरदितित्वं वेद ॥

He *reflected*. If I kill him, I shall have only little food. On this reflection he created by that word in union with that soul all this whatsoever, the Ṛk, the

Yajus, the Sāma Vedas, the metres, the sacrifices, mankind, the animals.

He resolved to devour all that he had created in this manner; for he eats all, therefore he has the name of Aditi. He is the eater of this whole universe, this whole universe is his food. He who thus knows him in his nature as Aditi, will obtain the reward of this knowledge.

"*He reflected.*" When death saw the terrified babe crying in such a manner, he reflected: "If I," however desirous of eating, kill at any time this babe, "I shall have only little food." On this reflection he abstained from eating him; for much food is required for eating a long time, not a little; for by eating this boy, there will be only little food, as by the eating of the seed there will be want of corn. After having thus reflected on the necessity of abundant food, he created by the union of the before-mentioned threefold speech with the soul, the mind, the whole moveable and immoveable universe, "all this whatsoever," *viz.*, the Ṛk, Yajus, Sāma Vedas, the seven metres, *viz.*, the Gāyatrī and others, the three kinds of Mantras, which are the parts of the body of the Stotra Sāstra with their Gāyatrī and other metres, the sacrifices to be performed by Mantras, mankind, as the performer of sacrifices, and all the wild and domestic animals, necessary for the performance of the sacrifices. "How is it possible, that he created by the threefold speech in its union with the mind, the Ṛk and the other Vedas when it was said before, that he created them in this manner?" There is no fault in this. The union, which the mind has with the three Vedas, does not exist as manifested, and the creation is the manifestation of the existing Vedas by their application to ceremonies. 'He,' Prajāpati, being thus aware of the increase of food, "resolved to devour all that he had created," all the actions, the causes of actions and the effects of actions. Death is therefore called Aditi, because he eats all; for Aditi is derived from Atti, he eats.—Thus it is in a Mantra " Aditi is the sky, he is the atmosphere, he is mother and father". He is the devourer of the whole world, considered as his food, by being the universal soul: otherwise there would be a contradiction; for no individual can be the eater of the universe. Therefore he is the universal soul. " This whole universe is his food." Therefore it is consistent that all becomes his food, because he, as the universal soul, is the eater,—he, who in the aforesaid manner knows this state of Prajāpati, death, or Aditi, *viz.*, this state, according to which he eats everything, will have such a reward.

6. सोऽकामयत भूयसा यज्ञेन भूयो यजेयेति सोऽश्राम्यत्स तपोऽतप्यत तस्य श्रान्तस्य तप्तस्य यशो वीर्यमुदक्रामत् प्राणा वै यशो वीर्यं तत्प्राणेषूत्क्रान्तेषु शरीरꣳश्वयितुमध्रियत तस्य शरीर एव मन आसीत् ॥

He desired: Let me perform again the great sacrifice. He became fatigued. He performed penance. When he was fatigued, when he had performed penance, glory and power departed. Life is glory, power; therefore, when life had departed from his body, his body assumed a swollen appearance; there was yet mind within his body.

" He desired," this is said for the purpose to give the description of the horse and the horse-sacrifice. " Let me perform again the great sacrifice." The word again refers to his former birth; Prajāpati made the sacrifice of a horse in his former birth. With this recollection he came again at the commencement of the present Kalpa.[1] Being impressed with the recollection of the ceremonies, the performer and the reward of the horse sacrifice, he

[1] Kalpa, a renovation of the universe, one of the great periods from the renovation to the destruction of the world.

desired: "Let me again perform the great sacrifice," and after he had thus desired the great work, he became fatigued like all other people. "He performed penance." When he was fatigued, when he had performed penance, as in the former description,[1] glory and power departed. The explanation of the words glory and power is given in the Upaniṣad itself; life, *viz.*, the organs of sense are glory, as being the cause of glory, for by the means of them renown is gained. In the same manner is power in this body; for if life is extinguished, no glory, no power is possible. Therefore the ǫrgnas of sense are like glory and power in this body; thus that glory and power of life departed from his body. When the organs of sense, the cause of glory and power, had departed from the body of Prajāpati, it presented the appearance of turgescence; and was unpurified. "There was yet mind in his body," although deserted by Prajāpati, in the same manner as the mind dwells on a beloved object, however distant it may be. When he thus remained in the body as mind, what did he do?

7. सोऽकामयत मेध्यं म इदꣳ स्यादात्मन्व्यनेन स्यामिति ततोऽश्वः समभवद्यदश्ववत्तन्मेध्यमभूदिति तदेवाश्वमेधस्याश्वमेधत्वम् । एष ह वा अश्वमेधं वेद य एनमेवं वेद तमनवरुद्ध्यैवामन्यत तꣳ संवत्सरस्य परस्तादात्मन आलभत पशून्देवताभ्यः प्रत्यौहत् तस्मात्सर्वदेवत्यं प्रोक्षितं प्राजापत्यमालभन्त । एष ह वा अश्वमेधो य एष तपति तस्य संवत्सर आत्मायमग्निरर्कस्तस्येमे लोका आत्मानस्तावेतावर्काश्वमेधौ सोपुनरेकैव देवता भवति मृत्युरेवापपुनर्मृत्युं जयति नैनं मृत्युराप्नोति मृत्युरस्यात्मा भवत्ये-तासां देवतानामेको भवति ॥

He desired: Let this my body be pure. Let me have a self by this body. Hence it became a horse,

[1] *Vide* p. 35.

because this became swollen. *And because* it became pure, therefore the ceremony gained the name of the As'vamedha. He who thus knows the As'vamedha, knows also him.

He knows the As'vamedha, who knows him in this manner. Having left it unrestrained, he considered himself as the horse. After a year he slaughtered it for his own sake, he gave up the animals to the gods. Therefore they slaughter the purified animal, representing in its nature as Prajāpati all deities. He is the As'vamedha who shines. His body is the year. This fire is Arka. These worlds are parts of his self. They in such a manner are Arka and As'vamedha. They are again one divinity, death. He thus conquers the second death. Death does not obtain him. Death becomes his soul. He becomes one of those deities.

The answer is: "He desired." What? "Let this my body be pure," worthy of the sacrifice. "Let me have a self," "let me have a body by this body". Thus he entered this body. "Because this," this body by my separation from it, destitute of glory and power, became swollen (Asvad) for this reason it became a horse (As'va). Hence the name of horse (As'va) is evidently intended for the praise of Prajāpati in this *ceremony*. Further, "because" that which was before impure (Amedhya) without glory and power, by his entering again "became pure" (Medhya), worthy of sacrifice, "therefore" the ceremony bearing the name of As'vamedha obtained the name of As'vamedha; for the nature of the sacrifice is to have ceremonies a performer and effects. This is like Prajāpati. That the horse, by which the sacrifice is accomplished, is to represent Prajāpati, is evident from the words of the S'ruti: "The dawn is the head of the sacrificial horse," etc.

The present passage, however: "He knows the As'vamedha," is commenced, in order that the worship of the sacrificial horse, as an emblem of Prajāpati and also of the fire, as it has been described, both of which are equal as being the sacrifice and effect, should be established. This view is obtained first, because in the former passage no verb, enjoining the action, is met with, and secondly because the rite (of the As'vamedha) requires such a verb.[1] "He knows the As'vamedha, who knows him," *viz*., the horse and Arka in his nature as fire, in this manner, he knows the As'vamedha, none beside, which means, that it should therefore be known in this manner. The Upaniṣad now explains, why *Prajāpati* is represented under the symbol of an animal. When Prajāpati had desired: "Let me again perform the great sacrifice," and had represented himself under the emblem of a sacrificial animal, he considered himself as the horse which he left unrestrained, *viz*., without rein. After the completion of a year, "he slaughtered it for his own sake," by his nature as Prajāpati representing all deities. "He gave up the animals," all the other animals, wild and domestic, according to the deities which they represent, "to the gods". Because Prajāpati considered himself as the horse, "therefore" any other person, who, according to the beforementioned manner, represents himself under the emblem of an animal, of the sacrificial horse, will thus think: "Let me as the representative of all deities, being purified, slaughtered, be the divinity of myself. Let the other wild and domestic animals, according to the deities of which they are symbols, be slaughtered for the other divinities which are my parts." In accordance with this, the priests slaughter at present the purified animal, which in its nature as Prajāpati represents all deities. "He is the As'vamedha who shines." He who is thus the sacrifice

[1] Ānandagiri supplies here the defect in the argument; for says he: a verb enjoining the action, has been mentioned in the former passage by the words 'He who knows the nature of Aditi'. The rite or action which is by this established, he continues, refers, however, only to a worship of secondary order; here, on the contrary, is the rule of the chief worship established.

which is performed by the means of animals is *also* described as the visible reward in the words : "He is the As'vamedha." Who ? He who "shines," *viz.*, Savitṛ (the sun) who manifests the world by his splendour. "His body," *viz.*, the body of him who is at the same time the reward and the sacrifice, "is the year," because his revolution is performed within a year.[1] And because the sacrifice which represents him, is only performed by means of fire, the reward is described by the symbol of the sacrifice. This terrestrial fire, Arka, is the cause *of performing the sacrifice.* "These worlds," these three worlds, "are parts of his self," of the body of this Arka, which is called Citi, when applied at the sacrifice. Thus it was before said : "His eastern quarter," etc. "They," the fire and Āditya, "in such a manner," as they are described, "are Arka and As'vamedha," the sacrifice and the reward. Arka, the terrestrial fire, as the visible action, is accomplished by fire. And because the reward (Savitṛ) is the effect of the sacrifice, it (the reward) is described by the emblem of sacrifice. Therefore it is said Āditya is the As'vamedha. "They," cause and effect, sacrifice and reward, Agni and Āditya "are again one divinity".[2] This is death. Being before also, one, he was divided to correspond to the division into sacrifice, performer and effect, as it was said : "He divided himself threefold." He becomes again in the time, when the ceremonies are accomplished, one divinity, *viz.*, death representing the reward. Whosoever again knows him, the As'vamedha as one deity in this manner :—I am this death, the As'vamedha, one deity, *the state of* this is gained by me as being like the horse and the fire,—"he conquers the second death," that is to say, one having died, he is not born again for the second death. Doubting whether death, although conquered, would still not get him again, it is said : "Death does not obtain him." Why ? "Death becomes his soul," the soul of him who knows death in this manner. Or, death being thus the

[1] The sacrifice is also performed in the space of a year.

[2] Life, according to Ānandagiri.

reward, "he becomes one of those deities".[1] This is his reward.

THIRD BRĀHMAṆA : UDGĪṬHA[2] BRĀHMAṆA

1. द्वया ह प्राजापत्या देवाश्चासुराश्च ततः कनीयसा एव देवा ज्यायसा
असुरास्त एषु लोकेष्वस्पर्धन्त ते ह देवा ऊचुर्हन्तासुरान्यज्ञ
उद्गीथेनात्ययामेति ॥

Twofold indeed is the offspring of Prajāpati, the gods and the demons.[3] Therefore the gods are thus few in number, the demons many. They rivalled in these worlds. The gods of a truth spoke. Let us now in this sacrifice overcome the demons by the Udgītha.

What is the connection of the words: "Two-fold indeed is the offspring of Prajāpati ?" The highest reward of ceremonial works, accompanied with knowledge, has been mentioned, *viz.*, the state of death is the reward of the As'vamedha. Therefore the Udgītha Brāhmaṇa is now commenced to expound, from whence[4] the origin of

[1] Savitṛ and Arka (sun and fire).

[2] The Udgīṭha, a part of the Sāma Veda (second chapter) is a kind of song, commencing with the mystic syllable Om, which the priest called Udgātā, sings at the Soma Yāga. The Soma Yāga is the general name for seven distinct rites, *viz.*, Agni Stoma, Atyagni Stoma, Ukthya, Ṣorasi, Vājapeya, Atirātra and Aptoryāma, where the Soma, or moon-plant juice is offered. 6th Chap. of Ās'valāyana's Sūtras.

[3] The same narrative, which here is given at the commencement of the Udgītha to show the power of life and its unity with the supreme soul, occurs in the chāndogya Upaniṣad, first Adhyāya, first Prapāṭhaka, where is also used as an introduction to the Udgītha.

[4] This source of all ceremonies and knowledge is the all-pervading life, as described in this Brāhmaṇa.

ceremonial works and knowledge which lead to a state identical with death, is derived.

If it should be said: 'The state of death has been before declared as the reward of the before-mentioned knowledge and ceremonies.[1] Now it will be asserted, that the reward of the knowledge and the ceremonies of the Udgītha is to overcome the condition of death. Therefore, since the reward is different it is of no use to explain the origin of the former ceremonies and knowledge.'

We answer, there is no fault in this; for as the reward of the Udgītha is the condition of Agni or Āditya, it is the same reward which has been mentioned for the former ceremonies and knowledge in the words: "He becomes one of those deities." 'Is it then not contradictory to say, that he overcomes death?'[2] No, because the overcoming of death means here to be liberated from the contact of innate sin.

To explain the meaning of the question: Who is that death which is the contact with innate sin? Whence is his origin? By whom is he overcome and how? A narrative is given commencing with the words: "Two-fold indeed." The word "indeed" is used to remind of a former state, *viz.*, it reminds of the present Prajāpati in his former birth. "The offspring of Prājapati, means his offspring in a former birth." Who are "the gods and the demons"? The organs[3] of Prajāpati, speech and the others. How again is the divine and demonical nature of the offspring? The answer is: The gods (Deva) who derive their name

[1] As reward of the As'vamedha, performed either symbolically, or in reality.

[2] *Viz.*, he who performs the Udgītha, overcomes death, while the reward of the As'vamedha has been stated as death.

[3] Remind here that the number of organs, according to the Vedānta, is eleven, *viz.*, the five organs of sense, sight, etc., five organs of action, speech, the hand, etc., and the internal organ, the mind. Here, however, the organs of Prajāpati, refer only to speech, smell, sight, hearing and mind, *viz.*, to those which are required for the performance of the Udgītha.

from manifesting (Dyotana) are such as are dedicated to knowledge and works, in accordance with the S'āstras ; the demons (Asura) as are dedicated to works and knowledge, the necessity of which is visible, in accordance with natural perception and inference. They are different from the gods or Suras, because they are satisfied within their own life[1] and also because the knowledge and works of the demons are directed to visible wants. "Therefore the gods are thus few in number, the demons many" ; for the desire of the organs to act in accordance with natural knowledge and works, is stronger than the desire to act in accordance with natural knowledge and works derived from the S'āstras, because the necessity of the former is evident. Therefore the number of the gods is less, because the desire to act in accordance with the S'āstras is less *strong*; for it can only be accomplished by excessive exertion. "They," the gods and the demons, being alike the parts of the body of Prajāpati, rivalled with each other for the sake of the enjoyment of these worlds, which may be obtained by actions and knowledge either in accordance with one's own nature, or in accordance with the S'āstras. The contest is for victory or defeat of the nature of the gods or demons. Sometimes the nature of the organs in accordance with knowledge and works derived from the S'āstras, is victorious. When it has the ascendancy, then the demonical power of the organs which refers to visible wants, and proceeds from knowledge and works in accordance with perception and inference, is defeated. This is the victory of the gods, and the defeat of the demons. Sometimes the reverse takes place, the nature of the gods is defeated, that of the demons is victorious. When the gods are victorious, then, by the prevalence of virtue, an ascension ensues up to the obtaining of the state of Prajāpati. When the demons are victorious, then, by the prevalence of vice, a descension ensues down to the state of inanimate matter. When both are alike, then the state of man is obtained. "The gods," who by their own small

[1] Asu here in the sense of vital air, life ; it means also fire, reflection.

number and the greater number of the demons, were defeated by them, of a truth spoke: "Let us in this sacrifice," *viz.*, the Jyoti-Ṣtoma,[1] "overcome the demons by the Udgītha," by taking refuge to the agent of the rite, called Udgātha. By defeating the demons, we shall obtain our own divine nature, as manifested by the S'āstras. Thus they spoke to each other.

To take refuge to the nature of the agent of the rite, called Udgātha, knowledge and works are required. The work consists in the recital of some (afterwards to be mentioned) Mantras, and will be established by such passages of the Yajus as: "Let him recite those Mantras." The knowledge will now be determined.

'But is this not rather Arthavāda,[2] as concluding the rite of reciting the Abhyāroha;[3] that an attempt to define knowledge?' No, because it is said in the S'ṛuti: "He who thus knows." 'But then it has the object to establish the rite of Udgītha, because in the topic of Udgītha it is authorized by the ancient narrative, *commencing with the words*: Two-fold indeed is the offspring of Prajāpati.' No,

[1] The Agniṣṭoma is a modification of the Jyotiṣṭoma, a sacrifice, offered by a person who is desirous of obtaining the enjoyment of heaven. The time of the sacrifice is the spring season. The performer is a brāhmaṇa who has read the Vedas, and entertains the sacred fire. The offering is the soma (moon-plant) juice, and the deities to whom the offering is made, are Indra, Vāyu, etc. The number of priests required to perform the rites, is sixteen, *viz.*, four Hotās (who read the Mantras of the Ṛg Veda), the same number of Adhvaryus (who recite the Mantras of the Yajur Veda), of Brahmās (who superintend and direct the rites of the sacrifice), and of Udgātas (who sing the Mantras of the Sāma Veda). Each of the priests of the four divisions has again a separate name and office. The ceremonies continue for five days.—Sabdakalpadruma.

[2] A kind of praise. The opponent reasons in this way. The Udgītha, is Arthavāda, a kind of praise and accordingly not knowledge; for praise of the deities does not contain a true knowledge of their nature and qualities, because it is merely offered for the purpose to make them propitious—Ā.G.

[3] Some Mantras of the Yajur Veda, recited by a person who is desirous of obtaining a divine state, as Ānandagiri explains: Devabhāvam anena ārohati, iti, Abhyāroha.

because it does not belong to this subject; further, because the Udgītha is established in another place;[1] further, because the rite of reciting the Abhyāroha is applied in two ceremonies[2] and is therefore not invariable; further, because the knowledge must be applied by a person who is perfect in his knowledge, and is declared invariable; further, because the S'ṛuti says: "He who overcomes this world," etc., further, because life is declared pure, speech and the other organs impure; for if life were no object of worship, it could not have been declared pure, nor speech, and the other organs which are mentioned in the same passage with life, impure, for by the reproof of speech, etc., the praise of the principal life is evident, as it was also intended. Lastly, because such and similar rewards are declared as: He who overcomes death, gets resplendent; for a state which resembles that life, for instance the state of the goddess of speech, when like Agni, is the reward.

'Let then the worship of life be granted, but no purity and similar qualities. If you say, this purity, etc., follows also from the S'ruti, we reply: it does not, because, as assigned in the act of worship, it is evidently intended as praise.'—(Arthavāda.)

We do not admit this; for, as in common life, by acquiring an object that is not contrary *to our wishes*, we acquire happiness; for in common life a person who obtains an object that is not contrary *to his wishes*, gets his desire, or he turns from the undesired object; but this is not the case by obtaining an object, contrary *to our desires*,—thus in

[1] In the Karma Kānda.—Ā.-G.

[2] There are two classes of ceremonies, the Havir Yāga, (Havis, a kind of oblation, usually clarified butter.—*Wilson Dict.*) including seven distinct ceremonies, *viz.*, Agñyādhan, Dars'apurṇamāsa, Cāturmāsya, Pas'ubandhana, etc., and Soma Yāga also including seven classes of rites which have been mentioned before (page 40). The rite of the Udgītha, which is performed by the Udgātha, is only performed in the Soma Yāga, while the Abhyāroha is included in either of the two classes. On this account it is said, the Abhyāroha, as occurring in two places, is variable, and is therefore no object of knowledge, as the Udgātha is.

our case also, by obtaining an object in accordance with the words of the S'ruti, we evidently obtain happiness, not otherwise. Moreover, there is no proof against the truth of the object of knowledge, arising from the word, which is mentioned for the sake of worship. Nor is there stated any impediment of the said knowledge. Therefore by proving, that we have acquired happiness, we also acquire the truth *of the object of knowledge*; otherwise we evidently acquire an unreal object; for he who in common life acquires an object, contrary to his idea, for instance, a trunk instead of a man, or an enemy instead of a friend, has evidently obtained something unreal. If *in this way*, the notions of the soul, of Īs'vara,[1] and of the gods in accordance with the S'ruti, were not true, then we should obtain by the S'āstra something illusive. *If this were the case*, it would be known, as in common life: but this is not admitted.

'This is not true, because Brahman is represented by differences of name, form, etc.; but such distinctions are evidently excluded from the nature of Brahman. In this perception of Brahman[2] the S'āstra is guilty of the same contradiction, as if a man is perceived as a trunk. Therefore we deny that with your obtaining the truth by the S'āstra, you also obtain happiness.

We do not admit this argument, on the ground that here is the same distinction, as it is with regard to an image. For your assertion, that the perception of Brahman by such distinctions, as name, form which are excluded from the nature of Brahman, etc., is in the same way contradictory as if a man is perceived as a trunk, is not right. Why not? Because by the distinctions of Brahman, who cannot be perceived by name, form and other properties; the perception of Brahman by name, form, etc.,

[1] Īs'vara, the supreme ruler. The soul, in which the universality of ignorance, or of unconsciousness, is inherent, and which has the attributes of omniscience, omnipotence . . . which is the cause of the world, is the universal ruler.—*Vedāntasāra*.

[2] That is to say, if Brahman is perceived, or comprehended by such distinctions.

is, established in the same way, as the perception of Viṣṇu by an image and similar things. The perception by name, form, etc., is, like the image, a mere appliance; for Brahman is by no means name, form, etc. The perception of Brahman by such distinction, as name, form, etc., by no means in the same way contradictory, as if a trunk, before it is ascertained as such, is perceived as a man.

If you say, 'that there is only a perception of Brahman, but Brahman himself does not exist; for the *perception of Brahman by name, form*, etc., is just like the presentation of Viṣṇu and other gods by an image, or of the forefathers by a Brāhmaṇa,'[1] we object; for the Ṛk and the other Vedas are represented under the form of the earth and other substances, that is to say, they are represented under the form of substances that really exist. Consequently, as the representation of Brahman, Īs'vara, etc., under name, form, etc., is the same with that just mentioned, the reality of Brahman, Īs'vara, etc., is proved. Hence also follows the objective reality of all those modes of perception, by which Viṣṇu and other gods are represented by images, or the forefathers by Brāhmaṇas.

This (the existence of Brahman, Īs'vara, etc.) follows also from the necessity, that every thing that is derived, depends upon the thing from which it is derived; for as in the five fires[2] the fire is only something derived, and hence proves the existence of an underived fire, so is the nature of Brahman in its distinctions of name, form, etc., only something derived, and hence proves the existence of an underived Brahman.

This follows also from the fact, that there is no difference between the passages of S'ruti referring to ceremonies, and those referring to knowledge; for as the ceremonies of the Dars'apūrṇamāsa have their peculiar

[1] The Brāhmaṇa who eats at S'rāddha the food intended for the manes, is a representative of them.

[2] Here the Vedic fires, by which the ceremonies the householder has to perform, are accomplished.

reward, their special rites, and a disposal of their parts in a certain order, and as by means of this a transcendent thing which cannot be proved by perception or inference is taught in its true nature by sentences of the Veda so also such beings, as the supreme soul, Īśvara, the gods, etc., who by their nature exclude the idea of corporeal composition, who overcome death and who have these and other distinctions, are taught by sentences of the Veda, that is to say, by proofs different from perception and inference, and it is therefore right that they should be true.

Nor is there a difference in passage of the Śruti referring to ceremonies, and in such referring to knowledge as to the formation of the true notion of them.

Likewise is the notion (Buddhi) whose object is the supreme soul and the like substance, neither indefinite nor contradictory. If you say : This is improper on the ground that knowledge is no object of ceremonial practice. We may grant, that any rite which has the three parts above mentioned,[1] although it is beyond common evidence, may be communicated by ceremonial practice through sentences, explaining the ceremonies ; but it is not so with the knowledge of the supreme soul, Īśvara and other substances, in which there is no possible object of ceremonial practice. Therefore the part of the Śruti explaining ceremonies, and the part referring to knowledge, have nothing in common.

We do not admit this, on the ground that knowledge has objective reality ; for the truth of that knowledge does not depend on its possibility to become an object of ceremonial practice, the rites of which have those three parts and can be performed,—but on its possibility to be obtained by proof. Nor has a notion, whose object is that knowledge, reality, because it can become an object of practice, but because it can be derived from sentences of the Vedas.

If you say : 'Admitting the truth of the substance (Brahman) obtained by sentences of the Vedas, it is either

[1] These three parts are special reward, special rites, and special arrangement.

an object of ceremonial practice, *or it is not so.* If it is such an object, it can be practised, if otherwise, it cannot be practised. As an object of practice, however, it is not proved by the evidence of sentences ; for there is no connection of words with a sentence, unless there is a ceremonial practice. On the other hand, if it is an object of practice, there is also connection of words for the sake of the ceremonies. Therefore, a sentence, dependent on practice, may be proved, as for instance: This, in this manner, is by this person to be performed ; but words, as this by this, thus, how many so ever you may string together, would never form a sentence, unless they be connected with such as: let do, may be done, etc. Therefore the supreme soul, Īs'vara, etc., cannot be proved by sentences. And if you say, it can be proved by the meaning of the words, we reply, that in this case another kind of proof is necessary.[1] Therefore this *Brahman* does not exist.'

We do not admit this argument, on the ground that there are sentences which do not require any actions *to be intelligible* ; as for instance, there is the four-coloured Meru ; for if this sentence is pronounced, there arises no notion referring to any possible practice with regard to Meru. If this is the case, how is it possible to prevent a connection of words in a sentence, expressing the idea of the supreme soul, Īs'vara, etc., with the word " exists," in the usual mode of connection between subject and predicate. If you say, 'this is inadmissible, because the knowledge of the supreme soul has no final end, as the knowledge of Meru, etc., has,' we deny this, for the reward is mentioned in such passages of the S'ruti, as : " He who knows Brahman, obtains liberation," and : " The bonds of the heart are broken," etc.

[1] I believe this to be the correct translation of the above passage, and the sense would be as follows : If you assume, that the supreme substance can be proved by the meaning of the words (Padārtha, the single words, in distinction from the whole sentence, Vākya) you have abandoned your argument, which was, that it should be proved by the Vedas ; for the meaning of words or ideas does not depend upon the Vedas, but upon their own contents, and requires therefore an investigation, different from the present.

The same is evident from the ceasing of the ignorance and other faults which are the origin of the world. And since the knowledge of Brahman does not depend upon any other *knowledge*, it cannot be considered as Arthavāda[1] (praise), as for instance, a special reward is declared by the use of the Juhū.[2]

Moreover the connection of prohibitions with punishment is learnt from the Veda which is also no object of practice. Nor is there, with regard to a forbidden object, any thing required but to refrain from an action; for prohibitory regulations depend in reality upon the knowledge that a certain thing is not to be done. If a hungry man, whose mind is impressed with the notion of food, forbidden on account of its nature or of accidental circumstances, falls in with poisoned[3] meat, or with impure rice, and the idea arises in him, that the one is eatable, and the other not impure, he is restrained *from eating* by the recollection, that food of this or that kind is forbidden to be eaten. The same is the case with regard to thirst, when a mirage produces the appearance of water. When by the knowledge of the real nature of a thing, the natural knowledge that is opposed to the former, has been removed, there no longer remains the injurious desire to eat what is forbidden by its nature or accidental circumstances. There is a cessation from the desire, which is caused by such an opposite knowledge and if that desire does not exist, no effort is again to be made. Hence it is evident, that the prohibitory regulations depend upon the knowledge of the nature of things, and not in any way upon the practice of a person. If this is true, then also in our case the regulations,

[1] Every praise depends upon a regulation, to which it supplies the motive.

[2] Juhū means a spoon of leaves, to the use of which in ceremonies, in preference to any other kind of spoon, a special reward is attached.

[3] Poisoned meat is the meat of an amimal, wounded by a poisoned weapon.

[4] Rice, etc., is impure by the touch of a person who has committed the murder of a Brāhmana, or similar crimes.

respecting the true knowledge of the supreme soul, etc., are founded solely upon the knowledge of the supreme soul itself. In this manner, when the worldly knowledge, produced by one's own nature, is removed by the recollection of the true knowledge of the supreme soul and of similar substances, a person, whose mind impressed with the knowledge of Brahman, has not any desire, caused by a knowledge, contrary to that Brahman, because he knows that those desires have no real object.

'The eating of poisoned meat having an undesirable (unreal) object, and there being at the same time a recollection of the knowledge of the real nature of a thing we may grant, that the natural knowledge, contrary to the former, which refers to its eating, is abolished; yet we must contend, that the absence of a desire to perform what is commanded by the Śāstra, is not admissible, because there is no object of prohibition, as there is such an absence of a desire to eat meat as before described.'

We deny this; for there is in reality no difference between the cause of the contrary knowledge and of the cause of the desire of an undesirable object. As the desire to eat poisoned meat, etc., is caused by a false knowledge and is the cause of danger, so it is also with regard to the desires of what is commanded by the Śāstras. Accordingly, a person who perfectly knows the reality of the supreme soul has consistently no desire of any actions commended by the Śāstras, because all such desires are the causes of false ideas and of danger, and because by the knowledge of the supreme soul, the contrary knowledge is abolished.

'This may be granted for the above mentioned prohibitions and commands, but it cannot be granted for the regular ceremonies; for these are solely produced by the Śāstra, and not directed to an unreal object.'

We do not agree; for the regular ceremonies are merely commanded on behalf of such persons who are tainted by ignorance, passion, hatred and other faults; for, as ceremonies whose object is a special desire, as those of the Darśapūrṇamāsa, are commanded on behalf of a person who is tainted by the fault of desiring heaven, etc., so are the regular ceremonies enjoined on behalf of a person who is stained by the fault of ignorance, the cause of all unreality, stained by love and hatred, etc., in obtaining the good and avoiding the evil, in accordance with the impressions of ignorance, and who is anxious to obtain the good and avoid the evil of his indiscriminate desires, caused by love and hatred ; hence they (the regular ceremonies) do not merely refer to the Śāstras. Nor can it be ascertained whether the Agnihotra, Darśapūrṇamāsa, Cāturmāsya, Paśubandha and Soma, are by their own nature, regular ceremonies, or ceremonies whose object is a special desire ; for, their reference to desire only arises, when they have found an agent, who is tainted with the desire of heaven, etc. Therefore the regular ceremonies behoof to one, who is tainted with the blame of ignorance, etc., and who is desirous to obtain the good and to avoid the evil, pointed out to him by the promptings of his own nature. On the other hand, for one who has the true knowledge of the supreme soul, no action is found to be commanded, except the subduing of his desires ; for, by the annihilation of the knowledge concerning all other motives, as ceremonies, causes, divinities, etc., the knowledge of the soul is established. And the knowledge with regard to actions, performer, etc., beings once annihilated, there does not arise a desire of any action, because this only takes place, if preceded by a knowledge of a special action, a special motive, etc. ; for there is no time to engage into actions for him who has the firm idea of Brahman, removed as it is from all notions of space, time, extension, duality, etc.

If you say 'there is the same time, as if one is about to eat,' we deny this ; there is no necessity to engage in eating, etc., all such acts are only necessary in consequence of ignorance and other faults ; for if an action is sometimes performed, and sometimes not, it cannot be called a regular action that has been fixed according to a rule. Because eating and other actions are merely done in consequence of faults, there is no certain rule for them, as there is no certain rule for desires and their objects, faults being sometimes prevalent, sometimes subdued. Hence, however, does not follow any uncertainty for regular actions, because time and other circumstances have been fixed for them by the S′āstra.

If you lastly say, 'even granted, that faults, etc., are the mediate cause of actions, (as eating, etc.), still there may have been fixed a time to engage in such actions, as eating, as according to the command of the S′āstra for ceremonies like the Agnihotra, times of morning and evening are appointed,'—we do not agree, because rule and action cannot be substituted for each other, *viz.*, a rule is no action, and an action no rule,—hence no objection remains against the supposition of knowledge. Consequently, in accordance with the rule of true knowledge of the supreme soul, which (knowledge) has the power to destroy its contrary knowledge of extension, duality, etc., the reality of the rule by which all actions are forbidden, is established; for the absence of any engagement in actions is the same, as if there were a prohibition. Therefore as the prohibitory regulation of the S′āstra is proved, so also the supreme soul, as produced by the S′āstra, and as the sole object of the S′āstra, has been proved.

2. ते ह वाचमूचुस्त्वं न उद्गायेति तथेति तेभ्यो वागुदगायत् यो वाचि भोगस्तं देवेभ्य आगायत् यत् कल्याणं वदति तदात्मने ते विदुरनेन वै न उद्गात्रात्येष्यन्तीति तमभिद्रुत्य पाप्मनाविध्यन्त्स यः स पाप्मा यदेवेदमप्रतिरूपं वदति स एव स पाप्मा ॥

The gods then said to speech: "Do thou for our sake sing the Udgītha." Speech, with the words: "Let it be so," sang the Udgītha for them. She sang to the gods all the enjoyment that is in speech. That she speaks well, is for herself.

The *demons* knew, by this Udgītha the gods will overcome us. Therefore, running up to him, they pierced him with their sin. That is this sin. That one speaks improper words, is the sin.

"The gods then," after having thus considered, said to speech, to the tutelary goddess of speech: "Do thou for our sake sing the Udgītha," perform the ceremony of Udgītha; for, they considered the ceremony of the Udgītha to be performed by the goddess of speech, and moreover by Mantras like this: "Do thou lead us from evil to good," her as the goddess called Japamantra. In this ceremony, speech and the other organs are pointed out as the agents of internal worship and external rites. For what reason?[1] Because their own objects and all intercourse concerning knowledge and ceremonies, are in truth only possible by their agency; for by the passage in the sixth chapter[2] *of this Upaniṣad*, "it thinks as it were," "it proceeds as it were," it is evidently declared, that the soul has no agency. In the end of this chapter also it will be proved, that these three, name, form and action, as resulting from work, performer and effect, in their unmanifested state, are the object of ignorance. That, however, which is different from all unmanifested things and which bears the name of the supreme soul, and is without name, form and work, will by such negations as: it is not this, it is not this, etc., be proved as something distinct, *to be* comprehended

[1] In assigning devotion and rites to the agency of speech and the other organs, an objection may be made, on the ground that all agency depends according to the S'āstra upon the soul. If this is the case, it depends either on the supreme soul, or upon the soul in its modification as life. Not on the first; for agency, etc., depending upon speech and other organs to which active power must be ascribed, cannot be assigned to the soul, which, considered in itself, is wholly without such a power. Moreover, all activity is the effect of ignorance, which is totally opposed to the supreme soul. Not on the second, because life is only the general idea of the sense, and has, therefore, in reality no agency. Hence, it is correct to assign agency and similar notions to the active senses.—A. G.

[2] *Vide* VIth chapter, 2nd Brāhmaṇa, 7th Khaṇḍikā.

under a different notion. But the mundane soul,[1] the existence of which, as arising from all the senses considered as one, is only a fiction, is plainly shown as arising from those senses, considered as one, by such passages as: "Arising from these elements it is *also* destroyed with them." Therefore, it is right to assign to speech and the other senses the reward, obtained by their being the agents of knowledge and ceremonies.

Speech, being addressed by the gods, with the words: Let it be so, performed for them, for the sake of their imploration, the Udgītha. Which is again the special work, which speech performed by the ceremony of Udgītha for the sake of the gods? The answer is: "All the enjoyment," which means, all the assistance of speech and all *the other* organs, which by means of speech is obtained in the intercourse of speaking; for the reward of all is the enjoyment, derived from speaking words, etc. It describes this enjoyment in three Stotras, called Pavamāna and in the nine remaining Stotras it assigns the reward: of the Ṛt-vik, as authorized *by the Upaniṣad*[2] by the words: "That it

[1] There are, according to the Vedānta, four sheaths or cases of the soul. The first is the intelligent case (Vijñānamaya Kos'a) and is formed by intellect and the five intellectual senses. The second case is the mental (Manomaya) and consists of mind (Manas) with the five organs of action, *viz*, speech, hand, foot, etc. [I may here observe that Colebrooke, in stating (M. E., p. 372) that the mental sheath consists of the intellect, joined to the five senses and the mind, is not quite correct, as it is mind joined with the five organs of action.] The third is the vital case (Prāṇamaya Kos'a) formed of the five vital airs, or faculties, (respiration, inspiration, circulation, etc.) and the five organs of action. The three cases united compose the subtle organism of the soul, which therefore comprehends 17 elements, *viz.*, intellect, mind, the ten organs, and the five vital airs. This subtle organism is inseparable from the soul, as long as it has to undergo transmigration; considered as one, it is universal organism, and the soul, to which this universality is ascribed, is Hiraṇyagarbha.—(*Vedāntasāra.*) In our passage the mundane soul means Hiraṇyagarbha, the soul which has the three cases, and is therefore in actual relation with the world. The last case is the nutrimental (Annamaya) which is composed of the gross elements.

[2] *Viz.* The Ṛtvik, or priest who performs the ceremonies, is not entitled to a reward for himself, because his services are hired,

speaks well," that it pronounces well the letters, "is for itself," for me; for the special work of speech is the entire pronunciation of the letters; therefore, it is mentioned, "that it speaks well"; but the effect of speaking as to the assistance of all, is for the sake of the sacrificer.

At that time (when the Udgītha was performed) by the contact which takes place between speech and the well-speaking, an opportunity was obtained *by the demons of entering* the deity like a hole.[1] "The demons knew." What! "By this Udgītha the gods will overcome us," *viz.*, natural knowledge and work by the light of the Udgītha, which is knowledge and work in accordance to the S'āstra. "Therefore," being aware of this, "running up to him," to the performer of the Udgītha, "they pierced," worried him with their sin, *viz.*, the sin of contact, which means they allied him with their sin. "That is this sin"; "that," the *sin* which was not cast *by the demons* upon the speech of Prajāpati in his former birth, "is this sin," which becomes manifest. Which is the sin? "That one speaks improper words," *viz.*, words contrary to themselves, forbidden by the S'āstra by which induced, one speaks indecorous, hateful, false and the like words, even against his own inclination, "is the sin," known by its before-mentioned effect, *viz.*, the speaking of improper words, which is found in the speech of the intelligent creatures of Prajāpati, which being implied by the speaking of improper words, is also in the speech of Prajāpati; for the effect is of the same nature as the cause.

3. अथ ह प्राणमूचुस्त्वं न उद्गायेति तथेति तेभ्यः प्राण उदगायद्यः प्राणभोगस्तं देवेभ्य आगायद्यत् कल्याणं जिघ्रति तदात्मने ते

and all the good resulting from the ceremonies, will be obtained by the sacrificer. Hence the special reward here mentioned does not follow from the sacrifice, but from the word of the Upaniṣad.—A. G

[1] This means, the deity of speech, having spoken well for its own sake, commits the sin of contact, of the connection of a desire with external objects. Therefore, by this sin of an opportunity is given, as it were, a hole of the deity, to pierce it with their sin.

विदुरनेन वै न उद्गात्रात्येष्यन्तीति तमभिद्रुत्य पाप्मनाऽविध्यन्त्स यः स पाप्मा यदेवेदमप्रतिरूपं जिघ्रति स एव स पाप्मा ॥

Then they spoke to the breath: Do thou sing these Udgītha for us. The breath, with the words: 'Let it be so,' sang the Udgītha for them. It sang to the gods all the enjoyment that is in breath. That it smells well, is for itself. The *demons* knew, by this Udgītha the gods will overcome us. Therefore, running up to him, they pierced him with their sin. That is this sin. That one smells improper odours, is the sin.

4. अथ ह चक्षुरूचुस्त्वं न उद्गायेति तथेति तेभ्यश्चक्षुरुदगायत् यश्चक्षुषि भोगस्तं देवेभ्य आगायद्यत्कल्याणं पश्यति तदात्मने ते विदुरनेन वै न उद्गात्रात्येष्यन्तीति तमभिद्रुत्य पाप्मनाविध्यन्त्स यः स पाप्मा यदेवेदमप्रतिरूपं पश्यति स एव स पाप्मा ॥

Then they spoke to the eye: Do thou sing the Udgītha for us. The eye, with the words: 'Let it be so,' sang the Udgītha for them. It sang to the gods all the enjoyment that is in the eye. That it sees well, is for itself. The *demons* knew, by this Udgītha the gods will overcome us. Therefore, running up to him, they pierced him with their sin. That is this sin. That one sees improper colours, is the sin.

5. अथ ह श्रोत्रमूचुस्त्वं न उद्गायेति तथेति तेभ्यः श्रोत्रमुदगायद्यः श्रोत्रे भोगस्तं देवेभ्य आगायद्यत्कल्याणꣳ शृणोति तदात्मने ते विदुरनेन वै न उद्गात्रात्येष्यन्तीति तमभिद्रुत्य पाप्मनाऽविध्यन्त्स यः स पाप्मा यदेवेदमप्रतिरूपꣳ शृणोति स एव स पाप्मा ॥

Then they spoke to the ear: Do thou sing the Udgītha for us. The ear, with the words: 'Let it be so,' sang the Udgītha for them. It sang to the gods all the enjoyment that is in the ear. That it hears well, is for itself. The *demons* knew, by this Udgītha the gods will overcome us. Therefore, running up to him, they pierced him with their sin. That is this sin.

That one hears improper sounds, is the sin.

6. अथ ह मन ऊचुस्त्वं न उद्गायेति तथेति तेभ्यो मन उदगायद्यो मनसि भोगस्तं देवेभ्य आगायद्यत् कल्याणꣳ संकल्पयति तदात्मने ते विदुरनेन वै न उद्गात्रात्येष्यन्तीति तद्भिद्रुत्य पाप्मनाऽविध्यन्त्स यः स पाप्मा यदेवेदमप्रतिरूपꣳ संकल्पयति स एव स पाप्मैवमु खल्वेता देवताः पाप्मभिरुपासृजन्नेवमनाः पाप्मनाऽविध्यन् ॥

Then they spoke to the mind: Do thou sing the Udgītha for us. The mind, with the words: 'Let it be so,' sang the Udgītha for them. It sang to the gods all the emjoyment that is in mind; that it imagines well, is for itself. The *demons* knew, by this Udgītha the gods will overcome us. Therefore running up to him, they pierced him with their sin. That is this sin. That one has improper notions, is the sin. In this manner the deities came in contact with sin, were pierced with sin.

When the gods had in this manner successively examined, whether by the performance of the Udgītha the deities were fit to be manifested by the Japamantra, and to become objects of devotion, they were convinced, that speech and the other deities whom they had successively examined, were unable to perform the Udgītha; for, by contact, which is their connection with the special *work* which *they* well *performed*, they were allied to the sin of the demons. Therefore they are not meant by the Mantra: "Do thou lead me from evil to good"; nor are they worthy to be worshipped, because they are not pure, and inferior to the principal life. In the same way as the deity of speech. etc., the deities of touch and of the other organs, although not especially mentioned *in this passage*, were pierced with sin by the manifestation of good and evil works, which means, they were allied to sin. Thus speech and the other deities, although gradually worshipped, were unable to protect from death.

7. अथ हेममासन्यं प्राणमूचुस्त्वं न उद्गायेति तथेति तेभ्य एष प्राण
उदगायत्ते विदुरनेन वै न उद्गात्रात्येष्यन्तीति तदभिद्रुत्य पाप्मना-
विध्यन्स यथाश्मानमृत्वा लोष्ठो विध्वꣳसेतैवꣳहैव विध्वꣳसमाना
विष्वञ्चो विनेशुस्ततो देवा अभवन् पराऽसुरा भवत्यात्मना
परास्य द्विषन्भ्रातृव्यो भवति य एवं वेद ॥

Then the gods spoke indeed to this life whose name is Āsanya: 'Do thou sing the Udgītha for us.' That life, with the words 'Let it be so,' sang the Udgītha for them. The *demons* knew, by this Udgītha the gods will overcome us. Therefore running up to him, they wished to pierce him with their sin. As a clod of earth, by falling upon a rock, is destroyed, so they were also altogether destroyed. Hence they became gods; the demons perished. *In this manner* he becomes *like him.* By the soul perishes the enemy, the brother's son, of him, who thus knows.

"Then the gods spoke indeed to this, (the word "this" is used to show respect) life, whose name is Āsanya," which means, produced in the mouth, which abides in the inner cavity of the mouth: Do thou sing the Udgītha for us. The principal life, with the words: 'Let it be so,' sang the Udgītha for the gods who had invoked its protection. This and what immediately follows, is all alike the former description. When the demon, desirous of piercing life with sin, in accordance with the practice which they had acquired by repeatedly entering speech and the other organs, attacked by their sin of contact the principal life which was free from sin, they became destroyed. To show how, an illustration is given. As in common life a clod of earth which is thrown upon a rock to reduce it to dust, is destroyed, reduced to dust itself, so were the demons, in different ways destroyed. By this destruction of the demons, speech and the other organs became free from the sins, which are the effect of the natural contact, and obstacles to their divinity; and obtained their own nature by the protecting power of the principal life which is free from contact. What did they obtain? The nature of fire, etc., in accordance with their own divinity, which (nature) will be explained hereafter, and which they had already before possessed. In this state, when their knowledge was darkened by their natural sin, they had a notion of an individual body alone. The meaning is: By the separation from that sin they left off the notion of an individual body, and obtained a notion of the nature of speech, etc., in its identity with fire, etc., as it is delivered in the S'āstra. Moreover their opponent, "the demons, perished". Perished means, they were destroyed. "*In this manner* he (the present sacrificer) becomes *like him*" (the ancient sacrificer) this means: As the former sacrificer,[1] described in the ancient narrative,—when he had comprehended the meaning of the S'ruti pointed out in this narrative, when he in the order mentioned in the S'ruti, had examined speech and the other deities, and abandoned them, because they are tainted with the sin of contact, when he had known by the idea of the soul the principal life free from sin and abandoned the idea, that the soul is different according to *the differences of*

[1] The sacrificer in a former birth.

the individual bodies, as speech and others, which are believed to be the soul, *as the former sacrificer* obtained the nature of the present Prajāpati, as manifested by the S'āstra, which is the notion of the body, as Virāj,[1] and which exhibits speech in its nature as fire,—so the present sacrificer obtains the state of Prajāpati in the same manner. "By the soul," in its modification of Prajāpati, his sin, contrary to the nature of Prajāpati, "the brother's son, perishes"; for the son of a brother, like Bharata and others, may be also not an enemy; but the sin produced by the contact of the senses with their objects, is at the same time a brother's son and an enemy, because it does not acknowledge the nature of the supreme soul. This sin then perishes, is reduced to dust, as a clod of earth, by its contact with life. Whose is this reward? The answer is: "He Who thus knows," which means, who thus, like the ancient sacrificer, comprehends life by the notion of the soul. Having described the reward, the S'ruti now shows the reward in the form of the narrative.[2] And for what reason? To prove, that the principal life, after the deities of speech, etc., have been rejected is alone to be worshipped by the idea of the soul, on the ground, that it is the common nature (soul) of such separate substances, as speech, etc., the S'ruti goes on in the narrative.

8. ते होचुः क्व नु सोऽभूद्यो न इत्थमसक्तेत्ययमास्येऽन्तरति सोऽयास्य
आङ्गिरसोऽङ्गानाꣳ हि रसः ॥

They spoke. Where was he, who thus established us? He is within the mouth; hence he is Ayāsya. *He is* Āṅgīrasa, because he is the essence of the members.

[1] *Vide* page 35.

[2] Ānandagiri explains this so: As the reward, following from the worship of the principal life has been set forth the next words of the Upaniṣad; "They spoke," etc., refer to a special worshisp of life. S'aṅkara says therefore, "Having described the reward," which means, having described the reward following from the worship of the principal life, he is to show the worship of life, endowed with special qualities.

"They," the organs of Prajāpati, having, by means of the principal life, obtained their divine nature and their reward, spoke thus: "Where then," the word where shows their reflection. "Where then was he who thus established us," that is to say, united us by the true notion of the soul with our divine nature, which was before separated from us; for whosoever is assisted by some body, remembers his benefactor. In the same manner the gods, when they had remembered their benefactor, had reflected on him, perceived him in the soul which is the whole of causes and effects. Why is he within the mouth? Because he is evidently in the ether of the mouth (Asya), as everybody will find on reflection. Thus also the gods. Life is called Ayāsya, because, excluding all distinctions of the nature of speech, etc., it was perceived by the gods within the internal ether; therefore is life like Ayāsya, since opposed to all distinctions, it united the organs, as speech, etc., with their divine nature. Hence it is called also Āṅgīrasa, the essence of causes and effects; for Āṅgīrasa is a compound of Aṅga and Rasa—Aṅga meaning members, causes and effects, and Rasa essence, substance; the whole meaning, therefore, is the substance, upon which causes and effects depend. It is the essence of every thing, because unless it were present, all would become without effect. The meaning of the whole is:—Life as the essence of causes and effects, and as annihilating all distinctions, is the common essence of causes and effects, and also purified; accordingly life, without further reference to speech, etc., is to be considered under the idea of the soul; for the soul can but be perceived by its own notion, since good is obtained by a notion that is not contradictory; otherwise evil is obtained.

9. सा वा एषा देवता दूर्नाम दूरꣳ ह्यस्या मृत्युर्दूरꣳ ह वा अस्मान्मृत्यु-
र्भवति य एवं वेद ॥

The name of that deity is Dūr; for death is far (dūr) from it. Far is death surely also from him who thus knows.

If it be thought, that the purity of life has not been proved, we ask, is not thus notion of the impurity (of life) removed, since life is no place for the sin of contact, as speech and the other organs are by well speaking, hearing, smelling., etc.? 'This may be so; but since it is called the essence of speech and the other organs as diffused through all, there is an apprehension that impurity may ensue through speech and the other organs, as it does by touching a person who has touched a corpse.' To this the S'ruti answers; "Life is pure." Wherefore? "The name of that deity is Dūr" (far). The demons, coming in contact with life, were destroyed, as a clod of earth is by a stone. This is the deity which, abiding in the body of the sacrificer of the present time, has been found by the gods as abiding in the mouth. It is a deity, because it is an object of devotion. Because its name is Dūr, (Dūrit,) its purity is proved by the name of Dūir. Whence again comes the name of Dūr the S'ruti answers, "because death, *viz.*, sin, which is defined by contact, is far (dūr) from that deity of life. Dūriti as the name of life, shows its purity, because death, although placed near, is yet removed from life, which by its nature is free from contact. The reward of the wise is then mentioned, *viz.*, "Far is death surely from him," from him means from the person who knows in the above described manner. Therefore, he worships thus the true life which is pure. Upāsana (worship) is derived from upa, which means, Manasa upa-āgamya (having perceived by the mind) the nature of a deity in the same way, as by passage of the S'ruti in the Arthavāda (praise) it is made known as an object of worship—and from Āsana, which means continued reflection without interposition of worldly notions until the idea is manifested, I am that deity, just as in the common notion, I am a man. This is evident from such passages of the S'ruti, as: "having thus become a god, he goes to the gods," and; "what god art thou in the eastern quarter?"

10. सा वा एषा देवतैतासां देवतानां पाप्मानं मृत्युमपहत्य यत्रासां
दिशामन्तस्तद्गमयांचकार तदासां पाप्मनो विन्यदधात्तस्मान्न
जनमियान्नान्तमियान्नेत्पाप्मानं मृत्युमन्ववायानीति ॥

This deity then, after having destroyed the sin of the deities, *viz.*, death, made him depart, where the end is of the quarters. There it fixed the abode of the sins of the deities. Hence let no one repair to the outer people, let him not follow sin, death.

"This deity then." It is said, that death is far from it, but why again is death far from him who knows? The answer is because death is opposed to a knowledge of such a kind; for sin, which is produced by the contact of the senses with their objects, is opposed to a person, who has the notion, that life is identical with the soul. He is at variance, because he has the notion, that the soul is different according to the differences of speech, etc., and because his knowledge is produced by his own nature. On the other hand, the notion, that life is identical with the soul, is produced by the S'āstra. In consequence it is proper to say, that sin is far from one who has such a notion of life, because both are opposed to each other. Therefore, by the words: "This deity," the S'ruti shows the said meaning to be sin, the death of speech and the other deities; for every body dies by the sin produced by contact of the senses with their objects in accordance with his natural ignorance. Sin is therefore called death. Life, by the soul notion of its identity with the soul, destroyed the death of the deities who had the notion of the identity of life with the soul, and is therefore called the destroyer. Sin, then, is removed from a person who thus knows by his being at variance with it. What did life again, when it has destroyed the sin, the death of the gods? The answer is: "life made him depart, where the end is of the quarters," *viz.*, of the eastern and the other quarters. But as there is no end of the quarters how can life make him depart there? The word "quarter" is made for the purpose to designate the abode of the people possessed of the knowledge of the Vedas; the country, therefore inhabited by people who do not follow the Vedas, is called the end of the country, the desert. Accordingly, there is no blemish in the expression. The deity of life made depart there the sins of the deities and by contempt fixed in various ways their abode among the outer people, who are without knowledge of the identity of life with the soul.

For, he is by his nature produced by the contact of the senses with their objects, and is therefore dependent upon the living creatures. Hence let them not go to the outer people, not approach them by intercourse in words or other actions. By intercourse with them, intercourse is made with sin; for he is the place of sin. The meaning is: Let none repair to his abode which is defined by the end of the quarters, although it may not be inhabited by the people, nor to that people, although it may be far from that country.

11. सा वा एषा देवतैतासां देवतानां पाप्मानं मृत्युमपहत्याथैनां मृत्युमत्यवहत ॥

That deity destroyed the sin, death, of those deities. Then life, having overcome death, saved them.

By the words: "That deity," the reward is mentioned, which for speech, etc., results from the knowledge, that life is the soul which reward is to acquire the nature of fire, etc. Then life, having overcome death, saved them. This means: Life is called the destroyer of sin death, because sin, death, which causes the separation of the soul *from life*, has been destroyed by the knowledge that life is one with the soul. Therefore this life, having overcome the natural sin, or death, saved them, which means, caused the deities of speech and the other organs to gain their divine nature as fire, etc., which is not separated from them (after the destruction of death).

12. स वै वाचमेव प्रथमामत्यवहत्सा यदा मृत्युमत्यमुच्यत सोऽग्निरभवत्सोऽयमग्निः परेण मृत्युमतिक्रान्तो दीप्यते ॥

Life, having overcome death, saved the first speech. When speech, having overcome death, was liberated, it became fire, that fire, having become free after its separation from death, shines forth.

"Life saved the first speech"; first means the principal, which is more efficacious than any other organ to perform the ceremony of the Udgītha. The nature of speech, which was saved after death was overcome, is thus described: When speech, after sin or death was overcome, had been liberated, it became fire which means, speech was fire, before it became united with death, and became fire again after its separation from death; so great is its difference after its separation from death. This fire, when released, shines forth after its separation from death. Before its liberation being allied with death, it was not shining, as it is at present; now again after its separation from death, it shines forth.

13. अथ ह प्राणमत्यवहत्स यदा मृत्युमत्यमुच्यत स वायुरभवत्सोऽयं वायुः परेण मृत्युमतिक्रान्तः पवते ॥

Then life, having overcome death saved the smell. That smell, having overcome death, became wind. That wind, having become free after its separation from death, purifies.

In the same manner the sense of smell became air, wind. Wind, liberated from death, purifies. All the particulars are as before.

14. अथ चक्षुरत्यवहत्तद्यदा मृत्युमत्यमुच्यत स आदित्योऽभवत्सोऽसावादित्यः परेण मृत्युमतिक्रान्तस्तपति ॥

Then life, having overcome death, saved the eye. When the eye, having overcome death, was liberated, it became Āditya. That Āditya, having become free after its separation from death, burns.

Thus the eye becomes Āditya. He burns.

15. अथ श्रोत्रमत्यवहत्तद्यदा मृत्युमत्यमुच्यत ता दिशोऽभवꣳस्ता इमा दिशः परेण मृत्युमतिक्रान्ताः ॥

Then life, having overcome death, saved the ear. When the ear having overcome death, was liberated, it became the quarters ; the quarters after their separation from death, are made free.

Thus the ear became the eatern and the other quarters.

16. अथ मनोऽत्यवहत्तद्यदा मृत्युमत्यमुच्यत स चन्द्रमा अभवत्सोऽसौ चन्द्रः परेण मृत्युमतिक्रान्तो भात्येवꣳ ह वा एनमेषा देवता मृत्युमतिवहति य एवं वेद ॥

Then life, having overcome death, saved the mind. When the mind, having overcome death, was liberated, it became the moon. That moon, having become free after its separation from death, is resplendent. In this manner that goddess having overcome death, saves *the present sacrificer*. Whosoever thus knows, obtains his due reward.

Mind is resplendent as moon. As the deity of life, having in its identity with speech, etc., as fire, etc., overcome death, saved the former sacrificer, so she saves also the present one. He who knows, that life is the same with speech and the other four organs in their state as fire, etc., obtains the state of life, which he has worshipped, be it as fire, etc.

17. अथात्मनेऽन्नाद्यमागायद्यद्धि किंचान्नमद्यतेऽनेनैव तदद्यत इह प्रति-
तिष्ठति ॥

Then life for its own sake praised by the Udgītha the primeval food ; for whatever food is eaten, the same is eaten by life. On this it subsists.

"Then for its own sake," that is to say, as by speech and the other organs for their own sake praise was offered, so also by the principal life, when it had praised in the three Pavamāna-Stotras the reward which is the state of Prajāpati, common to speech and the other organs, it praised it in the nine remaining Stotras food for its own sake. The connexion of desire with the agent is authorized by the Upaniṣad, as has been mentioned before. How again must it be understood, that life praised the primary food for its own sake? To explain this, the cause is mentioned in the words : "for whatever," etc. The word food means here common food ; for whatsoever food in this world is eaten by any living individual "the same is eaten by life". Prāṇa (life) with the preposition Pra is derived from Ana. Ana, with a final 's', (Prāṇas) means cart, with a final vowel (Prāṇa) life. The meaning is : this is eaten by life. And the primary food is not only eaten by life ; but life subsists on it, when it is transformed into the substance of its (life's) own body. Therefore the primary food is praised by life for the sake of its own subsistence.

All that is eaten by life, is for its own subsistence ; therefore the sin, which arises from the contact with the excellence of performance, is not in life as it is in speech, etc.

18. ते देवा अब्रुवन्नेतावद्वा इदꣳ सर्वं यदन्नं तदात्मन आगासीरनु नोऽस्मिन्नन्न आभजस्वेति ते वै माभिसंविशतेति तथेति तꣳ समन्तं परिण्यविशन्त तस्माद्यदनेनान्नमत्ति तेनैतास्तृप्यन्त्येवꣳ ह वा एनꣳ स्वा अभिसंविशन्ति भर्ता स्वानाꣳ श्रेष्ठः पुर एता

भवत्यन्नादोऽधिपतिर्य एवं वेद य उहैवं विदᳲस्वेषु प्रतिपत्तिर्बुभूषति न हैवालं भार्येभ्यो भवत्यथ य एवैतमनुभवति यो वै तमनुभार्यान्बुभूषति स हैवालं भार्येभ्यो भवति ॥

The gods spoke : ' All this is *only* so much. Whatsoever food there is, is praised by thee for thy own sake. Let us eat of that food.' *Life answered* : ' Do enter me.' They with the words : ' Let it be so,' everywhere entered life. Therefore whatsoever food is eaten by life, satisfies them. Him enter his own ; he is the preserver of his own, he is pre-eminent ; he walks before, he is an eater of food, he is the lord paramount who thus knows. He who against one who thus knows, amongst his own becomes a rival lord, is not able to support his dependents. On the other hand, whosoever becomes a follower, of such a one, and whosoever, following him, strives to support his own dependents, is able to provide for them.

"The gods." 'But it is not improper to assert, that the food was thus eaten *merely* by life, since it is evident, that food is also the cause of the support of speech, etc. ?' There is no fault in this, because the support is obtained by the means of life. How again is the food supplied by life, in support of speech and the other organs ? To explain this, it is said : "The gods." (Deva) speech and others, (they are called gods, Deva, because they manifest their own nature,) "spoke" to the principal life. "All this is only so much"; hence there is no more than this. "Whatsoever food," the cause of the support of life, is eaten in the world, is praised by thee for thy own sake, "which means is transformed by thy praise into thy own substance. We also are unable to subsist without food ; therefore let us afterwards for our own sake eat of thy food. Life answered :

All of you, if desirous of food, everywhere enter me." When, life had thus spoken, they surrounded and entered life with the words, 'Let it be so.' Thus the good food, the support of life, which is eaten by life, satisfies speech and the other organs which entered life by its command; but by their own will they have no connection with food. Therefore, it is proper to assert, that food is eaten merely by life. "Therefore" Because the deities of speech and the other organs by taking refuge to life had entered life in accordance with its command, "therefore whatsoever food people eat by life, the same satisfies them, *viz.*, speech and the other organs. Whosoever knows that life is the support of speech, etc., and also knows that the five organs depend upon life, "him enter also his own," his relations, as speech and the other organs enter life, which means, he is the supporter of his relations. "He is the preserver of his own" who have entered him, by his own food, as life is of speech, etc. Thus "he is pre-eminent". "He walks before," he has the precedence, as life among speech, etc. "Thus he is an eater of food," which means, he is without disease. "He is lord paramount," and to guide them he becomes their preserver as independent lord, as life of speech, etc. He "who thus knows," *viz.*, life, will obtain the above mentioned reward. But he who against one who thus knows, *viz.*, who thus knows life, "amongst his own," amongst his relations, "becomes a rival lord," like the demons who strove against life, "is not able to support his dependents". On the other hand, "whosoever amongst his relations becomes a follower of such a one," of a man who has that knowledge, as speech and others were of life, "and whosoever, following such a person, strives to support his own dependents," as speech and the other senses, following life, strove to support themselves, "is able to provide for them," not any other who acts on his own will.

19. सोऽयास्य आङ्गिरसोऽङ्गानाᳪँ हि रसः प्राणो वा अङ्गानाᳪँ रसः
प्राणो हि वा अङ्गानाᳪँ रसस्तस्माद्यस्मात्कस्माच्चाङ्गात्प्राण
उत्क्रामति तदेव तच्छुष्यत्येष हि वा अङ्गानाᳪँ रसः ॥

He who abides in the mouth, is Āṅgirasa; for he is the essence (Rasa) of the members (Aṅga). Life is the essence of the members; for life is the essence of the members; therefore, for the reason, that any member, from which life has departed, becomes dry, life is the essence of the members.

All this is declared to be the reward, resulting from the knowledge of the qualities of life. To establish the idea, that life is the essence of causes and effects, life is named Āṅgirasa. Before it was said: "This (life) is Āṅgirasa";[1] but there was no reason assigned, why it is Āṅgirasa; to explain this reason, it is now said: "He who abides within the mouth, is Āṅgirasa." For it depends upon this reason, that life is the essence of causes and effects; afterwards the dependence of speech and the other organs upon life is stated. How is this dependence to be proved? To answer this it is said; "He who abides within the mouth is Āṅgirasa." Hence it is taken according to its former description. The next sentence: "Life is the essence of the members," is to remind of the meaning that has been explained before. How is life the essence of the members? The answer is: "For life"; the word 'for' is used to show, that the essence of the members is well known. It is well known, that life is the essence of the members, but not that speech and the other organs of the essence. Therefore it is proper to remind of this by the words: "Life is." How is it again well known? To answer this, it is said. "Therefore." The word "therefore," which conveys the idea of conclusion, must be connected with the last part of the sentence. "For the reason that any member from which life has departed, becomes dry," without essence, "therefore" this is the conclusion, "life is the essence of the members". Hence it is evident, that life is the substance of causes and effects, because, when it is not there, dryness, death, ensues. Therefore all living creatures

[1] Page 61.

live through it. Therefore in preference to speech and the other organs, life is an object of worship. This latter is the meaning of the whole deduction.

20. एष उ एव बृहस्पतिर्वाग्वै बृहती तस्या एष पतिस्तस्मादु बृहस्पतिः ॥

This is also Bṛhaspati. Speech is Bṛhatī. Life is the preserver (Pati) of Bṛhatī ; therefore it is Bṛhaspati.

"This is" Life is not only the substance (soul) of causes and effects which have become forms and works, but also the substance of the Ṛk, Yajus and Sāma Vedas, which have become words. By the praise of life as the soul of all, it is exalted for the sake of worship. "This," well known "Āṅgirasa," is also Bṛhaspati. Why? The answer is: "Speech is Bṛhatī," the Vedic metre Bṛhatī, composed of thirty-six syllables. Further, Anuṣṭup is speech. Why? Because it is said in a passage of the Śruti: "Speech is Anuṣṭup." And this Anuṣṭup, which is like speech, is contained in the Bṛhatī metre.[1] Therefore it is proper to declare it as a well-known fact, that "speech is Bṛhatī". Moreover all the Mantras of the Ṛg Veda are contained in the Bṛhatī, because life is praised as 'Bṛhatī' as a passage of the Śruti says: "Life is Bṛhatī" "Let it be known, life is the Ṛk," says another passage of the Śruti. Further: The Ṛks are included in life, because they partake of the nature of speech. To prove this, it is said: 'This life is the preserver of this speech, Bṛhatī, Ṛk, because it produces the Ṛk; for the Ṛk is dependent upon the wind, produced by the digestive action of the stomach. Lastly, life is the preserver of speech for preserving it; for speech is preserved by life, because without life (breath) it is impossible to pronounce a sound. Therefore Bṛhaspati is the life, substance of the Ṛks. This is the meaning of the whole.

[1] The Anuṣṭup, of 32 syllables, is contained in the Bṛhatī of 36 syllables, as the smaller in the larger number.—A. G.

21. एष उ एव ब्रह्मणस्पतिर्वाग् वै ब्रह्म तस्या एष पतिस्तस्मादु ब्रह्मणस्पतिः ॥

This is also Brahmaṇaspati. Speech is Brahma. Life is the preserver (Pati) of speech ; therefore life is Brahmaṇaspati.

Life is also the substance of the Mantras of the Yajus. Why ? "This also Brahmaṇaspati. Speech is Brahma," that is to say, Yajus, which is a kind of speech, "Of this," speech, Yajus, Brāhmaṇa, "life is the preserver" (Pati). Therefore it is called Brahmaṇaspati, as before. How again is this known ? The answer is Bṛhatī and Brahman mean the Ṛk and Yajus, not any thing else ; for since at the conclusion of this subject it is said : "Speech is Sāma," it is evident that the Sāma Veda is the same with speech. In the same manner, if speech is Bṛhatī, speech Brahman, and both therefore the same with speech ; it is proper to maintain, Ṛk and Yajus are Bṛhatī and Brahman, for they are remaining ; for as the Sāma is mentioned last, the remaining two must be the Ṛk and Yajus. This follows also from the difference occurring in speech ; for Ṛk and Yajus are different kinds of speech. Therefore it is right to say, that they are the same with speech. And also from the fact that *if this were not the case*, there would not be any distinction between them. The word : "The Sāma is the Udgītha," clearly shows the use of a distinct name. Therefore it is also proper to employ the distinct names of Bṛhatī and Brahman ; otherwise, if distinct names were not fixed, there would be no sense. Further, if special names of them were a mere sound, there would be a repetition of the same.[1] And the names of the Ṛk, Yajus, Sāma, Udgītha, are also successively mentioned in the Śruti.

22. एष उ एव साम वाग् वै सामैष सा चामश्चेति तत्साम्नः सामत्वं यद्वेद समः प्लुषिणा समो मशकेन समो नागेन सम एभिस्त्रिभिर्लोकैः

[1] *viz.* Speech is speech.

समोऽनेन सर्वेण तस्माद्वेव सामाश्नुते साम्नः सायुज्यꣳ सलोकतां जयति य एवमेतत्साम वेद ॥

This is also Sāma. Speech is Sāma. Sāma is Sā and Ama. Therefore the Sāma has the nature of Sāma.—Because it is like (Sāma) a bee, like a gnat, like an elephant, like these three worlds, like this all, therefore again it is called Sāma. He obtains unity of nature with Sāma, or unity of place who thus knows this Sāma.

"This is also Sāma." Why? The answer is "Speech is Sā," *viz.*, whatsoever is included in the feminine gender is Sā, speech; for the demonstrative pronoun Sā denotes all that is included in the feminine gender. In the same manner this life is Ama, *viz.*, Ama means all that is included in the masculine gender. How hast thou obtained my masculine names? The answer is: By life. How hast thou obtained my feminine names? By speech, as another passage of the S'ruti says. Both, the names of speech and life are included in the sound of the Sāma. Accordingly the name of Sāma means a song, consisting of the whole of the letters, *words and sentences*, and depending upon life: therefore the name of Sāma is nothing else but a compound of the names of life and speech because each letter, etc., is produced by and dependent upon life. "This life is Sāma" and "speech is Sāma". Because the repetition of Sāma shows, that Sāma partakes of the nature of speech and life, *viz.*, as compounded of the words Sā and Ama, "therefore the Sāma," *viz.*, the songs, which consist of the whole of the letters, *words and sentences* must be comprehended under this idea of Sāma. The connection of the next sentence is: "Because it is like" (Sāma all which is afterwards mentioned, "therefore again it is Sāma".—The word "again" shows the possibility to explain *the meaning Sāma* in another way by the term of Sama (like). In what way is the likeness of life assumed? The answer is: It is "like (Sāma) a bee," *viz.*, the body of a bee, "like a gnat," *viz.*, like the body of a gnat, "like an elephant," *viz.*, "like the body of an elephant, "like these three worlds," *viz.*, like Prajāpati, whose body is the three worlds," "like this all," like Hiraṇyagarbha, whose form is the world, which is entirely found in all individual bodies, in the bee as well as in all others, as the idea of cow is found in all individual cows. This is the likeness (identity) of life. Again, this identity is not merely found in the different bodies in proportion to their size, because life has no shape and is everywhere; nor is the identity in the individual bodies on identity of contraction and expansion, as a light contracts in a jar and expands in a place; for the Śruti says: "All these are like, all are without end." There is, however, no contradiction between its being everywhere and its being limited to a certain size in the *different* bodies. He, who thus knows the life whose name is Sāma under the idea of sama (identity), *viz.*, *the life,* whose greatness is declared in the Śruti obtains this reward, *viz.*, "he gains unity of nature (Sāyujya) [1] with Sāma," *viz.*, with life, that is to say, unity of body organs and knowledge, or unity of place, that is to say, the same world, according to the power of his meditation, *viz.*, he who knows Sāma, life, who meditated on it, until the knowledge of the identity of life with the soul became manifest.

23. एष उ वा उद्गीथः प्राणो वा उत् प्राणेन हीदꣳ सर्वमुत्तब्धं वागेव
गीथोच्चगीथा चेति स उद्गीथः ॥

This is also Udgītha. Life is Ut; for by life all this is, upraised. Speech is Gītha. It is Ut and Gītha, therefore it is Udgītha.

"This is also Udgītha." The name of Udgītha means *here* neither a period, a special division of the Sāma

[1] Sāyujya, a kind of salvation, of which five kinds are stated. 1. Salokya, the abode in the same world. 2. Sārshti equal prosperity. 3. Samīpya, vicinity. 4. Sārupya, likeness of form. 5. Ekatva, unity or identity of nature.

Veda, nor the portion, referring to songs (Udgāna), because the Udgītha is included in the description of the Sāma, *which means here life* (Sāma). Why *then* is life Udgītha? The answer is; "Life is Ut; for by life is all this," the universe, "raised up" (Uttabdha), that is, supported. The name Ut, which elucidates the meaning of Uttabdha, shows a quality of life. Therefore in accordance with the single words in the compound of Udgītha, Ut means life, and Gītha speech. This Gītha after the meaning of the name derived from Gai (to sing) is speech; but with the exception of the sound Gītha (song) there is nothing in any part of the Udgītha *which refers to singing.* Therefore the assertion *that life is Udgītha* is proper, *viz.*, Ut is life, and Gītha speech dependent upon life; both terms, thus compounded in one term form Udgītha.

24. तद्धापि ब्रह्मदत्तश्चैकितानेयो राजानं भक्षयन्नुवाचायं त्यस्य राजा मूर्धानं विपातयताद्यदितोऽयास्य आङ्गिरसोऽन्येनोद्गायदिति वाचा च ह्येव स प्राणेन चोदगायदिति ॥

There is also a narrative: Brahmadatta, the grandson of Çikitāna when drinking the resplendent *Soma juice*, spoke: 'Let this resplendent *juice* cut off the head of this *man*, if Ayāsya Āṅgirasa performed the Udgītha by any other than this.' Therefore he performed the Udgītha by speech and life.

To show the firmness of the just explained meaning, a narrative is commenced with the words: "There," that is, with regard to the meaning just explained, a narrative is also known. "Brahmadatta," by name, the young grandson of Çikitāna when drinking at the sacrifice the resplendent Soma juice, spoke: "Let this resplendent juice," that is here in the sacrificial cup and drunk by me, "cut off the head of this *man*," of me speaking falsely, which means if I speak falsely. How again is the meaning of falsehood implied *in the words of the Upaniṣad?* "If Ayāsya (he is called Ayāsya Āṅgirasa, because his name is derived from the principal life), the performer of the Udgītha in the assembly of the former Ṛṣis, who created the word" "performed the Udgītha by any other," by another deity beside speech and life, "than by this," *viz.*, by the above described life in union with speech,—then let me be a speaker of falsehood, let the Soma cut off the head of me who has asserted something contradictory to the nature of the deity. In these words he made an imprecation, and shows therefore the necessity of the strength of the faith in the knowledge, *that life is the Udgītha.* The śruti confirms by its own word the meaning conveyed by the narrative, *viz.*, by speech, dependent upon life, and by life, transformed into his own nature, the Udgītha, Ayāsya Āṅgirasa, performed the Udgītha. This meaning is established by the imprecation.

25. तस्य हैतस्य साम्नो यः स्वं वेद भवति हास्य स्वं तस्य वै स्वर एव स्वं तस्मादार्त्विज्यं करिष्यन्वाचि स्वरमिच्छेत तया वाचा स्वरसंपन्नयार्त्विज्यं कुर्यात्तस्माद्यज्ञे स्वरवन्तं दिदृक्षन्त एवाऽथो यस्य स्वं भवति भवति हास्य स्वं य एवमेतत्साम्नः स्वं वेद ॥

He who knows the wealth of that Sāma here, obtains its wealth. The musical notes are its wealth. Therefore let one who is to perform the duties of a Ṛtvik, desire to acquire the musical notes together with speech. By that speech which has obtained the musical notes, let him perform the rites of the Ṛtvik. Therefore people are desirous to look during the sacrifice upon the sweet-toned *performer of the Udgītha* as *upon a rich man*; *for people desire to look upon him* who has obtained wealth. He obtains wealth, who in such a manner knows the wealth of this Sāma.

"Of that Sāma here." The word "that" connects it with the above-described life. The term "here" shows it as by a gesture as being present. He who knows the wealth of life which is called by the word Sāma, obtains what? "He obtains its wealth." This is the reward which the Śruti shows as an inducement to the hearer, *viz.*, "The musical notes are its wealth." The musical notes, the sweet sound, produced in the throat, are its wealth, its ornament; for a song, adorned with these notes, obtains wealth. Because this is so, "therefore let him who is to perform the duties of the Ṛtvik," the song of the Ṛitvik, *viz.*, the Udgāta—who is anxious to exhibit the wealth of the Sāma by its note, desire to acquire in speech the musical note, dependent upon speech. This, however, is established in the course of explaining the topic, that the tones of the Sāma are necessarily musical notes, and that the musical notes are not acquired by mere desire, but by the cleaning of teeth and the drinking of oil, etc. "By that speech," that purified speech, "which has obtained the musical notes, let him perform the rites of the Ṛtvik". "Therefore." Because the note has become the property (Svabhuta) of the Sāma, *and hence* the Sāma is adorned with the notes *as* with wealth (Sva), "therefore people are desirous to look during the sacrifice upon the sweet-toned performer of the Udgītha, as upon a rich man"; for it is well known, that "people desire to look upon him who has obtained wealth" (Sva). A person who has fully obtained the reward resulting from his knowledge of this quality, is described in the words: "He obtains wealth who in such a manner knows the wealth of this Sāma."

26. तस्य हैतस्य साम्नो यः सुवर्णं वेद भवति हास्य सुवर्णं तस्य वै स्वर
एव सुवर्णं भवति हास्य सुवर्णं य एवमेतत्साम्नः सुवर्णं वेद ॥

He who knows the gold of this Sāma, obtains verily its gold. The musical notes are its gold. He verily obtains gold, who in such a manner knows the gold of this Sāma.

Now another quality *of the Sāma* is explained, *viz.*, to be possessed of gold. This refers also to the sweetness of the notes, with the difference, however, that, while the former designated the sweetness of the notes, produced in the throat, the latter means gold only figuratively. "He who knows the gold of the Sāma, obtains verily its gold." The meaning is since the same word Suvarṇa, denotes a musical note, (Suvarṇa from Su, good, and Varṇa letter) and gold (Suvarṇa) common gold becomes the reward of him who knows this quality. Its musical note is, as it were, its gold. "He who knows the Sāma in such a manner, verily obtains its gold," just as it has been described before.

27. तस्य हैतस्य साम्नो यः प्रतिष्ठां वेद प्रति ह तिष्ठति तस्य वै वागेव प्रतिष्ठा वाचि हि खल्वेष एतत्प्राणः प्रतिष्ठितो गीयतेऽन्न इत्यु हैक आहुः ॥

He who knows the abode of that Sāma here, abides. Speech is its abode; for it is well known, that this life verily abides in speech, some say, that it abides in food.

Then the quality of abiding is explained, *viz.*, "He who knows the abode of this Sāma". The Sāma abides in speech; therefore speech is called the abode. He who knows this quality of abiding of the Sāma, "abides". It is proper to assign this quality to him, because it is said in the S'ruti, according to the manner in which "it is worshipped". To him, who, as in the former description, is desirous of the reward, and wishes to know which is the abiding place *of the Sāma*, the answer is given: "Speech is the abode of the Sāma." Speech means the organs of sound at the root of the tongue and elsewhere.[1] This speech is the abode. Therefore it is said: "For it is well known," because it is well known, that this life abides in speech, in the organs of speech, the root of the tongue, etc., therefore

[1] *Viz*, of the chest, throat, head, root of the tongue, teeth, nose, lips, and palate.—A.G.

speech is the abiding place of the Sāma. "Some," other, "say, that it abides in food," that it is well known to abide there. And because neither of these two opinions is blamed, therefore it is optional to assign the quality of abiding either to speech or to food.

28. अथातः पवमानानामेवाभ्यारोहः स वै खलु प्रस्तोता साम प्रस्तौति स यत्र प्रस्तुयात्तदेतानि जपेदसतो मा सद्गमय तमसो मा ज्योतिर्गमय मृत्योर्मामृतं । अगमयेति स यदाहासतो मा सद्गमयेति मृत्युर्वा असत्सदमृतं मृत्योर्मामृतं गमयामृतं मा कुर्वित्येवैतदाह तमसो मा ज्योतिर्गमयेति मृत्युर्वै तमो ज्योतिरमृतं मृत्योर्मामृतं गमयामृतं मा कुर्वित्येवैतदाह मृत्योर्मामृतं गमयेति नात्र तिरोहितमिवास्ति । अथ यानीतराणि स्तोत्राणि तेष्वात्मनेऽन्नाद्यमागायेत्तस्मादु तेषु वरं वृणीत यं कामं कामयेत तं स एष एवंविदुद्गातात्मने वा यजमानाय वा यं कामं कामयेत तमागायति तद्धैतल्लोकजिदेव न हैवालोक्यताया आशास्ति य एवमेतत्साम वेद ॥

Therefore afterwards the rite of the Abhyāroha of the Pavamāna-*Stotras* is defined. The praiser verily praises the Sāma. Where he praises it, there let him mutter these *Mantras*: From the unreal lead me to the real, from darkness lead me to light, from death lead me to immortality. In the words of the Mantra: From the unreal lead me to the real, death is the unreal, the real immortality; from death lead me to immortality, which implies, render me immortal. Further in the words: From darkness lead me to light, death is darkness, light immortality; from death lead me to immortality, which implies render me immortal. *In the last Mantra:* From death lead me to immortality, there is nothing concealed.—Then in the remaining Stotras let him praise the primeval food for his own sake. Therefore in those Stotras he may choose a blessing. Whatever desire he may desire, the same *he may choose*, *viz.*, the Udgâta who thus knows. Whatever desire he may desire, either for himself or the sacrificer, the same he accomplishes by the recital. This verily overcomes the worlds. There is verily no doubt to be worthy of the worlds for him who thus knows this Sâma.

For him who thus knows life, the rite of muttering prayers is appointed. The perfection in muttering prayers which one who thus knows has acquired, is called his knowledge "Therefore afterwards". Because the rite of muttering prayers, the reward of which is the ascension (Abhyāroha) to a divine state, must be performed by one, perfect in knowledge, "therefore" it is defined. The muttering of prayers by its connection with the Udgītha might be performed at any time but according to the word of the S'ruti: "Pavamānām," *a time is fixed for them*, and although the rite is *herewith* assigned to the three Pavamāna-Stotras, yet the time is again restricted *by the words*: "The praiser, verily praises the Sāma." "Where," at what time "he," the praiser, "praises," commences the Sāma, "there," at that time let him mutter these Mantras. The rite of muttering these Mantras, is called Abhyāroha (ascension), because a person who thus knows, directly ascends (Abhimukhyena ārohati) to the state of a god. The plural Etāni (these Mantras) shows that three Mantras of the Yajus are meant. *These Mantras* must be read according to the accent, which is in the Brāhmaṇa, and not as it is in the Mantras, as the second case (Etāni) proves,[1] and also their being found in the Brāhmaṇa.[2] The rite of muttering must be performed by the sacrificer.

[1] Otherwise the third case would be required.—A.G.

[2] *Viz.*, the Satapatha Brāhmaṇa.

The following are the Mantras of the Yajus: "From the unreal lead me to the real, from darkness lead me to light, from death lead me to immortality." As the meaning of the Mantras is concealed, the Brāhmaṇa itself explains it: "In the words of the Mantra: From the unreal lead me to the real, death is the unreal"; "death" it is called, because his knowledge and works arise from his own nature; "unreal" it is called from the very low degree of its existence. "The real immortality," "the real," knowledge and works, derived from the S'āstra, are "immortality," because they are the cause of it. Therefore "from the unreal," *viz.*, from unreal works and from ignorance, "lead me to the real," *viz.*, to such works and knowledge, as are derived from the S'āstra, that is to say, produce the state of the soul, by which the nature of a god is obtained. The meaning of the whole sentence is given in the words: "which implied, render me immortal." Thus also in the next Mantra: "From darkness led me to light, death is darkness"; for every ignorance, from its natural tendency to screen, is darkness; this as the cause of dying, is death, "Light immortality," the divine nature, contrary to the former (darkness); knowledge, by its natural tendency to manifest, is light; this is immortality, because its nature is exempt from destruction. Therefore: "From darkness lead me to light," as before, means: "From death lead me to immortality," which implies, "render me immortal," that is, grant me the divine state of Prajāpati as reward. The first Mantra means, from a state without causality produce a state that has causality. The second Mantra, however, means, from a state that has causality, but which is yet subject to ignorance, produce a state, where the *whole* effect *is accomplished.* In the third Mantra: "From death lead me to immortality," the whole meaning of the two preceding Mantras is given as conclusive. In the third Mantra, therefore, there is not, as in the two preceding, the meaning concealed, but it is the real meaning of the text. "Then," having made the song of the sacrificer in the three Pavamāna-Stotras, "in the remaining Stotras let him," the Udgātā[1]

[1] The priest who knows the Sāma Veda.

who knows life and has obtained the nature of life, "praise the primeval food for his own sake" in the same way, as life did. Because such an Udgātā knows life thus, in the manner, before described, and hence, like life, is able to accomplish the desire; "therefore he," the sacrificer, "may choose in those Stotras," at the recital of them, "a blessing". "Whatever desire he may desire, the same he may choose," ask as a boon, *viz.*, "the Udgātā who thus knows". "Whatever desire the Udgātā desires" asks, "either for himself or for the sacrificer, the same he accomplishes by the recital." In this sense it is said, that the acquirement of life in its identity with the soul takes place by knowledge and works, and therein is no apprehension of any doubt. It may, however, be matter of doubt, whether in the absence of works life is obtained or not. To remove this doubt, it is said: "This verily overcomes the worlds." "This verily," this knowledge of life alone, separated from works, "overcomes the worlds," is the cause of gaining the worlds. "There is verily no doubt to be worthy of the worlds," nor even a desire; for if one has the firm knowledge, that life is the soul, he has no doubt that he will obtain it; for a man, who is in a village, does not doubt, like one in the desert, whether he may arrive at the village. There may be indeed a doubt for one who has not the knowledge of the soul, which is yet far from him, but not for one who has it; he[1] therefore has no apprehension that he should not acquire the state of life as identical with the soul. For whom is there not such an apprehension? "For him who thus knows the Sāma" to be life, in accordance with the greatness, as has been explained, *for him therefore who knows*: I am the life, inaccessible to the sins of the demons, which consist in the contact of the senses with their objects; I am purified; I am speech and the other four organs,[2] which by their dependence upon me have obtained their *original* nature, as fire, wind, etc., which are free from the blemish of the sins of the demons, produced by the contact of the senses with their objects, in

[1] Who knows that life is identical with the soul.

[2] *Viz.*, nose, eye, ear and mind.

consequence of natural knowledge, and which by dependence upon me are the cause of the connection of the primeval food with all the elements; I am the soul of all the elements as the common essence of them; I am also the soul of speech, embodied in the Ṛk, Yajus, Sāma and Udgītha, because I pervade them and am their cause. When I have obtained the state of the song of the Sāma, my external wealth, or ornament is the sweetness of the notes. When I have obtained the golden state, figuratively speaking, the sweetness of the notes, the state of the song, my organs are the various places of the throat, etc. Possessed of such qualities, I pervade with my whole nature all living beings down to the smallest insect, for I am without shape and everywhere. *He will attain such a reward*, whose worship manifests such a knowledge.

FOURTH BRĀHMAṆA

1. आत्मैवेदमग्र आसीत् पुरुषविधः सोऽनुवीक्ष्य नान्यदात्मनोऽपश्यत्सोऽहमस्मीत्यग्रे व्याहरत्ततोऽहंनामाभवत्तस्मादप्येतर्ह्यामन्त्रितोऽहमयमित्येवाग्र उक्त्वाथान्यन्नाम प्रब्रूते यदस्य भवति स यत्पूर्वोऽस्मात्सर्वस्मात्सर्वान्पाप्मन औषत्तस्मात्पुरुष औषति ह वै स तं योऽस्मात्पूर्वो बुभूषति य एवं वेद ॥

This was before soul, bearing the shape of a man. Looking round, he beheld nothing but himself. He said first: 'This am I.' Hence the name of I was produced. Therefore even now a man, when called, says first: 'It is I,' and tells afterwards any other name that belong to him. *And* because he as the first of all of them consumed by fire all the sins, therefore he *is called* puruṣa. He verily consumes him, who before this strives to obtain the state of Prajāpati, he, namely, who thus knows.

"This was before soul." How the state of Prajāpati is obtained by the united effect of knowledge and works has been described, and also, how it is obtained by the mere knowledge of life, by passages as: "This verily overcomes the world," etc. By descriptions of the omnipotence and other attributes of Prajāpati, who is the embodied reward, in the creation, preservation and destruction of the world, the eminence of the reward, resulting from knowledge and works, in accordance with the Vedas is *further* to be described. For this object *the present Brāhmaṇa* has been commenced. This *description* sets forth the praise of the knowledge and works obtained by the practical [1] part, because they are of great power. But it is at the same time intended to show, that the whole reward, resulting from knowledge and works, has a worldly tendency; for it is said, that it is subject to fear and unhappiness; it is further involved in the connection between cause and effect, and as a manifestation of the gross organism [2] it is not eternal. The second part *of the Vedas*, on the other hand, is *intended* to show the liberation, resulting from the mere knowledge of Brahman, which will hereafter be explained; for he who is not dissatisfied with the objects of the world, subject as they are to the division of cause and effect, etc., has no desire *to obtain* the knowledge, that the soul is one *and all*, as a person who is not thirsty has no desire to drink. Consequently the description of the reward, resulting from knowledge and works, is made for the sake of the second part. With regard to this, it will be said: "This should be known by him." "This is better than a son."

"This was before the soul." The soul is here defined as Prajāpati, the first-born from the egg, the embodied soul, as

[1] Ceremonial part of the Veda.

[2] Vide p. 39 note.

the result from his knowledge and works in accordance with the Vedas. He was what? "This," produced by the division of body "was the soul," not separated from the body of Prajāpati; "before," before the production of other bodies. He was also bearing the shape of man, which means, that he was endowed with head, hands and other members; he was the Virāj, the first-born. "Looking round," reflecting, who am I, and of what nature, "he beheld nothing but himself," the fulness of life, the organism of causes and effects. He beheld only himself as the universal soul. Then endowed with the recollection of his Vedic knowledge in a former birth, "he said first; This am I," *viz.*, Prajāpati, the universal soul. "Hence," therefore, because from the recollection of his knowledge in a former world he called himself I, therefore his name was I. The name of I, as proved in this Upaniṣad, and therefore in the Śruti, will afterwards be explained.

"Therefore," because this happened to Prajāpati, as the cause, therefore it happens also to the living creatures, his effects; for even now a man "when called," addressed with: 'Who art thou?' says first: 'It is I,' denoting himself with the name of the soul as the cause, and when afterwards asked for his special name, the name of this special individual, he answers by: 'I am Devadatta, or Yajñadatta,' etc.; he tells the name, which was given to this individual person by father and mother. "And because he," Prajāpati in a former birth, which is the cause, as the first of those who were desirous to obtain the state of Prajāpati by the exercise of reflection on works and knowledge, *viz.*, "as the first of all of them," of all those desirous of obtaining the state of Prajāpati,—consumed by the perfect exercise of reflection on works and knowledge all the sins of contact, which are obstacles to the acquirement of the state of Prajāpati,—because such was the case,—therefore he is called Puruṣa, because he, Pūrvam Auṣad, (first burned). As that Prajāpati, by consuming all opposite sins, became this Puruṣa Prajāpati, so also any other consumes, reduces to ashes, by the fire of the practice of his reflection on knowledge and works, or only by the force of his knowledge. He verily "consumes". Whom? "Him who before this sage strives to obtain the state of Prajāpati." The sage is pointed out as he who thus knows, who according to his power manifests his reflection on knowledge. 'But is it not useless *for any one* to strive for the state of Prajāpati, if he is consumed by one who thus knows?' There is no fault in this; for consuming means here only, that the highest state, that of a Prajāpati, is not obtained, because the eminence of the reflection on knowledge is wanting. Therefore by the words: "He consumes him," is it meant, that the perfect performer obtains the highest state of Prajāpati, he, who is less perfect, does not obtain it, and by no means, that the less perfect performer is actually consumed by the perfect; thus it is said in common life, that a warrior who first rushes into battle, consumes his combatants, which means that he exceeds them in prowess.

2. सोऽबिभेत्तस्मादेकाकी बिभेति स हायमीक्षांचक्रे यन्मदन्यन्नास्ति कस्मान्नु बिभेमीति तत एवास्य भयं वीयाय कस्माद्ध्यभेष्यद्द्वितीयाद्वै भयं भवति ॥

He was afraid; therefore man, when alone, is afraid. He then looked round: Since nothing but myself exists, of whom should I be afraid? Hence his fear departed; for whom should he fear, since fear arises from another.

To show that the reward of knowledge and works, as set forth in the Karma Kāṇḍa, which is the state of Prajāpati, praiseworthy as it may be, does yet not overcome this world, it is said: "He was afraid," *viz.*, this Prajāpati, who is called the first-born embodied soul, bearing the shape of man, was afraid, as we and other creatures are. Hence it is said: Because he, bearing the shape of man, endowed with an organised body, was afraid in consequence of his desire against his destruction,[1] "therefore man," on account of his likeness with Prajāpati, also now, when alone, "is afraid". And further as with us, so also with Prajāpati, the true knowledge of himself (the soul) is the cause, that the desire against one's destruction is removed. *Hence it is said*: "He looked round." How? The answer is: "Since nothing but myself," but the soul, not a second thing, exists, "of whom should I be afraid," while there is no cause of my destruction. "Hence," from the true knowledge of himself (the soul) Prajāpati's "fear departed," for his fear is merely the effect of his ignorance, which cannot remain with true knowledge, wherefore it is said: "For whom should he fear," *viz.*, he who fears, and the meaning which is intended, is, when truth has been ascertained, fear is removed, since fear arises from a second, from another thing, and a second, another thing, is merely the production of ignorance; for a second thing, of which there is no knowledge, cannot be the cause of the origin of fear. Thus it is said in a Mantra: What blindness of mind, what distress exists for him who is conscious of the *universal* identity? And it is also proper, that by the knowledge that all is one, the fear is removed; for the knowledge of a second, from which fear may arise, is removed by the knowledge that all is one; hence there is nothing, from whence it could arise. Here it is asked: Whence was produced Prajāpati's knowledge, that all is one, or who instructed him?

Either the knowledge manifested itself without instruction. Then the same should be the case with us and similar beings. Or it is derived from impressions received in a former birth; then the knowledge that all is the soul, is useless; for *in this case,* as the knowledge of Prajāpati, although existing when he was in the state of a former birth, did not remove the cause of the contrary ignorance, because on account of his ignorance he was afraid, so also is the knowledge of the identity of the soul useless for every one. And if you, *lastly*, say, that the knowledge removes the

[1] Or of his desire for his preservation.

ignorance at the time of death, we also object, because, as before, it must again be connected with a prior *knowledge*, whence arises the logical fault of a too general argument. Hence it must be concluded, that the knowledge of the identity of the soul is useless.

We deny this, on the ground that the knowledge of Prajāpati is produced from the most powerful cause ; for as in common life strength of intellect and extent of memory are observed with him from the time of his birth, who has acquired various efficacious causes by his pious actions, so also with regard to the eminent birth of Prajāpati, united as it is with efficient causes, which are purified by his having consumed all sins, the effects of opposite causes, by the power of moral merit, of knowledge and of liberty from worldly desires. Hence it is proper to maintain, that Prajāpati's knowledge of the identity of the soul, produced at the time of his birth, has arisen without any instruction. In this respect says the Smṛti : " Whose four qualities, his unbounded knowledge, freedom from passion, power and moral merit are innate."

If you say, 'if they are innate, fear is impossible, for darkness does not rise with the sun,' we deny this on the ground, that the notion of innate knowledge has merely the meaning to exclude instruction from another. If your opinion is, 'that faith, devotion and reverence are no causes of knowledge, and that such causes of knowledge, as faith, devotion and reverence, assigned by the Śruti and Smṛti in such passages as : " The faithful whose mind is devoted to only one object, whose senses are subdued, gains knowledge,"[1] " Thou shalt know it by reverence,"[2]—have no causality,' and if you moreover say, 'that our moral merit in our former birth is the cause of our knowledge (in the next birth) as it is the case with Prajāpati,' we do not agree, because we must attend to the distinction of general and special causes, as well as of qualified and unqualified causes ; for in the common life obtains a manifold division of causes

[1] Bhagavad-Gīta, Fourth chapter.

[2] *Ibid.*, C. 1.

with regard to effects dependent upon a cause; in the same manner of general causes. These as well as special causes are again divided into qualified and unqualified causes. To show this by an instance we chose the perception of form, as an effect from a variety of causes. Here the perception of form in the dark, without light, by animals roaming at night, is caused by the contact of the eye with form. The cause or perception of form by the Yogis is the mind alone; for us it is the contact of the eye with form through light. Further by the division of light into sunlight, moonlight, etc., are produced the general divisions of the cause. Moreover there is the other divison of light, light especially qualified and light not qualified. In the same manner the cause of the knowledge of the identity of the soul is sometimes work performed in a former birth, as is the case with Prajāpati; sometimes penance, as the S'ruti says: By penance search for Brahman;[1] sometimes instruction from the teacher, as follows from such passages of the S'ruti and Smṛti: "A man, who has a teacher, knows." "The faithful acquires knowledge." "Do thou know it by reverence." "From the teacher he must be known, seen, heard," etc. Faith, devotion, etc., are direct causes to obtain that knowledge, as they effect separation from vice and from other causes *of the contrary*. The same is the case with the hearing, thinking and mental intuition of the Vedānta, because here is comprehended the present object of knowledge itself, and also because by the annihilation of sin and other obstacles the true knowledge of the soul and the mind from its very nature produces that knowledge. Therefore faith, reverence, etc., are real causes of knowledge.

3. स वै नैव रेमे तस्मादेकाकी न रमते स द्वितीयमैच्छत् स हैतावानास
यथा स्त्रीपुमाꣳसौ संपरिष्वक्तौ स इममेवात्मानं द्वेधा पातयत्ततः
पतिश्च पत्नी चाभवतां तस्मादिदमर्धबृगलमिव स्व इति ह स्माह
याज्ञवल्क्यस्तस्मादयमाकाशः स्त्रिया पूर्यत एव ताꣳसमभवत्ततो
मनुष्या अजायन्त ॥

[1] Taittarīya-Upaniṣad; Bhṛgu Valli, 5th Khanda.

He did thus not feel delight. Therefore no body, when alone feels delight. He was desirous of a second. He was in the same state as husband (Pati) and wife (Patni) are when in mutual embrace. He divided this two-fold. Hence were husband and wife produced. Therefore was this only a half of himself, as a split pea *is of the whole.* Thus verily has Yājñavalkya declared it. This void is thus completed by woman. He approached her. Hence men were born.

From this also follows the worldly state of Prajāpati, *viz.*, because "He," Prajāpati, "did thus not feel delight," which means, was unhappy, like us and others at the present time; "therefore," in consequence of the state of loneliness, etc., "no body, when alone, feels delight". Delight means the pleasure, derived from the union with a desired object. Unhappiness is called the state of mental distress, following the separation from an object of desire, to which one is attached. For the removal of this unhappiness "he was desirous of a second," of a wife able to destroy the unhappiness. And while he thus longed for his state was as of one, embraced by a wife. And because by wife this *state* he desired something real, he was of such a state. Of what state? In such a state, as in common life husband and wife are, when in embrace for the removal of unhappiness. "He," thus, divided this "self," which was of such a kind, "two-fold". The term "this" used in order to define the self and to distinguish it from the Virāj the first cause. He was by the removal of the state of Virāj, not in the same state, in which curd is, when *its former state*, that of milk is entirely removed. Which was then *the state of separation*? By the objective mental power of Virāj, entirely dependent upon himself, there was, beside himself, another body in the state of husband and wife in embrace. And this Virāj of such a kind, "was in the same state," because he is the same subject for two predicates.

"Hence," from this division (Pātanāt) husband (Pati) and wife (Patni) were produced, which is a description of the common state of husband and wife. "Therefore," because this wife is, as it were, the *other* separated half of himself, "therefore was this," this body, "*only* the half of himself, as a split pea is of the whole". Of whom was it only a half before his taking a wife? The answer is: "Of his self." Thus verily has Yājñavalkya, *viz.*, the son of Yajñavalkya (which denotes him who speaks at the sacrifice) Devarati, declared it. It may also mean a son of Brahmā. Because this male half is void, as wanting the female half, "therefore" again[1] after the taking of a wife, it is again completed by the female, as a split pea by its being joined *with its other half*. "He," "Prajāpati," under the name of Manu, "approached her," by name S'atarūpā,[2] his own daughter, under the notion that she was his wife. "Hence," from this union, "men were born".

4. सा हेयमीक्षांचक्रे कथं नु मात्मान एव जनयित्वा संभवति हन्त तिरोऽसानीति सा गौरभवदृषभ इतरस्तां समेवाभवत्ततो गावोऽजायन्त वडवेतराभवदश्ववृष इतरो गर्दभीतरा गर्दभ इतरस्तां समेवाभवत्तत एकशफमजायताऽजेतराभवद्बस्त इतरोऽविरितरामेष इतरस्तां समेवाभवत्ततोऽजावयोऽजायन्तैवमेव यदिदं किंच मिथुनमापिपीलिकाभ्यस्तत्सर्वमसृजत ॥

[1] Ānanda observes, that the word "again" refers to the same event in a former birth,—because the world is without commencement.

[2] The notion of Virāj dividing his own substance into male and female, occurs in more than one Purāṇa. So does that of an incestuous marriage and intercourse of the first Manu with his daughter Satarūpā, and the commentators on the Upaniṣad understand that legend to be alluded to in this place. But the institutes ascribed to Manu make Virāj to be the issue of such a separation of persons, and Manu himself to be his offspring. There is indeed, as the reader may observe from the passages cited in the present essay, much disagreement and consequent confusion, in the gradation of person interposed by Hindu theology between the supreme being and the created world. Col. M. E., Vol. I, p. 65. See also Wilson's Viṣṇu Purāṇa where, p. 51, note 5, a very lucid view of the opinions of the different Purāṇas on this subject is given.

She verily reflected: how can he approach me, whom he has produced from himself? Alas, I will conceal myself. Thus she became a cow, the other a bull. He approached her. Hence kine were born. The one became a mare, and the other a stallion, the one a female ass, the other a male ass. He approached her. Hence the one-hoofed kind was horn. The one became a female goat, the other a male goat, the one became an ewe, the other a ram. He approached her. Hence goats and sheep were born. In this manner he created every living pair whatsoever down to the ants.

"She," S'atarūpā, recollecting that it is forbidden in the Smṛti to approach one's own daughter, "verily reflected: How happens this improper action, that he can approach me," whom he has produced from himself. "Alas, I will now conceal myself," will conceal myself under the disguise of another kind. "Thus," having thus reflected, "she became a cow," by herself, and again and again was this the inclination of S'atarūpā, incited by the impulse of living creatures, as well as of Manu. Therefore "the other became a bull". "He approached her," in the same manner, as it has been related before. "Hence kine were born." Thus "the one became a mare, and the other a stallion," thus, "the one a female ass, the other a male ass". There, by the union of the mare with the stallion and the union of the other kinds "the one-hoofed kind," *viz.*, horses, mules and asses, "were" born. Thus "the one became a female goat, the other a male goat, the one became an ewe, the other a ram. He approached her," *viz.*, the one after the other in the order *as they are mentioned*. "Hence goats and sheep were born. In this manner he created every living pair, male and female, whatsoever, down to the ants," *viz.*, he created the world.

5. सोऽवेदहं वाव सृष्टिरस्म्यहꣳहीदꣳ सर्वमसृक्षीति ततः सृष्टिर-
भवत्सृष्ट्याꣳहास्यैतस्यां भवति य एवं वेद ॥

He knew : I am verily this creation ; for I created this all. Hence the *name of* creation ; is *derived*. Verily he who thus knows, becomes in this creation *like him*.

"He," Prajāpati, having created all this world, "knew". What? "I am verily this creation." The world is created, therefore the created world is called creation. Because the world is created by me, therefore, since it is not separated from me, am I the world ; it is not distinguished from me. Why is this I? "For I," because "I created this whole world," therefore. Because Prajāpati called himself the creation, "hence," therefore "the name of creation is derived". "Verily he becomes in this creation," in this world of Prajāpati, "like him"; he becomes like Prajāpati, a creator of the world, which is not different from his own self. Who? "He who thus knows," knows like Prajāpati, as has been said, that he is the world, depending upon the notion of the soul, of the elements and of the deities.

6. अथेत्यभ्यमन्थत्स मुखाच्च योनेर्हस्ताभ्यां चाग्निमसृजत तस्मादेतदु-
भयमलोमकमन्तरतोऽलोमका हि योनिरन्तस्तद्यदि तमाहुरमुं
यजामुं यजेत्येकैकं देवमेतस्यैव सा विसृष्टिरेष उ ह्येव सर्वे देवाः।
अथ यत्किंचेदमार्द्रं तद्रेतसोऽसृजत तदु सोम एतावद्वा इदꣳसर्व-
मन्नं चैवान्नादश्च सोम एवान्नमग्निरन्नादः सैषा ब्रह्मणोऽतिसृष्टिर्य-
च्छ्रेयसो देवानसृजताथ यन्मर्त्यः सन्नमृतानसृजत तस्मादति-
सृष्टिरतिसृष्ट्याꣳहास्यैतस्यां भवति य एवं वेद ॥

Then he churned. From his mouth, as the place of production, and from his hands he created the fire.

Both therefore are inside without hair; for the place of production is inside without hair.

That they speak there this word: Sacrifice to this, sacrifice to this, hence sacrifice to the one or the other god, is not proper. His is really this creation; for he verily is all the gods, fictitious view is obtained, if it is connected with a special fictitious attribute.[1] In this manner it is declared in the S'ruti:

[1] I translated Kalpanā with "fictitious view" and Upādhi with "fictitious attribute," as I was unable to find more adequate words. Kalpanā according to the dictionaries means: arrangement, distinction, artificial making; but these words do not express the meaning, which it has according to the Vedānta, where it is a predicate, which is assigned to a thing to which it really does not belong, or the conceiving of a thing under an idea which is contrary to its nature, as for instance, if Brahman (the infinite soul, infinite substance) is comprehended under the notion of infinite mind (manas) or infinite intelligence (Buddhi) which notions are mere anthropomorphisms. Thus far is the Kalpanā indeed an artificial notion, a notion made by some contrivance, or not founded on the real nature of the thing. Upādhi, (according to Wilson, discriminating or distinguishing property, disguise, in the Vedānta this is especially applied to certain natural forms or properties, considered as disguises of the spirit which I translated with fictitious attribute, is any quality which is assigned by a fictitious notion to the infinite soul; for instance, omnipotence, omniscience, etc. If the infinite substance is considered in its own nature, it has no attributes whatever, and the notions under which it is thought, *viz.*, existence, knowledge, happiness, are in reality no different attributes, but they constitute the one identical substance (Ātma, soul).

On the other hand, it is necessary to form fictitious views of the infinite substance; for the world cannot be thought by itself, and therefore requires to be thought by the infinite soul, as entirely depending upon it. The act of the mind by which it transfers the notions of the world upon Brahman or the infinite soul, is called Adhyāropa, which is in fact the same idea with that of Kalpanā. Under the condition, that the world is considered in Brahman, Brahma or the infinite soul is also considered under various attributes, as for instance, omniscience, universal providence, imminent cause of the world, etc. The Kalpanā, the view, although fictitious, is yet necessary, and the Upādhi, the attribute although not really an

"Sitting he proceeds afar, sleeping he goes everywhere. Who besides me, is able to know the god who is happy and not.

Then whatsoever is moist, the same he created from *his* semen, this is the Soma. So much is this whole universe, either food, or the eater of food. Soma is the food and Agni the eater of the food. This is the surpassing creation of Brahmā. Because he from the better parts created the gods, *and also*, because he, a mortal, created the immortals, therefore is it a surpassing creation. He who thus knows, becomes in this surpassing creation *like Prajāpati*.

Prajāpati, having thus created this world as a succession of pairs, was desirous of creating the guardian deities of the Brāhmaṇas and of the other castes, and at the commencement throwing his hands upon his mouth "he churned". Churning with his hands "he created from his mouth," as the organ of production, and also "from his hands," as organs of production, "the fire," the special benefactor of the caste of Brāhmaṇas. Because both the hands and the mouth are the organs of production of the fire, whose nature is to consume, "therefore both are without hair"; not the whole, however, but only the inside; for both resemble in this respect the female organ of production; "for this is inside without hair." Thus also the Brāhmaṇa was born from the mouth of Prajāpati. Therefore the fire is the special benefactor of the Brāhmaṇa, both being sprung

attribute of Brahman, is still indispensable, if he is considered in his relation to the world.

There is therefore, according to the Vedānta, no contradiction, if attributes are ascribed to Brahman, and denied of him, as long as the notions under which both is done, are kept separate; namely, he has no attributes, if considered in himself; he has attributes in his relation to the world.

from the same source, as the elder brother is of the younger. Therefore the Brāhmaṇa has the fire as his guardian deity, and the mouth as his strength, as proved by the S'ruti and Smṛti. Thus he produced from his arms, the seat of power, the slayer of Bala,[1] and other gods,[2] the ruling deities of the Kṣatriya caste and also the Kṣatriya. Therefore the Kṣatriya has Indra as his guardian deity, and the arm as his strength, as both S'ruti and Smṛti attest. Thus he created from his thigh, as the seat of endeavour—the Vasus,[3] and others, the ruling deities of the Vis', and also the Vis'. Therefore the Vais'ya is devoted to agriculture, *merchandize* and similar pursuits, and his guardian deities are the Vasus, etc., according to the evidence of the S'ruti and Smṛti. Thus he created from his feet Puṣaṇa,[4] the guardian deity of the earth, and also the S'ūdra, who is fitted for servitude, according to the evidence of the S'ruti and Smṛti. The Upaniṣad makes here for the praise of the whole creation, the supposition, as if the origin of the guardian deities of the Kṣatriya and the other castes had been related, although it has not been done, and yet remains to be related. By this passage of the S'ruti it is accordingly evident, that Prajāpati is all deities, because there is no difference between the creator and the creature, *and* because the gods are created by Prajāpati.

The meaning of the subject being thus established, the blame of the contrary notion[5] of ignorant people is introduced for the praise of the meaning, *as it has been established*; for the blame of the one is the praise of the other.

[1] Indra.

[2] Varuṇa, etc.

[3] The Vasus were the sons of Vasu. Their names are: Āpa, Dhruva, Soma, Dhaba (fire), Anila (wind), Anala (fire), Pratyūṣa (day break), and Prabhāsa (light)—W. V. P., p. 128.

[4] One of the twelve Ādityas, sons of Kas'yapa by Aditi, the daughter of Dakṣa.—L. C., p. 122.

[5] The contrary notion is, that the deities are independent beings; this view is blamed in the next sentence of the Upaniṣad.

"That they," the mere performers of sacrifices, "speak there," during the performance of the ceremonies at the time of offering, "this word: Sacrifice to this," to Agni, "sacrifice to this," to Indra, etc., they do so in accordance with the difference of name, S'astra, Stotra, work, etc., by considering this or the other different god, for instance Agni, etc., as one among others. This should not be thus understood, because "his," Prajāpati's, "is really this creation," the whole division of the gods; "for he," Prajāpati, as life, "is verily all the gods".

Here we meet with a contradictory opinion. 'Namely, some say, the supreme Hiraṇyagarbha is meant, others Hiraṇyagarbha, as being in a worldly state. According to the letter of the Mantras the supreme is meant; for the S'ruti says: "They call him Indra, Mitra, Varuṇa and Agni." And another passage. "He who is Brahman, who is Indra and Prajāpati, is all these gods." Also the Smṛti says: "Some call him Agni, others Manu, others Prajāpati." And further: He who is no object of the organs,[1] who is unapproachable,[2] who is infinitely little,[3] unmanifested, eternal, whose nature comprehends all elements, who is not conceived by thought,[4] sprung thus forth by himself. On the other hand he is also in a worldly state. This follows from the passage of the S'ruti, *stating*: "He consumed all sins"; for unless one is in a worldly state, he cannot consume sins. It follows also from the passage of the S'ruti, that he is subject to fear and unhappiness. Also from the other: "Being mortal he created immortals." Further, from the letter of the Mantra: "Lo the birth of Hiraṇyagarbha." Also from a passage of the Smṛiti *in the* chapter which treats on the results of works: Sages call Brahmā, the creators of the world, virtue, the great, the unmanifested, the best condition,

[1] The organs of action are here meant, according to Ānanda.

[2] To the senses of intellect, eye, ear, etc.

[3] This is the cause, that he cannot be perceived by the senses.

[4] No object of the mind, the internal sense.

which can be obtained by the quality of goodness.[1] Therefore a contradictory meaning being obtained, the argument is faulty.

"We do not grant this, because there is no contradiction, if it is considered under a different fictitious view, *and* a different happy."[2] Through attributes he is connected with the world; in reality by himself he is unconnected with the world. This is the identity and diversity of Hiraṇyagarbha, *and* in the same manner of all living creatures, which follows from the passage of the S'ruti: "That art thou." But while Hiraṇyagarbha, in consequence of the superlative purity of his attributes is, as it were, almost entirely supreme, as S'ruti and Smṛti declare, although they show his worldly state as it were, at some places, the worldly state of the living creatures, in consequence of the prevalent impurity of their attributes, is almost everywhere evident. Divested, however, of all distinction of attributes, every one obtains the name of supreme according to the evidence of the S'ruti and Smṛti. But the logicians who, abandoning the authority of the holy writings, reason much about existence and non-existence, agency and non-agency, confound the meaning of the S'āstra. Hence the determination of the meaning becomes difficult. But for those who

[1] This passage is taken from Manu 12, 50. According to Ānanda, by the creators are meant Manu and others, by virtue Yama, by the great one (Mahat), intelligence, Buddhi, the first production of Prakṛti, or self-existing nature, according to the Sāṅkhya stystem. Kullūka Bhaṭṭa, the commentator of Manu, explains it differently, *viz.*, Brahmā is the Brahmā with four faces, the creators Marici and the others, Mahat and Avyakta (unmanifested) two of the causes of the Sāṅkhya system, here the tutelary deity of the same, virtue the embodied virtue.

[2] Katha Upaniṣad, 2 V. 21. In this passage the contradictory predicates are founded upon different modes, by which the soul may be conceived. Thus "sitting" refers to its unchangeableness, "proceeding" to its worldly nature, where it proceeds faster than any other being. The Upaniṣads generally represent the difficulty to understand the infinite soul by assigning to it contradictory predicates. Thus it is said in the Vājasaneya Up., v. 5. If (the soul) proceeds, it does not proceed; it is far; it is near; it is within this universe; it is without this universe.

without pride follow the Śāstra alone, the meaning of the Śāstra with regard to deities is as clear, as if it were an object of perception. Here it is intended to introduce with reference to Prajāpati, although he is one God, such distinctions as food, etc., among them the fire has been mentioned; the Soma, as the first food, will now be mentioned.

"Then whatsoever is," in the world, "moist" in the form of a fluid, "the same he created from his semen," from his seed. Thus it is said in the Śruti: "From the semen sprang the waters." And the soma is also watery; therefore all that is moist, is created by Prajāpati from his semen. This is, "as it were, the soma'. "So much is this whole universe," that is, there is no more than this. What is it? "Either food," which is Soma, as nourishing by its fluidity, or "the eater of the food," Agni, by his heat and harshness. Hence Soma is defined as food. From the force of the meaning it is evident, that Soma is all that is eaten, and that Agni is the eater. Sometimes the fire, when offering is made by it, becomes Soma—Soma also, when offering is made to it, becomes fire, because it eats. Whosoever in this nanner perceives the world, as consisting of Agni and Soma, under the idea of the soul, is not tainted by any blame, and becomes also like Prajāpati. "This is the surpassing creation of Bṛahman," Prajāpati, surpassing, because it surpasses his own nature. Which is this creation? Because he from the better parts, "the parts" resembling him, "created the gods," therefore is the creation of the gods a surpassing creation. How is it again a creation which surpasses himself? The answer is: "And also, because he, a mortal," of a mortal nature, "created the immortals," the gods of immortal nature, after he had consumed all his sins by the fire of works and knowledge, therefore is this surpassing creation the effect of perfect knowledge. Therefore "he who knows" this surpassing creation of Prajāpati, as proceeding from himself, verily becomes in this surpassing creation like Prajāpati, becomes a creator like Prajāpati.

7. तद्धेदं तर्ह्यव्याकृतमासीत्तन्नामरूपाभ्यामेव व्याक्रियतेऽसौ नामाय-
मिदꣳरूप इति तदिदमप्येतर्हि नामरूपाभ्यामेव व्याक्रियतेऽ-
सौ नामायमिदꣳरूप इति स एष इह प्रविष्ट आनखाग्रेभ्यो यथा
क्षुरः क्षुरधानेऽवहितः स्याद्विश्वंभरो वा विश्वंभरकुलाये तं न
पश्यन्ति । अकृत्स्नो हि स प्राणन्नेव प्राणो नाम भवति वदन्
वाक्पश्यꣳश्चक्षुः शृण्वन् श्रोत्रं मन्वानो मनस्तान्यस्यैतानि
कर्मनामान्येव स योत एकैकमुपास्ते न स वेदाकृत्स्नो ह्येषोऽत
एकैकेन भवत्यात्मेत्येवोपासीतात्र ह्येते सर्वं एकं भवन्ति
तदेतत्पदवीयमस्य सर्वस्य यदयमात्मानेन ह्येतत्सर्वं वेद । यथा
ह वै पदेनानुविन्देदेवं कीर्तिꣳश्लोकं विन्दते य एवं वेद ॥

That which is this, was then verily unmanifested. That manifested itself by name and form, as it is *commonly* said: "He is of this name, of this form." In the same manner that which is this also then manifests itself, as it is said: "He is of this name, of this form." He entered this world.

Until the ends of the nails, as a razor is placed in a razor-case, or Vis'vambhara in the dwelling of Vis'vambhara. They do not behold him. For when incomplete, when inspiring only, it is called life. when speaking, speech, when seeing, sight, when hearing, ear, when minding, mind. These are the names of its actions. Whosoever worships one or the other special being, *separate* from that *totality*, does not know, for that soul is incomplete; it is *determined* by this or that individual function, the soul; considering this, *let a man* worship it; for in it all this *differences* become one.

This, even this is to be conceived in this all, *viz.*, this soul; for by this, one knows this all. As verily by a foot-print one finds *cattle*, so a person who thus knows, finds fame and completeness.

"That which is this[1] was then verily unmanifested." All Vedic causes,[2] denoted by knowledge and work, depend upon such distinctions as agent, etc., and their ultimate reward is the acquirement of the state of Prajāpati;[3] the effect is "so much," *viz.*, this manifested world. The Upaniṣad is now to show, how this manifested world, depending upon the connection of causes and effects, was before its manifestation in the shape of a seed (in its original shape) which is inferred, as the tree is inferred from its effect, the sprout; for this tree of the world, whose seed is work and whose field is ignorance, is to be taken up with its root, as by its taking up the liberation of man is accomplished. Thus it is said in the Kāṭhaka[4]: "Its root is above, its branches go downwards." The same is said in the Gīta: "Its root is above, its branches go downwards." It is also said in a Purāṇa: The eternal tree of Brahman. "That, the world in the state of a seed before its creation, is named, on account of its imperceptibility at that time, by the pronoun "that," which denotes anything that is no object of perception. The word "verily," which is the

[1] That which is this. Tad idam (that this) according to an idiotism in Sanskrit, where two demonstrative pronouns, this and that, are connected with the same subject, and where tad (that) refers to the past time, and idam (this) to the present time. The Vedānta frequently uses this form of expression to show the identity of the logical subject in its connection with predicates which exclude each other.

[2] Vedic causes are here causes of any mode or form of worldly existence as asserted by the Vedas; causes which lead to final liberation from the world, are accordingly in this passage not referred to; this is evident, says Ānanda, on the ground, that a multiplicity of causes cannot be a means of liberation which is of a uniform nature.

[3] Or in other words the ultimate reward is the state of death.—Ā. G.

[4] Kāṭhaka, 2 Adh., 6 Volli, V. I.

mark of a narrative,[1] is used *here* for the object to make it easily understood, that the world was in the state of non-manifestation, because it is connected with the past time. If it is said : Thus it verily was, it is easily understood, that the imperceptible state of the world is meant, in the same way, as if it is said : There verily was a king Yudhiṣṭira. "Which is this." This denotes the world as manifested by name, form and work, as being in the connection of cause and effect, in the manner in which it has been described. The terms "that" and "this" denote the state of imperceptibility and perceptibility of the world, and placed upon one and the same subject they express the identity of the world in its state of perceptibility and imperceptibility. The meaning is : That which is this, and this, which is that, was then unmanifested. If this is the case, it is evident that no effect can be produced from any thing that does not exist, and that it cannot, be destroyed from anything that exists.

"That," so described world, which was not manifested, manifested itself by name and form. The reflexive form[2] "manifested itself" shows, that the soul was manifested by itself. "It manifested itself," it clearly obtained a perceptible form of existence, the limits of whose knowledge are the differences of name and form, which by its own power[3] produced the *relations of* ruler, agent and depends upon the action of causes. "He is of this name"; by the pronoun,[4] "he," which is a name without distinction a name only is indicated. "He is of this name," *viz.*, Devadatta, or Yajñadatta is his name. In the same manner the pronoun "this," *in the sentence, he is of this colour*,

[1] The word for narrative is Itihāsa. Iti-hā-āsa ; thus verily it was, which formula commonly concluding a narrative in the Vedas, became the term of a narrative generally.

[2] Karma Kartṛ, where the agent (Kartṛ) is its own object (Karma).

[3] This is here mentioned, because according to the Vedānta it is necessary that the world as an effect must have a cause.

[4] The word for pronoun is in Sanskrit, Sarvanāma, a general name, on the meaning of which the exposition, as given above, is founded.

denotes colour generally, without distinction of white or black, etc. "That," unmanifested, substance, "which is this, then," at that time, manifests itself, by name and form, in the manner as it is said: He is of this name, this form.

"He,"[1] for whom the whole Śāstra[2] is commenced, upon whom by means of natural ignorance *the notions* of agent, ceremony and reward are transferred, who is the cause[3] of the whole world, from whom, identical with his nature, name and form, not manifested *before*, are manifested, as dirty foam from clear water, and who, different from either, name and form, of his own nature is eternal, pure, intelligent and free, "he," manifesting the before unmanifested name and form, which are identical with his own nature, "entered this world," these bodies from Brahman down to inanimate matter, dependent upon works and the consequences thereof, and subject to death and other evils.

'But it was said, that the unmanifested manifested itself; how can it now be maintained that even the supreme soul, manifesting the unmanifested entered this world?'[4]

There is no fault in this; *first*, because the supreme soul was meant under the notion of the unmanifested world; for we said, that the unmanifested world, which produces the relations of a creator, agent, etc., and which is dependent upon the action of causes, etc., manifested itself; *secondly*, because the term "this" is identical with the term "manifested". As "this" means manifested, when it has

[1] The Supreme Brahman.

[2] *Viz.*, the Veda in its two parts, the Karma Kāṇḍa, which relates to ceremonies, and the Jñāna Kāṇḍa, which relates to the knowledge of Brahma.

[3] *Viz.*, the only cause, without any difference of the mediate and material cause, as in the Sāṅkhya system.

[4] In other words, before it was not said of the soul, that it manifested the world, but it was said, that the unmanifested manifested itself. How is it therefore consistent with that doctrine to substitute here the notion of the soul for the notion of the unmanifested?

obtained the endless differences of ruler of the world and other agents, of cause, etc., so means "that" unmanifested, when it has not emitted any of its differences. The only difference[1] is, that the one is manifest, the other not manifest. In common life also the same word has different meanings according to the intention of the speaker, as if, for instance, it is said: The village is arrived, the village is empty. Sometimes the word village may only mean the dwellings, as in the sentence: the village is empty. Sometimes the inhabitants may be intended, as in the sentence: the village has arrived. Sometimes both meanings may be intended, as in the sentence: let him not enter the village. Thus also in the present case. If it is said: this manifested and unmanifested world, where there is no intention to separate them, the soul and the non-soul are meant. Further, this world subject to production and destruction, means the world alone. Further, the soul, which is great, not produced, not extended, which is not this, which is not that, means the soul alone.

But how can it be thought '*he* entered' the world, manifested by the supreme manifestor, and everywhere and at everytime pervaded by him? For a country, which is not entered before, may be entered by anything of limited extent, as for instance, a village by a man, etc., but not by *anything without limit,* as *for instance* the ether, because from its nature it is always present. If he entered it, as a snake[2] in a stone, by a modification of qualities, we may grant such a modification for the snake, but not for the supreme soul, because he entered even with his nature. If it be supposed, that, abiding in the effect (the world) he was produced by a modification of qualities, and that by this he entered, as a snake, which is

[1] Between the world in its former and in its present state.

[2] The snake can be considered as a modification of the stone, because according to the Vedānta both are productions of the five elements; therefore there is no contradiction in considering the snake a modification of the five elements which abide in a stone. In the same manner it may be thought, that the infinite soul entered the intellect and other creations by its modification as life.

produced at the same time; abides in the stone, or water in a cocoanut, we object, because the S'ruti says: having created that he entered it; for here it is evident, that the creater himself, without assuming another mode of existence, when he had created the world, entered it afterwards. Thus it is said: having enjoyed he goes. There also is a mutual difference between the actions of enjoying and going, referring to the past and present time, but the agent is the same. The same case is here, and it cannot be thought that a modification of existence of him who abides in this *effect*, is produced.

Nor accords *the idea of* an entrance, which denotes the separation from one place and the connection with another; with the *idea of the soul*, which is without parts and without limits. If it be supposed, that the S'ruti refers to an entrance, where parts are admitted, we deny this on the authority of such passages of the S'ruti as: for he is radiant, without forms, he is complete, without parts, without actions: we deny it also on the authority of such passages as prohibit the application of any differences of qualities whatsoever *to the soul.*

Nor entered he the world as an image, as there is no separation of a second thing.

Nor did he enter it as a quality enters a substance, because he does not depend upon anything; for a quality indeed, which in every way depends upon another thing, is considered to enter a substance, but not so Brahman, as depending upon himself according to the S'ruti.

• Nor as a seed the fruit, because such attributes as an increase and decrease of its parts, a production and destruction, are assigned to this relation: but there are no such attributes of Brahman, of whom it is said in the S'ruti: He is not produced, he is without age, etc.

Nor as another separate body: for, from the passage of the S'ruti: This deity reflecte let me manifest name and form, it is clear that the sam deity, which enters, also manifests and acts. Also from these passages: "Having created this he entered it," and: "Having opened the place, where the hairs divide, he entered by this door."[1] "Having considered all forms, having made all names, the hero sits inclined." "Thou, O youth, or thou, O maid, thou, old man with a staff, spends thy time," it follows, that no other enters but the supreme soul.[3]

If it be thought, there is a multiplicity in the supreme soul, in consequence of the natural differences of the things which he entered, we object from passages of the Śruti as: "One god he sits at many places; being one, he proceeded to many places. Thou, although one, hast entered many. One god art thou concealed in all beings thou pervadest all; thou art the soul within all beings."

'We shall at present not enquire, whether the idea of entering has been established or not; but it is clear, that the supreme soul has a worldly form, because the things which he entered, have a worldly form, and are not different from the soul?'

We deny this, because the Śruti says: He overcomes death.

If it is thought that he is in a worldly state on the ground that he is subject to happiness and unhappiness, we object; for the Śruti says: "He is not tainted with the unhappiness of the world, he is free from it."

If you say this is improper, because it is at variance with perception,[3] we do not agree, because the difference in objects of perception or other sources of knowledge is

[1] Aitareya-Upa., III, 12, that is to say, having opened the middle part of the skull, where the hairs divide, he entered the body by this opening.

[2] The first part of the argument was to prove, that it is the supreme soul which enters; the second is to show, that the supreme soul is not affected in its nature by his entrance.

[3] With individual perception, as in common life, people say: I am happy, I am unhappy.

only produced by *the notion* of dependance on attributes.[1] Such passages of the S'ruti as: "Thou does not behold the beholder of the visible." "How could one know him who knows?" Unknown is he who knows—prove that knowledge has no reference to the soul.[2]

To what then? Knowledge from perception, declared in such sentences as: I am happy, I am unhappy, is the object of the image of the soul, which is reflected in the intellect and in other attributes.

The same is also shown by the fiction of the identity of the perceptible object (the body) and the subject which perceives (the soul) in a sentence like this, I am [3] (body). It follows also *from the passage of the S'ruti*: "There is none else but him who sees," by which the idea of another *soul* is prohibited.

If you say, that happiness and unhappiness are qualities of the body because both must be predicated parts of the body,[4] and that therefore from the passage of the S'ruti: "For the sake of the desire of the soul,"[5] it is improper to maintain, that the soul is free from the world? —we do not agree, because the passage of the S'ruti: "Where it is, as it were, some other things," shows, that it is for the sake of the soul, which is in the state of ignorance. From such passages: "How can it behold any one." (B. Ā. 4th A. 5th B. 15. Bib. I. V. 11, p. 929.) "There is no difference whatsoever with regard to him." (K. U. 4th. V. 11. B. I. V.

[1] And therefore not by the soul, as attributes do not really belong to the soul.

[2] Accordingly no perception, for instance, I am happy, I am unhappy.

[3] Because here the soul, which is endowed with the perceptible object, the body; is an object of perception, and therefore the soul in itself is not in a worldly state.

[4] On the ground, that every one who feels pain or pleasure in any part of the body, refers this part to himself, as if one says, "my head aches."

[5] The desire of happiness is granted, the contrary must be also admitted, because both are inseparable.

VIII, p. 130.) "There is no delusion, no grief" (Vāj S. U. 7 B. I. Vol. VIII. 14) which refer to knowledge, it also follows, that unhappiness, as prohibited in them, is no quality of the soul.

If it is said, 'that the unworldly state of the soul cannot be admitted as contradictory to the argument of logicians,'[1] we deny this, because by reasoning also it can be proved that the soul is free from unhappiness; for unhappiness, which is an object of perception, cannot be attributed to the soul, which is no object of perception. If you say, 'that unhappiness is in the same manner a *quality* of the soul, as the sound is a quality of the ether,'[2] we deny this, because the soul and unhappiness are not objects of one and the same *kind* of knowledge;[3] for a knowledge of unhappiness, which is an object of perception, can never become an object of the soul, which is eternal, and can only be known by inference. *Unhappiness cannot become an object of the soul for this reason* also, that the soul, as one, is no object of anything whatsoever.

If you maintain, 'that, like a light, the soul, although one, is an object and manifests objects,' we do not agree, because this is impossible at one and the same time,[4] and because the soul has no parts. Hence the idea, that there is a perception of knowledge, and that knowledge is at the

[1] Of the Vais'eṣikas, according to whom the soul has the following fourteen qualities: intellect, pleasure, pain, desire, aversion, endeavour, number, quantity, severalty, conjunction and disjunction, faculty, merit and demerit.

[2] *Viz.*, the connection between substance and quality, which exists between ether and sound, of which the one (sound) is perceptible, the other (ether) not perceptible, may also exist between soul and happiness.

[3] This is in accordance with the principle, that where there is a relation between quality and substance, these are both perceived by one and the same kind (source) of knowledge, as for instance, a jar and its white colour.

[4] In accordance with the doctrine of the Nyāya, that the mind, through whose agency every object, external or internal, is represented to the soul, can only perceive one object at one time.

same time perceived, cannot be admitted *with reference to the soul*.

If it is said: 'Unhappiness and soul, the one of which is an object of perception, the other of inference are in relation of quality and substance, as may be known by inference; for unhappiness is constantly an object of perception, and has an equal dependence *upon a substance*, as form has,' etc. Accordingly, as unhappiness is *perceived by the soul* through its union with the mind, such attributes as multiplicity, changeableness and transientness, must be also assigned to the soul; for without a change in the substance which is in contact, it is nowhere found that a quality is added or removed. Nor has it any time been found that a substance which changes, is without parts, or that a substance whose qualities are transient, is eternal. Nor is the ether considered as an eternal thing by those who follow the S'ruti. Nor is there any other case.[1] If you say, "that a thing, although it changes may be eternal, because the knowledge, 'that is this,' yet remains"—we deny this, because the notion of change cannot be thought without the notion of a change of the parts of the thing.

And if you say, 'that a thing which has parts, may also be eternal,' we deny this because a thing that has parts, must before have been joined by a union of its parts, by which the idea of a separation is established.

If you say, 'that this is contrary to perception, as if you see lightning,' we object because we conclude that its parts have been joined before. Therefore it is impossible to conceive the idea that the soul is the site of unhappiness and other transient qualities.

And if you say, 'on the supposition that the supreme soul is without unhappiness, and that there exists no other soul which is unhappy; the S'āstra, which is commenced for the purpose to remove unhappiness, is useless, we object,

[1] The supposition of atoms is meant; for the existence of atoms cannot be proved by any evidence.

because it has the purpose to destroy the illusion of unhappiness, which is placed *upon the soul* by ignorance. And also because the unhappiness of the soul is only fictitious, *and is removed in the same way*, as a mistake in counting a common number, in which the person who counts, himself is included.[1]

As the image of the sun, etc., enters the water, so the entrance of the soul means the perceptibility *of the soul* in its effect which is manifested like a reflection. Before the production *of the world* the soul is not perceived; afterwards being perceived within the intellect in the effect which is created, manifested as the reflection of the sun, etc., *is perceived* in water, it is defined, as it were, as entering after the creation of the effect. This is evident, for example, from the following passages:

"He entered this world." (B. Ā. U. 1st Adh. 3d B. 7. B. I. Vol. II, p. 155.) "Having created this world, he verily entered it." (Taittarīya U. 2d Adh. 6th Anu. B. I. Vol. VII, p. 90.) "Having opened the place, where the hair is divided, he entered by this door." (Aitt. U. 3 Kh. 12 Varga B. I. Vol. VII, p. 198.) "This deity reflected: Verily, I am these three deities." (Chh. U. 6th Prapa. 3 Kh. B. I. Vol. III, p. 406.) "Having entered by this life, soul, etc." (Chh. U. 6th Prapa. 3d Kh. B. I. Vol. III, pp. 407—411.)

This is meant by the entering of the soul, but we say, it is impossible, that *the soul* which is all-pervading and without parts has ever a *real* entrance, the notion of which is to proceed from one part of space, place, or time to another.

[1] This seems to refer to the following tale. Ten friends having crossed a dangerous river, were anxious to know, whether any of them had been lost, and accordingly one of them commenced to count, but omitting himself (Ātma, meaning the soul and himself) found, of course, that there were only nine. The others successively counted also, but doing it in the same manner as the first, the result was the same. Upon this they thought, that one had perished in the river, and broke out in lamentations. A stranger who passed by, perceived the cause of their error, and explaining it to them satisfactorily, changed their distress into rejoicing.

Moreover there is nothing else but the supreme soul, as we said before in accordance with such passages of the S'ruti as the following: "There is nothing else that sees, hears, etc., but he." (B. A. 3rd A. 6th B. 11. B. I. Vol. II, p. 637.)

And the notions of creation, entrance, preservation, and destruction are *merely* formed for the apprehension *of the soul.* Again the apprehension *of the soul* is enjoined for the sake of final liberation, which is evident from such passages of the S'ruti as:

"He knew the soul." (B. Ā. 1st Adh. 4th B. 10. B. I. Vol. II, p. 198.) "Therefore he was this all." (B. Ā., p. 209.) "He who knows Brahman, obtains liberation." (Taitt. 2d A. 1 Anuv. 1 Kh. B. I. Vol. VII, p. 37.) "He who knows the supreme Brahman, verily becomes Brahma." (3 Mund. U. 2 Kh. 9 M. B. I. and Vol. VIII, p. 323.) "The person who has a teacher, knows *Brahman*." (Chh. U. 6 Prapa. 14 Kh. B. I. Vol. III, p. 459.) "He lives as long" (as he has not obtained liberation). (Chh. U. 6th P. 14th Kh. B. I. Vol. III, p. 460.) It is also evident from passages of the Smṛti as: "Then forthwith." (Bh. G. 18th Adh. 55.) Having known me in truth, he enters me. "For it (the knowledge of Brahman is the highest knowledge; immortality is thereby gained." (Manu S. 12th Add. 85.)

And the passages with regard to a creation, etc., serve for the purpose to establish the knowledge of the identity of the soul, because the notion of difference is prohibited. Therefore the entrance means the perceptibility *of the soul* as far as it abides in its effect.

"Until the ends of the nails" (*Vide* p. 104). This means, to the ends of the nails the consciousness of the soul extends. How did he enter the world? The answer is: As in common life, "a razor is perceived as placed in a razor-case," or as Vis'vambhara, which means fire,—so called from its supporting (bhara), the world, Vis'va,—is concealed in a nest, *viz.*, in wood, etc.—It is there; for on rubbing wood, etc., fire is perceived,—and as razor is placed on one side of the case, and as fire is everywhere pervading wood, etc., so, the soul, generally and specially, abides pervading the body. For there it is observed, performing the functions of inspiration, etc., and of seeing, etc. Therefore "they do not behold," do not apprehend "him" the soul, which has entered there, endowed as it is with inspiration, etc., seeing and other functions.

But is not in the sentence: "They do not behold him," a prohibition of a thing, which has not been obtained before? for *no doubt*, the beholding has not been obtained in our text.

There is no fault in this, for in the passages, relative to the creation, *preservation*, etc., which were directed towards the acquirements *of the knowledge*, that the soul is identical, the beholding (knowledge) of it (of the soul) has been introduced. Thus a Mantra declares: "Being of this and that form, he became every form for the sake of being seen." (Kath. U. 5 V. 9-10 Mantr. B. I. Vol. VIII, p. 138. B. Ā. U. 2 A. 5 Brāhm. 19 Kh. B. I. Vol. II, p. 600.)

The reason, why *the soul* having the functions of inspiration, *expiration*, etc., is not apprehended, is given in the words: "For when incomplete": because it is not perfect, when inspiring or performing other functions. Whence again *proceeds* the incompleteness? The answer is: for by "inspiring" performing the function of inspiration (Prāṇana) it is called life (Prāṇa) for by performing the function of inspiration (Prāṇana) life (Prāṇa) inspires, that is to say, performs no other function, as a *wood-cutter*, or a cook *is so called from special work*. Therefore because it does not include the other functions, it is incomplete.

In the same manner, "when speaking," performing the function of speaking, it is called speech, "when seeing," it is called sight; for because the beholder sees (caṣte) therefore it is called eye (cakṣu); when hearing (sṛṇvan), it is called ear (srotram). By the words: "when inspiring, it is called life, when speaking, speech," the origin of the power of action is shown, by the words "when seeing, sight, when hearing, ear," the origin of the power of knowledge; for the objects of the power of knowledge are name and form; for nothing is an object of knowledge, unless having name and form. The organs of perceiving them are the eye and the ear, and the action, to be performed by name and form, is intimately united with life. The organ of the manifestation *of this action*, which depends upon life, is the word. In this manner speech is mentioned here in illustration of the other organs of action, *viz.*, the hand, foot, and the organs of exertion and generation; for it will afterwards be said: "for this all is manifested, or this threefold, name, form and action." (B. Ā. 2d A. 1st Kh. B. I. Vol. II, p. 313.)

"When minding, mind." Mind (Manas) is derived from minding (manute), and it is the general organ of the manifestation of the power of knowledge.

These names of inspiration, etc., are the names of "its," the soul's 'actions,' that is to say, produced from actions. They are names of action, as it were, but not object of the substance, (of the soul) alone; therefore they do not manifest the whole substance of the soul; for in this manner the soul, although manifested by the action of inspiration, etc., and by its forms and names, derived from its different actions, *is still not completely apprehended.*

"Whosoever worships this or the other special being,—" separated from its totality as inspiration, etc., for instance life, or the eye, as a being, unmodified by the totality of the other special actions—*whosoever worships this* in his mind under the notion, that it is the soul, "does not know" Brahman. Why? "for that soul is incomplete," not whole, because this soul, *as* separated from this totality of inspiration, etc., *seeing*, etc., and determined *only* by one or the determining action, excludes all the other attributes. As long as a person knows himself *only* as determined by the activity of his own nature, which appears in such sentences as: "I see," "I hear," "I touch," etc., so long he does not know perfectly the complete soul.

How again seeing does he know? *The text* answers: "The soul"; for it is called soul (Ātmā) because it unites (obtains Āpnuvan) all the above mentioned different functions of life, etc. The soul, in this manner including all differences, becomes all; for only in its notion as substance it unites (obtains) the differences, produced by actions of inspiration, etc., which are the fictitious attributes *of the soul.* For instance, it will be said: "He thinks, as it were, he proceeds, as it were." (B. Ā. 4th A. 3rd B. 8th Kh. B. I. Vol. II, p. 730.) Therefore "the soul, considering this, let a man worship it"; for in this manner the whole soul is comprehended by its own notion as substance: Why is it the whole? Under this doubt it is said *in the text*: "For in it," "for," because, "in it," in this soul, when *considered* without fictitious attributes, like the different reflections of the sun in water, the above mentioned differences as life, etc., which are fictitious attributes *of the soul and* bear different names from their different functions as inspiration, etc., "become one," obtain indifference, therefore "the soul, considering this, let a man worship it".

The passage: "The soul; considering this, let a man worship it," is not a regulation, by which the acquirement of something not acquired before is enjoined, as it is acquired on our part; for the knowledge whose object is the soul, is produced by passages of the S'ruti, intended to produce *the idea of* the supreme soul, for instance: "That present, perceptible Brahman." (B. Ā. 3rd A. 4th B. 2 Kh. B. I. Vol. II, p. 575.) "Which is soul." (B. Ā 4th A 3rd B. 1st Kh. B. I. Vol. II, p. 723.) Whose nature is knowledge, etc. (B. Ā. p. 305.)

Thereby the knowledge of the nature of the soul has removed the ignorance, which is the misunderstanding that the non-soul is the soul, and which creates the fictions of agent, etc., rite and reward. If this *ignorance* is removed, the thinking of the non-soul is impossible, because desires and other faults are impossible. It remains at last only the thinking of the soul. Therefore the worship of the soul is on our part not enjoined ; for it is acquired.

We will not now discuss, whether the acquirement of the worship of the soul is called proceeding from the text, or permanent, but *at any rate* it is a regulation for something not acquired before, because, if knowledge and worship are the same, it was not acquired *before*, and the identity of the terms of "knowledge" and "worship" is evident from the passage *of the S'ruti*, commencing: "He does not know," where knowledge is praised, and concluding: "The soul ; considering this, let a man worship it," (B. Ā., p. 173), for by such passages of the S'ruti as: "By this he knows this all." (B. Ā., p. 185), and: "He knew the soul," etc. (B. Ā., p. 198), knowledge is the same as worship, and as it was not acquired before, it is also the object of a rule.

Nor show people any activity, if only the nature of a thing is related. Therefore that passage is a regulation for acquiring something not acquired before.

This follows also from its being identical with a regulation concerning rites. As the regulations concerning rites enjoin by such words as: "Let him sacrifice," "let him offer," so by similar words as: "Let a man worship it," and: "The soul should be seen," etc., *the worship of the soul is enjoined* wherefore there appears no difference between a regulation enjoining the worship of the supreme soul and the former *regulations*.

This follows also from the reason, that knowledge is an act of the mind. As a person, by whom an oblation is taken for a deity, should reflect on this deity in his mind, before performing a sacrifice, which is commenced by the word: "Vaṣad," by which this and other ceremonies are proved as acts of the mind, so the passage: "Let a man worship," indicates, that *the soul* is to be thought of, to be meditated upon, (B. Ā. Ā. 2d A. 4th B. 5th Kh. B. I. V. II, p. 450,) and that the act therefore refers to knowledge. In this manner we maintained that the terms "to know" (Veda) and "to worship" had the same meaning.

This follows also from the reason that *our passage* possesses the three parts of a regulation. For instance, in the regulation: "Let him sacrifice," etc., *viz.*, what, by what means, and how the three parts, by which future desires are removed, clearly appear. In the same manner, if the regulation: "Let a man worship," is about to be fixed, and at the same time the intention, what is to be worshipped, by what means or how, the three parts are established by a passage like this: "Let him who is intent on the duties of abstinence (from desires that are forbidden) of the observances of a religious student, of tranquillity and self-restraint, of resting (from all ceremonies), endurance, etc., worship the soul by the mind."

And as by the enunciation of the regulation for the Darśapūrṇamāsa, etc., the application of all its parts *is established*, so by the enunciation of the regulation for the worship of the soul *is established* the application of the subject of the worship of the soul as found in *all* the Upaniṣads. The application of passages as: "He is not this, he is not that." (B. Ā. 2d A. 3 B. 6th K., B. J. V. II, p. 435.) "Without gross body," one, without duality. (Ch. U. 6 P. 2 K. P. 387.) "He overcomes death," etc., is made by showing the speciality of the nature of the soul which is to be worshipped. And the reward is liberation or cessation from ignorance.

Others say: 'By worshipping should be produced another special knowledge whose object is the soul. By this alone the soul is known, and ignorance also removed. The knowledge, produced by the word of the Veda, has not the soul for its object. This sense is also supported by such passages as: "Having known, let him form *his* knowledge": "He is to be seen, to be heard, to be thought of, to be contemplated, to be searched, to be enquired."

We do not admit *the latter view*, because its meaning does not differ from the former. Nor is the passage: "The soul, therefore, let a man worship it," a regulation for something, not acquired before. Why ? The words, referring to the nature of the soul, have no other meaning, of anything to be done by the mind or the external senses, beside the knowledge, produced by the prohibiting sentences with reference to the non-soul.[1] For there a rule has taken effect, where, beside the knowledge produced by merely hearing the words, a person is observed as engaged in its execution, as by the rule of the Darśapūrṇamāsa : "Let him, who is desirous of heaven, sacrifice" ; for the knowledge, produced by the words for the regulation of the Darśapūrṇamāsa, is not *also* the performance of its ceremonies. This is dependent on a perfect knowledge and the other requisites ; but *here, on the other hand*, beside the knowledge, produced by the passage, *viz*., "He is not this, he is not that," establishing *the idea of* the soul, there arises no activity, as it does with regard to the ceremonies of the Darśapūrṇamāsa, etc., and this for the reasen, that the knowledge, produced by that passage causes the cessation of every activity ; for the knowledge of a person who is unconcerned in any worldly affair, does not produce activity, because such sentences as : "He is one without duality." (Ch. U. 6 Prap. 2 Kh. B. J. Vol. III, pp. 387, 389, 398.) "That art thou," (etc., pp. 448, 453, 455, 457, 461,) annihilate the knowledge relative to non-Brahman, or the non-soul. And this knowledge being annihilated, no desire for action arises ; for it would be contradictory.

If it is said, 'that by the knowledge alone, produced by such passages (as established nature of Brahman) there is no annihilation of the knowledge of a non-Brahman, or a non-soul,' we contradict, because it is proved by such passages as : "That art thou," "It is not this," "It is not that," "This is the soul," "One immortal Brahman without duality is this," "There is none who sees, etc., but him," "Know this alone as Brahman". (Kena U. 4, B. I. Vol. VIII, p. 43.)

[1] That is to say, the sentences which declare the nature of the soul, have the same meaning as sentences which prohibit to comprehend the soul by attributes of the non-soul.

Nor do those *passages* set forth the object of a rule with reference to *Brahman* to be seen, etc., because this, as we already said, does not differ from the meaning first stated. And we said before, that,—because by passages, setting forth the true nature of the soul, such as : "That art thou," the knowledge of the soul was established at the time of hearing them,—no performance, different from the regulation for the object of the seeing, was necessary.[1]

1. If you say, 'that, without a rule, by the mere declaration of the nature of the soul, a knowledge of the soul could not arise,' we object, because the knowledge of the soul is produced by hearing passages setting forth the soul, and why do you want to do once more what has been done already ?

2. If you say, '*knowledge* does not arise by hearing such passages,' we do not admit this, because we should otherwise have a retrogress in infinitum. For as (according to your opinion) by hearing the meanings of passages, declaring the soul, without a regulation, knowledge does not arise, it would follow that also by hearing the meanings of the words of the regulation, knowledge could not arise without a regulation, and this would require another regulation. The same would take place on hearing the latter, so that a retrogress in infinitum is evident (by your assumption).

3. Further, if you assume, 'that by the continuation of the recollection of the knowledge of the soul, arising from *Vedic* passages, a meaning is produced, different from the knowledge of what is merely heard, (and that therefore a regulation is necessary),' we do not agree on the ground, that the meaning has been obtained. At the time indeed that the knowledge, whose object is the soul, arises from

[1] Where then is the regulation ? If there is one, it either takes place—1, with reference to the knowledge of the soul, or 2, to the hearing of the passage, setting forth the knowledge of the soul, or 3, to the continuation of the recollection of the meaning, or 4, to the subduing of the state of the mind. But in all these cases it is impossible, as will be shown presently.—A.G.

hearing passages which produces *the idea of* the soul, at the same time this knowledge, at the moment of its production, annihilates the false knowledge with reference to itself. And if the false knowledge whose object is the soul, is annihilated, the natural recollections also, which are the effects of that *false knowledge* and which manifests the differences of a substance not the soul, cease to exist.

This follows also from the knowledge of the unreality *of every other thing*; for if the knowledge of the soul is true, it is also known, that every other substance is unreal, as tainted with transientness, unhappiness, impurity and many other faults; also from the fact, that the substance of the soul is free from them. Therefore, if the soul is known, there are no longer any recollections of a knowledge with reference to a non-soul. And as at last there exists in reality a continual recollection of the knowledge only of the soul, no regulation can be established.

This follows also from the annihilation of *all* faults, as grief, delusion, fear, weariness and other kinds of unhappiness;[1] for grief, delusion and other faults arise from a knowledge contrary to that recollection, as is proved by such passages of the S'ruti as; "What delusion is there." (Vajan. S. U. B. I. Vol. VII, p. 14.) "The wise is not afraid." "You have, O, Janaka, obtained fearlessness." (Br. Ā., p. 702.) "The bonds of the heart are broken," etc. (Muṇḍ. 2d. Kh. 8th M. B. I. Vol. VII, p. 302.)

If you say, 'but then subduing has another meaning; therefore there ought to be *a regulation*; for the subduing of the state of the mind (Citta) has a meaning different from the knowledge, produced by the words of the Veda. And in other philosophical system,[2] also the nature of a rule is known by that which is to be done.' We deny this,

[1] This may also be rendered . . . and other kinds of unhappiness, which is effected by that recollection; for grief, delusion and other faults arise from a contrary knowledge.

[2] In the Yogas'āstra.

because it (the subduing of the state of the mind) is not known as effecting liberation; for in the Vedānta nothing else but the knowledge of the soul as Brahman is considered as effecting the final end of man. This follows from a hundred passages such as these: "He knows the soul alone; hence he became this all." (B. Ā., p. 209.) "The knower of Brahman obtains the supreme Brahman." (Taittirīya U. 2d. A. 1. A. I. M. B. I. Vol. VII, p. 51.) "Whosoever verily knows the supreme Brahman, becomes Brahman." "A person who has a teacher, knows." (Ch. 6th P. 14th K. B. J. V. III, p. 459.) "To him all becomes for ever without fear." "Whosoever thus knows, becomes Brahman," etc.

Moreover the *aforesaid* subduing depends not upon another cause; for beside the uninturrupted recollection of the knowledge of the soul, no other cause exists for the subduing of the state of soul, and in this sense it has been stated before;[1] without a knowledge of Brahman, however, nothing can be thought as cause of liberation.

Further, there is no intention, and therefore is no regulation. What has been said *before*, 'that, as an intention with regard to a regulation,—for instance when it is said: "Let him sacrifice,"—where the three parts of a regulation, *viz.*, what, by what means, and how, are present, —is removed by *understanding* the effect, cause and the necessary acts, so it is also here established with reference to the regulation for the knowledge of the soul,' *we say*, this is not true, because every intention is annihilated at the very time, when the meaning of passages as the following is understood: "One even without duality." "That art thou."

'He is not this, he is not that.' "That soul, which is not within, which is not without, is Brahman," etc.

Nor is the application of a regulation possible, in order to understand the meaning of a sentence. And we have already explained the fault of a regress in infinitum, following from the application of another rule.

[1] *Viz.*, that the state of the mind, beside the knowledge of the soul, has no other cause.

Further, no rule can be understood to proceed from passages such as: "One Brahman even without duality," because it is abolished by the declaration of the nature of the soul.

And if you say, 'there is no proof that this takes place by the mere declaration of the nature of a substance. For instance, as in the passage: "He wept (arodit); because he wept, therefore Rudra (a name of fire) obtained the name of Rudra," (Taitt. S. 5th Pr. 1st Kh.) there is no proof by the mere declaration of the nature of the substance, so there is also no proof in passages setting forth the nature of the soul,'—we object, because there is a difference. Neither the declaration of the nature of a thing, nor the declaration of rites is the cause of the proof or non-proof of a passage *of the Vedas*, but it is the production of knowledge, united with its necessary effect. Where such a passage is met with, it is also proved, and where not, it is not proved.

Moreover we would ask you: Do you admit that in passages, engaged in declaring the nature of Brahman, a determined knowledge, which is at the same time united with its effect, is produced, or is not produced? If it is produced, why is it not produced? Do you not see the effect of the knowledge in the disappearance of the faults of ignorance, grief, delusion, fear, etc., which are the causes of the world? Or do you not hear: What delusion, what grief is there for one who knows the identity. (V. U. Ā. 7, p. 14.) "I know even Mantras, not the soul." "Being such, O most venerable, I am grieved. O venerable, do teach me to overcome grief," and of the same kind there are a hundred other passages of the Upaniṣads.

Is then in such passages as: "He wept," etc., the knowledge a determined one and united with its effect, *or is it not*? If it is not, we may admit, that there is no proof for it. If there is no proof for it, what does it matter with reference to the passage, producing the knowledge, which is determined and united with its effect? And if there is no proof for the latter, what confidence can be placed in passages, referring to the Darśapūrṇamāsa and other ceremonies ?

'But are the passages, referring to the Darśapūrṇamāsa and other ceremonies, not proved by their producing a knowledge causing man to act ? The same is not found in passages, referring to the knowledge of the soul.'

This is true ; however, it is no fault, because we have obtained that which is the cause of proof. The cause of proof, namely, is what has before been mentioned,[1] and nothing else.[2] This, however, is rather a merit *than a fault*, because, if there is something, producing a knowledge united with its effect, which annihilates the cause of every action, it cannot be maintained, that there is no proof of the passages producing the knowledge of the soul.

'But passages, mentioned before, such as : "Having known, let him form *his* knowledge," are rather destined for the cause of worship, without the knowledge of the meanings of the passages.' This we admit ; but they do not refer to a rule for something not acquired before, but to what has been necessarily acquired in our text.

'How again can the worship *of the soul* have been acquired in the text ? For it has been said, that *by the annihilation of the non-soul* there remains at last the permanent continuation of the recollection of the knowledge of the soul.'[3] Very good. If this is the case, although perfect knowledge has been obtained, yet by the necessary

[1] *Viz.*, such passages as produce a knowledge which is determined and at the same time united with its effect.

[2] For the cause of a proof is neither that which produces a knowledge, by which action is produced, because otherwise no proof of passages were possible by which something is forbidden,—nor that which produces a knowledge prohibitory of an action, because otherwise no proof of passages were possible which enjoin action,—nor that which is different from either, because, in this case, no proof were possible in accordance with the first supposition.

[3] That is to say, it has not been obtained from the text, but from something else, not connected with it, *viz.*, the annihilation of the idea of the non-soul.

effects of works which are the causes of the assumption of a body (transmigration) activity will be indispensible ; for action having gained entrance in word, thought and body, is powerful than is the *velocity of* arrows, etc., when in motion. Hence the efficacy of knowledge, acquired in the course of discussion, is weak. Therefore we said before, that the uninterrupted recollection of the knowledge of the soul is to be effected by dependence upon the force of abandoning all worldly desires, of indifference to them and of the other essential causes ; but it is not a regulation for something, not acquired before, because *the idea of* a necessity to act has not been obtained. Accordingly such passages as : " Having known let him form his knowledge," are intended to establish a rule for the uninterrupted recollection of a knowledge, which is obtained ; for another meaning is impossible.

" By employing the term 'considering this' (*Vide* p. 100) the worship of the non-soul,[1] (under the idea of the soul) is rather enjoined, as if it were said : " the dear, considering this worship it." Here is not the quality of 'dear' to be worshipped, but *the worship of* life, etc., which has the quality of 'dear,' etc., is here enjoined. In the same manner it must also be understood in the passage under consideration, that by employing the term 'the supreme soul,' the substance of the non-soul determined by the qualities of the soul, is to be worshipped. This is also clear from the difference of that passage from any other, where the worship of the soul is enjoined. Thus, for instance, it will afterwards be said : 'Worship the soul as the place *of dependence*.' In this sentence the worship of the soul is evidently intended by using the accusative case. In the sentence under consideration, however, the accusative is not employed, and there 'the soul, considering this worship' the term 'soul' means something different. Therefore it

[1] This is an objection in the view of the Sāṅkhyas, *viz.* the non-soul is the pradhāna (the chief) or Mūlaprakṛti (nature as the root of all things) which, according to the passage, would obtain the attributes of the soul, or the non-soul is to be thought of under the attributes of the soul.

is evident, that not the worship of the soul is enjoined, but of something else possessed of the qualities of the soul."

We deny this, for as at the end of the passage the idea of the worship of the soul is understood; it is also understood, that the soul alone is to be worshipped, *viz.*, "This, even this is to be conceived in this all, *viz.*, this soul," "Because this soul is more internal," "He knew the soul".

If you say "that there does not arise the notion of the worship (of the soul) as the beholding is prohibited for him who entered; for which soul is said to enter, for the same the beholding is forbidden, as it is evident from the passage, obtained in the text, *viz.*, 'They do not behold *him*' (p. 100). Accordingly the soul is no object of worship."

We deny this, for the beholding is *merely* prohibited, in consequence of the fault of non-totality, with the intention to guard against the fault of non-totality, not with the intention to guard against the worship of the soul, because the soul is determined *in that passage* by the differences of inspiration and other actions.

And if you say, "that the worship of the soul was not intended," the consequences were, that the passage, referring to the non-totality of the soul, which is determined by individual functions, as inspiration, etc., would be without use, *viz.*, "for that soul is incomplete; it is *determined* only by this or the other individual functions". (*Vide* p. 100.) Hence it is proved that the soul, possessed of many functions, on account of its totality, is an object of worship. The final application, however, of the term "soul" after the term "considering this," is in truth only to show that the real notion of the soul is no object whatever of the inflective base of the word ātman (soul) and its inflectional terminations, (that is to say, the supreme soul cannot be described by any words,) otherwise the accusative case would have been used: "Let him worship the soul." If this were the meaning, (that is, if, without the formula "considering this" the word ātmā should be applied) then the inflective base and one of its terminations would be applied to the soul. But this is not admitted, as is clear from such passages of the S'ruti as: "It is not this, it is not that," "How should one know him who knows," "Unknown is he who knows." (B.Ā., p. 473). "From whom words and the mind return, without having obtained him" (Taitt. U. 2d A. 9 A B. J. Vol. VII, p. 119). The *passage*, however: "Let him worship the soul as the place," is not a different word, because it is designed to remove the worship of the non-soul.

If it is said: "Both the soul and non-soul are to be known, as they have the common notion of not being perfectly known. Why then is here made an effort to worship the soul alone, as it is said: 'The soul, considering this let one worship it,' and not also *an effort* with regard to the other knowledge?" The answer to this is: "This, even this," which is obtained in the text, "is to be conceived," to be comprehended, nothing else, "in this all" (the sixth case *in Saṁskṛt*, "Asya Sarvasya," is, for the sake of determination, used for the seventh, "Asmin Sarvasmin,") "this soul," the nature of the soul. Shall this not be known? *If so*, why not also what is different? Because, when known, another knowledge is not required, different *from the knowledge of the soul*. Why? "for," because, "by this," knowledge of the soul, "one knows this all," all this other which is non-soul.

If the objection is made, 'by another knowledge is not known another thing,' we shall refute it *afterwards* by the passage, referring to the drum, etc.

How again is this to be conceived? The answer is: "As verily," in common life, "by a foot-print" (a foot-print is called a place marked by the hoof of a cow, etc.) "one" who makes a search by means of a foot-print, "finds," recovers, cattle that had been lost, and whose recovery is desired, thus, when the soul is obtained, all is obtained.

If the soul is known, all other is known, and knowledge, *we may admit*, is obtained in the text. But then how can it be called obtaining, *a term which* is not authorized by the text? This is not the case, because the terms of knowledge and of "obtaining" have one and the same meaning according to the intention of the speaker; for the non-obtaining of the soul is even ignorance. Therefore is knowledge the obtaining of the soul, *and* the obtaining of the soul is not—like the obtaining of anything which is not the soul—to be comprehended by the notion of an acquiring of what was not acquired before, because there is no difference (here) between the obtainer and what is to be obtained; for where the non-soul is to be obtained by the soul, there is the soul the obtainer, and the non-soul what is to be obtained. This (non-soul) is not acquired, as concealed by the action of producing, etc., and is to be obtained when producing a special action by the production of a special agent; but it falls under the notion of an acquirement of something not acquired before, and is transient, because it is the effect of an action in accordance with a desire, produced by false knowledge, as the obtaining of son in a dream. But the soul, which is contrary to the former (non-soul), is by its nature as soul not concealed by the actions of production, etc. Therefore, as there exists the nature of something eternally obtained, is ignorance only concealment. As the non-apprehension of mother-of-pearl, although apprehended,[1] which appears through error as silver, is merely a concealment of the opposite knowledge, so is apprehension even mere knowledge, because knowledge has destroyed the concealment by the opposite knowledge. Thus in this case also is the non-obtaining of the soul the concealment *of it* merely by ignorance. Therefore by knowledge must be understood an obtaining, which annihilates *ignorance* merely, and no other *obtaining*. Therefore we shall say *afterwards*, that in respect of the obtaining of the soul, any cause, which has any meaning different from knowledge, is useless. Therefore the text, without any doubt, intending to set forth the identity *of the terms* of "knowledge" and "obtaining," after having mentioned knowledge in the text, says: "One finds" (as Vindati, "to find," has the meaning

According to its nature, adds A.

of Lābha, "obtaining," this is stated as the effect from the knowledge of the qualities).

As that soul, by entering with name and form, acquired fame, *viz.*, with the names and forms of the soul, etc., and as it obtained completeness (Śloka), that is to say, the totality of life and other *actions*, so a person who thus knows, "finds," obtains, "fame," (kīrti) celebrity, and "completeness" (Śloka) a multitude *of followers*, together with his friends.

Or *the passage may also thus be understood.* A person, who knows the substance in the declared manner, obtains the knowledge of identity (which is understood by the term "kīrti,") desired by those who strive for liberation, and the fruit of that *knowledge* (which is understood by the term Sloka) liberation, that is to say, the principal fruit.

8. तदेतत्प्रेयः पुत्रात्प्रेयो वित्तात्प्रेयोऽन्यस्मात्सर्वस्मादन्तरतरं यदयमात्मा स योऽन्यमात्मनः प्रियं ब्रुवाणं ब्रूयात् प्रियꣳ रोत्स्यतीतीश्वरो ह तथैव स्यादात्मानमेव प्रियमुपासीत स य आत्मानमेव प्रियमुपास्ते न हास्य प्रियं प्रमायुकं भवति ॥

This is dearer than a son, dearer than wealth, dearer than any other thing, *dearer* than all, because this soul is more internal. Whosoever says to one, saying anything else to be dearer than the soul: "What is dear, is to perish," he is the lord, *therefore* verily it should be so. A person should worship as dear even the soul. Whosoever worships as dear the soul, to him is not dear a perishable object.

And why *then* is the nature of the soul to be known without regard to other things? The answer is: "This," the nature of the soul, "is dearer," more beloved, "than a son," for a son is generally known as dear. By saying, that is more beloved even than this, it is shown, how exceedingly dear it is. In the same manner it is dearer than "wealth," gold, jewels, etc., in the same manner "*dearer than* any other thing," which is generally known as dear, that is to say, therefore *dearer* than all.

Why then is the nature of the soul more beloved, *why* not *rather* life, etc. ? The answer is : The totality of life is more internal, is nearer the soul than what is external, a son, wealth, etc., "because this soul," this nature of the soul, "is more internal" than what is more internal. For a person who in common life is exceedingly dear, must be obtained by every effort. In this manner is the soul the dearest of all that is dear in common life, that is to say, great efforts should be made to obtain it. Why again, discarding an effort, considered as a duty, with regard to the obtaining of other dear objects, shall—by the abandonment of either of the dear *objects the* soul and non-soul—with reference to the obtaining of the production of one, the abandonment of the other rather be made by the obtaining of the production of the soul,—why not the contrary ?

In reply to this it is said : "Whosoever (*viz.*, a person who holds that the soul is the dearest object) says to one saying anything else," some particular non-soul, for instance a son, etc., "to be more beloved than the soul," what ? "What is dear," in thy opinion, a son or the like, "is to perish" (rotsyati) is to obtain concealment, or ceasing of life (Prāṇasaṁrodham) that is, "is to be destroyed". On what ground can he say so ? Because "he is the lord," because he is able, fit to say so, therefore it should be so, that he obtains the ceasing of life, as has been said by him : for he is a speaker of truth : therefore he is the lord to say every thing. Some understand by the term "Īsvara" (which has before been explained by able, and whose original meaning is ruler, lord) "quick." If it is accomplished, then, abandoning every other dear object, a person should worship as dear only the soul. "Whosoever worships as dear even the soul, to him, it is considered, is the soul alone dear, *and* no other object. Having come to the certainty, that any other worldly object which is dear, is even *in reality* not dear, he worships, he meditates; "to him," who thus knows, "is not dear a perishable object," an object whose nature is subject to death. The *sentence* (let him worship as dear even the soul) is *either* only a repetition of what is certain (of the sentence by which knowledge of the soul is produced) because for one who knows the soul, nothing is dear or not dear, or it is said for the praise of the knowledge, that the soul is dear, or for the determination of the fruit of the attribute of "dear," because it is producing faith in the perishable nature of all dear objects in *the mind of* one whose knowledge of the soul is of a sluggish kind.

9. तदाहुर्यद्ब्रह्मविद्यया सर्वं भविष्यन्तो मनुष्या मन्यन्ते किमु तद्ब्रह्मा-
वेद्यस्मात्तत्सर्वमभवदिति ॥

This they declare to be the knowledge of Brahman by which men think, we shall become all. What then knew that Brahman, by which he became all?

The knowledge of Brahman has been declared in the aphorism: "The soul, considering this, let a man worship it." Wishing to explain this very aphorism, for which the whole Upaniṣad has been *composed*, the text exemplifies *it* under the desire of setting forth *its* necessity (end).

"This," *viz.*, the thing to be set forth, to be manifested in the next sentence, "they declare," they, *viz.*, the Brāhmaṇas, those who are desirous to know Brahman, having repaired to the Guru (spiritual teacher) the vessel over the future shoreless ocean of the pain of exertion, caused by the uninterrupted revolution of the wheel of birth, old age and death, who are desirous of crossing over to its shore, who are separated from the nature of cause and effect, *viz.*, the cause of virtue and vice and its consequences, and who are desirous of obtaining the eternal incomparable good, free from those *causes*.

What do they declare? The answer is: "the knowledge of Brahman"; Brahman means the supreme soul, the knowledge by which this is comprehended, is the knowledge of Brahman, "men, think, we shall become all" the totality. The term "man" is used for the purpose to indicate the special subject of this knowledge[1] for men alone are the subjects of effecting in a special manner either a state of elevation[2] or of liberation. This is the intention *of the text.* As with regard to works they think, that fruits will necessarily follow from works, so they think, that from the knowledge of Brahman the fruit which is the state of universal identity, will necessarily follow; for as to their being proved by the Veda, there is no difference between them (the works and Brahman).

There[3] is something[4] contradictory indicated. Therefore we ask: "What then knew that Brahman," by whose knowledge men think, we shall become all? What knew that, "by which," knowledge he became this all, and Brahman is all according to the Śruti.

If he, (Brahman) not entirely knowing anything, became all, then it (all) may also belong to others, *and* of what use would *then* be the knowledge of Brahman? If knowing *something* it became all, then, as it is effected by knowledge, *all* (the effect from knowledge) is like the effect from work, and therefore the notion of transientness is in fact applied. Moreover, the effect from a knowledge of Brahman, which (effect) is the state of the nature of all, has the fault of a regress into infinitum, namely, knowing something else than this, he became all, and further knowing something else, etc., etc. *However*, if knowing all, it became all, there is not the fault of a contradiction of the meaning of the Śāstra, and therefore not the fault of a

[1] In the text is adhikāra, which means "possession," "competent knowledge". I translated adhikāri, as conveying the idea more exactly.

[2] In the scale of existence, *viz.*, the state of happiness in the different worlds.

[3] In assigning to man the notion of subject.

[4] Something means here the effect from knowledge.—Ā.G.

transientness of the effect. If, knowing something *only*, this Brahman became all, we ask: "What then knew that Brahman, by which he became all?"

10. ब्रह्म वा इदमग्र आसीत्तदात्मानमेवावेदहं ब्रह्मास्मीति तस्मात्तत्सर्वम-
भवत् तद्यो यो देवानां प्रत्यबुध्यत स एव तदभवत्तथर्षीणां तथा
मनुष्याणां तद्धैतत्पश्यन्नृषिर्वामदेवः प्रतिपेदेऽहं मनुरभवꣳ सूर्यश्चेति
तदिदमप्येतर्हि य एवं वेदाहं ब्रह्मास्मीति स इदꣳ सर्वं भवति
तस्य ह न देवाश्च नाभूत्या ईशते आत्मा ह्येषाꣳ स भवत्यथ
योऽन्यां देवतामुपास्तेऽन्योऽसावन्योऽहमस्मीति न स वेद यथा
पशुरेवꣳ स देवानां यथा ह वै बहवः पशवो मनुष्यं भुंज्युरेव-
मेकैकः पुरुषो देवान् भुनक्त्येकस्मिन्नेव पशावादीयमानेऽप्रियं
भवति किमु बहुषु तस्मादेषां तन्न प्रियं यदेतन्मनुष्या विद्युः ॥

Brahman verily was this before; therefore he knew even the soul (himself).

I am verily Brahman. Therefore he became all.

Whosoever among the gods comprehended it, he alone became it; thus *whosoever* among the Ṛṣis, *whosoever* among men.

Knowing that this is that, the Ṛṣi Vāmadeva verily obtained these Mantras: I became Manu, I became the Sun. Whosoever knows this *Brahman* also in this time in the said manner: "I am Brahman," even the gods verily are not able to prevent him from its possession. (The possession of the state of all.)

For he becomes the soul of them.

Then whosoever worships another deity in such a manner, as: "He is another, another am I," does not know; like a beast, he is *used* by the gods.

As verily many beasts maintain a man, so every man maintains the gods. It is not pleasant, even if only one beast is taken away, how then, if many ? Therefore it is not pleasant to them, that men should know this.

Having thus said, the text gives an answer, untouched by any blemish : "Brahman," "*viz.*, the inferior *Brahman*," because it is obtained under the notion of a "cause of the nature of all" ; for it is impossible to obtain by knowledge the nature of all with regard to the supreme Brahman, and the text speaks of an obtaining of the nature of all by means of knowledge, in the words : "Therefore this became all." Therefore the words : "Brahman verily was this before," cannot mean anything else but the inferior Brahman.

Or : "By making man the subject of the knowledge, a Brāhmaṇa who is to become this *Brahman*, may be *designated*. For in the passage : 'Men think, we shall become all,'[1] men *are obtained* in the text, and it is said that they are in a special manner the subjects to effect elevation or liberation ; *this is* not *said* either of the supreme Brahman, or of the inferior Prajāpati. Therefore, on account of *his* knowledge of Brahman, is here designated a Brahman, (Brāhmaṇa), who is to become a supreme Brahman, who, by the knowledge of the inferior Brahman, *viz.*, the knowledge, that duality is identity, a knowledge which is connected with works, has obtained the state of an inferior Brahman, who has renounced *all* enjoyment, and who by obtaining all, has broken the bonds of desire and work. It appears also in common life, that a term is applied with reference to its future state, for instance, in the sentence : 'He cooks the boiled rice ; (Odana means rice which is boiled,) and also in the Śāstra, for instance : Let a Parivrājaka (a person who has already obtained a

[1] Here the opinion of the Vṛttikṛts is given, which is the view of the Bhartṛprapañca Bhāṣya, *viz.*, because the nature of all is obtained under the notion of something to be accomplished (of an effect, *viz.*, from knowledge) it is impossible, that the supreme Brahman should have obtained the nature of all by knowledge.

state, entirely devoted to the contemplation of God) give to all beings *the blessing of* fearlessness.' In this manner some explain a Brāhmaṇa as a person who is to become Brahman."

This is not right, because, if the nature of all is obtained, the fault of transientness is committed ; for it is impossible that in this world any person should in reality obtain by any cause another state, and *at the same time* be eternal. In the same manner, if by means of the knowledge of Brahman, the nature of all should be obtained, and *this state be at the same time* eternal, there is a contradiction. If, *on the other hand*, it (*viz.*, the nature of all) is considered as non-eternal, the before mentioned fault takes place, *viz.*, that there is a resemblance with the effects from works. But if you think, 'that the abolition of the nature of non-totality (individual existence) which (nature of non-totality) is the effect of ignorance *and* the obtaining of the nature of all, is the effect of a knowledge of Brahman,' then the fiction of a person who is to become Brahman, is useless. *But if you think*, that even before the knowledge of Brahman every creature by *its possessing* the nature of Brahman, has eternally obtained the nature of all, that the state of non-Brahman and of non-totality is superimposed in reality by ignorance, and that, as silver is superimposed on mother-of-pearl, or as any special place (Atala means, literally, a division of the infernal regions) of standing or unclearness on the sky, so are also here the notions of non-Brahman and of non-totality superimposed by ignorance and removed by the knowledge of Brahman ; if you think thus, then it is right to say that in reality the supreme Brahman was, because in the passage : "Brahman verily was this before," the literal meaning of the term "Brahman" is supreme Brahman : for the veda declares a meaning, as it in reality is ; but the fiction, according to which a person who is to become Brahman, is called Brahman, at variance with the meaning of the term "Brahman," is not right, because *a hypothesis*, by which *the meaning of* the Śruti is lost, and a fiction is made of something, not acquired in the Śruti, is inadmissible, unless there be some strong necessity.

If you say 'that, without being produced by ignorance, there may exist the nature of non-Brahman and non-totality,' we object, because it is impossible that *in this case* they could be removed by the knowledge of Brahman; for it is never observed that knowledge either destroys or creates attributes of any actual thing, but it is everywhere observed as the destroyer of ignorance. In the same manner let also in our case the knowledge of Brahman remove the nature of non-Brahman and non-totality, as the productions of ignorance; but the knowledge of Brahman is never able to create or destroy any real thing. Therefore *the hypothesis*, by which *the meaning of* the S'ruti is lost, and a fiction is made of something, not found in the S'ruti, is even without use.

If you say, 'that ignorance with regard to Brahman is impossible,' we do not agree, because knowledge is enjoined with regard to Brahman; for if mother-of-pearl has become an object of the eye, then its nature is never known by such a sentence: This is mother-of-pearl *and* not silver, unless there is a superimposition of (the notion of) silver upon it. In the same manner, from such passages as: "This all alone existing," "This all alone Brahman," "This all merely the soul," "This is not duality, non-Brahman," the knowledge of identity with reference to Brahman could never be enjoined, unless there is a superimposition of ignorance upon Brahman. We do not say (like you), as there is *a superimposition* with regard to mother-of-pearl, so there is not a superimposition of the nature of non-Brahman (atad). What then? Brahman is not the cause of the superimposition of the nature of non-Brahman upon his own self, and is not the producer of ignorance.

We admit, that Brahman is not producer of ignorance nor deluded; but do not admit, that there is another deluded conscious *being* (beside Brahman which could be the producer of the ignorance of non-Brahman. This is evident from such passages of the S'ruti as: "There is no other knower than him." "There is nothing else which knows but him," "That art thou" (Ch. U. P. 448). "He knew the soul" (B. U. 184). "I am the soul" (B. Ā., p. 205). "Another is he, another am I." "He does not know." And also from such passages of the Smṛti as: "Whosoever beholds God as the same in all beings," etc. (Bhag.-Git., 13 Adh., 27th S'l.) "I am the soul, O Guḍākes'a, dwelling in the heart of all beings" (Bh. G., 10th Adh., 20th S'l.). "The wise see the same . . . in the dog and the man who lives upon dog's-meat" (Bh. G., 5th Adh., 18th S'l). And from such Mantras as: "Who beholds all beings in the soul," and "In whom all beings are like the soul" (Vaj. S. U. M. 6 and 7 B. I. Vol. VII. p. 13).

'But if this is the case, the advice of the S'āstra is without any use?' Well, this may in this manner be admitted, if *Brahman* is known; but if you say, 'also the knowledge is useless', we object,[1] because the cessation of non-understanding is visible., If it is said: 'That cessation is even impossible, because there is identity,' we object, because this is contradictory to what is visible; for it is visible, that there is a cessation from non-understanding by the knowledge of identity.

If any one says, 'that even, when seen, it is impossible,' it is contradictory to what is visible; and a contradiction to what is visible, is by no body admitted.

Nor, when visible, is anything in reality impossible, because it is even seen.

If it is said, 'that the seeing is impossible,' the same argument holds good.

If it is said 'From such passages of the S'ruti,' as the following: "He becomes holy by holy work" (B.Ā., p. 546) "knowledge and work entered him". "The Puruṣa is the comprehender, agent, the knowing soul," it is evident, that there is another mundane soul, different from the supreme

[1] The cessation of non-knowledge is either different from Brahman, and then there non-duality is lost, or it is not different, and then it cannot be comprehended under the idea of knowledge.

soul. And this different *soul* is the supreme *Brahman*, which follows from such passages of the S'ruti as: "He is not this, he is not that" (B.Ā., p. 435). "The soul liberated from sin, without old age, without death." "The ruler of this universe" (B.Ā., p. 628).

Also in the S'āstra of Kaṇāda, Akṣapāda[1] and others God (Īs'vara) is proved as different from the mundane soul; for through the desire to remove the unhappiness, *arising* from the world, activity is perceived *with the embodied soul* (and not with God), and hence the difference between God and mundane soul is clear.

And the S'ruti and Smṛti declare: "He, without speech, without honour": "There is nothing, O Pārtha, to be done by me *in the three worlds*" (B. G. 3d A. 22). "He is to be searched, to be enquired into" (Ch. U., p. 571). "A person, knowing him is not contaminated" (B. Ā. B. I. Vol. II, p. 913). "Whosoever knows Brahman, obtains the supreme Brahman" (T. U. 2d A. 1st An. 1st M). "He (Brahman) is to be contemplated in a uniform manner" (B. Ā. 6th Adh. 4th Br. 20. B. I. Vol. II, p. 889). "Knowing that which is undestroyable, O Gargi" (B.Ā. 5th Ad. 8th B. 10. B. I. Vol. II, p. 636). "The firm knowing him" (B.Ā., p. 829). "The great word (the letters A U M being joined) is like a bow, and the soul like the arrow; and Brahman what is aimed at by it" (2d Muṇḍ. U. 4th M. B. I, p. vol. vii, p. 228). In all these passages there is a declaration of agent and action.

This is also evident from the declaration, that the roads to elevation are different from *the road of* him who strives after liberation. If there were no difference, to what place could there be proceeded by any one? And if there were not, a difference of the northern and southern roads and of the places to be proceeded to, would be impossible; but if *the mundane soul* is different from the supreme, all this is possible.

[1] A name of Gautama, the founder of the Nyāya.

"This follows also from the declaration with reference to the causes of knowledge and work. If the mundane soul is different from Brahman, the declaration *addressed* to the former about work and knowledge, as being the cause either of elevation or liberation, is consistent, but it is not with reference to God because all desires are obtained by him."

If it is therefore (on all those grounds) said, "It is proper that the term 'Brahman,' means a person who is to become Brahman," we object, because the application of the declaration with regard to Brahman would be useless; for if the mundane soul,—which is not Brahman, *but* is to become Brahman, *on the strength of the passage*: "knowing the soul, I am verily Brahman"—should become all, the advice with regard to Brahman, would be undoubtedly useless, because the effect which is the state of the nature of all, would be accomplished by the knowledge of the soul which is to be accomplished;[1] because that knowledge (*viz.*, the knowledge of the regulation concerning work) could never be applied to the accomplishment of the last aim of man.

If it is said, "that the declaration *with regard to Brahman*, in the passage: 'I am Brahman,' is for the sake of transforming the mundane soul to the nature of Brahman," we object; for, if the nature of Brahman is not perfectly known, what can the passage, "I am Brahman" transform? If his nature is known a transformation is possible. By passages in our text such as: "That soul is verily Brahman" (B. Ā. 6th Adh. 4th Br. 5 B. I. Vol. II, p. 849). "That present perceptible Brahman" (B.Ā., 5th Ad. 4th Br. I. B. I. Vol. II, p. 575). "Which soul" (B.Ā., p. 575). "This is true." "This is soul." "He who knows Brahman, obtains the supreme" (T. U. 2nd A. 1st A. 1st M.), and by such a conclusion as: "From this very soul," the term "Brahman" and "soul" are more than a thousand times placed on the

[1] If it is said, that the advice with reference to Brahman is useful, under the condition, that it is the object of a regulation, we ask, whether it is regulation regarding work, or regarding worship? Either assumption is contradictory.

same ground, and therefore it is evident, that they have the same meaning; for transformation of another takes place to the nature of another, and not to identity.

And the passage: "Because this all is that soul," proves the identity of the soul, which has been set forth in the text, and which is to be seen *afterwards*. Therefore, it is impossible, that the soul could be transformed to the nature of Brahman.

It is also impossible to conceive with regard to Brahman any other effect because in such passages as: "He who knows Brahman becomes Brahman," the obtaining of Brahman *only* is declared.

"If the transformation is the obtaining of Brahman," we object; for another state of another is impossible.

If it is said, "that, according to the word of the S'ruti the obtaining of the state of Brahman, even implies transformation," we object, because transformation is only a notion "not something real," and we said, that knowledge had no other agency but to destroy a false knowledge; a word has no power to produce any thing, for the S'āstra teaches, but does not create: this is evident.

From such passage as: "He entered this world"; (B. Ā., p. 77) it is certain, that it is the supreme Brahman who entered; therefore it is not right to explain the term "Brahman" by a person who is to become Brahman.[1]

This is also evident on the ground, that *the meaning which you wish to establish,* is an obstacle to the admitted meaning; for the knowledge that, like a lump of rock-salt, Brahman is of the same taste (substance) without difference without or within,—which is the meaning intended to be expressed in all Upaniṣads, is clearly established at the end of two Kāṇḍas (of this Upaniṣad, *viz.*, the Madhu Kāṇḍa and Muni Kaṇḍa), *viz.*, "This is the declaration" (p. 503)

[1] For instance, the road which leads upwards through the fire, that is to say, through sacrifices, etc.—Ā. G.

and: "So far extends *this cause of* immortality" (B. Ā. B. I. Vol. II, p. 930).

In the same manner is the knowledge of the identity of Brahman the certain meaning of the Upaniṣads of all the S'ākhas.

If by the passage: "He knew even the soul" (p. 62), a mundane soul, different from Brahman, is assumed, it would be an obstacle to the admitted meaning. If it were so, then, by the contradiction of the commencement and of the conclusion of this S'āstra, an inconsistency would be assumed.

Also the declaration would be impossible; for if by the passage: "He knew even the soul," a mundane soul were assumed, there could not be a declaration of the knowledge of Brahman, because *then* the passage: "He knew even the soul," would refer to the knowledge of the mundane soul alone.

If it is said, "that the term 'soul' means something different from the knower," we object, because it is the predicate *of I*, in the passage: "I am verily Brahman," *and* if anything else were the object of knowledge, it would have been determined: "This is that," but not: "I am." As in the passage: "I am verily Brahman." Brahman is the predicate, and as it is determined in the passage: "He knew even the soul," it is distinctly understood, that the soul alone is Brahman. If this is the case, the declaration of the knowledge of Brahman is possible, not otherwise; for the knowledge would be otherwise.

Nor is the knowledge of Brahman possible if the nature of Brahman and non-Brahman were to belong to one *subject*, because there would be in reality a contradiction, as darkness *is contradictory* at the manifestation of the sun.

Nor if both (Brahman and non-Brahman) were the objects of knowledge, would the definite declaration of a knowledge of Brahman be proper, because in this case there should be a knowledge of Brahman and of the mundane soul.

Nor is it proper to assume a substance with contradictory attributes ; for in this case, the knowledge of the truth being declared, doubt would arise *in the mind of* the hearer, and a definite knowledge is required to accomplish the last end of man. From the following passages of the S'ruti and Smṛti : " Of whom there is even no doubt," " A person who doubts perishes," it is evident, that whosoever is desirous of the welfare of others must not say the meaning of a sentence which is doubtful.

If it is maintained, " that in (your explanation of) the passage : 'He knew even the soul ; therefore he became all,' the not very skilful assumption is made of Brahman being like us and similar beings, an agent " (*viz.*, as the subject of knowledge) we protest, because *this notion* is conceived in the S'āstra ; for it is not our assumption, but that of the S'āstra ; therefore the S'āstra is to be blamed (which you would probably not do). And by him, who is anxious about his welfare, must not be given up the literal meaning of Brahman by an assumption at variance with the meaning of the S'āstra.

An obstinacy on your part which goes so far, is also not proper ; for all difference with regard to Brahman is only a fiction, and must be considered under the notion of identity, as follows from a hundred passages, such as : " Here is nothing different " ; " for where there is duality, as it were " ; " one alone without duality ". Every action of man in fact with regard to Brahman, is a fiction, wherefore it is said very little, that this assumption is not skilful.

Therefore (in the passage : Brahman verily was this before) " Brahman " means the Brahman who entered, who is the creator. The term " verily " is *used* for the sake of determination. " This," all that is perceived as embodied (in the shape of a body) " Before ". Previously even to apprehension (awakening) was Brahman alone, and all this ; but from the moment of the apprehension *there is the opinion,*—" I am non-Brahman," I am not all,—the effect of superimposition; hence the superimposition. " I am agent, I am performer of ceremonies, I am the mundane soul, the enjoyer of fruits, happy, unhappy, etc., but in reality there is Brahman alone, and this all which is separate from him." " He " (tat), who has in any manner been made known by a merciful teacher in the sentence: " Thou art not the mundane soul,"—" knew even the soul," in its own nature, and the term " even " means *the soul* free from any differences, superimposed by ignorance.

" Say *then* which is the soul in its own nature which Brahman knew as the soul ? " Do you not recollect the soul ? for it has declared thus: " He who having entered this world, inspires, causes to descend, diffuses, expires and equalises ?"

" But then you declare him in the same manner, as if you say: 'This is a cow,' 'this is a horse'; you do not show him directly."

Well then, the soul is the beholder, the hearer, the thinker, the knower.

" But then, here also you do not show directly the nature of the agent of the actions of seeing, *hearing*, etc.; for the action of going is not the nature of the goer, nor the action of cutting the nature of the cutter."

Then let us say, the soul is the beholder of the beholding, the hearer of the hearing, the thinker of the thinking, the knower of the knowing.

" But how differs this from the *mere* beholder ? Where there is a beholder of the beholding, or the beholder of a jar, there is in every instance a beholder alone; but whether it is a beholder of the beholding, or a beholder of a jar, there is no difference; for it is even a beholder."

There is a difference. The beholder of the beholding, if there is a beholding, constantly sees the beholding; the beholding is at no time not seen by the beholder; therefore the beholding belongs permanently to the beholder. If the beholding of the beholder is transient, then the beholding, which is to be seen, does at some or the other time not behold, as for instance, where a jar and the like is seen by a transient beholding. Moreover, the beholder of that beholding sees never the beholding.

"But then there are two beholdings of the beholder, one, the permanent, which is invisible, and the other a transient one, which is visible."

Be it so. On the one hand, the transient beholding of the beholder is evident from the appearance of blindness and non-blindness; for if *this beholding* were constant, no one would be blind. The permanent beholding of the beholder, on the other hand, is evident from the passage of the S'ruti: "For there is no variance between the beholder and the beholding" (B. Ā. B. I. Vol. II, p. 803). It follows also from inference; for it is observed that in a dream there is a beholding of the blind, by which a jar, for instance, is an object of manifestation. This beholding of the beholder, then, is not destroyed by the destruction of the other beholding. By this unperishable permanent beholding, which is identical with itself, which is called self-manifesting light, seeing the other transient beholding, which remains in a dream, and which, among the two *beholdings*, resembles the knowledge of an impression, the beholder is *the beholder* of the beholding. If this is the case, the beholding is even his nature, like the heat of the fire, and there is not another conscious beholder, as is the opinion of the followers of Kaṇāda. "This," Brahman, "knew even the son," *viz.*, *the soul*, like the permanent beholding, *and* free from the transient beholding, superimposed by ignorance.

"But then the knowledge of the knower is prohibited, as follows from the passage of the S'ruti: 'Thou dost not know the knower.'"

We say, No; for there is no prohibition of knowledge. In the same manner must be understood the beholder of the beholding.

This follows also from its independence of another knowledge; for, if it is known, that the beholding of the beholder is permanent, no other beholding, of which the beholder is the object, is expected; for it ceases the desire of a beholding, which is the object of the beholder, as this is improbable; for no one has a desire, if there is no object (of the desire). Nor has the visible beholding the power to make the beholder its object, so that one could desire it. Nor is there any desire of any one whose object is one's own nature. Accordingly, by the passage: "He knew even the soul," it is said, that there is a cessation from ignorance, but not that the soul is made an object.

How did he know? The answer of the text is: "I," the beholder of the beholding, the soul, "am verily Brahman" *and* "Brahman," *means* the present, perceptible soul, which is within all, has overcome *hunger*, etc., which is not this, which is not that, and has therefore the characteristics, not to be of gross body, not to be an atom, etc.

This alone am I, not another mundane soul, as you said. Therefore from a knowledge of such a kind "he" Brahman "became all". From the disappearing of the superimposition of non-Brahman by the cessation of the effect of it (the superimposition of non-Brahman) he became all. Therefore it is alone proper *to say*, "men think, that by the knowledge of Brahman we shall become all." What has been asked before: "What then knew that Brahman, from which he became all," is *now* defined, *viz.*, "Brahman in truth was this before, he knew even the soul, therefore he became this all".

In respect of this "whosoever among the gods comprehended" the soul, in the manner explained (*viz.*, according to its true notion) "he alone," the enlightened soul "became it" Brahman; "thus *whosoever* among the Ṛṣis, thus whosoever among men" (comprehended the soul, became this all).

By the terms "among the gods," etc., a reference is made to the *different* worlds, and therefore the knowledge of

Brahman is not mentioned thereby, but we declared, that by the passage: "Brahman (Puruṣa) entered before," Brahman everywhere entered within. Therefore the terms "among the gods" are used with reference to the knowledge of the *different* worlds, which is produced by the superimposition of body, etc. In reality, however, was Brahman here and there before, *viz.*, before comprehension, in the bodies of the gods, etc.; otherwise he would be an object of investigation.

The meaning of the passages: "He knew even the soul," and also "he became all" *is*, that the fruit of this knowledge of Brahman is the obtaining of the nature of all. To establish this meaning firmly, the S'ruti quotes some Mantras. How? "knowing, that this" Brahman, "is that," the soul: "I am Brahman," from this knowledge of Brahman alone "the Ṛṣi Vāmadeva," by name, verily "obtained" *these Mantras*. He, firmly established in the knowledge of the nature of Brahman, saw these Mantras: "I became Manu, I became the sun," etc.

By the words: "Knowing that this is that," Brahman, the knowledge of Brahman is shown; by the words: "I became Manu, I became the sun," etc., the text shows that the fruit of the knowledge of Brahman is the obtaining of the state of all. Knowing, he obtained the fruit, the state of the nature of all; thus by this declaration *the text* makes known the liberation, which is effected by means of the knowledge of Brahman, as he who eats gets satisfied.

Some one may have the impression: "The obtaining of the state of all by the knowledge of Brahman was *possible* for the great gods by their extraordinary power, but not at present for beings of the present Yuga, especially not for men, because they have only little power. To remove this objection, the text says: "Whosoever," free from external desires, "knows this" Brahman,—set forth in the text, *as* having entered all beings and possessed of the characteristics of knowledge, action, etc., "also in this," the present, "time," *whosoever knows* this as the soul alone in the said manner: I am Brahman, who having discarded *all* differences superimposed no knowledge by delusions, produced by fictitious attributes (upādhi), knows: I am only Brahman, not affected by *any* worldly characteristics, who is not within, who is not without,—he, from the cessation of the state of non-totality, becomes this all by the knowledge of Brahman. There is no difference with regard to Brahman or to the knowledge of him among persons of great power, such as Vāmadeva, and persons of little power, *such as* the present men. But there is a doubt, whether the present men are adequate to obtain the fruit of the knowledge of Brahman. *To remove this*, the text says: "Even the gods," of extraordinary power, "are not able to prevent him," who knows Brahman in the said manner, "from its possession," from obtaining the state of all like Brahman. How then others? But there is no doubt, that the gods and the like are able to create obstacles to obtaining the fruit of the knowledge of Brahman as it is said: "The mortals are in the condition of debtors towards the gods"; for the Śruti shows, that man, even when born, is indebted to the Ṛṣis by the duties of a religious student, to the gods by sacrifices, *and* to the forefathers by *his* offspring. This follows from the declaration, *that men are like beasts to the gods*, and also from the passage: "Then that soul is the place of all beings."

From this argument: that the gods from the desire to preserve the state of the soul, create obstacles to men, subject to another's will, like debtors, to obtain the state of immortality,—arises that apprehension. The gods preserve their beasts like their bodies; for the text shows afterwards that the maintenance of gods, etc., which depends upon work, becomes greater, because each single man worth many beasts; for it will be said: "Therefore it is not pleasant to them, that men should know this" (p. 82). "As one for his own body verily wishes welfare, so also wish all beings welfare for one who knows thus" (B. Ā., p. 255). If *a man* has the knowledge of Brahman, then, with the ceasing of dependance, there exists no longer the nature of one's own body and of a *dependance* like cattle; this is the intended meaning, as is evident from the two passages about "the not being pleasant," and the "welfare". Therefore the gods raise, even to the knower of Brahman, obstacles to obtaining the fruit from the knowledge of Brahman; for they are powerful.

'But then, if this is the case, the gods raise obstacles also to obtaining other effects of works, like the drinking of what is drinkable. Alas, then, there is an end of the faith, that practice (of ceremonies and knowledge) is the cause of elevation and liberation. In the same manner, on account of his inconceivable power, god is able to raise obstacles, in the same manner, time, action, charms, drugs and penances; for that they are causes of obtaining or not obtaining the fruit, is evident from the Śāstra and common belief; hence there is no faith in any practice in accordance with the Śāstras.

We reply to this, No; for all things are produced by their necessary causes, and the world shows a variety (of happiness and unhappiness), both of which is impossible under the supposition, that all arises from its own nature. But when the supposition, that (ceremonial) work is the cause of (the enjoyment of) happiness and unhappiness and of other consequences, is firmly established *and* confirmed by the statements of the Veda, Smṛti, argument, and common belief, *it is clear that* the gods, Īśvara and time are not opposed to *the acquirement* of the fruit of works, because works are the causes of what is desired; for the good or bad work of men, independent of the gods, time, Īśvara and other agents, is by itself without effect (liter. does not produce itself), and if it should even have effect by itself, it is not able to give the fruit, as it is the nature of action to be produced by agents and other numberless causes. Therefore the gods, Īśvara, etc., favour actions, and hence there cannot be a disbelief as to the obtaining of the fruit. Sometimes actions are subject also to them (to the gods) because their power cannot be destroyed; but whether the nature of action or time, gods, thing, etc., is the first or second, is not determined, and is difficult to be understood; hence arises the delusion of the people. Some say, action is the cause, and not anything else, with reference to the obtaining of the fruit; others, it is the gods; others, time; others, the nature of the thing; others, all these together. With regard to this, the statements of the Veda and the Smṛti acknowledge action as the principal cause, as for instance: "Holy gets a person by holy action, sinful by sinful." Even if one or the other of those *agents* with regard to its own object should become principal, while at the same time the principal power of the others were stopped, yet it could not be said, that works is not the principal agent as to the acquirement of the fruit, because the principal agency of work is established by the S'āstra and argument.

(But if it be asked, whether the gods do not hinder the acquirement of the effect of knowledge, we answer): No, because on the mere cessation of ignorance the effect is the obtaining of Brahman. In respect of what has been said, "that the gods raise obstacles to the effect, which is the obtaining of Brahman," the gods have no power to raise obstacles. Why? because there is no time intervening between the knowledge *of Brahman* and the effect, which is the obtaining of Brahman. How? As in common life at the very time when light is in contact with the eye of the beholder, there is the manifestation of colour, so at the very time when the knowledge, whose object is the soul, takes place, there is the disappearance of the ignorance, whose object is the soul. Therefore, when the knowledge of Brahman exists, an effect contrary to it is impossible, just as it is impossible that the effect of light is darkness. Where (When the knowledge of Brahman exists) the knower of Brahman is the *very* soul (substance) of the gods, how can they in any way raise obstacles to him?

The text *then* declares, what is this very nature, *viz.*, Brahman identical with himself (whose nature is the soul) who is to be thought of, who may be known from all the S'āstras; "for he," the knower of Brahman, "becomes *the soul* of them," of the gods, at the very time, when there exists the knowledge of Brahman, by the mere cessation of the screen of ignorance, like the nature of mother-of-pearl, which appears as silver, as we said before. Therefore the endeavour of the gods has no success against the soul; for where an effect ensues, not referring to the nature of the soul, and where there is a difference of space, time and causes, there, in respect of any thing whose object is not the soul, the endeavour of the gods to raise obstacles is successful, but not in respect of the effect referring to the nature of the soul, which takes place at the time of the knowledge without any difference of space, time and causes, because an opportunity (to raise obstacles) is impossible.

"But then, since there is no continuation of the (first) apprehension of the knowledge *of Brahman*, and since (after the first apprehension) the contrary apprehension (=non-soul), and its effects are apparent, only the last apprehension of the soul destroys the ignorance, and not the first."[1] (If the last knowledge destroys ignorance, it is either, because it is the last, or because its object is the soul. Not under the first alternative, because the last could not be determined. (Not under the second) for if the first apprehension, whose object is the soul, does not destroy the ignorance, then also not the last, because the object is the same.

If it is said, "this being the case, the continuation of knowledge destroys the ignorance, not á single *act* of

[1] As S'aṅkara has set forth his argument rather enigmatically, I give it in the more explicit form of Ānandagiri. "'But then, an opponent may say, the knowledge which destroys the ignorance, cannot be the first, because after the first knowledge there is no continuation of it, and because afterwards the opposite knowledge and its effects take place.' To show the futility of this objection, S'aṅkara assumes the following alternative, if the first knowledge does not destroy the ignorance, either the last knowledge destroys it, or the continuation of knowledge.

If the last knowledge destroys the ignorance, it is either, because it is the last, or because its object is the soul; but not under the first of these alternatives, because it could not be determined (which is the last); not under the second, (because its object is the soul) because in this respect it is the same as the first knowledge, which, according to admission, does not destroy ignorance." The second part of the argument is clearly given by S'aṅkara, wherefore we do not repeat it here.

knowledge," we object; for as long as life, etc., remains a continuation (of knowledge) is impossible; for as long as there is an apprehension, of which life, etc., is the cause, the continuation of the apprehension of knowledge is impossible, because it is contradictory.

If you say: 'But then by the disappearance of the apprehension, of which life, etc., is the cause, there remains a continuation of knowledge until death,' we object, because the continuation of a so-much-ness of the apprehension is not defined, and there is hence the fault, that the meaning of the S'āstra is not defined. By saying,—the continuation of a so-much-ness of the apprehension destroys the ignorance,—there is nothing defined, and hence the meaning of the S'āstra is undefined. And this is not desired.

If it is said, 'that the meaning of the S'āstra is even defined, when there is a mere continuation,' we object, because there is no difference between the first and the last *knowledge*; for either the first knowledge is the continuation of the apprehension, or the last until the time of death; but as in this way no difference is found between the first and last apprehensions, the two above mentioned faults apply.

If it is said: 'This being the case, then *knowledge* does not even destroy *ignorance*,' we object, because our text declares: "Therefore he became all," the same is also declared in other passages of the S'ruti. "The bond of the heart is broken," and "There is no delusion, etc."

If it is said: 'It is *merely* for the sake of praise' (Arthavāda), we object, because *otherwise* the same applies to the Upaniṣads of all the S'ākhās (Vedic schools), *viz.*, that they are merely for the sake of praise; for the Upaniṣads of all the S'ākhās set forth neither more nor less than this meaning.

If it is said: 'Let it be so, (that they are for the sake of praise,) since the object of the soul is evident from perception; we object, because from the said statement (that knowledge destroys ignorance) ignorance, grief, delusion, fear and other faults have ceased.

If it is said "from perception," the answer has already been given. Therefore it cannot be fixed, whether the *knowledge* is the first, or the last, a continuation or not a continuation, because the ultimate effect of knowledge is the cessation of ignorance and other faults. That apprehension, whether the first or the last, continuation or no continuation, is alone knowledge, which produces the effect, *viz.*, the cessation of the faults of ignorance, etc. Having come to this conclusion, there remains nothing to be fixed.

But what has been said before : "Since the contrary apprehension and its effects are apparent, only the last apprehension of the soul destroys the ignorance and not the first," (p. 148) this *also* holds not good, because the last action (in a former birth) is the cause of the production of a body (in this world). The action,—which is the cause of the production of the body, *and* which, by means of the fault of the opposite apprehension of the work, which is of such a nature and which has the fault of the opposite apprehension, is able to produce the fruit,—*this action* puts into effect the opposite apprehension, and the faults of passion, etc., by the continuation of the enjoyment of the effect, as long as life lasts, and only so long, because the entering upon the enjoyment of the effects follows necessarily from their cause, *viz.,* action, like arrows which are shot (continue their course, until their velocity is spent). Therefore knowledge does not destroy action of such a kind (which is the effect of actions in a former world) because it is not opposed to it. What then (does it destroy) ? The effect of ignorance, opposite to its own (knowledge's) nature, which (effect) has the tendency to produce *another body* (in a future world) even from *ignorance, which is its* support, (it destroys it,) because it determines it ; for it (the action) has not yet arrived, (not yet been done) the other action (which is the cause of the present body) has been produced, (is passed, and cannot therefore be destroyed by knowledge). Moreover, the opposite apprehension (opposite to true knowledge) is not produced for the knower, because it (the opposite apprehension) is without object; for the opposite apprehension, when produced, is produced as dependent upon generality when the nature of its particular object has not been ascertained, as silver is no mother-of-pearl. But this (opposite apprehension) by the destruction of the site of opposite apprehensions without number, does not arise for one who has ascertained the differences of objects, as the *delusion of silver* does not again appear, when a perfect apprehension of mother-of-pearal has taken place.

If you say, 'that recollections,—manifesting opposite apprehensions, *and* arising from impressions, produced from opposite apprehensions, which were made previously to the knowledge,—*that these recollections* in the moment of their birth sometimes cause of a sudden the obtainment of opposite apprehensions, *and that*, in the same manner, as for one who is perfectly acquainted with the divisions of space, *yet* of a sudden a confusion may arise with regard to space, so also for the perfect knower an opposite apprehension may be produced, as it *was* before (the attainment of knowledge) *then it would follow*, that there is no confidence also in pertect knowledge that hence an activity with regard to the knowledge and the works in accordance with the meaning of the Śāstra would be inconsistent, and that proof had become non-proof: for a difference between proof and non-proof were impossible.

Hereby it is ascertained, for what reason there is no liberation from the body (immediately) after the attainment of perfect knowledge. *But* that consequent to knowledge, from the very same time, there is a destruction of the actions which are collected for a future birth and whose fruits have not commenced, has been proved from our text, which prohibits any obstacle to the obtaining of the fruit; also from such passages of the Śruti as "His actions also are annihilated" (1st Muṇḍ. B. I. Vol. VII, p. 302). "All is his forever," "All sins are shaken off," "Having known him, they are not tainted by sin," (B. Ā. B. I. Vol. II, p. 913). "Him alone do those two not trouble, him good and bad actions do not torment" (l. c., p. 910). "Him he does not torment, he is not afraid of anything (S'. U. B. I. Vol. VII, p. 119); also from passages of the Smṛti such as this: "The fire of knowledge burns all actions to ashes" (Bh. G. 4th Adh. S'l. 37).

But what *before* (p. 144) has been said, that he is bound by debts, is also not applicable, because this refers to ignorance; for the ignorant is a debtor; for him the notion of agency, etc., is true; thus it will be said afterwards: "Where some other thing exists, there another sees it otherwise," and the term "other" means here, what differs from the true substance, the soul. Where ignorance exists, there it is another thing, as it were; there like the moon on the second day after its darkness, is an action of showing (one saying, It is this, another, It is not this, etc.), depended on the many agents through ignorance; and the effect, arising from this 'ignorance,' is also shown by passages such as this: "Another sees it otherwise" (B. Ā., p. 813). Where, however, knowledge exists, by the removal of the numberless illusions, arising from ignorance, there is shown the impossibility of actions by such passages as: "Therefore he sees all" (p. 122). Therefore the *state of a debtor* is described as referring to ignorance alone,—because that state is the consequence of actions,—not as referring to knowledge. This we shall in the next passage explicitly show by our explanation, as follows: "Then whosoever," not knowing Brahman, by praise, reverence, offering (of flowers, scents, etc.), oblation (gift of eatables), attention and contemplation, "worship" (represents to himself the state of the excellencies of a deity) "another deity," a deity different from the soul "in such a manner as: Hé is another," not the soul, different from me, "another am I," subject *to him*, I, like a debtor have to propitiate him,—whosoever through such a belief worships, "he," through such a belief, "does not know" the truth. Such a person is not only ignorant, or has the faults of ignorance and the like, but like a beast, a cow, etc., is used for the benefit of conveyance, of giving milk, etc., so far the various benefits he affords through offerings, etc., is he used by each of the gods. Therefore he is, like a beast subject to works of all kinds—this is the meaning. For the effect of the work in accordance with the word of the S'āstra, be it work, united with knowledge, or be it work alone, done by a person who is ignorant, a partaker of the division of caste and the orders of life,[1] and dependent, *the effect of such a work* is elevation from man, etc., to Brahman ; the effect, however, of work, which is at variance with the word of the S'āstra and which is done by the promptings of one's own nature, is descension from man, etc., down to inanimate matter. For as here, so we shall say *the same* at the end of this chapter by the passage : "Again there are three worlds, etc." (B. Ā., p. 301.)—That the effect of knowledge is the obtaining of the state of all, has been briefly shown ; for this whole Upaniṣad is engaged to show the divisions of knowledge and ignorance (or the whole knowledge within this Upaniṣad is not very extensive as it describes the division of ignorance).

And that this is the meaning of the whole S'āstra, we shall *afterwards* show. Because it is so, therefore the gods are able to raise obstacles or to show favour to an ignorant man. This is said in *the words* : "As verily" in common life, "many beasts," cows, horses, etc., "maintain, a man," their owner, ruler, "so every" ignorant "man" who stands for many beasts, "maintains the gods" (the plural, "the gods," is here used to indicate also the forefathers, etc.), under the idea : "Indra and the other gods, who are different from me, or my lords ; I am like a servant of them. If I adore them by praise, reverence, gifts, etc., I shall obtain the rewards, given by them, *viz.*, elevation and liberation." Thus as in this world it is very unpleasant for a possessor of many beasts, "even if only one beast is taken away," is seized by a tiger, etc., so, if one man who stands for many beasts, rises from the state of a beast, it is not

[1] These are four, *viz.*, of the religious student, of the householder, of the anchorite (Vānaprastha, who retires to the wood), and of the mendicant.

surprising, that it is unpleasant to the gods, as the taking away of many beasts is to the householder. Therefore "it is not pleasant to them," to the gods—what? "that men should" in any way "know this," truth of the nature of Brahman. In this view it is said by the venerable Vyāsa in the Anugitas (a part of the Mahābhārata): "The world of the gods is closed for the performers of works; for the gods do not wish that men abide above." Therefore the gods try to exclude, like a cattle from tigers, *men* from the knowledge to Brahman, as it is their desire, that they should not be elevated above *the sphere of* their use. Whom they wish to liberate, to him they impart belief, etc., and unbelief to him whom they wish not to liberate. Therefore let a person, desirous of liberation, be intent on the adoration of the gods, on reverence and faith, submissive, and assiduously striving for the acquirement of knowledge, or for knowledge, as is implied in the words of fear: "How then, if many." This is the meaning of the passage: "It is not pleasant to the gods."

11. ब्रह्म वा इदमग्र आसीदेकमेव तदेकꣳ सन्न व्यभवत्तच्छ्रेयो रूपमत्यसृजत क्षत्रं यान्येतानि देवत्रा क्षत्राणीन्द्रो वरुणः सोमो रुद्रः पर्जन्यो यमो मृत्युरीशान इति तस्मात् क्षत्रात्परं नास्ति तस्माद्ब्राह्मणः क्षत्रियमधस्तादुपास्ते राजसूये क्षत्र एव तद्यशो दधाति सैषा क्षत्रस्य योनिर्यद्ब्रह्म तस्माद्यद्यपि राजा परमतां गच्छति ब्रह्मैवान्तत उपनिश्रयति स्वां योनिं य उ एनꣳ हिनस्ति स्वाꣳ स योनिमृच्छति स पापीयान् भवति यथा श्रेयाꣳसꣳ हिꣳसित्वा ॥

Brahman verily was this before one alone. Being one, he did not extend. He with concentrated power created the Kṣatra of elevated nature, *viz*, all those Kṣatras who are protectors among the gods, Indra, Varuṇa, Soma, Rudra, Parjanya, Yama, Death, and

Īs'āna. Therefore none is greater than the Kṣatra; therefore the Brāhmaṇa, under the Kṣatriya, worships at the Rājasūya ceremony. The Kṣatra alone gives *him* his glory. Brahman is thus the birth-place of the Kṣatra. Therefore, although the king obtains the highest dignity, he at last takes refuge in the Brahman as in his birthplace. Whosoever despises him destroys his birth-place. He is a very great sinner, like a man who injures a superior.

The meaning of the S'āstra has been declared in the Sūtra: "The soul, considering this, *let a man* worship it" (p. 100). The relation and the necessity of this Sūtra, which was to be explained, has been determined by the words: "They declare, that by the knowledge of Brahman, etc." (p. 129) together with its Arthavāda by the words: "Therefore, whosoever among the gods," etc. (p. 130),—and the subjection of ignorance to the world in the words: "Then whosoever worships another deity, etc." (p. 150).

There it has been said, that the ignorant is a debtor, *and* subject to *the will of* another by the necessity to perform, like a beast, the works of the gods and others. What again is the means of performing the necessary works of the gods and others? The *different* castes and orders of life. Which then are the castes? In reply to this the present passage is commenced, *viz.*, to show how that ignorant person, dependent on another's will and subject to works in connection with their agents, is busy, *like a beast*, in this world.

The creation of Indra, etc., has not been described above after the creation of Agni (p. 94); but the creation of Agni has been described to complete the creation through Prajāpati. The creation of Indra, etc., *however*, should there have been shown, because it is its conclusion; but it is here told in order to show, that the ignorant is the proper subject for the performance of works.

"Brahman verily was this before." "Brahman," by the creation of Agni having obtained the nature of Agni (he is called Brahman by believing himself to be of the caste of Brāhmaṇas) "verily was this," the caste of Kṣatras, etc., the undivided Brahman, "one alone". Therefore was no distinction of the Kṣatriya and other castes. "Being one," without *the distinctions of* Kṣatra, etc., of preserver, etc., "he," Brahman, "did not extend," which means, was not sufficient for extensive work.

Then "he," Brahman reflecting, I am a Brāhmaṇa, I who by nature desire to perform the work to be done by the Brāhmaṇa caste, have to discharge such and such duties, "created" for the amplification of work and agent, "with concentrated power the Kṣatra of elevated nature". Which again is the Kṣatra, the Kṣatriya caste, created by him? To show this, the text specifies the individuals, *viz.*, "all those Kṣatras who are protectors among the gods". Those who are anointed kings, are here specified "Indra," the king of the gods (Devas) "Varuṇa" of the aquatic animals, "Soma," of the Brāhmaṇas, "Rudra," of beasts, "Parjanya," of lightning, etc., "Yama" of the forefathers, "Death," of persons in ill health, etc., *and* Īśana of splendours. These and others are Kṣatras among the gods. After them (the divine Kṣatras) *he created* the Kṣatras who are ruled by Indra and other Kṣatra deities, *viz.*, the families of the moon and sun, as *the king* Purūravas, etc. For this reason the creation of the Kṣatras among the gods has been set forth.

Because the Kṣatra was created by more concentrated power than the Brāhmaṇa, "therefore none is greater than the Kṣatra," who is also the ruler of the Brāhmaṇa caste. "Therefore the Brāhmaṇa," although the source of the Kṣatriya, placed "under the Kṣatriya," "worships" him who is placed above. Where? "At the Rājasūya ceremony." "The Kṣatra alone gives him his glory," his repute as Brahman. Ṛtvik,—at the Rājasūya ceremony addressed by the king who is anointed and seated on the royal chair, by the words: "O Brahman."—replies again to the king:

"O king, thou art Brahman." He alone is called Kṣatra who bestows glory. "Brahman is thus the" well-known "birth-place of the Kṣatra". "Therefore, although the king obtains the highest dignity"; in virtue of the anointing at the Rājasūya ceremony, "he at last," at the completion of the ceremony, "takes refuge in the Brahman," in the Brāhmanical caste, "as in his birth-place," that is, he appoints a family priest. "Whosoever," again from the pride of power, "despises," lowers, "him" his birthplace, the Brāhmanical caste, the Brāhmaṇa, destroys his "own birth-place". "He," by so doing, "is a very great sinner"; (in former times the Kṣatriya was also a sinner) by his wickedness, because he injures his producer, "like," in common life, "a man who injures," defeats, "his superior" is a very great sinner.

12. स नैव व्यभवत् स विशमसृजत यान्येतानि देवजातानि गणश
आख्यायन्ते वसवो रुद्रा आदित्या विश्वेदेवा मरुत इति ॥

He did not extend. He created the Viṭ. He is all those gods who, according to their classes, are called Vasus, Rudras, Ādityas, Viśvedevas, and Maruts.

(As Brahman did not extend before the creation of the Kṣatra), so even after the creation of the Kṣatra "he," Brahman, "did not extend" for the work. He did not extend, because there was none to procure wealth. "He created the Viṭ," to procure wealth for the performance of ceremonies. Who again is the Viṭ? "He is all those gods according to their classes" (for almost all the Viṭs are called so, as they are counted in classes; for commonly they are only capable of collecting wealth, when jointed together, and not singly); the class of "the Vasus" is eight in number, of "the Rudras," eleven, of "the Ādityas," twelve, of "the Vis'vedevas," means "either the thirteen sons of Vis'va, or all (sarve-vis've) the gods, and of the Maruts," is seven times seven.

13. स नैव व्यभवत् स शौद्रं वर्णमसृजत पूषणमियं वै पूषेयꣳ हीदꣳ सर्वं पुष्यति यदिदं किंच ॥

He did not extend. He created the caste of the S'ūdras as the nourisher. This *earth* is the nourisher; for it nourishes all this whatsoever.

"He" in want of servants, "did not extend. He created the caste of the S'ūdras". Which again is the caste of the S'ūdras, created by him? "The nourisher" (Pūṣan) because he nourishes. Who again is that Pūṣā? The text determines this in a special manner. "This," earth, "is Pūṣā; for it nourishes all this whatsoever."

14. स नैव व्यभवत्तच्छ्रेयोरूपमत्यसृजत धर्मं तदेतत् क्षत्रस्य क्षत्रं यद्धर्मस्तस्माद्धर्मात्परं नास्त्यतो अबलीयान् बलीयाꣳसमाशꣳसते धर्मेण यथा राज्ञैवं यो वै स धर्मः सत्यं वै तत्तस्मात् सत्यं वदन्तमाहुर्धर्मं वदतीति धर्मं वा वदन्तꣳ सत्यं वदतीत्येतद्ध्येवै-तदुभयं भवति ॥

He did not extend; he created with concentrated power justice of eminent nature. This justice is the preserver (Kṣatra) of the Kṣatra. There is nought higher than justice. Even the weak is confident *to defeat* the more powerful by justice, as *a house-holder* by the king. Verily justice is true. Therefore they say of a person who speaks the truth, he speaks justice, or of a person who speaks justice, he speaks the truth, in this manner verily it is both.

"He," after having created the four castes, did not extend. "He," from a fear of the ungovernableness of the Kṣatra on account of his fiery nature, "created by concentrated power justice of eminent nature." "This justice," created of eminent nature, is the preserver, the governor even "of the Kṣatra," more fiery even than the fiery. "There is nought higher than justice," because it governs even the Kṣatra ; for all are ruled by it. In what manner ? To this it is replied : "Even the weak is confident to defeat the more powerful" than himself, "by" the power of "justice," "as" in common life "the house-holder by the king," who is the most powerful. Therefore it is in this manner evident, that justice is governing all, because it is more powerful than all. "Verily justice," *viz.*, a case which has been decided according to legal evidence, "is true". Here "true" means, in accordance with the meaning of the S'āstra, and justice means, what is transacted in such a manner: it is true, if understood in accordance with the meaning of the S'āstra. Because this is so, "therefore they," those who are sitting near, who are aware of the arguments on both parts, "say of a person who speaks," at the time when a suit is transacted, the "truth," that is, according to the S'āstras. "He speaks justice," *viz.*, he speaks according to fitness, which is well known and pursuant to usage. Thus, on the other hand, they say "of a person who speaks in accordance with justice," to usage, "he speaks in accordance with truth," he speaks what does not deviate from the S'āstra. "In this manner verily it," which has been mentioned before, "is both," *viz.*, the justice, which must be made known and which must be practised. Therefore justice, as an object of knowledge and of practice, governs all, as well those who know the S'āstra as those who do not know them. Therefore, it is the preserver even of the Kṣatra. Hence an ignorant person, who is proud of justice, acknowledge for the practice of its different parts, its difference which is the cause of the Brahma, Kṣatra, Vais'ya and S'ūdra castes. These *differences* are by their own nature the causes of the *different* agents.

15. तदेतद्ब्रह्म · क्षत्रं विट् शूद्रस्तदग्निनैव देवेषु ब्रह्माभवद्ब्राह्मणो मनुष्येषु क्षत्रियेण क्षत्रियो वैश्येन वैश्यः शूद्रेण शूद्रस्तस्मादग्नावेव देवेषु

लोकमिच्छन्ते ब्राह्मणे मनुष्येष्वेताभ्याꣳ हि रूपाभ्यां ब्रह्माभवत् ।
अथ यो ह वा अस्माल्लोकात्स्वं लोकमदृष्ट्वा प्रैति स एनमविदितो
न भुनक्ति यथा वेदो वाननूक्तोऽन्यद्वा कर्माकृतं यदिह वा
अप्यनेवंविद् महत्पुण्यं कर्म करोति तद्धास्यान्ततः क्षीयत
एवात्मानमेव लोकमुपासीत स य आत्मानमेव लोकमुपास्ते
न हास्य कर्म क्षीयते अस्माद्ध्येवात्मनो यद्यत्कामयते तत्तत्सृजते ॥

This *is the creation of* the Brahma, the Kṣatra, the Viṭ *and* the S'ūdra. He was in the form of Agni (fire) among the gods as Brahman, he was the Brāhmaṇa among men, in the form of Kṣatriya, Kṣatriya; in the form of Vais'ya, Vais'ya; in the form of S'ūdra, S'ūdra. Therefore among the gods the place (loka) is desired like through Agni only, among men through the Brāhmaṇa, because in their forms Brahman became *manifest.*

Then whosoever, through this world not seeing the self-like world, dies, him the latter, because unknown, does not preserve, as the Veda which is not read, or as other work, which is not done. Even the great *and* holy work, which a person who does not know in this manner, performs, all this work of him, verily perishes at last. Let a man worship the soul as *his* place. Whosoever worships the soul alone as his place, his work does verily not perish. For whatsoever he desires from the soul, the same he obtains.

The passage: "This is the creation of the four castes" "of the Brahma, the Kṣatra, the Vais'ya and S'ūdra," serves as an introduction into the next sentence. "He," Brahmā, the creator, "was in the form of Agni among the gods," that is to say, in no other form. "As Brahmā," "the Brāhmaṇa caste, he was the Brāhmaṇa," in the form of a Brāhmaṇa Brahmā was among men. Assuming other modifications among the other castes, he became in the Kṣatriya form a Kṣatriya, whose tutelary deities are Indra and other gods (devas); in the Vais'ya form a Vais'ya and in the S'ūdra form a S'ūdra.

Because Brahmā the creator assumed *other and other* modifications among the Kṣatriya and other castes, and remained unmodified only in Agni's form, "therefore among the gods the place," the fruit of works, "is desired through Agni only," that is to say, by the performance of works, dependent on Agni; for on this ground is this Brahman evidently represented under the form of Agni, the locality of works. Therefore it is established, that by the performance of work through Agni, the fruit, resulting from it, is desired. "Among men through the Brāhmaṇa." If among men there is a desire of the fruit to be derived from works, there is no dependence upon works, of which Agni, etc., is the cause. How then? The object of man is effected only by reliance upon the nature of the castes. Where, however, the accomplishment of the subject of man is subject to the gods, there it is dependant upon work in conjunction with Agni, etc. This follows also from the passage of the Smṛti: "By muttering prayers, the Brāhmaṇa, no doubt, is successful, whether he performs other work (work, dependant upon fire) or not. Friend is called the Brāhmaṇa."[1] This is also evident from his leading the life of a religious mendicant.[2] Therefore among men the place, the effect of works, is desired through the nature of the Brāhmaṇa alone, "because Brahmā," the creator, "in their forms," in the forms of the Brāhmaṇa and Agni, the forms upon which the agents of work are dependent, "became manifest".

With reference to this, some[3] say, 'it is the place of the supreme soul, *the obtainment of* which is desired through

[1] By giving to all beings the blessing to be without fear.
[2] Which is to renounce all worldly objects—the cause of obtaining the world of Brahman.
[3] The commentary, called Bhartṛprāpañcika.

Agni and the Brāhmaṇa.' This is not true; because a subjection to ignorance existing, the division of the castes is introduced for the subjection to works, it is not true, moreover, because it differs from the next passage; for if here (in the present passage) by the term "place," even the supreme soul were declared, then in the next passage: "Not having seen the self-like place," the predicate "self-like" would be absurd; for if there the common place (world) which is desired by dependance upon Agni, is different from the self-like place, then the predicate "self-like" is proper, because the meaning is the annihilation of the common place (world) after death, and because by the term "self-like" there is no going astray from the place of the supreme soul; but the works, performed by ignorance would go astray by the term "self-like". And by the passage: "Perishes certainly," the going astray of all the effects by works will be set forth. By Brahmā the castes were created for the sake of work, and this work, because it rules all *castes* by the notion of duty and accomplishes the object of man, has the name of virtue.

If therefore by this work alone the self-like place which is called the supreme soul, is obtained, although it is unknown, why then is it necessary to do anything with reference to its production? On this ground it is said in the text: "Then," which is to remove the objection of the opponent. Whosoever through this "world," which is subject to transmigration, whose nature is the assumption of a body, whose causes are the desire and work of ignorance by believing in the work, dependent upon Agni, or by believing in work to be performed by the Brāhmaṇa caste alone, on account of the world which is transient, and whose nature is not self-like, "not seeing the self-like world," which is called soul from not going astray from the nature of the soul, *not seeing* "I am Brahman,"—"dies," the latter, (although "the latter" means the self-like world, yet it is unknown, concealed by the ignorance, as a horse, which is not recognised) "does not preserve him,"—as the tenth soul in the well-known example (*vide* p. 110), does not preserve himself,—by the removal of grief, delusion, fear and other faults. And "as" in common life, "the Veda, which is not read," does not teach work and whatsoever arise from it, "or as other work," in common life, for instance ploughing, "which is not done," is not manifested by its own nature, does not preserve him by the yielding of its fruit, so the soul, if unmanifested by its self-like nature, which is the eternal soul does not preserve *him* by the annihilation of ignorance.

"But then, does it not follow from the necessity that work obtains its effect by preserving the cause of the knowledge of the self-like world, and from the abundance of work, which is the cause of the desired effect, that 'its preserving cause is undestroyable?' No, because *every* effect is liable to destruction. Therefore it is said in the text: 'Even the great,' as for instance many Aśvamedha sacrifices, '*and* holy work,' which obtains its fruit, as if it were desired (although there has been no desire of its fruit) 'which a person,' of extraordinary magnanimity, 'who does not know in this manner,' who does not know the self-like place in the said manner, continually 'performs,' under the notion that he shall thereby gain immortality, '*all* this work of him,' of the ignorant person, 'verily perishes at last,' at the end of the enjoyment of the fruit, because desire, the effect of ignorance, is its cause, like some *wonderful* superhuman power (perished) which appeared by the delusion of a dream. Since the causes of it (of the work), *viz.*, ignorance and desire, are not permanent, it is necessary that its effects are also liable to destruction. Therefore there is no hope to preserve for ever the fruit of holy work. 'Therefore let a man worship the soul alone' as the self-like place; the soul is the self-like place; for in this meaning is the self-like place set forth in the text, and here is the term of 'self-like' not applied. 'Whosoever worships the soul as *his* place,' what of him? It is replied in the text: 'his work does verily not perish,' because there is even no work; this is repeated here in order to establish it firmly. The meaning is, as there is constantly worldly unhappiness, consisting in the decrease *of the effect* derived from work, so there is not for him (the wise) as if one thinks: if Mithila is burned, nothing burns me. Others[1] explain it to mean, that the work of the knowing worshipper of his ownself (soul) does not perish by the connection with a person who does not know. Further, for the term of 'place' intimately connected with work, they in fact assume two meanings; one is the place in the state of manifestation, depending upon work, and bearing the name of Hiraṇyagarbha. Whosoever worships this place, which is intimately connected with work, which is manifested and finite, the work of him, who knows the finite self as engaged in work, verily perishes. But whosoever worships the world, which is intimately connected with work, comprehending it in its unmanifested state under the notion of cause, his work does not perish, because he knows the infinite self (soul) as engaged in work. This assumption is ingenious, but it does not accord with the S'ruti, because by the term 'the place of self' the supreme soul, set forth in the text, is denoted.

The text having mentioned (before) "the place of self," omits (now) the term "of self" and introducing the term "soul," shows its identity with the former by the words: "whosoever worships the soul alone as his place." There is here no possibility for the assumption of a place, intimately connected with work.

Moreover it (the place intimately connected with work) is different from the supreme *place*, whose object is knowledge alone. By the passage: "The soul is not the place," it is distinguished from the places, which are gained by inferior knowledge and the work of a son. Therefore "the soul is not the place," and also: "His place is not measured by any work; this is his highest place." By these sentences, because they are determined, a corresponding meaning is proper. Thus here also, because by the words "the place of self," the predicate is fixed.

[1] *Viz.*, the explanation, given by the Bhartṛprāpañca.

If it is said "that according to the passage: 'for whatsoever,' it is improper, that the place of self is the supreme soul; for if it is certain, that by the worship of him he becomes the supreme soul: whatsoever he desires, he obtains from the soul, then the declaration with regard to the fruit is improper, unless it is to obtain that soul." We contradict, because it has the object to extol the worship of the world of self; for the meaning is, from the place of self alone all that is desired is obtained; anything different from it is not to be asked for, because all desires are satisfied, as it is said in another passage of the S'ruti (Ch. U. 7th Pr. 16th Kh. B. I. Vol. III, p. 524): "From the soul is life, from the soul hope." Or it means to show the state of the universal soul as before (p. 66). For if the supreme soul is declared, it is right to apply the term "soul" in the passage: "for . . . from the soul" (p. 93), and it means, from the place of self, which is set forth as soul in the text. Otherwise it would have been said with a predicate, "from the place of work in its unmanifested state", in order to remove *thereby the idea of* a place of the supreme soul in accordance with the text, and to remove the state of manifestation; for since it set forth in the text and determined, another state, not authorized by the S'ruti, is impossible.

16. अथो अयं वा आत्मा सर्वेषां भूतानां लोकः स यज्जुहोति यद्यजते
तेन देवानां लोकोऽथ यदनुब्रूते तेन ऋषीणामथ यत्पितृभ्यो
निपृणाति यत्प्रजामिच्छते तेन पितृणामथ यन्मनुष्यान्वासयते
यदेभ्योऽशनं ददाति तेन मनुष्याणामथ यत्पशुभ्यस्तृणोदकं
विन्दति तेन पशूनां यदस्य गृहेषु श्वापदा वयाꣳस्यापिपीलिकाभ्य
उपजीवन्ति तेन तेषां लोको यथाह वै स्वाय लोकायारिष्टि-
मिच्छेदेवꣳ हैवंविदे सर्वाणि भूतान्यरिष्टिमिच्छन्ति तद्वा
एतद्विदितं मीमाꣳसितम् ॥

Next that soul (self) verily is the place of all beings.

He is the place of the gods by what he offers and sacrifices, further of the Ṛṣis by what he learns, further of the forefathers (Pitṛs) by what he gives to the forefathers, and by his exertions about offspring, further of men by housing them and giving them food, further of cattle by finding them grass and water, further of beasts of prey, birds, etc., down to ants, by sustaining their life in his dwelling. As every one desires the continuance of his place, so verily desire all beings welfare for one who thus knows. This verily is declared and considered.

"Next that soul verily." It has before (in the last section, describing the state of ignorance) been said, that the ignorant in the conscious pride of caste and order of life, etc., and governed by the law, is, like a beast, subject to another by the necessity of performing the works of the gods and others. Which again are the works by the necessary performance of which he becomes, like a beast, subject to another? And who are the gods and others whom he assists, like a beast, by works? Both is explained in the text. The term "next" is intended as an introduction to *the present* sentence. The house-holder, as set forth in the text, who is subject to work, ignorant, and endowed with body, senses, etc., is here called "that soul". The meaning is "he is the place," the object of enjoyment, "of all beings," from the gods down to the ants, because he affords assistance to all by works which are commanded with reference to the different castes and others. By what special again affording assistance does he become the place, for what special being? The answer is: "By what he," the house-holder, "offers and sacrifices". Sacrifice with reference to the deity is an abandonment of wealth (to the deity). If it is performed until the sprinkling *of the water* (on the head of the sacrifice), it is Homa. By this work, *viz.*, by Homa (offering) and sacrifice (Yāga) which it is his duty to perform, "he is," like a beast, subject to the will of another, "the place of the gods". "Further by what he reads," *viz.*, his daily reading of the Vedas, "he is the place of the Ṛṣis". "Further by what he gives to the forefathers," *viz.*, the oblation, water, etc., "and by his exertions about offspring," by that work, which he is bound to perform, "he is the place of the forefathers". "Further by housing men," by giving them place, water, etc., in his house, "and giving them food," *viz.*, them who ask him for it, whether they live in his house or not, "he is the place of men". "Further by finding," giving "them grass and water," he is the "place of cattle". "Further of beasts of prey, birds together with ants by sustaining their life in his dwelling," with grains and (particles of food gained) by the cleaning of the sacrificial vessels, "he is the place of them". Because by those works he affords assistance to the gods, etc., therefore "as every one desires continuance of his own place," of his own body, desires the preservation of his nature, from the fear of losing his nature sustains it always by nourishing, protecting it, etc., "so verily desire all beings," the gods and others, the above mentioned continuance of life "for him who thus knows," who thus frames his soul: "I am to be enjoyed by all beings, I, like a debtor, am bound to make return"; *that is to say*, they preserve him for the continuance of their own existence, as house-holders *preserve* cattle. Therefore it is said: "It is not pleasant to them." "This verily," that the said works must necessarily be done, like the paying of a debt, "is declared," in the chapter of the five great sacrifices, (the five great sacrifices, *viz.*, to all beings, to men, to the forefathers, to the gods, and to Brahman) "and considered," and proved as necessary by consideration in the chapter of the distribution of the things, required for the five great sacrifices (Avadānaprakaraṇa).

17. आत्मैवेदमग्र आसीदेक एव सोऽकामयत जाया मे स्यादथ प्रजायेयाथ वित्तं मे स्यादथ कर्म कुर्वीयेत्येतावान् वै कामो नेच्छꣳश्च नातो भूयो विन्देत्तस्माद्प्येतर्ह्येकाकी कामयते जाया

मे स्यादथ प्रजायेयाथ वित्तं मे स्यादथ कर्म कुर्वीयेति स यावदप्येतेषामेकैकं न प्राप्नोत्यकृत्स्न एव तावन्मन्यते तस्यो कृत्स्नता मन एवास्यात्मा वाग्जाया प्राणः प्रजा चक्षुर्मानुषं वित्तं चक्षुषा हि तद्विन्दते श्रोत्रं दैवꣳ श्रोत्रेण हि तच्छृणोत्यात्मैवास्य कर्मात्मना हि कर्म करोति स एष पाङ्क्तो यज्ञः पाङ्क्तः पशुः पाङ्क्तः पुरुषः पाङ्क्तमिदꣳसर्वं यदिदं किंच तदिदꣳ सर्वमाप्नोति य एवं वेद ॥

Self (the soul) alone was this before ; he was even one. He desired: Let me have a wife ; again,—let me be born ; again,—let me have wealth ; again,—let me perform work. So far extend verily desire. For without desire one does not get more than this. Therefore also now a person, when alone, desires: Let me have a wife,--again, let me be born,—again, let me have wealth,—again, let me perform work. As long as he does not obtain one of them, so long he thinks himself incomplete. His completeness is this, that the mind is his self (soul) and speech his wife.

Life is their offspring, the eye the wealth of man ; for by the eyes one obtains it,—the ear *the wealth* of the gods; for by the ear one hears it; self is even his work,—for by self one performs work.

The sacrifice is five-fold, the animal, five-fold, the man five-fold, five fold this all whatsoever. Whosoever thus knows, the same obtains this all.

"Self alone was this before." If the knower of Brahman is liberated from the state of cattle, which consists in the bondage of duty, by whom then has he been made subject to the bondage of work, and not again to the practice of knowledge, which is the means of liberation? Is it not said: "The gods preserve?" Certainly, but they preserve those who by the performance of work obtained their own (the gods') state; otherwise it would be in their power to bestow the effects of actions not done, or destroy *the effects* of actions done, (that is to say; otherwise, they would be partial) but they do not preserve a common man, who has not obtained a special perfection. Therefore it must be the same (who makes him subject to the bondage of work) by whose power a *person* subject to *work* is getting out of his own place. Is that not ignorance? for the ignorant getting out of himself, is engaged in work? No, ignorance also is not the cause which makes one to engage in work; for its character is to conceal the true nature of a thing; but it may be the cause of making one to engage in work, in the same manner, as blindness in the cause, that one is liable to fall into holes, etc. If this is the case, then say, what cause one to engage in work? This is set forth, *viz.*, it is willing, desire. Thus it is said in the Kāṭhaka (4 to P. 2. B. I. Vol. VIII, p. 123): "Remaining in their nature ignorance, youths engage in actions; follow external object of desire." In the Bhagavad-Gīta: "It is desire, it is anger, etc." (B. G. 3rd A. 37.) And in Manu: "Desire is the cause of all engagements in action" (M. S. 2d. A. 4.) This meaning is in all its detail proved throughout this whole chapter. "Self alone was this before." Self alone, *viz.*, the person who is ignorant by his own nature, who is to be comprehended under the notion of effect and cause, the Brahmacāri (the religious student). "Before." Previous to the union with a wife he is called self.

There was no object of desire, as a wife, etc., different from this self. "He was even one," possessed of ignorance, the cause of the desire of a wife, etc., he was even alone; he was pervaded by ignorance, the nature of which is to assign to one's own soul the assumptions of agent, action and fruit. "He desired." What? "Let me have a wife." Let me, the agent, have a wife, the cause of the performance of work; without her I am not a fit agent for work; therefore to accomplish the performance of work, let me have a wife. "Again,—let me be born," let me be produced as offspring. "Again,—let me have wealth," cows, etc., by which work is accomplished. "Again let me perform work," the cause of elevation and liberation, *viz.*, let me perform work,—by which—liberated from my debt, I may obtain the places (worlds) of the gods, etc.,—and the ceremonial rites for objects of desire which are the causes by which a son, wealth, heaven, etc., are effected. "So far extends verily desire," which means, desire is limited to those objects. So far extend the objects which are to be desired, *viz.*, a wife, son, wealth and works, *viz.*, the desire or cause. The three worlds, the world of man, the world of the forefathers, and the world of the gods, are the effects of this desire as cause; for the desire, as cause referring to wife, son, wealth and work, is for their sake. Therefore this is one desire; and the *other*, the desire of the worlds, which is also a desire, depends upon a cause; in this manner desire is two-fold. Hence it will be afterwards (B.Ā., p. 592), said: "These two desires." Because every action is undertaken on account of its effect, therefore it should be understood, that by the passage: "So far extends desire" the worlds are necessarily implied, and *therefore* declared, for if eating is mentioned, it is not necessary to mention also satisfaction, because eating is merely for the sake of it. These two desires, characterised as cause and effect, are the longing, by which compelled, the ignorant, who is subject *to work*, like the silk-worm, encases his self (soul); *that is to say*, on the road of action not attending to himself (the soul), *and* having got out (of himself,) he does not know his own place (the place which is like himself). Thus it is said in the Taittirīya: "Bewildered by fire, teased by smoke, he does not know his own place." How again is it ascertained, that *desire* extends so far, because desires are infinite, for desires have no end? On this account the reason is stated: Because "without desire one does not get more than this," which consists of effect and cause; for, beside cause and effect, nothing, either perceived or not perceived, is to be gained in *this* world; for the object to be obtained is desire, and as this does not exist without them (cause and effect) it is proper to say; "So far extends verily desire." Hereby it is said: Which, the object of action of the ignorant subject, is two-fold desire, *viz.*, either desire as effect, or as cause, whether its object is perceived or not perceived. Above this wish the wise must be elevated. Because in this manner the ignorant self (soul) being desirous, before desired, *and* also he who preceded him,—(*for* this is the law of the world, and in the same manner was this the creation of Prajāpati; *for* it is said, (p. 64) "he was afraid by ignorance." Then (pp. 67-68); "Hence, excited by desire, a person is not happy when alone; to remove the unhappiness, he desired a wife; he approached her; hence sprang forth this creation,"—Therefore after this creation, "also now," at the present time, "a lonely person," before his being married, desires in accordance with what has been said: "Let me have a wife,—again, let me be born,—again, let me have wealth,—again, let me perform work." "As long as he," who is thus desirous and endeavouring of getting all, a wife, etc., "as long as he does not obtain one of them," one of what has been mentioned, a wife, etc., "so long he thinks himself incomplete". At last when he obtains all of them, his completeness ensues; but when he cannot accomplish his completeness, he is in the state of incompleteness; then for the accomplishing of his completeness, the text says: "His completeness," the completeness of him, who, as before mentioned, is conscious of incompletenesses "is this". What? (to show this), the totality of effect and cause is divided. Here (in this division) "the mind is" (for everything else, produced from *the totality* of cause and effect, is governed by it), by its superiority, "his self (the soul)" which means like his self, as the master of the family is like the soul of the wives, etc., because his wife, son, etc., follow him. In the same manner is the mind here assumed as the self for the sake of completeness: "and" thus also "speech his wife," on account of speech being in like manner governed by the mind. Speech, *viz.*, sound whose characteristic is directing, etc., is received by the mind through the ear, etc., considered and revered; in this manner is speech the wife of the mind. From both, speech and mind, represented as wife and husband, was produced life for the *performance of* work; therefore "life is their offspring," as it were. There (if self, wife and offspring are present) work characterised by the effort of life, etc., is to be accomplished by the wealth perceived by the eye, and therefore is "the eye the wealth of man". Wealth is two-fold, wealth of man and other wealth; therefore it is said, "of man," to distinguish it from other wealth; for cattle the wealth connected with man *and* perceptible by the eye, is accomplishing action; therefore *it* represents it. Hence by connection is the eye the wealth of man; "for," because, "one obtains," perceives "it," the wealth of man, cattle, etc., "by the eye" (therefore is the eye the wealth of man). What again is the other kind of wealth? "The ear the wealth of the gods," because knowledge is the object of the gods. Knowledge is the wealth of the gods. Therefore in our case is the ear even the object of wealth. Why? "For by the ear"; because by the ear "one hears it," the wealth of the gods, knowledge, therefore is the ear even the wealth because knowledge is the dependent on the ear. How again is work to be performed by those agents, the first of which is self, and the last wealth? The answer is: "Self is even." Self means *here* the body. How again is self (the body) the representative of work? because it is the cause of work for him (the sacrificer). How is it the cause of work? "For by self," by the body, "one performs work". In this manner is the completeness, whose characteristics are external objects, as a son, etc., accomplished for him, who thinks himself incomplete. In this manner, therefore, "The sacrifice is five-fold," to be performed by five, even in the case of a person who has ceased from work, where it is to be performed by symbols alone. How again is the symbol by the mere apprehension of five, called a sacrifice? Because an external sacrifice also is accomplished by men and animals, and there are five men and five animals, by the application of the mentioned five, mind, speech, etc.

Therefore it is said : " The animal five-fold,—the man five-fold.' 'Although the notion of animal is found also in man, yet there is a difference betwen them, wherefore " man " has been separately mentioned. What more ? " Five-fold this all," the cause and effect of the work " whatsoever ". " Whosoever thus knows," whosoever in this manner represents the five-fold sacrifice as himself, " the same obtains this all," the world under the notion of himself.

FIFTH BRĀHMAṆA

1. यत्सप्तान्नानि मेधया तपसाजनयत्पिता । एकमस्य साधारणं द्वे देवानभाजयत् । त्रीण्यात्मनेऽकुरुत पशुभ्य एकं प्रायच्छत्त-स्मिन्सर्वं प्रतिष्ठितं यच्च प्राणिति यच्च न कस्मात्तानि न क्षीयन्तेऽद्यमानानि सर्वदा । यो वैतामक्षितिं वेद सोऽन्नमत्ति प्रतीकेन स देवानपि यच्छति स ऊर्जमुपजीवतीति श्लोकाः ॥

Of the seven provisions which the father created by understanding and penance, he as assigned one as the common to *all and* two to the gods, three he made for himself, one he gave to the animals ; for upon this all is founded, whatsoever breathes and whatsoever not breathes. Why are they not destroyed although always consumed ? Whosoever knows the cause of the non-destruction, eats the principal food ; he goes to the gods, he lives eternally.

There (in the last Brāhmaṇa) ignorance has been introduced by the words : " Whosoever worships another deity in such a manner " : " He is another, another am I," " the same does not know" (B., Ā., p 118). It has also been said (p. 200), that the person, who has the consciousness of caste and of the different conditions of life (*viz.*, of a religious student, a house-holder, of one who retires to the forest, and of one who lives merely for the contemplation of God), who is ruled by his duties, who, compelled by desire, affords assistance to the gods, forefathers, etc., through sacrifice and other rites, is the place for all beings. And as by each and all of his works he has been created as the place to be enjoyed by all beings, thus he has created all beings and the whole world for his own enjoyment. The meaning is, in this manner, everybody, in accordance with his knowledge and work, is the enjoyer and enjoyment, the agent and the object of action of the whole world. To understand the identity of the soul, we shall say with reference to knowledge in the chapter treating on the knowledge of the universal essence (madhu lit. honey): "All is the effect of all, one universal essence."

He created by the five-fold work whose object in desire, *viz.*, by the *five-fold* sacrifice, etc., the world for *his* enjoyment, and also by knowledge (for his consideration). This whole world is seven-fold divided according to it being cause and effect. They (these parts) are called provisions, because they are objects of enjoyment. Hence (by the creation of them through work and knowledge) he is the father of those provisions. Those Mantras: "Of the seven provisions," etc., are here assumed as: Sūtras, because they show, compendiously, the meaning of those provisions together with their application. (The term "Yad" is here an adverb in connection with 'he created'.) By "understanding," knowledge, and "penance," work; for knowledge and work are the meanings of the terms "understanding," and "penance," because they are topics of the text, and not "the literal meanings of them "understanding" and "penance," because they are not topics of the text; for the five fold work, to be accomplished by a wife, etc., and afterwards knowledge by the words: "who thus knows, etc.," have been set forth in the text. Therefore it must not be doubted, that understanding and penance are well known.

Again: "The seven provisions which the father created," by knowledge and work, here it must be supplied: the same I will mention.[1]

2. यत्सप्तान्नानि मेधया तपसाऽजनयत्पितेति मेधया हि तपसाऽजनयत्पितैकमस्य साधारणमितीदमेवास्य तत्साधारणमन्नं यदिदमद्येत स य एतदुपास्ते न स पाप्मनो व्यावर्तते मिश्रꣳ ह्येतद्द्वे देवानभाजयदिति हुतं च प्रहुतं च तस्माद्देवेभ्यो जुह्वति च प्र च जुह्वत्यथो आहुर्दर्शपूर्णमासाविति। तस्मान्नेष्टियाजुकः स्यात्पशुभ्य एकं प्रायच्छदिति तत्पयः पयो ह्येवाग्रे मनुष्याश्च पशवश्चोपजीवन्ति तस्मात् कुमारं जातं घृतं वैवाग्रे प्रतिलेहयन्ति स्तनं वानुधापयन्त्यथ वत्सं जातमाहुरतृणाद इति। तस्मिन् सर्वं प्रतिष्ठितं यच्च प्राणिति यच्च नेति पयसि हीदꣳ सर्वं प्रतिष्ठितं यच्च प्राणिति यच्च न। तद्यदिदमाहुः संवत्सरं पयसा जुह्वदपपुनर्मृत्युं जयतीति न तथा विद्याद्यदहरेव जुहोति तदहः पुनर्मृत्युमपजयत्येवं विद्वान्सर्वꣳ हि देवेभ्योऽन्नाद्यं प्रयच्छति। कस्मात्तानि न क्षीयन्तेऽद्यमानानि सर्वदेति पुरुषो वा अक्षितिः स हीदमन्नं पुनः पुनर्जनयते यो वै तामक्षितिं वेदेति पुरुषो वा अक्षितिः स हीदमन्नं धियाधिया जनयते। कर्मभिर्यद्धैतन्न कुर्यात्क्षीयेत ह सोऽन्नमत्ति प्रतीकेनेति मुखं प्रतीकं मेखेनेत्येतत्स देवानपि गच्छति स ऊर्जमुपजीवतीति प्रशꣳसा॥

"Of the seven provisions which the father created by understanding and 'penance'; for the father created by understanding and penance; he assigned one as the common to all." The common provision to all, is that which is eaten. Whosoever worships it, the same does

[1] There is no necessity for assuming the proposed ellipsis and I have therefore, not followed S'aṅkara's explanation in the translation.

not turn from sin; for it is mixed. "*And* two to the gods," *viz.*, the sacrifice and the oblation. Again, others say they mean the ceremonies at the new and full moon. Therefore it is not their nature to be associated with desires. "One he gave to the animals." This is milk; for before men as well as animals subsist on milk alone. Therefore they feed the child, when born, either with melted butter, or put him to the breast. Then they call the babe born; for he does not eat grass.

Upon this all is founded, whatsoever breathes and whatsoever not breathes; for on milk all is founded, whatsoever breathes and whatsoever not breathes. The saying: "a person, offering throughout the year with milk, overcomes the second death," let none understand this in such a manner. Which day a person sacrifices, the same day he overcomes the second death. A person who thus knows, will overcome the second death that day on which he offers; for he gives all the eatable food to the gods. For what reason do they not decrease, although they are continually consumed? The soul is verily the cause that they do not decrease, for he again and again produces this provision.

"Whosoever knows the cause that they do not decrease,—the soul is the cause that they do not decrease; for he produces this provision by understanding, by understanding and by works; if he did not produce it, it would verily decrease,—" he eats food in the true manner," true means principal; therefore he eats food in the principal manner, he goes to the gods, he lives upon strength ; this is said for the sake of praise.

Here is the sense of the Mantras on account of their obscurity difficult to be understood; hence the Brāhmaṇa is engaged in the explanation of them. There what means *the Mantra*: "Of the seven provisions which the father created." "The answer is given by the term for" which is to show, that the meaning is well-known ; for the meaning is that the meaning of the Mantra is well-known, and therefore by the repetition of the Mantra: "The provisions he produced," is to indicate, that the meaning is well-known. Therefore the Brāhmaṇa says without hesitation: "For the father created by understanding and penance. But how then is the meaning well-known ?" The answer the causes are: The nature of a father with regards to those causes, producing the worlds, of which the first is a wife and the last work, is evident, and it is also declared by such passages as: "Let me have a wife." There it has been declared, that the wealth of the gods,—*viz.*, knowledge, —work and a son are the cause of the creation with reference to the worlds in their nature as effects (that is to say, as the result of good or bad actions). And also that which will be said, is well-known. Therefore it is proper to say: "By understanding, etc.," for desire, whose object is (enjoyment of) fruit, is well-known in common life, and also desire, whose object is a wife, etc., which is set forth in the passage: "So far extends desire"; but as to the object of the knowledge of Brahman (which is liberation), desire is impossible, because then all is one and the same. Thereby (by showing, that the cause of the world is desire, produced by ignorance) it is also said, that the world is created by natural, unscriptural knowledge and penance. This follows also from the reason, that work and knowledge are the cause of consequence which are not desired, down to the state of inanimate matter. But it was intended to explain the relation of effect and cause in accordance with the S'āstra ; for in the desire to establish the knowledge of Brahman, there is included the intention to describe the state, in which the world is disregarded ; for this whole world, whose nature is manifested and not manifested, is impure, transient, a compound of cause and effect, the object of unhappiness and ignorance, and therefore for him who has no regard for this world, the knowledge of Brahman is to be commenced.

There, by the division of the provisions, their application is set forth. " He assigned one as the common to all," this is a part of the Mantra. Its explanation is as follows : " The common provision to all " to all enjoyers, what is it ? " that which is eaten," enjoyed by all beings day by day ; this common *food,* the object of all enjoyers, the father assigned after the creation of the provision.

" Whosoever worships,"—which means is attached to, (for worship means *also* attachment, as it is clear from common expressions such as : " He worships the teacher," " he worships the king,") " it "—*viz.*, the common provision, which is to be enjoyed, the cause of the preservation of all living beings, whose principal object is the enjoyment of provision for the sake of the preservation of the body, and not work for the sake of something unseen,—" the same," being of such a nature, " does not turn," is not liberated, " from sin," from vice. Thus a Mantra says : " He enjoys useless food," etc. (Kr. Yajur Brāhmaṇa 2d Adh. 8th Pr. 8th Anva). Also the Smṛti : " Let him not cook food for himself " (alone). " He, who eats, without giving to the guests, is a thief. Even a person who procures abortion,[1] becomes free from sin if he eats food after he has first distributed it."

Why again does he not turn from sin ? " for it is mixed " ; for the property, which is enjoyed by the living creatures, is undivided (and therefore it does not belong to one as the property, left by a father, does not belong to any of his sons, before it is divided) because it is the object of enjoyment for all. Even the morsel which is put into the mouth is observed to cause pain in the mind of another for,

[1] According to Ānanda, a person who kills a high caste Brāhmaṇa.

while there is the desire, let me have it, the hope of every one is thereby excluded. Therefore it is impossible to take even a mouthful of food, without giving pain to another. Thus it is said in the Smṛiti: "It is the guilt of man," etc.

Some (the Bhartṛprapañca) say: The food called that of the Vis'vedevas which is daily given by the house-holder, is *here* meant. This is not evident, like the food which is an object of enjoyment for all living beings; nor does it agree with the passage: "that which is eaten." Because the food which is called the food of the Vis'vedevas, is included in the food, which is an object of enjoyment for all living beings, therefore it is proper to understand the food which may be eaten by a dog, a Caṇḍāla, etc., for it is the food which, beside the Vis'vedevas, is taken by a dog, Caṇḍāla, etc. In this case the expression: "that which is eaten" is proper, for if food is not to mean general food, then it must be said, that it has neither been created nor applied by the father; but it has been granted, that all food, has been created and distributed by the father; and it is very improper to say that a person who has performed the work which is called that of the Vis'vedevas, and which is in accordance S'āstras, is not released from all sin. Nor is there a prohibition of it; nor is it like the action of catching fish, blamed for its own nature because it is performed by good people, and because the S'ruti declares it sin, if it is not done, moreover otherwise also sin is obtained: for it is said in a Mantra: "I am food, I eat him who eats food."— "*And* two to the gods." This is a part of the Mantra. Which are the two provisions, which after their creation he assigned to the gods? The answer is: "The sacrifice (Hutam) and the oblations (Prahutam)."[1] Sacrifice is an offering in the fire. The oblation is the taking of the offerable food after the sacrifice. Because the father made over these two provisions, the sacrifice and the oblation, to

[1] The Brāhmaṇa has twice daily to perform the ceremony of Homa (the offering of ghee in fire). When the food is ready, a part of it is to be offered in the fire to the gods; this is called Hutam, while another part is thrown on the ground as an offering to those gods, who are called Dharmādi.

the gods, therefore at this time house holders also "sacrifice to the gods," thinking, this food must be given by us to the gods, "and offer," which means, and having sacrifice, take the offering. "Again others say," the two provisions which were given by the father to the gods, are not the sacrifice and the oblations; what then? "They *mean* the ceremonies at the new and full moon (Dars'apūrṇamāsau). Here, according to the first supposition, it will be said, because there is no difference with reference to the dual number (dve, two provisions, which may be as well applied to Hutaprahuta as to the Dars'apūrṇamasau) and because *they* (the Huta and Prahuta) are otherwise known, it means the sacrifice (Huta) and the oblation (Prahuta). But although the dual number accords also with the sacrifice and the oblation, yet the ceremonies at the new and full moon are also performed by the S'rauta fire, 1 and the notion of their being provisions, is yet better known, because they are declared in a Mantra.[1] And if a quality and the thing to which it refers, are obtained (at the same time) the latter must first be comprehended; but to the ceremonies at the new and full moon the idea of priority must be assigned rather than to the sacrifice and oblation. Therefore it is proper to think of them by the words: "*And* two to the gods." Because those two provisions under the name of the provisions at the new and full moon, were designed by the father for the gods, "therefore," in order to remove any objection, that they are made for the gods, "it is not their nature to be associated with desires" (iṣṭi,) that the term "iṣṭi" means desire, is clear from the S'atapatha Brāhmaṇa, (the affix uka in the word "Iṣṭiyayuka," means a natural inclination).

"One he gave to the animals." Which is the one provision which the father gave to the animals? "This is milk": How again is it known, that the animals are the possessors of that provision? The text answers: "For

[1] The house-holder has to perform his daily ceremonies, etc., by the Smārta fire (the fire ordained by the Smṛti) and the ceremonies at the new and full moon by the S'rauta fire (the fire ordained by the S'ruti).

before," because before, at first, "men as well as animals subsist on milk alone," therefore this provision is proper for them; how could they otherwise before subsist on it in accordance with a law? How do they before subsist on it? The answer is: Because men as well as animals subsist on that provision (as this application is made at the commencement, although there existed also *other* provisions) "therefore they," the three castes, "either feed," cause to eat, "the child, when born," at the ceremony of its birth, "with melted butter," together with gold,[1] "or they put him afterwards to the breast," they cause him afterwards to drink *milk*. As it is natural for the others, (*viz.*, for animals, different from men) they put *the young animal* first to the breast. "Then they call the babe born." Of what size (that is to say, "age,") is the babe? To this question it is replied: "for he does not eat grass," even until this day he does not eat grass, which means, that a very young child even until this day lives upon milk. And what has before been said, "that at first at the ceremony after birth they subsist on melted butter, and others on milk (*viz.*, that they subsist upon milk merely; this makes no difference) for melted butter is of the same nature as milk, being a modification of it. Why is the provision for animals, which was before (in the Mantra) given in the seventh case, explained *here* in the fourth? *This is done*, because thereby the work is accomplished; for all work which refers to burnt-offerings, etc., depends upon milk as its cause.

And this work (milk) which is to be effected by wealth, is to effect the three provisions which will be mentioned, as the before mentioned two provisions of the ceremonies at the new and full moon (are the cause of the three provisions); therefore it (milk) being a part of the work (ceremonial work) it is declared to be identical with work. Moreover, since there is no difference as to its being a cause (as this provision, milk, is a cause in the same way as the former two

[1] It is only a touching of the tongue with melted butter, mixed with gold.

provisions are) and hence the meaning (of the two former provisions with milk) is similar, the succession (in which the topics are described in the Mantra) is disregarded (*lit.* is no reason, that the explanation should not have been made in a different order). It is also done, because the explanation is *thereby made more* easy; for the provisions, when *treated* one after another, can be easily explained, and, when explained, are easily understood.

"Upon this all is founded, whatsoever breathes and whatsoever not breathes." What is the meaning of this? The answer is: "Upon this," the animal provision, "all," be it characterized as belonging to the soul, or to the material sphere or to the superintendence of deities, the whole world, is founded, "whatsoever breathes," endowed with the effort of breathing, "and whatsoever not breathes," immoveable matter, as rocks, etc. And there (in the text) it is explained by the term "for," which illustrates anything already well known. How *can it be said that* the notion "to be the foundation of all," belongs to milk? On account of its being considered as cause. And it is the intimate cause of all the works connected with burnt-offering, and by its nature a modification of the oblation of a burnt-sacrifice. That it is the whole world (which is founded thereon) is established by a hundred passages of the Śruti and Smṛti, wherefore it is proper to explain it by the term "for". "The saying": in other Brāhmaṇas, "a person, offering throughout a year with milk, overcomes the second death" (here by the year are in fact meant three hundred and sixty days, and in them there are seven hundred and twenty burnt-offerings). The bricks [1] which are collected *by the sacrificer* in accordance with the Yajur Veda and the days and nights of the year, obtain Prajāpati in the shape of the fire, which is called Saṁvatsara (the annual fire). Having performed in this manner offering throughout the year, a person overcomes the second death; having died he becomes like the gods, and does not die again. This, which

[1] The sacrificer, or in his stead his appointed substitute, is after every daily ceremony to put down a brick to mark the number of ceremonies he has performed in the year.

is said in the passages of other Brāhmaṇas; "let none understand this in such a manner," let it not be explained thus. "Which day a person sacrifices; the same day he overcomes the second death," it does not depend upon the practice of the whole year. "A person who thus knows," *viz.*, what has been said, that "Upon milk all is founded," because all is a modification of the burnt-offering of milk, obtains the nature of the world (of Prajāpati) in one day. Thus it is said: "He overcomes the second death"; the sage once dying, being separated from the body, becomes the universal soul (the nature of all) which means, does not assume a finite body for dying again. What again is the reason, that by gaining the nature of all he overcomes death? It is replied: "for he gives" because he gives all "the eatable food to the gods," to all of them, by his morning and evening burnt-offerings; therefore it is proper, that he—after having made his whole self like a burnt-offering, after having gained one identical nature with all the gods by his being the provision of all the gods, and after being like all the gods—should not die again. In this manner it is also said in a Brāhmaṇa. "The self-existing Brahman (in the form of Hiraṇyagarbha) performed penance." Then he reflected: "Verily, there is a limit of penance; alas, let me offer myself in all beings, and all beings in myself," therefore, having offered himself in all beings and all beings in himself, he obtained by his excellency over all beings, his kingdom, his dominion. "For what reason do they not decrease, although they are continually consumed?" From the time that the provisions after their creation were given by the father to the seven different enjoyers, they are consumed by them. Since they (the provisions) are the cause of their (of the enjoyers') preservation, and since there "continually," without interruption, is a decrease of what has been made, their decrease is proper. But they do not decrease, as is evident, from the world continuing in an unshaken manner; hence there must be a cause for it, that they do not decrease. Therefore it is asked: "For what reason," again, "do they not decrease". The reply is: "The soul is verily the cause, that they do not decrease."

As the father was before the creator of the provisions by understanding, and *as he was* enjoyer by the five-fold work in connection with a wife, etc., in the same manner also those, to whom the provisions are given, although they are enjoyers of those provisions, are fathers ; they produce by understanding and penance those provisions. It is then declared : the soul which is the enjoyer of the provisions, is the cause, that they do not decrease. How is it the cause, that they do not decrease? The answer is : "For he," because he "again and agian produces this provision," *viz.*, this seven-fold provision, which is to be enjoyed, the characteristic of which is to be cause and effect, and which consists in the effect of work,—"by understanding, by understanding," by knowledge which will take place at this or the other time, "and by works," the effects of speech, mind and body. "If he did not produce it," the mentioned seven-fold provisions, even for an instant, by knowledge and works, then he would be separated from the permanent enjoyment, "it would verily decrease". And the meaning is therefore, because the soul, the enjoyer of the provisions, uninterruptedly produces *them* according to *his* knowledge and action, therefore is the soul the cause that they do not decrease, as it is a constant agent ; therefore the provisions, although consumed, do not decrease. Hence the whole world, the totality, characterized by knowledge and the result of action, consisting of effect and cause, being the effect resulting from action,—because it is an expanse, concreted by the actions and desires of numberless embodied souls, joined together,—of a moment's duration, impure, without substance like the continuation of a light *reflected* on the current of a river, without substance like the trunk of the plantain-tree, like foam, like a deception, like the water in a mirage, like a dream, etc., although changeable and transient, appears to be substantial to those whose knowledge is formed by it. For the sake of disregarding the world it is said : "He produces this provision by understanding *and* by works. If he did not produce it, it would verily decrease"; for in this manner *the disregard* of those who disregard the world has success :—therefore the science of Brahman will be commenced in the fourth chapter. "Whosoever knows the cause that they do not decrease," —the three provisions to be mentioned are by this opportunity explained; in this manner the effect of true knowledge is set forth. "Whosoever knows the cause that they do not decrease,—the soul is verily the cause that they do not decrease; for he produces this provision by understanding, by understanding and by work; if he did not produce *it,* it would verily decrease,—he eats food in the true manner." The sense of this is explained: "in the principal manner"; whosoever knows in the principal manner that the cause of the non-decrease of the provisions is the father, the soul, "he eats the food"; a person who knows is not placed, as the ignorant is, in accidental relation to the food; having become the substance of the provisions, he is alone the enjoyer; he does not become an object of enjoyment (for others) "he goes to the gods," obtains a godlike state; "he lives upon strength," and immortality, "this is said for the sake of praise," it has not another meaning relative to an invisible effect.

3. त्रीण्यात्मनेकुरुतेति मनो वाचं प्राणं तान्यात्मनेऽकुरुतान्यत्रमना अभूवं नादर्शमन्यत्रमना अभूवं नाश्रौषमिति मनसा ह्येव पश्यति मनसा शृणोति। कामः संकल्पो विचिकित्सा श्रद्धाऽश्रद्धा धृतिरधृतिर्ह्रीर्धीर्भीरित्येतत्सर्वं मन एव तस्मादपि पृष्ठत उपस्पृष्टो मनसा विजानाति यः कश्च शब्दो वागेव सैषा ह्यन्तमायत्तैषा हि न प्राणोऽपानो व्यान उदानः समानोऽन इत्येतत्सर्वं प्राण एवैतन्मयो वा अयमात्मा वाङ्मयो मनोमयः प्राणमयः ॥

"Three he made for himself," *viz.*, mind, speech, *and* life; these he made for himself. "I was absent in mind, I did not see. I was absent in mind, I did not hear"; in this manner it is evident, that a person sees with the mind, hears with the mind. Desire, determination, uncertainty, belief, unbelief, steadiness, non-steadiness, shame, intellect, fear, all this is the mind alone. Therefore, when touched from behind, a person knows by the mind. Every sound whatsoever is speech; for it extends as far as the end; for it is not an object of *manifestation.* The vital air, which goes forwards, the vital air, which goes downwards, the vital air, which goes everywhere, the vital air, which goes upwards, and the vital air, which equalises, vital air, all this is life (Prāṇa). Thus modified the soul is the modification of mind, the modification of speech, *and* the modification of life.

The three provisions, mentioned before which are the effects of the five-fold work, exceed in value the others on account of their native as effects and of their extensiveness. For the separate explanation of them, the present section, from the words: "Three he made for himself," until the end of *this* Brāhmaṇa is commenced. What is its meaning? The answer is: "Mind, speech *and* life, these" three provisions, these mind, speech and life, "*he,*" the father, at the commencement of the creation, "made for himself," for his own sake. With reference to them there is a doubt as to the existence and nature of the mind; hence it is said the mind exists as something different from the ear and the other external organs, because it is well known, that, although there is a connection of the soul with the objects of the external organs, yet a person does not (always) apprehend a present object. A person, when mind wandered somewhere else, "I was absent in mind, I did not see". In the same manner when asked: Dost thou hear my word? *he answers*: "I was absent in mind, I did not hear." Therefore, it is evident that that,—in the absence of which a knowledge of form, sound, etc., by the eye, ear, etc., (*the instruments* fit to apprehend forms, sounds, etc.,) does not take place, although they (eye, ear, etc.,) are in connection with their respective objects, and by the presence of which such a knowledge takes place,—is something different, named the mind, the internal organ, connected with the objects of all the *other* organs. Therefore " in this manner it is evident, that a person " every person " sees with the mind, hears with the mind," because, the mind being disturbed, there is no seeing, hearing, etc. The existence of the mind having been proved, the following is said with reference to its nature : " Desire,"—the wish to be united with a woman, etc. ; " determination,"—the ascertaining of a present object of white, blue, etc. ; " uncertainty,"—doubt ; " belief,"—the knowledge of the existence of actions whose effects are not perceived, of deities, etc. ; " unbelief,"—the knowledge, opposite to the former ; " steadiness,"—the firmness in pain of body, etc. ; " non-steadiness,"—the opposite of the former ; " shame "—bashfulness ; " intellect,"—knowledge ; " fear,"—apprehension ; " all this, etc., is the mind," are forms of the mind, of the internal organ. Another reason is also mentioned for the existence of the mind. Because, " when touched from behind," by some body unperceived by the eye, a person is aware by discrimination, this is a touch of hand, that a touch of the knee, therefore exists an internal organ, called mind. If there were nothing which discriminates, called mind, how could there be discrimination by the mere skin ; therefore the mind, the cause of the possibility of discrimination, exists. Its nature has already been shown.

The three provisions, the effects of actions, *viz.*, mind, speech and life, are here to be explained inasmuch as they are subservient to the soul, as they have their material sphere, and as they are superintended by deities. Among them, *viz.*, among mind, speech and life, as subservient to soul, the mind has been explained. Now speech will be explained. " Every sound whatsoever," *viz.*,—either that which is characterized as a letter, etc., to be pronounced through the palate and other organs by the agency of living beings, or the other *kind*, produced by drums, clouds, etc.,—every sound " is speech ". Such is the nature of speech, now its effect will be mentioned. " For it," for speech "extends as far as the end," the conclusion of what is to be named, the determination of the same; "for it" again, as being the manifester, is not to be manifested, as is what is to be named, because its nature is to manifest like a light, etc., for what manifests, as a light and the like, is not manifested by some other manifestation. In the same manner speech which manifests, is not manifested itself. Thus the śruti removes the *regres sum in infinitum* (that anything which manifests, supposes something else by which it is manifested, etc.). It is not an object of manifestation, and the meaning is, manifestation is the effect of speech.—Now "the vital air, which goes forwards," (respiration, Prāṇa) is explained. Respiration is the function of the heart which is to be discharged by the mouth and nose. Respiration (Prāṇa is derived from Praṇayana; taking forwards). "The vital air which goes downwards," (flatulence, Apāna) whose function is downwards, from the carrying away of excrements, urine, etc., the vital air which goes everywhere," (circulation: Vyāna) has its place from the navel (throughout the whole body) and is called Vyāna from its function of regulating (Vyāyamāna); it is the union of the functions of respiration and flatulence and the cause of energetic action. "The vital air, which goes upwards," (Eructation, Udāna) is the getting stout, it is the cause of going upwards, the function of rising from the sole of the feet to the head; "the vital air, which equalises," (assimilation, Samāna) because it equally (Samam) carries (distributes) what is eaten and drunk; its place is the stomach, and its function to digest the food; vital air (Ana) is the common function of all those special functions, and united with the common effort of the body. "All this," the whole of the mentioned functions of respiration, etc., is life (Prāṇa),—Life, as having a function and subservient to the soul, is not mentioned; but its action has been explained by showing the division of its functions. Explained are the provisions called mind, speech and life, in their relation as subservient to the soul. "Thus modified," *viz.*, by the modifications commenced by mind, speech and life, as referring to Prajāpati.

Which is that soul, the whole of causes and effects, the thus or thus modified totality, which by those who do not discriminate, from want of distinction, is thought to be of the nature of the soul ? The mentioned totality is the modification of speech, the modification of mind *and* the modification of life; this also is said for the purpose to determine life.

4. त्रयो लोका एत एव वागेवायं लोको मनोऽन्तरिक्षलोकः प्राणोसौ लोकः ॥

They are even the three worlds; speech is even this world, mind the atmospheric world, life that world.

The material sphere (Ādhibhautika) of these provisions of Prajāpati will *now* be stated. "They" speech, mind and life, are even "the three worlds," earth, atmosphere and heaven. Their distinction is "speech is even this world," mind the atmosphere, and life that world.

5. त्रयो वेदा एत एव वागेवर्ग्वेदो मनो यजुर्वेदः प्राणः सामवेदः ॥

They are even the three Vedas; speech is even the Ṛg Veda, mind the Yajur Veda, *and* life the Sāma Veda.

6. देवाः पितरो मनुष्या एत एव वागेव देवा मनः पितरः प्राणो मनुष्याः ॥

They are even the gods, the forefathers *and* men, speech is even the gods, mind the forefathers, *and* life men.

7. पिता माता प्रजैत एव मन एव पिता वाङ्माता प्राणः प्रजा ॥

They are even father, mother and child ; mind is even the father, speech the mother, *and* life the child.

In the same manner: "They are even," etc. ; the meaning of these words is plain.

8. विज्ञातं विजिज्ञास्यमविज्ञातमेत एव यत् किंच विज्ञातं वाचस्तद्रूपं वाग्घि विज्ञाता वागेनं तद्भूत्वाऽवति ॥

They are even that which is known, which is wished to be known, and which is not known ; whatsoever is known, is of the nature of speech ; for speech is known ; speech being of such a nature, preserves a person.

"They are even that which is known, which is wished to be known, and which is not known." Their distinction is, "whatever is known," fully known, "is of the nature of speech"; and the text gives the reason for this ; "for speech is known," because its nature is to manifest. How can that be unknown which makes other things also known ? "By speech the universal king is known as a companion," will be said afterwards. The effect of knowing the nature of speech is "speech being of such a nature, being known, preserves him," *viz.*, the person who knows the mentioned perfections of speech, that is to say, in the form of knowledge becomes a provision, an enjoyment, for him.

9. यत्किंच विजिज्ञास्यं मनसस्तद्रूपं मनो हि विजिज्ञास्यं मन एनं तद्भूत्वाऽवति ॥

Whatsoever is wished to be known, is of the nature of the mind ; for the mind is desired to be known ; the mind being of such a nature, preserves a person.

10. यत्किंचाविज्ञातं प्राणस्य तद्रूपं प्राणो ह्यविज्ञातः प्राण एनं तद्भूत्वाऽवति ॥

Whatsoever is not known, is of the nature of life, for life is not known; life being of such a nature, preserves a person.

In the same manner, "whatsoever," how indistinct soever desired to be known distinctly, "is wished to be known, is of the nature of the mind, for," because, "the mind" on acconnt of its doubtful nature, "is desired to be known," As before, is described the reward for one who knows the perfection of the mind. "The mind," being of such a nature, *viz.*, which is wished to be known, "preserves him," obtains the nature of a provision by its own characteristic to be some thing wished to be known. In the same manner "whatsoever is not known," is not an object of knowledge, nor doubted, "is of the nature of life; for life is not known," not known in its nature, since it is not heard to be determined. As the distinction of speech, mind and life is established by the division into what is known, what is wished to be known, and what is not known (*viz.*, by a division, comprehending all objects of knowledge) the three worlds, etc., are only mentioned for the sake of illustration. By the passage showing, that the nature of what is known is everywhere, etc., its rule is to be remembered. "Life, being of such nature, preserves him," which means life with its unknown nature becomes his provision. Teachers, fathers, etc., appear to be doubted and their assistance to be not known by disciples, sons, etc. In the same manner is obtained the nature of the provisions of mind and life, which are doubted and not known.

11. तस्यैव वाचः पृथिवी शरीरं ज्योती रूपमयमग्निस्तद्यावत्येव वाक्तावती पृथिवी तावानयमग्निः ॥

Of this speech is earth the body, its illuminating nature that fire. Therefore as far as speech *extends*, so far *extends* the earth, so far fire.

The material extent of speech, mind and life has been explained; now their sphere as superintended by deities, is commenced. "Of this speech," which is shown in the text under the notion of a provison of Prajāpati, "is earth the body," the external locality; "its illuminating nature," the manifesting organ, located upon the earth, "that" earthly, "fire"; for twofold is Prajāpati's speech, *viz.*, effect, locality, which does not manifest, and secondly organ, which is placed *in that locality* and which does not manifest. Both of them, earth and fire, are the speech of Prajāpati. "Therefore (tat, explained by S'aṅkara with tattra, with reference to this)" as far as, in measure "speech, extends," in its divisions, *viz.*, in its subserviency to the soul and in its material sphere, "so far extends the earth," which is established everywhere under the notion of locality as effect, "so far goes that fire," as located in the form of sense, it entered so far with its illuminating nature the earth. The last (relation, *viz.*, the sphere superintended by deities) is the same (and therefore not commented on).

12. अथैतस्य मनसो द्यौः शरीरं ज्योती रूपमसावादित्यस्तद्यावदेव मनस्तावती द्यौस्तावानसावादित्यस्तौ मिथुनꣳ समैतां ततः प्राणोऽजायत स इन्द्रः स एषोऽसपत्नोऽद्वितीयो न सपत्नो नास्य सपत्नो भवति य एवं वेद ॥

Again, of this mind is heaven the body, its illuminating nature Āditya. Therefore as far as mind extends, so far extends heaven, so far that Āditya. They united in love. Hence life was produced. He is Indra, he is without rival. A second verily is a rival. Whosoever knows this, has no rival.

"Again of this mind," which has been declared a provision of Prajāpati, "is heaven," the place of heaven, "the body," the effect, the locality, "its illuminating nature," its organ, that which is to be located, "that Āditya". There "as far as," in measure, "mind," as subservient to the soul, or in its material sphere, "extends, so far" in expanse, in measure, is fixed heaven to be the locality for the illuminating organ of the mind "so far that Āditya," the illuminating organ, which requires to be located. They, Agni and Āditya, speech and mind, in their nature as superintending deities, mother and father, "united in love". *Both having the intention,* I will do the action, it was—between the two places (heaven and earth),—produced by the mind, Āditya as father, and manifested by speech, Agni, as mother. "Hence" by the union of both of them, "life," air, "was produced" for the sake of motion, of work. "He," who was born, "is Indra," the supreme lord (Parameśvara) and not only Indra, but "without rival". Without rival means a person for whom there exists no rival. Who again has really a rival ? "A second verily," a second who approaches with *the intention of* contention, "is" called "a rival". Accordingly, although speech and mind have the nature of a second, yet they entertain no rivalry ; for they have a friendly intention towards life.—The fruit, arising from the knowledge, that there is no rivalship from those who were united in love, is like that *derived* from the subserviency to the soul, as follows : "Whosoever knows this," life as it has been described, as being without rival, *viz.*, he who has true knowledge, "has no rival," no antagonist.

13. अथैतस्य प्राणस्यापः शरीरं ज्योती रूपमसौ चन्द्रस्तद्यावानेव प्राणस्तावत्य आपस्तावानसौ चन्द्रस्त एते सर्व एव समाः सर्वेऽनन्ताः स यो हैतानन्तवत उपास्तेऽन्तवन्तꣳस लोकं जयत्यथ यो हैताननन्तानुपास्तेऽनन्तꣳ स लोकं जयति ॥

Again of this life are the waters the body, the illuminating nature that moon. Therefore as far as life extends, so far extend the waters, so far extends that moon. They are even all alike, all infinite. Whosoever worships them as finite (beings) conquers a finite world; again whosoever worships them as infinite (beings) conquers an infinite world.

"Again of this life,"—of the life, set forth in the text, which is a provision of Prajāpati, not the life which has been declared as offspring, *and* described immediately before, are "the waters the body," the effect, the locality for the organs, "illuminating nature," as before, "that moon". There "as far as," in measure, "life extends," in its divisions as subservient to the soul and as material sphere, "so far extend" pervade, "the waters," in their measure, "so far" "extends that moon" which is to be located, so far, having entered the waters, and being of the nature of sense, it extends, as far as the sphere, subservient to the soul, and the material sphere extend.—Those three provisions, created by the father through the five-fold work, bear the names of speech, mind and life. The whole world in its sphere, subservient to the soul, and in its material sphere, is pervaded by them, or, besides them, there is nothing whatsoever, either effect or cause. But all these are Prajāpati. "They," speech, mind and life, "are even all alike," having the same extent, are as far pervading, as the objects of living beings together with the sphere subservient to the soul and the material sphere. Therefore they are "infinite"; because they are present in all bodies; for a body cannot be conceived without cause and effect, for it is said that they consist of cause and effect. "Whosoever worships them," which are of the nature of Prajāpati, "as finite," limited, under the notion of their material sphere and their sphere, subservient to the soul, "conquers" as the reward in accordance with his worships, "a finite world," a world which is limited, which means, "he does not get their nature". "Again, whosoever worship them as infinite," as possessing the nature of all, living beings, as unlimited, "conquers an infinite world".

14. स एष संवत्सरः प्रजापतिः षोडशकलस्तस्य रात्रय एव पञ्चदशकला ध्रुवैवास्य षोडशी कला स रात्रिभिरेवा च पूर्यतेऽप च क्षीयते सोऽमावास्याꣳ रात्रिमेतया षोडश्या कलया सर्वमिदं प्राणभृदनुप्रविश्य ततः प्रातर्जायते तस्मादेताꣳ रात्रिं प्राणभृतः प्राणं न विच्छिन्द्यादपि कृकलासस्यैतस्या एव देवताया अपचित्यै ॥

That Prajāpati in his likeness of the year consists of 16 parts (Kalā). His nights are even 15 parts; his fixed part is the sixteenth. He becomes full and wanes by the nights. At the day of the new moon, during the night entering with this sixteenth part all that is endowed with life, he is then the next day born in the morning. Therefore let in that night nobody cut off the life of any one endowed with life, not even of the chameleon. It is intended for the honour of this deity.

It has been said that the father, after having created seven provisions by the five-fold work, produced three provisions for his own sake. They are explained to be the effects of the five-fold work. How again are they called the effect of the five-fold work? Because even in these three provisions the five-fold work is perceived, as wealth and works are there probable, *therefore is their cause also similar*. There (as to the three provisions) the earth and fire are the mother, heaven and Āditya the father, and, the life (air) which is in the middle of them, is *their* offspring, as it has been explained. On account of this wealth and work should be produced; this means to imply the commencement: "That Prajāpati, in his likeness of the year," who has been set forth in the text as consisting of three parts, is determined in a special manner by the nature of the year as consisting of sixteen parts. He, consisting of sixteen parts, is the year, the nature of time. "His" prajāpati's, as the substance of time, "nights," days and nights—meaning lunar days (tithi) are fifteen parts. "His fixed," permanent, "part" remains, as "the sixteenth," as the part (Kalā); which completes the sixteenth. "He" becomes full and wanes by the nights; by the lunar days which are called parts (Kalā); for by the first day of lunation, and by those which succeed it, the moon Prajāpati, gets full in the light half of the lunation, it grows by the increasing parts (Kalās) until the orb is full at the day of the full moon; it wanes by the decreasing parts in the dark half of the lunation, until the one permanent part remains in the dark night. "He," Prajāpati, the substance of time, "at the day of the new moon during the night," "entering with this sixteenth part," which has been called the permanent part, "all that is endowed with life," all living beings, *viz.*, all that drinks water and all that eats annual plants, pervading all this by his identity with the annual plants (or with water) *and* abiding during the dark night, "is then" the next day, "born in the morning," united (the moon) with its second part.—In the following manner is Prajāpati of five-fold nature. The heaven and the sun are the mind the father,—the earth and fire speech, the wife, the mother; and their offspring is life, the days of the moon, the parts (Kalā) are the wealth, because by their increasing and decreasing they are like wealth, and the work of those parts is what effects the change of the world. In this manner the whole Prajāpati has become the effect of the five-fold work, in accordance with the desires: "Let me have a wife,"—again "Let me be born,"—again, "Let me have wealth," again,—"Let me perform work," for as the cause so is the effect, is a principle even with the common people. Because the moon, having that night entered all living creatures, is possessed of its permanent part, "therefore," on this ground, "let in that night nobody cut off the life of any one endowed with life," let him not destroy a living creature, "not even of a chameleon," for the chameleon, as being wicked, is naturally destroyed, since it is considered to forebode bad luck, when it is seen. "But then enmity to living beings is prohibited according to the passage *of the Smṛti*": "Not killing living creatures except at holy places." Very good, it is prohibited; but yet it must not be said, that the sentence means to make an exception for any other time than the day of the dark night, or an exception for the killing of the chameleon. What then does it mean? "It is intended for the honour," the adoration, "of this deity, *viz.*, the deity of the moon".

15. यो वै स संवत्सरः प्रजापतिः षोडशकलोऽयमेवं स योऽयमेवं-वित्पुरुषस्तस्य वित्तमेव पञ्चदशकला आत्मैवास्य षोडशी कला स वित्तेनैवा च पूर्यतेऽप च क्षीयते तदेतन्नभ्यं यदयमात्मा प्रधिर्वित्तं तस्माद्यद्यपि सर्वज्यानिं जीयत आत्मना चेज्जीवति प्रधिनागादित्येवाहुः ॥

That Prajāpati who under the likeness of the year is possessed of sixteen parts, is even this. That "this" is a person who thus knows. His wealth is the fifteen parts, his soul (self) is his sixteenth part. He gets full and wanes even by wealth.

It *is well known*, that the soul is like the nave of a wheel, wealth like its periphery. Therefore, although he suffers the loss of all, if he lives, he is bare of the periphery, as it is said.

"That Prajāpati," bearing the name of the invisible, "who under the likeness of the year is possessed of sixteen parts," must not be thought as absolutely invisible, because he is even this, he is perceived visibly. Who is that "this"? "He is the person who thus knows," who knows, that Prajāpati whose nature consists of the three provisions, is like himself. By the similarity with what is he Prajāpati? The answer is: "His wealth," the wealth in cows, etc., of a person who thus knows, "is the fifteen parts". For the sake of his completeness "his soul," the individual self, "is his" (the knowing person's) sixteenth part, representing the permanent Kalā. "He," like the moon, "gets full and wanes even by wealth". "It is well known" in common life, that "the soul," the "individual" self, "is like the nave of a wheel, wealth like its periphery," represented by the family, the external part of the wheel, *viz.*, spokes and circumference, etc. "Therefore, although he suffers the loss of all," of his property, suffers distress, "if he lives," "by the soul," represented by the nave of the wheel, "he is bare of," he has lost "the periphery," the external wealth, the family, as a wheel, deprived of spokes and circumference, "as it is said," and the meaning is, if he lives, he is again increasing in wealth, represented by the spokes and circumference.

16. अथ त्रयो वाव लोका मनुष्यलोकः पितृलोको देवलोक इति सोऽयं मनुष्यलोकः पुत्रेणैव जय्यो नान्येन कर्मणा कर्मणा पितृलोको विद्यया देवलोको देवलोको वै लोकानाꣳ श्रेष्ठस्तस्माद्विद्यां प्रशꣳसन्ति ॥

Again there are verily three worlds, the world of man, the world of the forefathers, and the world of the gods. The world of man is to be conquered by a son, and not by any other work, (or knowledge,) by work the world of the forefathers, by science the world of the gods. The world of the gods is the best among the worlds. Therefore they praise science.

It has been explained, how by five-fold work in connection with science, the wealth of the gods, Prajāpati is possessed of the nature of the three provisions; it has afterwards been said, how the wealth of a wife, etc., is represented by the family. There (in the former section) it has only generally been understood, that a son, work and inferior science (knowledge of the Vedas with reference to ceremonies), are causes of obtaining the worlds, but the rule of the special connection of a son, etc., with the effect, which is the obtaining of the worlds, has not been understood. To explain the special connection of the effects with their causes, *viz.*, a son, etc., the present section is commenced. The term "again" has the object to introduce the sentence "there are verily," verily is to show certainty, "three worlds," alone fit to be causes, stated by the S'āstra, neither more nor less. Which are they? The answer is: "The world of man, the world of the forefathers, and the world of the gods." Among them "the world of man" is to be gained by, is the effect of "a son," as cause (how it is to be gained by a son, will afterwards be said) "and not by any other work," or knowledge, as must be supplied here; "by work," alone, as for instance, the daily burnt-offering (Agnihotra) "the world of the forefathers," is to be gained, and not by a son, nor by knowledge,—"by science the world of the gods," not by a son, nor by work. "The world of the gods is the best," the one most deserving of praise, "among the" three, "worlds". "Therefore they praise science," because it is the cause of it.

17. अथातः संप्रत्तिर्यदा प्रैष्यन्मन्यतेऽथ पुत्रमाह त्वं ब्रह्म त्वं यज्ञस्त्वं लोक इति स पुत्रः प्रत्याहाहं ब्रह्माहं यज्ञोऽहं लोक इति यद्वै किंचानूक्तं तस्य सर्वस्य ब्रह्मेत्येकता । ये वै के च यज्ञास्तेषाꣳ सर्वेषां यज्ञ इत्येकता ये वै के च लोकास्तेषाꣳ सर्वेषां लोक इत्येकतैतावद्वा इदꣳ सर्वमेतन्मा सर्वꣳ सन्नयमितोऽभुनजदिति तस्मात् पुत्रमनुशिष्टं लोक्यमाहुस्तस्मादेनमनुशासति स यदेवंविदस्माल्लोकात्प्रैत्यथैभिरेव प्राणैः सह पुत्रमाविशति स यद्येनेन किंचिदक्ष्णया कृतं भवति तस्मादेनꣳ सर्वस्मात्पुत्रो मुञ्चति तस्मात्पुत्रो नाम स पुत्रेणैवास्मिँल्लोके प्रतितिष्ठत्यथैनमेते देवाः प्राणा अमृता आविशन्ति ॥

Hence again the making over. When *the father* thinks he is to die, then he says to his son; "Thou art Brahman, thou art the sacrifice, thou art the world." The son repeats: "I am Brahman, I am the sacrifice, I am the world." Of all that has been read, is Brahman the identity. Of all the sacrifices that *are to be performed*, is sacrifice the identity. Of all the worlds that are to be conquered, is world the identity. Thus far extends verily all this. All this multitude preserves me from this *world.* Therefore they call a son who is instructed, Lokya ; therefore they instruct him. When he, having such a knowledge, departs from this world, then he enters together with those lives the son. If by him anything through negligence, remains undone, the son liberates him from all this. Hence the name of a son (Putra). He continues by a son alone in this world. Then those divine, immortal lives enter him.

In this manner the three causes, *viz.*, a son, work, and knowledge, find their application according to the division of the effect, *viz.*, the three worlds which are to be accomplished. But a wife, because it is necessary for the sake of a son and of work, is not a separate cause, and is therefore not separately mentioned. Also wealth, as it is the cause of work, is not a separate cause. It is evident, that knowledge and work are means of conquering the worlds in consequence of their recovering their own nature. But a son not being of the nature of work, it is not clear, in what manner he is the means of conquering the worlds. "Hence," it is to be explained, in this manner "again," afterwards is commenced, "the making over" ; this is the name of the work which is to be *now* related ; for the father makes over the duties he has himself to perform, in the manner to be mentioned, to his son ; hence this work bears the name of "making over". At what time is this to be done. "When the father thinks, he is to die," by inauspicious signs and the like, then he says to his son (after having called him): "Thou art Brahman, thou art the sacrifice, thou art the world." Thus addressed, he "repeats". That is to say, being instructed before, he knows, I have to do this. In this manner he says the three sentences : "I am Brahman, I am the sacrifice, I am the world." Under the idea that the sense of the same is concealed, the S'ruti continues for its explanation. "Of all that has been read" the remainder of what has been read, that is to say, read or not read "is Brahman the identity," is the identity in the term of Brahman. The practice of reading with reference to the Vedas, which was hitherto thy duty, is henceforth thou, Brahman ; which means, must be done by thy agency. In the same manner, "Of all the sacrifices that were to be performed by me," may they be performed by me or not performed, "is sacrifice the identity," is the identity in the term sacrifice. The sacrifices which were to be performed by my agency, are henceforth "Thou sacrifice," which means, are to be performed by thy agency. "All the worlds that are to be conquered," by me, whether they are conquered or not conquered is world the "identity," is the identity in the term "world". Hence forward they are "thou world," to be conquered by thee henceforward the sacrifice which it was my duty to perform by reading (the Vedas), offerings and conquering of the worlds, is laid by me upon thee, but I am free from the sacrifice consisting in the bondage of duty. And the son has understood all in this manner, because he was instructed (before). The S'ruti, having considered there the intention of the father, gives this explanation: "Thus far extends verily all this," this is the limit of all the duties of a householder, *viz.*, that the Vedas are to be read, the sacrifices to be performed and the world to be conquered. "All this multitude" (for all this burden, to which I am subject, when taken from me and placed upon you) preserves me, saves me from this world. (The past Abhunajat in Saṁskṛt, has in the S'ruti the meaning of the future : Pālayiṣyati). Because a son, who thus knows, is to liberate *his* father from this world, from the bondage of duty, "therefore they," the Brāhmaṇas, "call a son who is *thus* instructed, Lokya," which means, good for his father obtaining the worlds. "Therefore they," the fathers,

" instruct a son " under the expectation that he will be there Lokya (procurer of the worlds). " When he," the father, " having such a knowledge," after having delivered to the son the sacrifice of duty, " departs from this world," dies, " then he enters with those lives the son," pervades him with the speech, mind and life set forth in the text. When the cause of distinction relative to the soul (which cause is ignorance) is removed, the speech, mind and life of the father enter all with their nature as superintended by deities, *viz.*, in their likeness with the earth, the fire and the son. Together with those lives the father also enters, because the father is transformed into the nature of speech, mind and life; for the father is transformed in such a manner as: " I am the infinite speech, mind and life, extending as far as the distinctions of what relates to the soul, to matter and to the superintendance of deities." Therefore his life is continuation of the father's, and it is hence properly said, " then together with those lives he enters the son "; for it is said, he becomes the soul (substance) of all and (therefore also) of the son; and the meaning is, the father who has a thus instructed son, continues in this world, is by the likeness with the son not to be thought dead. In this manner it is said in another passage of the Śruti : " He is made his other soul by holy works." (A. U. B. I. vii, p. 226th, M. 4.) Now the text gives the derivation of Putra (son). " If by him," by the father at anytime, " anything through negligence, remains," meanwhile, " undone," which ought to be done, " the son liberates him from all this," which bearing the nature of duty, was left undone by the father, and which is an obstacle to gaining the worlds,—*he liberates* him, by completing it (Pūrayitvā) through its own practice. " Therefore," because he saves the father by completing (Pūraṇena) hence the name of a son (Putra). This is the true notion of a son (Putrasya Putratvam) that by filling (Pūrayitvā) the whole of the father he saves *him*. " He," the father, " continues," although dead, yet immortal, " by a son," of such a kind, " in this world". In this manner the father conquers (obtains) by the son this world of man,—not so, however, the worlds of the gods and the forefathers by knowledge and work, but (he conquers them) by assuming their nature alone; for without assuming their own nature, knowledge and work cannot possibly become causes of conquering the world by dependence upon another, as it is the case with a son. "Then," after the father has made over *his duties*, "those divine" belonging to Hiraṇyagarbha, "immortal," whose nature it is not to die, "lives," speech and the others, "enter him". How? The answer is given *in the next section* by the words: "The divine speech, etc."

In this manner it has shown by the Śruti itself, that a son, work and inferior knowledge have the power of accomplishing the worlds of men, of the forefathers and of the gods. In respect of this some wranglers (the Mīmāmsakas as are meant) not knowing the special meanings of the words of the Śruti, say, that a son and the other causes have the power to effect liberation. To silence them this passage has been given by the Śruti, commencing with: "Let me have a wife," and all the other five-fold work which accomplishes desire, continuing with, "*So far goes the desire*," of a son, etc., and concluding with the application to the special *effects* to be accomplished. Hence it is evident, that the passage of the Śruti about debt refers to an ignorant person, and not to the knowledge of the supreme soul. And it will be said (p. 903): "of what use is a son to us to whom the soul is the world." Others, (the Bhartṛprāpañcika) on the other hand, maintain, that the conquering of the world, of the forefathers and gods is even an exclusion from them. Therefore a person, who, by the joint performance of a son, of work and of the inferior knowledge, is excluded from those three worlds, obtains liberation by the knowledge, of the supreme soul; in this way the causes of a son, etc., successively have the power to effect liberation. To silence them also the other subsequent passage of the Śruti is engaged in showing the effect, resulting for the father, whose duty is the performance of works, who has the knowledge of the nature of the three provisions and who makes over *the performance* of what has been left undone. But it cannot be said, that the effect is that of liberation, because it has been shown, that by the effect derived from understanding and penance in connection with the three provisions, the provisions are again produced. This follows also from the passage, referring to the decrease (of the provisions). "For what even does not produce it, decreases," also from the nature of the means of the effect in the passage ; "the body is like light," and lastly from the conclusion with the nature of name, form and work, in the passage ? "Three-fold is this," etc. Nor is it possible to infer from this passage, that the three causes when united, have the power to effect one's liberation and another's, obtaining the nature of the three provisions, because the passage merely intends to show, that the effect of a son and of the other causes is the obtaining of the nature of the three provisions.

18. पृथिव्यै चैनमग्नेश्च दैवी वागाविशति सा वै दैवी वाग्यया यद्यदेव वदति तत्तद्भवति ॥

From the earth and the fire the divine speech enters him. That speech is verily divine, by which whatever he says comes to pass.

"From the earth and the fire the divine speech, (divine refers to its superintending diety,) enters him," after he has made over *his duties* ; that is to say, the divine speech, as characterised by earth and fire, is the last cause of the speech of all ; for speech is obstructed by the faults of the attachment, etc., with reference to the material elements, *and* as the faults of a person who has knowledge are removed, it (speech) pervades him, like water and the manifestation of a light, on the breaking of what concealed them (for instance a vessel). This is the sense of the words : "From the earth and the fire the divine speech enters him." "That speech is verily divine," free from the faults of untruth and the like, pure, "by which" (divine speech) "whatever he says," either for himself or another, "comes to pass," that is to say, his word is not in vain, is not obstructed.

19. दिवश्चैनमादित्याच्च दैवं मन आविशति तद्वै दैवं मनो येनानन्द्येव
भवत्यथो न शोचति ॥

From the sky and the sun divine mind, enters him. That verily is the divine mind, by which he becomes joyful; henceforth he does not grieve.

In the same manner: "From the sky and the sun the divine mind enters him." And, "that is the divine mind," by the purity of its nature, "by which he (the father) becomes joyful," happy, "henceforth" moreover, "he does not grieve," because there is no connection of such a cause as grief (with him).

20. अद्भ्यश्चैनं चन्द्रमसश्च दैवः प्राण आविशति स वै दैवः प्राणो यः
संचरꣳश्चासंचरꣳश्च न व्यथतेऽथो न रिष्यति स एवंवित्सर्वेषां
भूतानामात्मा भवति यथैषा देवतैवꣳ स यथैतां देवताꣳ सर्वाणि
भूतान्यवन्त्येवꣳ हैवं विदꣳ सर्वाणि भूतान्यवन्ति यदु किंचेमाः
प्रजाः शोचन्त्यमैवासां तद्भवति पुण्यमेवामुं गच्छति न ह वै
देवान् पापं गच्छति ॥

From the waters and the moon the divine life enters him. That verily is the divine life, which, whether issuing forth, or not issuing forth, is not afraid, again which is not lost. The person who thus knows, becomes the soul of all beings. As that deity, so also he. As all beings preserve that deity, so also preserve all beings a person who thus knows.

Whatever grief the children suffer together with *their children*, remains united with them alone; what is holy approaches him; for sin does not approach the gods.

In the same manner: "From the waters and the moon the divine life enters him. That verily is the divine life"; *viz.*, of what nature? The answer is,—"Which, whether issuing forth," in all the distinctions of life, "or not issuing forth," in its nature as totality or speciality, or also, issuing forth in all moveable things, and not issuing forth in all immoveable things, "is not afraid," is not connected with fear, of which unhappiness is the cause, "again, is not lost," is not destroyed, is not injured. "The person who knows thus," the before mentioned view of the nature of the three provisions, "becomes the soul of all beings," becomes the life of all beings, becomes the mind of all beings, becomes *their* speech, that is to say becomes omniscient by being the nature of all; and also, omnipotent. "As that deity," the before mentioned deity named Hiraṇyagarbha, "so also" (also shows that there is no obstacle to his omniscience and omnipotence) "he" *which term* concludes the illustration. Moreover:[1] "As all beings," "preserve" worship, "that deity," the deity called Hiraṇyagarbha with offerings, etc. "So also preserve all beings a person who thus knows," which means, they worship him always with offerings and the like.

It has been said, "he becomes the soul of all beings." Now it may be questioned, whether, by his being the nature of cause and effect of all beings, he is not also allied to the happiness and unhappiness of them. This is not the case, because his intellect is unlimited. As to persons whose intellect and nature are limited on beings censured, etc., a connexion with unhappiness is evident, as if we say: "I am censured by that man"; but in virtue of *his* being the soul of all, there is no unhappiness from such causes

[1] Kiñca (moreover) is in text connected with the preceding sentence, commencing with "Sa," I believe, by a clerical error, as in this place it has no meaning, or a meaning which destroys the simplicity of the text.

produced, as there is no distinction of intellect with regard the nature of the soul between the one who is censured and the other who censures, and also, as, like the unhappiness of death, there is no cause. For instance: If any body dies, unhappiness is produced for somebody (showing itself in such words as:) He is my son, my brother, where the cause (of the distress) is a son, a brother. If there is no cause of such a kind, unhappiness is not produced, even should a person behold the death of a person, etc. (who is not related to him). In this manner no unhappiness arises for god whose nature is unlimited, because he has not the faults of false knowledge, etc., which produce the uuhappiness of pride, etc. This is meant by the words,—" Whatever grief his subjects suffer together with their children," " the same," the unhappiness which is the cause of the grief, etc., " remains united with them," with his subjects, because it is produced from a limited intellect. But what of the universal soul can be united with or disunited from what thing? " What is holy," what is good,—the desired reward means here holy; for a great many holy actions are done by him, therefore its reward " approaches him who now occupies the place of Prajāpati". " For sin does not approach the gods," and the meaning is, sin, its effect, unhappiness does not approach the gods, because there is no opportunity for the effect of sin.

21. अथातो व्रतमीमांसा प्रजापतिर्ह कर्माणि ससृजे तानि सृष्टान्यन्योन्येनास्पर्धन्त वदिष्याम्येवाहमिति वाग्दध्रे द्रक्ष्याम्यहमिति चक्षुः श्रोष्याम्यहमिति श्रोत्रमेवमन्यानि कर्माणि यथा कर्म तानि मृत्युः श्रमो भूत्वोपयेमे तान्याप्नोत्तान्याप्त्वा मृत्युरवारुन्धत्तस्माच्छ्राम्यत्येव वाक् श्राम्यति चक्षुः श्राम्यति श्रोत्रमथेममेव नाप्नोद्योऽयं मध्यमः प्राणस्तानि ज्ञातुं दध्रिरे अयं वै नः श्रेष्ठो यः संचरंश्चासंचरंश्च न व्यथतेऽथो न रिष्यति हन्तास्यैव सर्वे रूपमसामेति त एतस्यैव सर्वे रूपमभवंस्तस्मादेत एतेनाख्यायन्ते प्राणा इति तेन ह वाव तत्कुलमाचक्षते यस्मिन्कुले भवति

य एवं वेद य उहैवंविदा स्पर्धतेऽनुशुष्यत्यनुशुष्य हैवान्ततो म्रियत इत्यध्यात्मम् ॥

Next therefore the deliberation of observance. Prajāpati verily created the actions. When they were created, they vied with each other. With the words,—“ I will speak,” speech kept they observance ; with the words,—“ I will see,” eye ; with the words—“ I will hear,” ear ; in the same manner the other actions (Karmāṇi) according to their action. Death, being *there* as fatigue, seized them, be made them his own ; having made them his own, he arrested them. Therefore speech gets even fatigued, the eye gets fatigued, the ear gets fatigued. Again he did not make his own that *life.* They resolved to know that central life. “ He verily is amongst us the best, who moving and not moving, not suffers, is not injured. Well then, let us all become of the nature of him.” Thus all of them became of his nature. Therefore they are named by this “ Prāṇāh”. After him, who thus knows, is verily called the family in which he is *born.* Whosoever rivals one who thus knows, after having wasted, dies at last. This is what refers to the soul.

By the words,—“ They are all alike, they are all infinite ” (p. 194), the worship of speech, mind and life has been declared in general, that is to say, without their mutual distinction. Must this now be understood in the mentioned manner, or is there any possible distinction with regard to observance on considering *the case* ? The answer is,—“ Next therefore,” then *follows* “ the deliberation of observance,” of worship, which means the consideration of the action of worship. And the consideration turns upon this, which is it among those organs, whose work is to be conceived under the idea of observance? "Prajāpati verily," after having created *his* offspring, "created the actions," which means the organs, speech and others (for being capable of action, they are called actions) and the meaning is: He created speech and the other organs. Again "when they were created, they vied," rivalled, "with each other". How? "With the words—I will speak," let me not rest from my business, speaking "speech kept the observance". If there is likewise another, my equal, who does not require rest from his business, let him show his prowess. In the same manner, "with the words,—'I will see,' eye; with the words, 'I will hear,' ear; in the same manner the other actions," organs, "according to their action". "Death," the destroyer, "being *there as* fatigue," in the form of fatigue "seized them," took hold of them. How? "He made them," the organs engaged in their business, "his own," he appeared under the form of fatigue, and "having made them his own, he" death, "arrested them, made them cease from their work". "Therefore," even now, "speech," having entered upon its work, "gets even fatigued," is made to cease from its work, seized by death in the form of fatigue. In the same manner "the eye gets fatigued, the ear gets fatigued". "Again he," death in the form of fatigue, "did not make his own that *life*," the principal life. "They," the other organs, "resolved," made up their mind, "to know that central life" which even now not fatigued by him (death) enters upon its work.

"He verily is amongst us the best," the most praiseworthy, the greatest, "who moving and not moving not suffers," again, "is not injured. Well then" now "let us all become of the nature of him," of life, that is to say, let us consider ourselves as life. Having "thus" ascertained, "our observances are sufficient to protect *us* from death," "all of them became of his nature," considering themselves as the nature of life, kept the observances of life. Because by the nature of life, *viz.*, by its nature to move and by its nature to manifest, the other *organs* get their nature,—namely, without life nothing could move: for only after the action of moving they are observed to engage in their own work—" therefore they," speech and the others, " are named by this," name of life, " Prāṇāh " (lives). " After him," the wise person, who in this manner knows that all the organs have the nature of life, and are called by the term " life " (Prāṇa), " is verily called the family," by the people. The family, in which he who thus knows, " is born," gets famous by the name of the wise person, it is his family, as this is the family of Tapati. " Whosoever thus," in the manner mentioned, " knows " that speech and the other organs have the nature and the name of life, gets a reward of such a kind. Again, " Whosoever rivals," being his antagonist " one who thus knows," knows the nature of life, wastes in this body, " after having wasted, dies at last " not on a sudden. " This is what refers to the soul," in the mentioned manner, the knowledge of the nature of life. This conclusion is intended to introduce the exposition of what refers to the superintendence of deities.

22. अथाधिदैवतं ज्वलिष्याम्येवाहमित्यग्निर्दध्रे तप्स्याम्यहमित्यादित्यो भास्याम्यहमिति चन्द्रमा एवमन्या देवता यथादैवतꣳस यथैषां प्राणानां मध्यमः प्राण एवमेतासां देवतानां वायुर्निम्लोचन्ति ह्यन्या देवता न वायुः सैषानस्तमिता देवता यद्वायुः ॥

Next what refers to the superintendence of deities. With the words,—" I will burn," fire kept the observance, with the words,—" I will heat," the sun, with the words,—" I will shine," the moon. In the same manner the other deities according to their divine nature. As this central life amongst those organs, so *appears* Vāyu (the air), amongst those deities; for the other deities decline, not Vāyu. This Vāyu indeed is an unrestrained deity.

"**Next** what refers to the superintendence of deities," the thinking as to the deities is described. It is the question, of which special deity is it best to keep the ordinance ? All is *here* like *the former description about* what referred to the soul. "With the words,—'I will burn,' fire kept the observance, with the words,—'I will heat,' the sun, with the words,—'I will shine,' the moon. In the same manner the other deities according to their divine nature." Here is an illustration. "As this central life," with reference to the soul "amongst those organs," speech and the others, was not seized by death, was not compelled to cease from its work, was not disturbed in its own observance of life, so also not "Vāyu amongst those deities," Agni and others: "for the other deities," Agni and the rest, like speech, etc., with regard to the soul, according to their divine nature, "decline," go down, cease from their works, "not Vāyu, goes down as the central life" (does not decline). Therefore "this Vāyu indeed is an unrestrained deity". The reference to the soul and the superintendence of deities having in this manner been considered, it is ascertained, that the observance of the nature of Vāyu (alone) remains unbroken.

23. अथैष श्लोको भवति यतश्चोदेति सूर्योऽस्तं यत्र च गच्छतीति
प्राणाद्वा एष उदेति प्राणेऽस्तमेति तं देवाश्चक्रिरे धर्मꣳ स
एवाद्य स उ श्व इति यद्वा एतेऽमुर्ह्यध्रियन्त तदेवाप्यद्य कुर्वन्ति ।
तस्मादेकमेव व्रतं चरेत्प्राण्याच्चैवापान्याच्च नेन्मा पाप्मा मृत्यु-
राप्नुवदिति यद्युचरेत्समापिपयिषेत्तेनो एतस्यै देवतायै सायुज्यꣳ
सलोकतां जयति ॥

Here follows this S'loka—"Whence the sun rises and where he sets,"—he verily rises from life and sets into life,—"this the gods made Their sacred law This *sways* to-day, this *sways* to-morrow". What they kept then they will also observe to-day. Therefore let a man follow only one *observance*; let him breathe, let him expel. Alas, let death not seize me. If a person follows it, let him strive to accomplish it. Thereby a person gains union and dwelling in the same world with that deity.

"Here" in elucidation of the said meaning "follows this śloka". "Whence," from which wind "the sun rises" (with reference to divine superintendence) and from which life (as regards its reference to the soul) *he rises* by the nature of the eye, again into which wind and life at evening and at the sleeping-time of men he sets, "this the gods made," kept, "their sacred law". This means, the gods, speech and others, and fire and others, having before considered the observance of life and the observance of Vāyu, "this sways to-day, this sways to-morrow," this will be followed by them at the present and future time. Here the Brāhmaṇa explains briefly the meaning of the Mantra. "He" the sun, "verily rises from life and sets into it". "This the gods made their sacred law; this *sways* to-day, this *sways* to-morrow." What does this mean? It is answered *by the text*: "What," what observance, observance of life and of Vāyu, "they," speech and the rest, and Agni and the rest, "kept then," at that time, "the same they will also observe to-day," the same observance they will keep unbroken. But any observance of speech, etc., gets even broken, as it has been shown, that at the time of their setting they decline into Vāyu and life. It is said elsewhere,—"When man sleeps, then speech, mind, eye, ear, all become life: when he awakes, then they are born again from life. This is their reference to the soul. Next their reference to divine superintendence. When fire is extinguished, it disappears in Vāyu (air). Therefore it is said, it is lost in it; for it is extinguished in the air. When the sun sets, he enters into the air, into the air the moon *enters*; in the air are placed the quarters. From the air they are born again." Because then the observance is found in speech and the rest, and also in Agni and the rest, because the observance, whose nature is to move is to be obeyed by all the gods, "therefore let a man follow only one observance". Which is it? "Let him breathe," let him perform the function of breathing (Prāṇa), "let him expel," let him perform the function of expelling (of the descending air); for there no ceasing of the function of life (Prāṇa) of which the functions of breathing and expelling are here given as examples. "Therefore let a man follow only one observance," abandoning the functions of all other organs. "Alas" (this term expresses apprehension) "let not death," as fatigue—"seize me". The meaning is, let a person, who is afraid that he will be seized by death on his abandoning that observance, keep the observance of life. "If a person follows it," once has commenced the observance of life, "let him strive to accomplish it," for if he ceases from the observance, life is despised, and also the gods are; therefore let him accomplish it even. "Thereby" by that observance,—*for* by the obtaining of the nature of life, my functions, for instance speech, etc., and Agni, etc., are in all beings, and (my) soul as life is the moving cause of all—by the keeping of that observance, "a person gains," obtains, "union," identity of nature, and dwelling in the same "world," identity of place, "with that deity," with the deity of life.

SIXTH BRAHMAṆA

1. त्रयं वा इदं नामरूपं कर्म तेषां नाम्नां वागित्येतदेषामुक्थमतो हि सर्वाणि नामान्युत्तिष्ठन्त्येतदेषाꣳ सामैतद्धि सर्वैर्नामभिः सममेतदेषां ब्रह्मैतद्धि सर्वाणि नामानि बिभर्ति ॥

This (world) is a triad, name, form and work. The names are speech; the latter is the foundation, for from the same all names spring forth This is their community ; for it is in common to all the names ; it is the Brahman of them ; for it upholds all names.

"This" manifested world, characterised as cause and effect, further the reward, which consists in obtaining the nature of life (Hiraṇyagarbha), both of which have been set forth as being included in the idea of ignorance, and lastly the state of the world before its manifestation, which is called "unmanifested" like the seed of a tree, "is a triad". What is this triad ? The answer is,—"name, form, and work," that is to say, non-soul, not the soul which is the present, visible Brahman. Therefore the Brāhmaṇa, of which the first words are,—"this is a triad," is commenced for the object, that man should turn from this (world) ; for the knowledge, resulting from the great sentence,—"I am Brahman,"—to adore the soul alone as the proper place, is without effect for one whose thought is not averted from this (world) which is not the soul—the actions (of the mind) with regard to external objects and the absolute soul being at variance. In this manner it is said in the Kaṭha (4, 1). "The self-existence subdued the senses which turn to external objects ; therefore (man) sees the external objects, not the internal soul (but) the wise with eye averted (from sensual objects) and desirous of immortal nature, beholds the absolute soul." Why again falls this world, which is manifested and not manifested, and at the same time effect, cause and reward, under the notion of name, form and work, why should it not rather be thought by the notion of the soul ?

To answer this, it is said,—"the names" in the order in which they are introduced, "are speech," as he called the general term of all sounds. Every sound is even speech ; it is speech in consequence of being spoken, the meaning of a sound is merely the general term of sound. "The latter is their foundation," the special cause, of the special names, as a hill of rock-salt is the cause of (all) the grains of rock-salt. For this reason it is said,—"for from the same," general term of names, "all names," as Yajñadatta, Devadatta, according to this or any other division, "spring forth," are produced, separated, as grains of salt from a rock of salt; and the effect is not different from the cause. In the same manner the special (names) being included in the general term how can there be a state of generality and of special objects? (To show this it is said),—"This" the general term of the sounds, "is their community," of the special names, community from its being common, *viz.*, the general term; "for it is common to all the names," which are different from it, (and) moreover, because the special names are not different (from it) by having obtained it (the general idea), (for) nothing is perceived to differ from that whose nature it has assumed, as a jar differs not from the earth (of which it is made). How are the special names said to have obtained it (the general idea of speech)? The answer is, because "it" the thing called by the name of speech, "is the Brahman of them," their soul; for hence the names obtain it (the generality); for nothing is found differing from the nature of sound. This the text explains: "for this," the general notion of sound, "upholds all names" by giving them its own nature. This, the relation of cause and effect, of the general idea and the special objects and of the communication of the own nature (of one thing to other things) being proved, it is evident, that the special names are only sound. The same explanation holds good for the two other things.

2. अथ रूपाणां चक्षुरित्येतदेषामुक्थमतो हि सर्वाणि रूपाण्युत्तिष्ठन्त्येतदेषाꣳ सामैतद्धि सर्वैं रूपैः सममेतदेषां ब्रह्मैतद्धि सर्वाणि रूपाणि बिभर्ति ॥

Further, the forms are objects of the eye; the latter is their foundation, for from the same all forms spring forth; this is their community; for it is common to all the forms. It is the Brahman of them; for it upholds all forms.

"Further, the forms," white, black, etc., "are objects of the eye," are the general idea, named "object of the eye," the general idea of forms, all that may be manifested. "For from the latter all forms spring forth; the same is their community; for it is common to all the forms. It is the Brahman of them; for it upholds all forms."

3. अथ कर्मणामात्मेत्येतदेषामुक्थमतो हि सर्वाणि कर्माण्युत्तिष्ठन्त्येतदेषाꣳ सामैतद्धि सर्वैः कर्मभिः सममेतदेषां ब्रह्मैतद्धि सर्वाणि कर्माणि बिभर्ति तदेतत्त्रयꣳ सदेकमयमात्माऽत्मो एकः सन्नेतत्त्रयं तदेतदमृतꣳ सत्येन छन्नं प्राणो वा अमृतं नामरूपे सत्यं ताभ्यामयं प्राणश्छन्नः ॥

Further, the works are self (Ātmā), the latter is their foundation; for from the same all works spring forth; this is their community; for it is common to all works; it is the Brahman of them, for it upholds all works. Those three are existing, one that self (Ātmā); that self, one existing, is the three. This immortal (being) is concealed by existence. Life is verily the immortal being, name and form existence. By them that life is concealed.

Further all special works, as well such as thinking, seeing, etc., as also such as refer to motion, are said to be contained in the general notion of effect. How? All special works are "self," the body, the general notion; self are called the works of self; for it is said, that by the self, by the body, people perform their work. Moreover, in the body every work is manifested. Therefore by its being sited there (in the body) "the latter" work, the general idea of work, "is the foundation of them," just the same as before. "Those three," name, form and work, as mentioned before, being in mutual dependence, being the mutual cause of manifestation and being united for their mutual destruction, "are," like the (mutual) support of the three vows of the devotee,[1] "existing, one". Why is the idea of unity connected with the self? It is answered,—"That self," that lump, the combination of cause and effect; in the same manner as in the following passage (B.Ā., 1, 5, 3) "Thus modified is the soul," the modifications of mind, speech and life, "for so far extend this all both manifested and unmanifested, as name, form and work".

"The self (soul) one," the combination of effect and cause, "existing," in relation to the soul, the elements and the deities, "is the three," as defined, name, form and work. "This immortal being to be mentioned, "is concealed by existence". The text itself explains the meaning of the preceding sentence, *viz.*, "Life is the immortal being," in its nature as cause, the internal support of work, being the same with the soul, immortal, indestructible. "Name and form are existence"; they have the nature of effects and abide in the body; but life having the nature of cause and being the support of them, "is concealed," not manifested, by them, which are external, corporeal, liable to increase and decrease, and mortal. The fourth[2] chapter is commenced for the purpose to show, that the soul, the object of knowledge, must be comprehended.

---

[1] To subdue his mind, his senses and his speech.

[2] The fourth chapter of the Brāhmaṇa, the second of the Upaniṣad.

SECOND CHAPTER

FIRST BRĀHMAṆA

1. दृप्तबालाकिर्हानूचानो गार्ग्य आस स होवाचाजातशत्रुं काश्यं ब्रह्म ते ब्रवाणीति स होवाचाजातशत्रुः सहस्रमेतस्यां वाचि दद्मो जनको जनक इति वै जना धावन्तीति ॥

There was a great speaker, Gārgya the proud son of Balākā. He said to Ajātas'atru, the king of Kās'i—"Let me explain to thee (the nature of) Brahman" (1). Ajātas'atru said—"For such a word (2), I will give thousand (of cows)." (Hearing) "Janaka, Janaka" (3). people verily run (after a man of such a character).

(1) In the first chapter the difference between knowledge and ignorance has been defined, and ignorance generally described; in the second, knowledge, or the science treating on Brahman, is set forth. This is done in the form of a narrative—in which the Brāhmaṇa Gārgya represents the imperfect ideas, entertained on the nature of Brahma, while king Ajātas'atru represents the perfect knowledge of Brahman—with a view of showing, that this knowledge cannot be obtained by mere arguing, in consequence of the subtle nature of its object, and that it requires both a disciple believing in the existence of Brahman, and a teacher who has a full knowledge of him.—S'.

(2) Even for the mere words, whether thou be able or not to explain Brahman.

(3) "Janaka is a liberal donor, Janaka is a zealous hearer."—S'.

2. स होवाच गार्ग्यो य एवासावादित्ये पुरुष एतमेवाहं ब्रह्मोपास इति स होवाचाजातशत्रुर्मा मैतस्मिन्संवदिष्ठा अतिष्ठाः सर्वेषां भूतानां मूर्धा राजेति वा अहमेतमुपास इति स य एतमेवमुपास्तेऽतिष्ठाः सर्वेषां भूतानां मूर्धा राजा भवति ॥

Gārgya said,—"I adore as Brahman the spirit who abides in the sun" (1). Ajātas'atru said,—"Do not boast, do not boast of him. Knowing that, excelling all beings he is their head, their king, I adore that spirit. Whoever thus adores him, excels all beings and becomes their head, their king."

(1) The spirit who abiding in the sun and in the eye has entered the heart through the eye.—S'.

3. स होवाच गार्ग्यो य एवासौ चन्द्रे पुरुष एतमेवाहं ब्रह्मोपास इति स होवाचाजातशत्रुर्मा मैतस्मिन्संवदिष्ठा बृहत्पाण्डरवासाः सोमो राजेति वा अहमेतमुपास इति स य एतमेव मुपास्तेऽहरहर्ह सुतः प्रसुतो भवति नास्यान्नं क्षीयते ॥

Gārgya said,—"I adore as Brahman the spirit who abides in the moon" (1). Ajātas'atru said,—"Do not boast, do not boast of him. Knowing, that he is great, clothed in a white dress (2), Soma (3), (and) king, I adore that spirit. (For him) who thus adores him, is day by day produced and reproduced (the Soma); his food does not decrease."

(1) And in the mind.—S'.

(2) Because water is the body of life, in the form of the moon.—S'.

(3) As Soma, the moon-plant, in the sacrifice.—S'.

4. स होवाच गार्ग्यो य एवासौ विद्युति पुरुष एतमेवाहं ब्रह्मोपास इति स होवाचाजातशत्रुर्मा मैतस्मिन्संवदिष्ठास्तेजस्वीति वा अहमेतमुपास इति स य एतमेवमुपास्ते तेजस्वी ह भवति तेजस्विनी हास्य प्रजा भवति ॥

Gārgya said,—" I adore as Brahman the spirit who abides in lightning " (1). Ajātas'atru said—" Do not boast, do not boast of him. Knowing, that he is glorious, I adore that spirit. Whoever thus adores him, becomes glorious ; glorious becomes his offspring."

(1) In the lightning, in the skin, and in the heart.—S'.

5. स होवाच गार्ग्यो य एवायमाकाशे पुरुष एतमेवाहं ब्रह्मोपास इति स होवाचाजातशत्रुर्मा मैतस्मिन्संवदिष्ठाः पूर्णमप्रवर्तीति वा अहमेतमुपास इति स य एतमेवमुपास्ते पूर्यते प्रजया पशुभिर्नास्यास्माल्लोकात्प्रजोद्वर्तते ॥

Gārgya said,—" I adore as Brahman the spirit who abides in the ether " (1). Ajātas'atru said,—" Do not boast, do not boast of him. Knowing, that he is full and immoveable, I adore that spirit. Whoever thus adores him, has plenty of offspring and cattle, and his offspring is never removed from this world."

(1) In the ether as element, and also in the ether of the heart.—S'.

6. स होवाच गार्ग्यो य एवायं वायौ पुरुष एतमेवाहं ब्रह्मोपास इति स होवाचाजातशत्रुर्मा मैतस्मिन्संवदिष्ठा इन्द्रो वैकुण्ठोऽपराजिता सेनेति वा अहमेतमुपास इति स य एतमेवमुपास्ते जिष्णुर्हापराजिष्णुर्भवत्यन्यतस्त्यजायी ॥

Gārgya said,—"I adore as Brahman the spirit who abides in the wind" (1). Ajātas'atru said,—"Do not boast, do not boast of him. Knowing, that he is Indra, whose strength is indomitable and whose hosts are unconquerable, I adore that spirit. Whoever thus adores him, becomes a conqueror, is unconquerable by foes, and conqueror of his step-brothers."

(1) In the wind, in the vital air of the body, and in the heart.—S'.

7. स होवाच गार्ग्यो य एवायमग्नौ पुरुष एतमेवाहं ब्रह्मोपास इति स होवाचाजातशत्रुर्मा मैतस्मिन्संवदिष्ठा विषासहिरिति वा अहमेतमुपास इति स य एतमेवमुपास्ते विषासहिर्ह भवति विषासहिर्हास्य प्रजा भवति ॥

Gārgya said,—"I adore as Brahman the spirit who abides in the fire" (1). Ajātas'atru said,—"Do not boast, do not boast of him. Knowing, that he is a destroyer, I adore that spirit. Whoever thus adores him, becomes a destroyer, and his offspring becomes a destroyer."

(1) And in the understanding of the heart.—S'.

8. स होवाच गार्ग्यो य एवायमप्सु पुरुष एतमेवाहं ब्रह्मोपास इति स होवाचाजातशत्रुर्मा मैतस्मिन्संवदिष्ठाः प्रतिरूप इति वा अहमे-

तमुपास इति स य एतमेवमुपास्ते प्रतिरूपꣳ हैवैनमुपगच्छति नाप्रतिरूपमथो प्रतिरूपोऽस्माज्जायते ॥

Gārgya said,—" I adore as Brahman the spirit who abides in the waters" (1). Ajātas'atru said,—Do not boast, do not boast of him. Knowing, that he is the same (2), I adore that spirit. Whoever thus adores him, obtains him as the same, not as not the same. Again from him is born what is the same with him " (3).

(1) In the waters, in the semen and in the heart.—S'.

(2) In the Sruti and Smṛti.—S'.

(3) A son like himself.

9. स होवाच गार्ग्यो य एवायमादर्शे पुरुष एतमेवाहं ब्रह्मोपास इति स होवाचाजातशत्रुर्मा मैतस्मिन्संवदिष्ठा रोचिष्णुरिति वा अहमेतमुपास इति स य एवमेतमुपास्ते रोचिष्णुर्ह भवति रोचिष्णुर्हास्य प्रजा भवत्यथो यैः सन्निगच्छति सर्वाꣳस्तानतिरोचते ॥

Gārgya said,—" I adore as Brahman the spirit who abides in the looking-glass" (1). Ajātas'atru said,— " Do not boast, do not boast of him. Knowing, that he is resplendent, I adore that spirit. Whoever thus adores him, becomes resplendent, and resplendent his offspring; he overcomes in splendour all those with whom he meets."

(1) In the looking-glass, in other reflective things, and in the heart.—S'.

10. स होवाच गार्ग्यो य एवायं यन्तं पश्चाच्छब्दोऽनूदेत्येतमेवाहं ब्रह्मोपास इति स होवाचाजातशत्रुर्मा मैतस्मिन्संवदिष्ठा असुरिति

वा अहमेतमुपास इति स य एतमेवमुपास्ते सर्वꣳ हैवास्मिँल्लोक आयुरेति नैनं पुरा कालात्प्राणो जहाति ॥

Gārgya said,—" I adore as Brahman the spirit who, when proceeding, is followed by noise (1). Ajātas'atru said,—" Do not boast, do not boast of him. Knowing, that he is life, I adore that spirit. Whoever thus adores him, obtains the full age in this world ; life does not leave him before the (appointed) time."

(1) Life.

11. स होवाच गार्ग्यो य एवायं दिक्षु पुरुष एतमेवाहं ब्रह्मोपास इति सहोवाचाजातशत्रुर्मा मैतस्मिन्संवदिष्ठा द्वितीयोऽनपग इति वा अहमेतमुपास इति स य एतमेवमुपास्ते द्वितीयवान् ह भवति नास्माद्गणश्छिद्यते ॥

Gārgya said,—" I adore as Brahman the spirit who abides in the quarters" (1). Ajātas'atru said,—" Do not boast, do not boast of him. Knowing, that he is double and inseparable (2). I adore him. Whoever thus adores him, becomes double (3), and his followers never part from him."

(1) In the quarters, in the ear and in the heart.—S'.

(2) Like the As'vins who are the tutelary deities of the quarters.

(3) By the number of his servants.—Ā.G.

12. स होवाच गार्ग्यो य एवायं छायामयः पुरुष एतमेवाहं ब्रह्मोपास इति स होवाचाजातशत्रुर्मा मैतस्मिन्संवदिष्ठा मृत्युरिति वा अहमेतमुपास

इति स य एतमेवमुपास्ते सर्वꣳ हैवास्मिँल्लोक आयुरेति नैनं पुरा कालान्मृत्युरागच्छति ॥

Gārgya said,—"I adore as Brahman the spirit who abides in the shadow (1). Ajātas'atru said,—"Do not boast, do not boast of him. Knowing, that he is death, I adore that spirit. Whoever thus adores him, obtains (his) full age in this world; death does not approach him before the time."

(1) The spirit, abiding in the shadow, externally as darkness and internally in the heart as ignorance.

13. स होवाच गार्ग्यो य एवायमात्मनि पुरुष एतमेवाहं ब्रह्मोपास इति स होवाचाजातशत्रुर्मा मैतस्मिन्संवदिष्ठा आत्मन्वीति वा अहमेतमुपास इति स य एतमेवमुपास्त आत्मन्वीह भवत्यात्मन्विनीहास्य प्रजा भवति स ह तूष्णीमास गार्ग्यः ॥

Gārgya said,—"I adore as Brahman the spirit who abides in the soul" (1), (in self). Ajātas'atru said,—"Do not boast, do not boast of him. Knowing, that he is possessed of soul (2), adore that spirit. Whoever thus adores him, becomes in this world possessed of soul, and also his offspring." Then Gārgya was silent.

(1) The spirit, abiding in the soul, in Prajāpati, and in the intellect of the heart.—S'.

(2) Of much understanding.

14. स होवाचाजातशत्रुरेतावन्नू३ इत्येतावद्धीति नैतावता विदितं भवतीति स होवाच गार्ग्य उपत्वायानीति ॥

Ajātas'atru said,—" Does (Brahman) so far extend ?" (He answered),—" So far."—(Ajātas'atru said),—" Brahman is not comprehended by (a knowledge) which so far extends only " (1). Gārgya said,—" Let me approach thee as disciple."

(1) Why then sayest thou boasting,—I will teach thee the nature of Brahman ?

15. स होवाचाजातशत्रुः प्रतिलोमं चैतद्यद्ब्राह्मणः क्षत्रियमुपेयाद्ब्रह्म मे वक्ष्यतीति व्येव त्वा ज्ञपयिष्यामीति तं पाणावादायोत्तस्थौ तौ ह पुरुषꣳ सुप्तमाजग्मतुस्तमेतैर्नामभिरामंत्रयांचक्रे बृहन् पाण्डरवासः सोमराजन्निति स नोत्तस्थौ तं पाणिना पेषं बोधयांचकार स होत्तस्थौ ॥

Ajātas'atru said,—" It verily goes against the grain that a Brāhmaṇa should approach a Kṣatriya for the purpose of learning (the nature of) Brahman from him. I will explain (him) to thee." (Thus saying) he took him by the hands and rose. They went to a man who slept. They called him by the name, " Mighty one, clad in white garments, Soma, king." He did not rise. Squeezing him with the hand, he awoke him. He then arose.

16. स होवाचाजातशत्रुर्यत्रैष एतत्सुप्तोऽभूद्य एष विज्ञानमयः पुरुषः क्वैष तदाभूत्कुत एतदागादिति तदु ह न मेने गार्ग्यः ॥

Ajātas'atru said,—" Where was the spirit whose nature is like knowledge, at the time when he thus profoundly slept ? Whence did he come ?" Gārgya did not know this.

17. स होवाचाजातशत्रुर्यत्रैष एतत्सुप्तोऽभूद्य एष विज्ञानमयः पुरुषस्तदेषां प्राणानां विज्ञानेन विज्ञानमादाय य एषोऽन्तर्हृदय आकाशस्तस्मिञ्छेते तानि यदा गृह्णात्यथ हैतत्पुरुषः स्वपिति नाम तद्गृहीत एव प्राणो भवति गृहीता वाग् गृहीतं चक्षुर्गृहीतꣳ श्रोत्रं गृहीतं मनः ॥

Ajātaśatru said,—" When the spirit whose nature is like knowledge, thus profoundly slept, then the ether (1), in the midst of the heart drawing in, together with the knowledge of the senses (2), (their actual) knowledge (3), slept therein (in the ether) (4). When the spirit draws in that (knowledge of the senses), then he sleeps indeed. Then life is drawn in (5), speech is drawn in, the eye is drawn in, the ear is drawn in (and mind is drawn in).

(1) The soul in its independent nature.—Ś.

(2) The intellect of the heart in which Brahman reflected.

(3) The faculty of the senses of manifesting the respective objects; that is to say, in sleep intellect withdraws the senses from their objects, and concentrates them in the heart, where intellect itself is absorbed in the nature of the soul.

(4) The soul within its own self.

(5) Means here, according to Śaṅkara, the sense of smelling.

18. स यत्रैतत्स्वप्नयया चरति ते हास्य लोकास्तदुतेव महाराजो भवत्युतेव महाब्राह्मण उतेवोच्चावचं निगच्छति स यथा महाराजो जानपदान्

गृहीत्वा स्वे जनपदे यथाकामं परिवर्तेतैवमेवैष एतत्प्राणान्
गृहीत्वा स्वे शरीरे यथाकामं परिवर्तते ॥

"When he is in the state of dream, then become such (conditions as the following) his worlds, then he becomes like a great king, like a great Brāhmaṇa, he proceeds as it were to higher and lower places. As a great king, assembling his followers, sends them about in his kingdom according to his pleasure, so that (spirit resembling knowledge drawing in) the organs, sends them about in his body according to his pleasure.

19. अथ यदा सुषुप्तो भवति यदा न कस्यचन वेद हिता नाम नाड्यो
द्वासप्ततिसहस्राणि हृदयात्पुरीततमभिप्रतिष्ठन्ते ताभिः प्रत्यवसृप्य
पुरीतति शेते स यथा कुमारो वा महाराजो वा महाब्राह्मणो
वातिघ्नीमानन्दस्य गत्वा शयीतैवमेवैष एतच्छेते ॥

"Again when he profoundly sleeps, he does not know of anything. There are 72,000 (1) arteries called the good, which from the heart proceed everywhere to the body. Returning with them he sleeps in the body. As a youth, or a great king or great Brāhmaṇa, sleeps, enjoying excessive bliss, so does he (the spirit resembling knowledge) sleep.

(1) *Vide* Prasna Upaniṣad, 3, 6.

20. स यथोर्णनाभिस्तन्तुनोच्चरेद्यथाग्नेः क्षुद्रा विस्फुलिङ्गा व्युच्चरन्त्येवमे-
वास्मादात्मनः सर्वे प्राणाः सर्वे लोकाः सर्वे देवाः सर्वाणि भूतानि
व्युच्चरन्ति तस्योपनिषत्सत्यस्य सत्यमिति प्राणा वै सत्यं तेषामेष
सत्यम् ॥

"As the spider proceeds along with its web, as little sparks proceed from fire, so proceed from that soul all organs, all worlds, all the gods, all beings. The nearest conception of him is this, that he is the truth of truth. The organs are the truth, he is the truth of them" (1).

(1) What "the truth of truth" means, will be explained in the two next Brāhmaṇas.—S'.

SECOND BRĀHMAṆA (1)

1. यो ह वै शिशुꣳ साधनꣳ सप्रत्याधानꣳ सस्थूणꣳ सदामं वेद सप्त ह
द्विषतो भ्रातृव्यानवरुणद्ध्ययं वाव शिशुर्योऽयं मध्यमः प्राणस्तस्ये-
दमेवाधानमिदं प्रत्याधानं प्राणः स्थूणान्नं दाम ॥

Whoever knows the young animal with its abode, the upper part of its abode, its pillar (and) its rope, destroys the seven inimical brother's sons (2). The young animal is the central life (3). This (4) is its abode, this (5) the upper part of its abode, life (6) is the pillar, food the rope (7).

(1) The connection between the former and the present Brāhmaṇa is shown by S'aṅkara, as follows. The topic of Brahman has been introduced by the words,—"I will explain Brahman" (p. 137), and declared,—The one Brahman is he from whom the world is produced, of whom it consists and into whom it is dissolved. Of what nature again is the world, which is produced and

dissolved ? It consists of the five elements, which consist of name and form. Moreover it has been said, that name and form are truth (satya). The truth of truth (consisting of the five elements), is Brahman. Why again are the elements truth ? This question is answered in the Brāhmaṇa, whose subject, is to show the nature of what has form and what is without form. On account of their having form and not having form, the elements, consisting of effect and cause (are truth, and thus) also the organs (Prāṇāḥ). To define the nature (Satva) of the elements, consisting of cause and effect the two next Brāhmaṇas are commenced. This Upaniṣad is to be explained, for Brahman is determined as the truth of the truth by the determination of the reality (satva) of effect and cause. There (in the former Brāhmaṇa) it has been said,—" The organs are the truth ; he is the truth of them." Here by the connection of the Brahma Upaniṣad in this manner,—" Which are the organs, of which nature, their objects and which the Upaniṣads," the text determines the nature of the causes in the same way, as wells, gardens, etc., seen on a road, are determined.

(2) For the sons of a brother may be inimical or friendly. Here the attachment to the objects of the senses is denoted by the brother's sons. The senses are the seven orifices by which objects are perceived, the attachment produced by them is the brother's sons.—S'.

(3) The subtle body, dwelling in the midst of the body : subject to it are the organs ; it is a babe, because it is unwitted, while the senses are keen with regard to their objects.—S'.

(4) The body.—S'.

(5) The head with its seven orifices.—S'.

(6) Life means, according to S'aṅkara, the strength produced by food ; according to others, respiration.

(7) By which the young animal is bound to the pillar.

2. तमेताः सप्ताक्षितय उपतिष्ठन्ते तद्या इमा अक्षन् लोहिन्यो राजय-स्ताभिरेनꣳ रुद्रोऽन्वायत्तोऽथ या अक्षन्नापस्ताभिः पर्जन्यो या

कनीनका तयादित्यो यत्कृष्णं तेनाग्निर्यच्छुक्लं तेनेन्द्रोऽधरयैनं वर्तन्या पृथिव्यन्वायत्ता द्यौरुत्तरया नास्यान्नं क्षीयते य एवं वेद ॥

The seven (deities) who cause (its) indestructibility (1), surround it (2) (the infant) worshipping, *viz.*, Rudra adores it with the red lines in the eye, Parjanya with the water in the eye, Āditya with the sight, Agni with the black in the eye, Indra with the white, the earth adores it with the lower, and the heavens, with the upper eye-lash. The food of him is not destroyed who thus knows it.

(1) Thus I rendered "Akṣiti" after S'. They cause the indestructibility of food.

(2) The babe, when dwelling in the upper part of the abode it rises to the eye.—S'.

3. तदेष श्लोको भवति। अर्वाग्बिलश्चमस ऊर्ध्वबुध्नस्तस्मिन्यशो निहितं विश्वरूपं। तस्यासत ऋषयः सप्त तीरे वागष्टमी ब्रह्मणा संविदानेत्यर्वाग्बिलश्चमस ऊर्ध्वबुध्न इतीदं तच्छिर एष ह्यर्वाग्बिलश्चमस ऊर्ध्वबुध्नस्तस्मिन्यशो निहितं विश्वरूपमिति प्राणा वै यशो विश्वरूपं प्राणानेतदाह तस्यासत ऋषयः सप्त तीर इति प्राणा वा ऋषयः प्राणानेतदाह वागष्टमी ब्रह्मणा संविदानेति वाग्घ्यष्टमी ब्रह्मणा संवित्ते ॥

This is said in the following memorial verse,—"There is a Soma-cup, whose mouth is below, and whose foot is above; therein is put glory of various kinds. On its margin there are seven Ṛṣis, and speech is the eighth, as holding communication with Brahman." The Soma-cup whose mouth is below and whose foot is above, is the head: for it is like a cup with mouth below and foot above. "Therein is put glory of various kinds." With the various kinds put therein (1), it (the memorial verse) means the vital airs (2). "On its margin there are seven Ṛṣis." "With the Ṛṣis it means the vital winds."

"Speech is the eighth, as communicating with Brahman"; for speech as the eighth communicates with Brahman (3).

(1) As the Soma-juice in the cup.—S'.

(2) The vital airs by which the senses are moved to the performance of their functions.

(3) Brahman is the whole of sounds, and speech has communication with it, by pronou'ncing it.—Ā. G.

4. इमावेव गोतम भरद्वाजावयमेव गोतमोऽयं भरद्वाज इमावेव विश्वामित्रजमदग्नी अयमेव विश्वामित्रोऽयं जमदग्निरिमावेव वसिष्ठकश्यपावयमेव वसिष्ठोऽयं कश्यपो वागेवात्रिर्वाचा ह्यन्नमद्यतेऽत्तिर्ह वै नामैतद्यदत्रिरिति सर्वस्यात्ता भवति सर्वमस्यान्नं भवति य एवं वेद ॥

These (ears) are Gautama and Bharadvāja, this (ear) is Gautama, the other Bharadvāja. These (eyes) are Vis'vāmitra and Jamadagni; this is Vis'vāmitra, the other Jamadagni. These (nostrils) are Vasiṣṭha and Kas'yapa; this is Vasiṣṭha, the other Kas'yapa; speech is Atri; for by speech food is consumed; for Atri is verily derived from the root Attid (to eat, consume); he is the consumer of all. All becomes the food of him who thus knows.

THIRD BRĀHMAṆA

1. द्वे वाव ब्रह्मणो रूपे मूर्तं चैवामूर्तं च मर्त्यं चामृतं च स्थितं च यच्च सच्च त्यच्च ॥

There are two modes (1) of Brahman (2), what has form, and what has no form (3), the one mortal, the other immortal, again finite the one, and the other infinite (4), again the one existing and the other beyond.

(1) I use mode here in the sense of "accidental modification of substance".

(2) Brahman the supreme soul, who, in his absolute nature, is without those two modes.—Ś.

(3) At the time that their differences are not evolved. Their differences are stated afterwards.—Ś.

(4) Sthitañ ca yacca, explained by Śusthistam paricchinnam gatipūrvakam yat sthāsnu yacca yātīti yadvyāpyaparicchinnam, what is stationary limited, what after motion has the tendency to stand, and what moves, therefore what is pervading, unlimited

2. तदेतन्मूर्तं यदन्यद्वायोश्चान्तरिक्षाच्चैतन्मर्त्यमेतत्स्थितमेतत्सत्तस्यैतस्य मूर्तस्यैतस्य मर्त्यस्यैतस्य स्थितस्यैतस्य सत एष रसो य एष तपति सतो ह्येष रसः ॥

What has form (1), is what is different from the air and the ether (2), this is mortal, this is finite, this is visible. The essence of what has form, what is mortal, finite and visible, is the being that heats (the sun); for he is the essence of what exists.

(1) What is formed of parts, a compound.—Ś.

(2) Namely, the other three elements, earth, water and light.

3. अथामूर्तं वायुश्चान्तरिक्षं चैतदमृतमेतद्यदेतत्त्यन्तस्यैतस्यामूर्तस्यैतस्या-
मृतस्यैतस्य यत एतस्य तस्यैष रसो य एष एतस्मिन्मण्डले पुरुष-
स्त्यस्य ह्येष रस इत्यधिदैवतम् ॥

Again what has no form is the air and the ether; this is immortal, this is infinite, this is beyond. The essence of what has no form, what is immortal, infinite and beyond, is the spirit who (abides) in this universe (1). This refers to the divine relation.

(1) Hiraṇyagarbha.

4. अथाध्यात्ममिदमेव मूर्तं यदन्यत्प्राणाच्च यश्चायमन्तरात्मन्नाकाश एत-
न्मर्त्यमेतत्स्थितमेतत्सत्तस्यैतस्य मूर्तस्यैतस्य मर्त्यस्यैतस्य स्थि-
तस्यैतस्य सत एष रसो यच्चक्षुः सतो ह्येष रसः ॥

Now the relation to the soul. What has form is different from the air and from the ether in the midst of the body (1). This is mortal, this is finite, this existing. The essence of what has form, what is mortal, finite and existing, is the eye (2); for this is the essence of what exists.

(1) That is to say, the three elements, light, water and earth, as constituents of the body, independent of ether and air.—Ś.

(2) Because by the eye the whole body assumes substance, and because the eyes were first produced, in

accordance with the passage, "Āditya (the sun), the becoming eye," entered the eyes.—S',

5. अथामूर्तं प्राणश्च यश्चायमन्तरात्मन्नाकाश एतदमृतमेतद्यदेतत्त्य तस्यैतस्यामूर्तस्यैतस्यामृतस्यैतस्य यत एतस्य त्यस्यैष रसो योऽयं दक्षिणेऽक्षन्पुरुषस्त्यस्य ह्येष रसः ॥

Now what has no form is the air, and the ether in the midst of the body. This is immortal, this is infinite, this is beyond. The essence of what has no form, what is immortal, infinite and beyond, is the spirit (Puruṣa) in the right eye ; for is the essence of what is beyond.

6. तस्य हैतस्य पुरुषस्य रूपं यथा महारजनं वासो यथा पाण्ड्वाविकं यथेन्द्रगोपो यथाऽग्न्यर्चिर्यथा पुण्डरीकं यथासकृद्विद्युत्तꣳ सकृद्विद्युत्तेव या वा अस्य श्रीर्भवति य एवं वेदाथात आदेशो नेति नेति न ह्येतस्मादिति नेत्यन्यत्परमस्त्यथ नामधेयꣳ सत्यस्य सत्यमिति प्राणा वै सत्यं तेषामेष सत्यम् ॥

The form of this spirit (1) is, as cloth dyed by turmeric (2), as the smoke colour of sheep-wool, as the red colour of the Indragopa insect, as the bright colour of the fire-flame, as the white colour of the lotus, as the lightning shines forth at one moment (thus are the modifications of the desires of that spirit). The glory of him who thus knows, shines forth at one moment. After this, therefore, the definition (of Brahman),—"He is not this, he is not this, etc" (3). There is another name, different from that (definition),—"He is not this, he is not this," *viz.*, the truth of truth ? The organs are the truth he is the truth of them.

(1) The subtle spirit, the spirit, who is the cause of manifestation.

(2) As cloth, dyed by turmeric, so is the desire of that spirit in contact with special objects.

(3) If it is asked, how by those negations the "truth of truth" is defined the answer is,—by the prohibition of any allegation which may be made with regard to the nature of Brahman, name, form, action, quality, etc., must be denied of Brahman; for there is no distinction in Brahman; if he is defined, this definition refers only to qualities which are alleged of him; but his own nature, can in no manner be determined, except by stating, that every attribute is denied of him.

FOURTH BRĀHMAṆA (1)

1. मैत्रेयीति होवाच याज्ञवल्क्य उद्यास्यन्वा अरेऽहमस्मात्स्थानादस्मि हन्त तेऽनया कात्यायन्यान्तं करवाणीति ॥

"Maitreyī," said Yājñavalkya (2), "Behold, I am desirous of raising myself from the order (3) (of householder); therefore, let me divide (my property) amongst thee and Kātyāyanī there."

(1) It is the object of this Brāhmaṇa to show that the state of a Sanyāsi, *viz.*, the retiring from the world of the forest and the renunciation of all ceremonies, is indispensable for the knowledge of Brahman.—S'. The same conversation between Yājñavalkya and his wife Maitreyī is with slight variations, repeated in the 5th Brāhmaṇa of the 4th chapter.

(2) A Ṛṣī, Yājñavalkya by name.—S'.

(3) To the higher stage of a Sanyāsi.

2. सा होवाच मैत्रेयी यन्नु म इयं भगोस्सर्वा पृथिवी वित्तेन पूर्णा स्यात्कथं तेनामृता स्यामिति नेति होवाच याज्ञवल्क्यो यथैवोपकरणवतां जीवितं तथैव ते जीवितꣳ स्यादमृतत्वस्य तु नाशास्ति वित्तेनेति ॥

Maitreyī said,—" If, O Venerable, this whole world with all its wealth were mine, could I become immortal thereby?" Yājñavalkya said,—" Life the life of the wealthy thy life might become; by wealth, however, there is no hope of (obtaining) immortality."

3. सा होवाच मैत्रेयी येनाहं नामृता स्यां किमहं तेन कुर्यां यदेव भगवान्वेद तदेव मे ब्रूहीति ॥

Maitreyī said,—" Of what use would be wealth to me, if I did not become thereby immortal. Tell me, O Venerable, any (means of obtaining immortality) of which thou knowest."

4. स होवाच याज्ञवल्क्यः प्रिया बतारे नः सती प्रियं भाषस एह्यास्स्व व्याख्यास्यामि ते व्याचक्षाणस्य तु मे निदिध्यासस्वेति ॥

Yājñavalkya said,—" Behold, (thou wast) dear to us before, (and now) thou sayest what is dear. Come, sit down; I will explain to thee (the means of obtaining immortality); endeavour to comprehend my explanation."

5. स होवाच न वा अरे पत्युः कामाय पतिः प्रियो भवत्यात्मनस्तु कामाय पतिः प्रियो भवति न वा अरे जायायै कामाय जाया प्रिया भवत्यात्मनस्तु कामाय जाया प्रिया भवति न वा अरे पुत्राणां कामाय पुत्राः प्रिया भवन्त्यात्मनस्तु कामाय पुत्राः प्रिया भवन्ति

न वा अरे वित्तस्य कामाय वित्तं प्रियं भवत्यात्मनस्तु कामाय वित्तं प्रियं भवति न वा अरे ब्रह्मणः कामाय ब्रह्म प्रियं भवत्यात्मनस्तु कामाय ब्रह्म प्रियं भवति न वा अरे क्षत्रस्य कामाय क्षत्रं प्रियं भवत्यात्मनस्तु कामाय क्षत्रं प्रियं भवति न वा अरे लोकानां कामाय लोकाः प्रिया भवन्त्यात्मनस्तु कामाय लोकाः प्रिया भवन्ति न वा अरे देवानां कामाय देवाः प्रिया भवन्त्यात्मनस्तु कामाय देवाः प्रिया भवन्ति न वा अरे भूतानां कामाय भूतानि प्रियाणि भवन्त्यात्मनस्तु कामाय भूतानि प्रियाणि भवन्ति न वा अरे सर्वस्य कामाय सर्वं प्रियं भवत्यात्मनस्तु कामाय सर्वं प्रियं भवत्यात्मा वा अरे द्रष्टव्यः श्रोतव्यो मन्तव्यो निदिध्यासितव्यो मैत्रेय्यात्मनो वा अरे दर्शनेन श्रवणेन मत्या विज्ञानेनेदꣳ सर्वं विदितम् ॥

He said,—"Behold, not indeed for the husband's sake the husband is dear (1), but for the sake of the self (2), is dear to the husband. Behold, not indeed for the wife's sake the wife is dear, but for the sake of the self is dear the wife. Behold, not for the sons' sake the sons are dear, but for the sake of the self are dear the sons. Behold, not for property's sake property is dear, but for the sake of the self is property dear. Behold, not for the Brahman's sake the Brahman is dear, but for the sake of the self is the Brahman dear. Behold, not for the Kṣattra's sake the Kṣattra is dear, but for the sake of the self the Kṣattra is dear. Behold, not for the worlds' sake the worlds are dear, but for the sake of the self are dear the worlds. Behold, not for the gods' sake the gods are dear, but for the sake of the self are dear the gods. Behold, not for the Vedas' sake the Vedas are dear, but for the sake of the self are dear the Vedas (3). Behold, not for the elements' sake the elements are dear, but for the sake of the self are dear the elements. Behold, not for the sake of the universe the universe is dear, but for the sake of the self is dear the universe. Behold, the self (ātmā) is verily to be seen, heard, minded (and) meditated upon. Behold, O Maitreyī, by seeing, hearing, minding, knowing the self, all this (universe) is comprehended.

(1) To the wife.

(2) Ātma, the self, the soul: for the self of the wife, for her own soul.

(3) The last sentence is omitted in the Saṁskṛt text, published by the As. Soc.

6. ब्रह्म तं परादाद्योऽन्यत्रात्मनो ब्रह्म वेद क्षत्र तं परादाद्योऽन्यत्रात्मनः
क्षत्रं वेद लोकास्तं परादुर्योऽन्यत्रात्मनो लोकान्वेद देवास्तं
परादुर्योऽन्यत्रात्मनो देवान्वेद भूतानि तं परादुर्योऽन्यत्रात्मनो
भूतानि वेद सर्वं तं परादाद्योऽन्यत्रात्मनः सर्वं वेदेदं ब्रह्मेदं
क्षत्रमिमे लोका इमे देवा इमानि भूतानीद९ सर्वं यदयमात्मा ॥

The Brahman should disown a person (1), who considers the Brahman (caste) as something, different from (his) self (ātmā); the Kṣattra should disown a person who considers the Kṣattra (caste) as something different from (his) self; the worlds should disown a person who considers the worlds as something different from (his) self; the gods should disown a person who considers the gods as something different from (their) self ; the elements should disown a person who considers the elements as something different from (their) self ; the universe should disown a person who considers the universe as something different from (its) self. This (own) self is this Brahman, this Kṣattra, these worlds, these gods, these elements, is this universe.

(1) A person, belonging to the Brāhminical caste.

7. स यथा दुन्दुभेर्हन्यमानस्य न बाह्याञ्छब्दाञ्छक्नुयाद्ग्रहणाय दुन्दुभेस्तु ग्रहणेन दुन्दुभ्याघातस्य वा शब्दो गृहीतः ॥

As a person, when a drum (unseen by him) is beaten, is unable to perceive the sounds proceeding from it (as sounds of a drum), but on the perception of the drum the sounds of a drum beaten is perceived,

8. स यथा शङ्खस्य ध्मायमानस्य न बाह्याञ्छब्दाञ्छक्नुयाद्ग्रहणाय शङ्खस्य तु ग्रहणेन शङ्खध्मस्य वा शब्दो गृहीतः ॥

As a person, when a shell (unseen by him) is blown, is unable to perceive the sounds, proceeding from it (as sounds of a shell) but on the perception of the shell the sound of a shell blown is perceived,

9. स यथा वीणायै वाद्यमानायै न बाह्याञ्छब्दाञ्छक्नुयाद्ग्रहणाय वीणायै तु ग्रहणेन वीणावादस्य वा शब्दो गृहीतः ॥

As a person, when a lute (unseen to him) is played, is unable to perceive the sounds proceeding from it, but on the perception of the lute the sound of a lute played is perceived (1),

(1) S'aṅkara supplies the above comparisons with,—so is the identity of Brahman with the individual soul only apprehended by general and special knowledge.

10. स यथार्द्रैधाग्नेरभ्याहितात्पृथग्धूमा विनिश्चरन्त्येवं वा अरेऽस्य महतो भूतस्य निःश्वसितमेतद्यदृग्वेदो यजुर्वेदः सामवेदोऽथर्वाङ्गिरस इतिहासः पुराणं विद्या उपनिषदः श्लोकाः सूत्राण्यनुव्याख्यानानि व्याख्यानान्यस्यैवैतानि सर्वाणि निःश्वसितानि ॥

As from fire, made of damp wood, proceed smoke, sparks, etc. (1), of various kind, thus, behold, is the breathing of this great being the Ṛg Veda, the Yajur Veda, the Sāma Veda, the Atharvāṅgirasa, the narratives (Itihāsa) (2), the doctrines on creation (Purāṇa), the science (Vidyā), the Upaniṣads, the memorial verses (S'lokas), the aphorisms (Sūtras), the explanation of tenets (Anuvyākhyānāni), the explanation of Mantras (Vyākhyānāni), all these are his breathing.

(1) Dhūmaḥ (smoke), the plural denotes, according to S'., smoke, sparks, ashes, etc.

(2) S'. ascerts that the Itihāsa, etc., are the eight topics of the Brāhmaṇas, *viz.*, Itihāsa, narrative, as for instance, that of Uvāsi, and Purūravas ; Purāṇa doctrines on creation, as for instance, "this was before"; vidyā, the science of the gods, for instance, "he knows"; Upaniṣads, doctrines about adoration, for instance, "the soul, therefore let it be adored"; S'lokas, Mantras, occurring in the Brāhmaṇas, as "there follow these S'lokas"; Sūtras, sentences, which give the pith of a thing, as "the soul, therefore, it should be adored"; Anuvyākhyānāni, explanation of Mantras ; Vyākhyānāni, praise in honour of a deity, etc.

11. स यथा सर्वासामपाᳫं समुद्र एकायनमेवᳫं सर्वेषाᳫं स्पर्शानां त्वगेकायनमेवᳫं सर्वेषां गन्धानां नासिके एकायनमेवᳫं सर्वेषाᳫं रसानां

जिह्वैकायनमेवꣳ सर्वेषां रूपाणां चक्षुरेकायनमेवꣳ सर्वेषाꣳ शब्दानाꣳ श्रोत्रमेकायनमेवꣳ सर्वेषाꣳ संकल्पानां मन एकायनमेवꣳ सर्वासां विद्यानाꣳ हृदयमेकायनमेवꣳ सर्वेषां कर्मणाꣳ हस्तावेकायनमेवꣳ सर्वेषामानन्दानामुपस्थ एकायनमेवꣳ सर्वेषां विसर्गाणां पायुरेकायनमेवꣳ सर्वेषामध्वनां पादावेकायनमेवꣳ सर्वेषां वेदानां वागेकायनम् ॥

As the only site of all the waters is the sea, thus is the only site of every touch the skin, thus the only site of every taste the tongue, thus the only site of every smell the nose, thus the only site of every colour the eye, thus the only site of every sound the ear, thus the only site of every determination the mind, thus the only site of every knowledge the heart, thus the only site of every act the hands, thus the only site of every pleasure the organs of generation, thus the only site of every evacuation the anus, thus the only site of every motion the feet, thus the only site of every Veda speech.

12. स यथा सैन्धवखिल्य उदके प्रास्त उदकमेवानुविलीयेत न हास्योद्ग्रहणायेव स्याद्यतो यतस्त्वाददीत लवणमेवैवं वा अर इदं महद्भूतमनन्तमपारं विज्ञानघन एवैतेभ्यो भूतेभ्यः समुत्थाय तान्येवाऽनु विनश्यति न प्रेत्य संज्ञास्तीत्यरे ब्रवीमीति होवाच याज्ञवल्क्यः ॥

As a piece of salt, when thrown into water, is dissolved into mere water, and none is capable of perceiving it, because, from whatever place a person might take (water), it would have the taste of salt (but be no piece of salt, thus), behold, the great being, which is infinite, independent and mere knowledge.

Springing forth together with those elements (1), (he) (2) is destroyed, when they are destroyed. After death, no conscience remains (3) ; thus, "O Maitreyī, I hold," thus said Yājñavalkya.

(1) I give here, in a somewhat different language, some of the images which S'aṅkara uses, in explanation of this passage. As the appearance of the sun and moon in water is a mere reflection, and nothing real, or as the appearance of red in a white crystal is a mere reflection from a red substance and nothing real;—for on removing the water, the sun and moon only remain, not their reflections, or on removing the red substance, the whiteness of the crystal continues unchanged,— thus the elements and the individual souls are reflections of the one soul upon ignorance, and nothing real ; for on removing the ignorance by knowledge the soul alone remains, while those reflections cease to exist.

(2) He, the individual soul, or as S'aṅkara has it, the division of a particular soul.

(3) For him who has the true knowledge of the eternal soul.

13. सा होवाच मैत्रेय्यत्रैव मा भगवानमूमुहन्न प्रेत्य संज्ञास्तीति स होवाच याज्ञवल्क्यो न वा अरेऽहं मोहं ब्रवीम्यलं वा अर इदं विज्ञानाय ॥

Maitreyī said,—" With regard to him (Brahman) thou hast bewildered me, O Venerable, by the saying (1), —After death no conscience remains." Yājñavalkya said,—"Behold, I verily do not create bewilderment, behold, this (Brahman) is sufficient for knowledge."

(1) Because this seems contradictory to the former statement, that Brahman is the fulness of knowledge.

14. यत्र हि द्वैतमिव भवति तदितर इतरं जिघ्रति तदितर इतरं पश्यति तदितर इतरꣳ शृणोति तदितर इतरमभिवदति तदितर इतरं मनुते तदितर इतरं जानाति यत्र वा अस्य सर्वमात्मैवाभूत्तत्केन कं जिघ्रेत्तत्केन कं पश्येत्तत्केन कꣳ शृणुयात्तत्केन कमभिवदेत्तत् केन कं मन्वीत तत् केन कं विजानीयाद्येनेदꣳ सर्वं विजानाति तं केन विजानीयाद्विज्ञातारमरे केन विजानीयादिति ॥

For where (1) there is duality (2), as it were, there sees another (3), thing; there smells another, another thing; there hears another, another thing; there speaks another of another thing; there minds another, another thing; there knows another, another thing; but how does one to whom all has become mere soul (Ātmā), smell anything, how see anything, how hear anything, how speak of anything, how mind anything, how know anything? How should he know him by whom he knows this all; behold, how should he know the knower (4)?

(1) In the individual soul, produced by the substrata of ignorance as the totality of causes and effects.—S'.

(2) Difference from the supreme soul.

(3) Any individual soul.

(4) The argument which S'aṅkara advances in support of this doctrine is essentially as follows,—Every effect requires a cause; or without cause there is no effect; therefore, if there is ignorance, there is the assumption of effect, cause and reward as the effect of ignorance; but this assumption is not made on a knowledge of Brahman; for if all is soul or Brahman, there is, besides the soul neither cause, nor effect, nor reward. A knowledge of a cause can take place, if there is a difference between the cause and the object of knowledge, and there may be an

enquiry on the subject of the knowledge (the knowing soul) and the object of the same, but not of the soul. If the latter be the case, such a knowledge (the knowledge of the knowing subject, the soul) would be either produced by the soul itself, or by something else. Not the first; for the soul is not an object of the soul, not by something else; for there is nothing else but the soul, and there is therefore no object of its knowledge.

FIFTH BRĀHMAṆA (1)

1. इयं पृथिवी सर्वेषां भूतानां मध्वस्यै पृथिव्यै सर्वाणि भूतानि मधु
यश्चायमस्यां पृथिव्यां तेजोमयोऽमृतमयः पुरुषो यश्चायमध्यात्मं
शारीरस्तेजोमयोऽमृतमयः पुरुषोऽयमेव स योऽयमात्मेदममृतमिदं
ब्रह्मेदं सर्वम् ॥

The earth is honey (2) for all beings, for the earth are all beings honey (3). Both the immortal, luminous spirit (4) (abiding) in the earth, and the immortal, luminous spirit, who exists in the body according to his relation to the soul (are honey for all beings and all beings are honey for them). This (5) is that soul, this (6) is immortal, this is Brahman, this all.

(1) S'aṅkara explains the connection between the present and the preceding Brāhmaṇa, as follows:—The Maitreyī Brāhmaṇa has been composed for the purpose to state that that which is independent of ceremonies and the cause of immortality, is worthy of explanation. This is the knowledge of Brahman pertaining, as has been declared, to all the duties of a Sanyāsī. Moreover, since by the knowledge of the soul the whole universe is known, and the

soul is dearer to every one than every thing else, "the soul should be beheld". "It is to be heard, to be minded, to be pondered upon." The different modes of beholding the soul have been stated before. To be heard is the soul, by means of the teacher, to be pondered on by means of disquisition, and disquisition has been explained. The proposition, "the soul is the all," is proved by the argument, that the one soul is the only cause of the generality, of the production and of the dissolution of the world, and as this may be doubtful, the present Brāhmaṇa, is composed to remove any doubt regarding it. Because the whole world, earth, etc., is in the mutual dependence of support and supported, it is dependent upon one cause of generality, production and dissolution. Or with other words, after the proposition (Pratijñā) "soul alone is this all" has been proved by the argument, that the soul is the cause of the creation, preservation and dissolution of the world; the conclusion (Nigamana) of the proposed meaning is again made in the Madhubrāhmaṇa, conformably to the definition of logicians, that the conclusion in a syllogism is the repetition of the proposition, after the argument has been stated.

(2) *Vide* Chānd. Up.. 3, 1—5, where a similar comparison is made.

(3) As the bees collect honey from every kind of flower, which again serves as nourishment for the bees, so all the beings are nourishment for the one earth, are changed into its very substance, and again the earth is nourishment for all beings; it is changed into all; that is to say, they are mutually dependent; there is no real difference between them; they are the same,—Brahman.

(4) The Saṁskṛt term is Puruṣa.

(5) This ayam, this fourfold division, *viz.*, the earth, all beings, the spirit abiding in the earth, and the spirit abiding in the body.—S'.

(6) This idam, the knowledge, whose object is the fourfold division.—S'.

2. इमा आपः सर्वेषां भूतानां मध्वासामपाᳬ सर्वाणि भूतानि मधु यश्चाय-
मास्वप्सु तेजोमयोऽमृतमयः पुरुषो यश्चायमध्यात्मᳬ रेतसस्तेजो-
मयोऽमृतमयः पुरुषोऽयमेव स योऽयमात्मेदममृतमिदं ब्रह्मेदᳬ
सर्वम् ॥

The waters are honey for all beings ; for the waters are all beings honey. Both the immortal, luminous spirits, abiding in the water and the immortal, luminous spirit, abiding in the semen according to his relation to the soul (are honey for all beings and all beings are honey for them). This is that soul, this is immortal, this is Brahman, this all.

3. अयमग्निः सर्वेषां भूतानां मध्वस्याग्नेः सर्वाणि भूतानि मधु यश्चाय-
मस्मिन्नग्नौ तेजोमयोऽमृतमयः पुरुषो यश्चायमध्यात्मं वाङ्मयस्ते-
जोमयोऽमृतमयः पुरुषोऽयमेव स योऽयमात्मेदममृतमिदं ब्रह्मेदᳬ
सर्वम् ॥

The fire is honey for all beings ; for the fire all beings are honey. Both the immortal, luminous spirit, (abiding) in the fire, and the immortal luminous spirit, abiding in speech according to his relation to the soul, (are honey for all beings and all beings are honey for them). This is that soul, this is immortal, this is Brahman, this all.

4. अयं वायुः सर्वेषां भूतानां मध्वस्य वायोः सर्वाणि भूतानि मधु
यश्चायमस्मिन्वायौ तेजोमयोऽमृतमयः पुरुषो यश्चायमध्यात्मं
प्राणस्तेजोमयोऽमृतमयः पुरुषोऽयमेव स योऽयमात्मेदममृतमिदं
ब्रह्मेदᳬ सर्वम् ॥

The wind is honey for all beings: for the wind all beings are honey. Both the immortal, luminous spirit, (abiding) in the wind, and the immortal, luminous spirit, who is life according to his relation to the soul (are honey for all beings, and all beings are honey for them). This is that soul, this is immortal, this is Brahman, this all.

5. अयमादित्यः सर्वेषां भूतानां मध्वस्यादित्यस्य सर्वाणि भूतानि मधु यश्चायमस्मिन्नादित्ये तेजोमयोऽमृतमयः पुरुषो यश्चायमध्यात्मं चाक्षुषस्तेजोमयोऽमृतमयः पुरुषोऽयमेव स योऽयमात्मेदममृतमिदं ब्रह्मेदꣳ सर्वम् ॥

Āditya is honey for all beings; for Āditya all beings are honey. Both, the immortal, luminous spirit, (abiding) in that Āditya, and the immortal, luminous spirit, abiding in speech according to his relation to the soul, (are honey for all beings, and all beings are honey for them). This is that soul, this is immortal, this is Brahman, this all.

6. इमा दिशः सर्वेषां भूतानां मध्वासां दिशाꣳ सर्वाणि भूतानि मधु यश्चायमासु दिक्षु तेजोमयोऽमृतमयः पुरुषो यश्चायमध्यात्मꣳ श्रोत्रः प्रातिश्रुत्कस्तेजोमयोऽमृतमयः पुरुषोऽयमेव स योऽयमात्मेदममृतमिदं ब्रह्मेदꣳ सर्वम् ॥

The quarters are honey for all beings; for the quarters all beings are honey. Both, the immortal, luminous spirit, (abiding) in the quarters, and the immortal, luminous spirit, abiding in the ear according to his relation to the soul, (are honey for all beings, and all beings are honey for them). This is that soul, this is immortal, this is Brahman, this all.

7. अयं चन्द्रः सर्वेषां भूतानां मध्वस्य चन्द्रस्य सर्वाणि भूतानि मधु यश्चायमस्मिँश्चन्द्रे तेजोमयोऽमृतमयः पुरुषो यश्चायमध्यात्मं मानसस्तेजोमयोऽमृतमयः पुरुषोऽयमेव स योऽयमात्मेदममृतमिदं ब्रह्मेदꣳ सर्वम् ॥

The moon is honey for all beings; for the moon all beings are honey. Both, the immortal, luminous spirit (abiding) in the moon, and the immortal, luminous spirit, abiding in the mind according to his relation to the soul (are honey for all beings, and all beings are honey for them). This is that soul, this is immortal, this is Brahman, this all.

8. इयं विद्युत्सर्वेषां भूतानां मध्वस्यै विद्युतः सर्वाणि भूतानि मधु यश्चायमस्यां विद्युति तेजोमयोऽमृतमयः पुरुषो यश्चायमध्यात्मं तैजसस्तेजोमयोऽमृतमयः पुरुषोऽयमेव स योऽयमात्मेदममृतमिदं ब्रह्मेदꣳ सर्वम् ॥

The lightning is honey for all beings; for the lightning all beings are honey. Both, the immortal, luminous spirit, (abiding) in lightning, and the immortal, luminous spirit, abiding in the light (skin) according to his relation to the soul, (are honey for all beings, and all beings are honey for them). This is that soul, this is immortal, this is Brahman, this all.

9. अयꣳ स्तनयित्नुः सर्वेषां भूतानां मध्वस्य स्तनयित्नोः सर्वाणि भूतानि
मधु यश्चायमस्मिन्स्तनयित्नौ तेजोमयोऽमृतमयः पुरुषो यश्चाय-
मध्यात्मꣳ शाब्दः सौवरस्तेजोमयोऽमृतमयः पुरुषोऽयमेव स
योऽयमात्मेदममृतमिदं ब्रह्मेदꣳ सर्वम् ॥

The thunder is honey for all beings; for the thunder all beings are honey. Both, the immortal, luminous spirit, (abiding) in thunder, and the immortal, luminous spirit, abiding in sound and musical note according to his relation to the soul, (are honey for all beings, and all the beings are honey for them). This is that soul, this is immortal, this is Brahman, this all.

10. अयमाकाशः सर्वेषां भूतानां मध्वस्याकाशस्य सर्वाणि भूतानि मधु
यश्चायमस्मिन्नाकाशे तेजोमयोऽमृतमयः पुरुषो यश्चायमध्यात्मꣳ
हृद्याकाशस्तेजोमयोऽमृतमयः पुरुषोऽयमेव स योऽयमात्मेदममृतमिदं
ब्रह्मेदꣳ सर्वम् ॥

The ether is honey for all beings; for the ether all beings are honey. Both, the immortal, luminous spirit, (abiding) in the ether, and the immortal, luminous spirit, abiding as ether in the heart according to his relation to the soul, (are honey for all beings, and all beings are honey for them). This is that soul, this is immortal, this is Brahman, this all.

11. अयं धर्मः सर्वेषां भूतानां मध्वस्य धर्मस्य सर्वाणि भूतानि मधु
यश्चायमस्मिन्धर्मे तेजोमयोऽमृतमयः पुरुषो यश्चायमध्यात्मं धर्मस्ते-
जोमयोऽमृतमयः पुरुषोऽयमेव स योऽयमात्मेदममृतमिदं ब्रह्मेदꣳ
सर्वम् ॥

Justice is honey for all beings; for justice all beings are honey. Both, the immortal, luminous spirit (abiding) in justice, and the immortal, luminous spirit, produced in justice according to his relation to the soul, (are honey for all beings and all beings are honey for them). This is that soul, this is immortal, this is Brahman' this all.

12. इदꣳ सत्यꣳ सर्वेषां भूतानां मध्वस्य सत्यस्य सर्वाणि भूतानि मधु यश्चाऽयमस्मिन्सत्ये तेजोमयोऽमृतमयः पुरुषो यश्चाऽयमध्यात्मꣳ सात्यस्तेजोमयोऽमृतमयः पुरुषोऽयमेव स योऽयमात्मेदममृतमिदं ब्रह्मेदꣳ सर्वम् ॥

Truth is honey for all beings; for truth all beings are honey. Both the immortal, luminous spirit, (abiding) in truth, and the immortal, luminous spirit, produced in truth according to his relation to the soul, (are honey for all beings, and all beings are honey for them). This is that soul. this is immortal, this Brahman, this all.

13. इदं मानुषꣳ सर्वेषां भूतानां मध्वस्य मानुषस्य सर्वाणि भूतानि मधु यश्चाऽयमस्मिन्मानुषे तेजोमयोऽमृतमयः पुरुषोऽयमेव स योऽयमात्मेदममृतमिदं ब्रह्मेदꣳ सर्वम् ॥

Mankind is honey for all beings; for mankind all beings are honey. Both, the immortal, luminous spirit (abiding) in mankind, and the immortal luminous spirit produced in mankind according to his relation to the soul, (are honey for all beings, and all beings are honey for them). This is that soul, this is immortal, this Brahman, this all.

14. अयमात्मा सर्वेषां भूतानां मध्वस्यात्मनः सर्वाणि भूतानि मधु यश्चाय-मस्मिन्नात्मनि तेजोमयोऽमृतमयः पुरुषो यश्चायमात्मा तेजोमयोऽमृ-तमयः पुरुषोऽयमेव स योऽयमात्मेदममृतमिदं ब्रह्मेदꣳ सर्वम् ॥

The soul is honey for all beings; for the soul all beings are honey. Both, the immortal, luminous spirit, (abiding) in the soul, and the immortal, luminous spirit who is that soul, (are honey for all beings, and all beings are honey for them). This is that soul, this is immortal, this is Brahman, this all.

15. स वा अयमात्मा सर्वेषां भूतानामधिपतिः सर्वेषां भूतानाꣳ राजा तद्यथा रथनाभौ च रथनेमौ चाराः सर्वे समर्पिता एवमेवास्मि-न्नात्मनि सर्वाणि भूतानि सर्वे देवाः सर्वे लोकाः सर्वे प्राणाः सर्व एत आत्मानः समर्पिताः ॥

This soul is verily the lord of all beings, the king of all beings. As all spokes are fastened in the nave and the circumference of the wheel (1), thus also all beings, all gods, all worlds, all organs, all souls, are fastened in that soul.

(1) See a similar comparison, 2 Muṇḍ., 2, 6.

16. इदं वै तन्मधु दध्यङ्ङाथर्वणोऽश्विभ्यामुवाच तदेतदृषिः पश्यन्नवो-चत् । तद्वां नरा सनयेदꣳस उग्रमाविष्कृणोमि तन्यतुर्न वृष्टिं । दध्यङ् ह यन्मध्वाथर्वणो वामश्वस्य शीर्ष्णा प्रयदीमुवाचेति ॥

This honey Dadhyaṅ (1), the son of Atharvaṇa explained to the two aśvins. Beholding their deed the

Ṛṣi (2) said—"O ye men, I will manifest your cruel deed (3) (undertaken) for your advantage, as Tanyatu (4) (manifests) rain (from a cloud). The honey which Dadhyaṅ, the son of Atharvaṇa, explained to you through the head of the horse (is this honey)."

(1) The tale, alluded to in the text, is contained in the Taittiriya Brāhmaṇa in the part which treats on the Pravargya sacrifice, and is given by S'aṅkara. Its drift is as follows,—Dadhyaṅ, the son of Atharvaṇa, explained to the two As'vins, the physicians of the gods, the Madhu Brāhmaṇa. When they came to him for instruction, he told them, that Indra had threatened him to cut off his head, if he repeated the Madhu Brāhmaṇa to any body else. The As'vins promised to save him from the consequence of Indra's anger. They would place his head somewhere else, and meanwhile put a horse's head on his body; when Indra should cut off the head, they would replace it by his own. He consented, and explained to them the Madhu Brāhmaṇa by means of the head of a horse which they had placed upon his body instead of his own, and on Indra cutting off the horse-head, they restored to him his own. This tale, says S'aṅkara, is to illustrate the superiority of the knowledge of Brahman, for the knowledge possessed by Indra is difficult even for the gods to gain, and was gained but with great trouble by the As'vins.

(2) The Mantra.—S'.

(3) The cutting off the head of Dadhyaṅ.

(4) Parjanya.

17. इदं वै तन्मधु दध्यङ्ङाथर्वणोऽश्विभ्यामुवाच तदेतदृषिः पश्यन्नवोचदाथर्वणायाश्विना दधीचेऽश्व्यꣳ शिरः प्रत्यैरयतं । स वां मधु प्रवोचदृतायन्त्वाष्ट्रं यद्दस्रावपि कक्ष्यं वामिति ॥

This honey explained Dadhyaṅ, the son of Atharvaṇa, to the two As'vins. Beholding this deed, the Ṛṣi said,—" O As'vins, ye placed a horse-head on Dadhyan, the son of Atharvaṇa. To keep his promise, he explained to you, O Destroyers, the honey of Tvāṣṭra (Āditya) and also the honey, which is to be concealed " (1)

(1) The honey of Tvāṣṭra is knowledge, referring to rite; the honey to be concealed, the knowledge of Brahman.—S'.

18. इदं वै तन्मधु दध्यङ्ङाथर्वणोऽश्विभ्यामुवाच तदेतदृषिः पश्यन्नवोचत् । पुरश्चक्रे द्विपदः पुरश्चक्रे चतुष्पदः पुरः स पक्षी भूत्वा पुरः पुरुष आविशदिति स वा अयं पुरुषः सर्वासु पूर्षु पुरिशयो नैनेन किंचनानावृतं नैनेन किंचनासंवृतम् ॥

This honey explained Dadhyaṅ, the son of Atharvaṇa, to the two As'vins. Beholding their deed, the Ṛṣi said,—" (He) (1) created the bodies (purah) of bipeds (and then) the bodies of quadrupeds. At first, (puraḥ) being a bird (2) he entered as Puruṣa the bodies (puraḥ). This Puruṣa is called thus, because he sleeps in all bodies (Puris'aya)." From him nothing is concealed (within), from him nothing is concealed (without).

(1) Parmes'vara.—S'.

(2) That is to say, being of subtle body.

19. इदं वै तन्मधु दध्यङ्ङाथर्वणोऽश्विभ्यामुवाच तदेतदृषिः पश्यन्नवोचद्रूपं रूपं प्रतिरूपो बभूव तदस्य रूपं प्रतिचक्षणाय । इन्द्रो मायाभिः पुरुरूप ईयते युक्ता ह्यस्य हरयः शतां दशेत्ययं वै हरयोऽयं वै दश च सहस्राणि बहूनि चानन्तानि च तदेतद्ब्रह्मापूर्वमनपरमनन्तरमबाह्यमयमात्मा ब्रह्म सर्वानुभूरित्यनुशासनम् ॥

This honey explained Dadhyaṅ, the son of Atharvaṇa, to the two As'vins. 'Beholding this deed, the Ṛṣi said,—" He became to every nature of every nature; therefore to manifest the nature of him, Indra appears of manifold nature by his Māyās; for his hundred and ten senses are attached (to the body as horses (1) to a car), it (the soul,) is the senses; it is ten, it is many thousands, nay, infinite, it is Brahman who has not a Before nor an After, nor a Beside, nor a Without; this is the soul, Brahman, the perceiver of all (2). Such is the doctrine.

(1) The word "Hari," means in Saṁskṛt "sense" as well as "horse," and denotes here both of them.

(2) This passage may also be translated,—This Brahman is without a Before, without an After, without a Beside, without a Without, is this soul (the individual soul); Brahman is the enjoyer of all.

Or,—This is Brahman, who is without a Before, without an After, without a Beside, without a Without, it is this soul (the individual soul), it is Brahman, the enjoyer of all (the universal soul).

SIXTH BRĀHMAṆA

1. अथ वꣳशः पौतिमाष्यो गौपवनाद्गौपवनः पौतिमाष्यात्पौतिमाष्यो गौपवनाद्गौपवनः कौशिकात्कौशिकः कौण्डिन्यात्कौण्डिन्यः शाण्डिल्याच्छाण्डिल्यः कौशिकाच्च गौतमाच्च गौतमः ॥

Next follows the school (1) Pautimāṣya succeeded Gaupavana,—Gaupavana, Pautimāṣya,—Pautimāṣya, Gaupavana,—Gaupavana, Kaus'ika,—Kaus'ika, Kauṇḍinya,—Kauṇḍinya, S'āṇḍilya—S'āṇḍilya, Kaus'ika and Gautama,—Gautama.

(1) Two more lists of teachers are given in this Upaniṣad, *viz.*, 4, 6, and 6, 5. S'ankara observes about the present list, that it is the list of the Madhu Kāṇḍa and given for the praise of the knowledge of Brahman. The school itself means the succession of teachers for the four preceding chapters of the Brāhmaṇa, or the two first chapters of the B. Ā. U.

2. आग्निवेश्यादाग्निवेश्यः शाण्डिल्याच्चानभिम्लाताच्चानभिम्लात आनभिम्लातादानभिम्लात आनभिम्लातादानभिम्लातो गौतमाद्गौतमः सैतवप्राचीनयोग्याभ्याः सैतवप्राचीनयोग्यौ पाराशर्यात्पाराशर्यो भारद्वाजाद्भारद्वाजो भारद्वाजाच्च गौतमाच्च गौतमो भारद्वाजाद्भारद्वाजः पाराशर्यात् पाराशर्यो बैजवापायनाद्बैजवापायनः कौशिकायनेः कौशिकायनिः ॥

Āgnives'ya,—Āgnives'ya,—Sāṇḍilya and Anabhimlāta,—Ānabhimlāta, Ānabhimlāta,—Ānabhimlāta, Ānabhimlāta—Ānabhimlāta, Gautama,—Gautama, Saitava and Prācīnayōgya,—Saitava and Prācīnayōgya, Pārās'arya,—Pārās'arya, Bhāradvāja,—Bhāradvāja, Bhāradvaja, and Gautama,—Gautama Bhāradvāja,—Bhāradvāja, Pārās'arya,—Pārās'arya, Baijavāpāyana,—Baijavāpāyana, Kaus'ikāyani—Kaus'ikāyani.

3. घृतकौशिकाद्घृतकौशिकः पाराशर्यायणात्पाराशर्यायणः पाराशर्यात्पाराशर्यो जातूकर्ण्याज्जातूकर्ण्य आसुरायणाच्च यास्काच्चासुराय-

णस्त्रैवणेस्त्रैवणिरौपजन्धनेरौपजन्धनिरासुरेरासुरिर्भारद्वाजाद्भारद्वाज आत्रेयादात्रेयो माण्टेर्माण्टिर्गौतमाद्गौतमो गौतमाद्गौतमो वात्स्याद्वात्स्यः शाण्डिल्याच्छाण्डिल्यः कैशोर्यात्काप्यात्कैशोर्यः काप्यः कुमारहारितात्कुमारहारितो गालवाद्गालवो विदर्भीकौण्डिन्याद्विदर्भीकौण्डिन्यो वत्सनपातो बाभ्रवाद्वत्सनपाद्बाभ्रवः पथः सौभरात्पन्थाः सौभरोऽयास्यादाङ्गिरसादयास्य आङ्गिरस आभूतेस्त्वाष्ट्रादाभूतिस्त्वाष्ट्रो विश्वरूपात्त्वाष्ट्राद्विश्वरूपस्त्वाष्ट्रोऽश्विभ्यामश्विनौ दधीच आथर्वणाद्दध्यङ्ङाथर्वणोऽथर्वणो दैवादथर्वा दैवो मृत्योः प्राध्वꣳसनान्मृत्युः प्राध्वꣳसनः प्रध्वꣳसनात्प्रध्वꣳसन एकर्षेरेकर्षिर्विप्रचित्तेर्विप्रचित्तिर्व्यष्टेर्व्यष्टिः सनारोः सनारुः सनातनात्सनातनः सनगात्सनगः परमेष्ठिनः परमेष्ठी ब्रह्मणो ब्रह्म स्वयंभु ब्रह्मणे नमः ॥

Ghṛtakaus'ika,—Ghṛtakaus'ika, Pārās'aryāyaṇa,—Pārās'aryāyaṇa, Pārās'arya,—Pārās'arya, Jātūkarṇya,—Jātūkarṇya, Āsurāyaṇa and Yāska,—Āsurāyaṇa, Straivaṇi —Straivaṇi, Aupajandhani,—Aupajandhani, Āsuri,—Āsuri, Bhāradvāja,—Bhāradvāja, Ātreya,—Ātreya, Māṇṭi—Māṇṭi, Gautama—Gautama, Gautama,—Gautama, Vātsya,—Vātsya, Sāṇḍilya—Sāṇḍilya, Kais'orya Kāpya,—Kais'orya Kāpya, Kumārahārita,—Kumārahārita, Gālava,—Gālava, Vidarbhi Kauṇḍinya,—Vidarbhi Kauṇḍinya, Vatsanapāt Bābhrava—Vatsanapāt Bābhrava, Panthah Saubhara,—Panthāh Saubhara, Ayāsya Āṅgirasa,—Ayāsya Āṅgirasa, Abhuti Tvāṣṭra,—Abhuti Tvāṣṭra, Vis'varūpa Tvāṣṭra,—Vis'varupa Tvāṣṭra, the As'vins,—the As'vins, Dadhin, Ātharvaṇa—Dadhyaṅ Ātharvaṇa, Atharvaṇa Daiva,—Atharvā-Daiva, Mṛtyu

Prādhvaṁsana,—Mṛtyu Prādhvaṁsana, Pradhvaṁsana, —Pradhvaṁsana, Ekarṣi,—Ekarṣi, Vipracitti,—Vipracitti, Vyaṣṭi,—Vyaṣṭi, Sanāru,—Sanāru Sanātana,—Sanātana, Sanaga,—Sanaga, Parameṣṭi,—Parameṣṭi, Brahman (1). Brahman is the self-existent ; salutation to Brahman.

(1) Parameṣṭi Virāṭ and Brahman, denotes Hiraṇyagarbha.—Ś.

THIRD CHAPTER

FIRST BRAHMAṆA (1)

1. जनको ह वैदेहो बहुदक्षिणेन यज्ञेनेजे तत्र ह कुरुपञ्चालानां ब्राह्मणा अभिसमेता बभूवुस्तस्य ह जनकस्य वैदेहस्य विजिज्ञासा बभूव कः स्विदेषां ब्राह्मणानामनूचानतम इति स ह गवाꣳ सहस्रमवरुरोध दश दश पादा एकैकस्याः शृङ्गयोराबद्धा बभूवुः ॥

Janaka, the king of the Videhas, performed the sacrifice, named Bahudakṣiṇa (2). There were assembled the Brāhmaṇas of the kurus and the Pāñcālas. Janaka the king of the Videhas, had a great desire to know, who among those Brāhmaṇas knew best the Vedas ; for this purpose he tied a thousand cows (in a stable) ; the horns of each of them were surrounded with ten Pādas (of gold) (3).

(1) The present Kāṇḍa, or the Yājñavalkya Kāṇḍa, treats the same subject as the Madhu Kāṇḍa ; but it is no repetition, for while the latter exhibits the knowledge of Brahman in the form of mere enunciation, the former establishes it by argument. The narrative is given in praise of the knowledge of Brahman, and also to show liberality as a means conducive to that knowledge.—S'.

(2) Bahudakṣiṇa is either a sacrifice of this name, which has been explained in another S'akhā, or the

As'vamedha sacrifice, as in the latter great donations are required.—S'.

(3) A Pāda is, according to S'ankara, equal to the 4th part of a Pala, or equal to Suvarṇa of gold, which, according to Wilson, is equal to about 176 grains Troy.

2. तान्होवाच ब्राह्मणा भगवन्तो यो वो ब्रह्मिष्ठः स एता गा उदजतामिति
ते ह ब्राह्मणा न दधृषुरथ ह याज्ञवल्क्यः स्वमेव ब्रह्मचारिणमु-
वाचैताः सोम्योदज सामश्रवा ३ इति ता होदाचकार ते ह
ब्राह्मणाश्चुक्रुधुः कथं नो ब्रह्मिष्ठो ब्रुवीतेत्यथ ह जनकस्य वैदेहस्य
होताश्वलो बभूव सहैनं पप्रच्छ त्वं नु खलु नो याज्ञवल्क्य
ब्रह्मिष्ठोऽसि ३ ति स होवाच नमो वयं ब्रह्मिष्ठाय कुर्मो गोकामा
एव वयꣳ स्म इति तꣳ ह तत एव प्रष्टुं दध्रे होताश्वलः ॥

He said to them,—" O Venerable Brāhmaṇas, whoever amongst you is the best knower of Brahman, shall drive home those cows." The Brāhmaṇas did not venture (to come forward). Then said Yājñavalkya to his Brahma student,—" O gentle one, drive home those (cows)." " (As you command), O knower of the Sāma Veda " (1), with these words (the disciple) drove them home. The Brāhmaṇas became angry (thinking),—How dare he call himself amongst us the best knower of Brahman? There was then As'vala, the Hotā (2) of Janaka, king of the Videhas. He asked him,—Art thou in very deed amongst us the best knower of Brahman, O Yājñavalkya?" He said,—" We bow to him who is the best knower of Brahman ; we are even desirous of getting the cows." Hence the Hotā As'vala undertook to question him.

(1) That is to say, knower of the four Vedas, as the Sāma Veda was to be studied after the three other Vedas.

(2) The Ṛtvik, one who knows the Ṛg-Veda, or he who arranges the sacrifices.

3. याज्ञवल्क्येति होवाच यदिद१ सर्वं मृत्युनाप्त१ सर्वं मृत्युनाभिपन्नं केन यजमानो मृत्योराप्तिमतिमुच्यत इति होत्रर्त्विजाग्निना वाचा वाग्वै यज्ञस्य होता तद्येयं वाक् सोऽयमग्निः स होता स मुक्तिः सातिमुक्तिः ॥

He said,—"Yājñavalkya, all this is pervaded by death, all this is subject to death. By what means overcoming the grasp of death is the sacrificer liberated?" (He replied),—"By speech which is fire in the shape of the priest, called Hotā. The speech of the sacrificer (1), is verily the Hotā. This speech (2) is this fire; this (fire) is the Hotā, this (fire of the Hotā) is liberation (3), this (liberation) absolute liberation." (4)

(1) With reference to the sacrifice.—S'.

(2) With reference to the deities.—S'.

(3) Cause of liberation.—S'.

(4) Absolute liberation is here the gaining of the state of speech and of the deity of fire.—S'.

4. याज्ञवल्क्येति होवाच यदिद१ सर्वमहोरात्राभ्यामाप्त१ सर्वमहोरात्राभ्यामभिपन्नं केन यजमानोऽहोरात्रयोराप्तिमतिमुच्यत इत्यध्वर्युणर्त्विजा चक्षुषादित्येन चक्षुर्वै यज्ञस्याध्वर्युस्तद्यदिदं चक्षुः सोऽसावादित्यः सोऽध्वर्युः स मुक्तिः सातिमुक्तिः ॥

He said,—"Yājñavalkya, all this is pervaded by day and night (1), all this is subject to day and night.

By what means, overcoming the grasp of day and night, is the sacrificer liberated?" (He replied,)—"By the eye, which is Āditya (the sun) in the shape of the priest called Adhvaryu. The eye of the sacrificer is verily the Adhvaryu. This eye is the Āditya, this (Āditya) is the Adhvaryu, this (Adhvaryu) is liberation, this (liberation) absolute liberation."

(1) The cause of the continual change of such rites as the Darśa and Pūrṇamāsa, is time; for although time is included in work, yet, independent of the performance of work, time, before and after work is observed to change the causes of rites, for which reason the liberation from time must be separately explained.—Ś.

5. याज्ञवल्क्येति होवाच यदिदꣳ सर्वं पूर्वपक्षापरपक्षाभ्यामाप्तꣳ सर्वं पूर्वपक्षापरपक्षाभ्यामभिपन्नं केन यजमानः पूर्वपक्षापरपक्षयोराप्तिमतिमुच्यत इत्युद्गात्रर्त्विजा वायुना प्राणेन प्राणो वै यज्ञस्योद्गाता तद्योऽयं प्राणः स वायुः स उद्गाता स मुक्तिः सातिमुक्तिः ॥

He said,—"Yājñavalkya, all is pervaded by the light and dark halves of the lunar mouth (1); all this is subject to the light and dark halves of the lunar months. By what means, overcoming the grasp of the light and dark halves of the lunar month, is the sacrificer liberated?" (He replied),—"By the vital breath, which is the wind in the shape of the priest, called the Udgātā. The vital breath of the sacrificer is verily the Udgātā. This vital breath is this wind, this (wind) is the Udgātā, this (Udgātā) is liberation, this (liberation) absolute liberation."

(1) Although time, as containing lunar days, is included in time, characterized by day and night, and although the sun is the Ruler of day and night, yet this is only the case in general, but not with regard to days and nights, where there is an increase or decrease which are ruled by the moon, and in this respect a liberation from time as represented by lunar days, is necessary.—S'.

6. याज्ञवल्क्येति होवाच यदिदमन्तरिक्षमनारम्भणमिव केनाक्रमेण यजमानः स्वर्गं लोकमाक्रमत इति ब्रह्मणर्त्विजा मनसा चन्द्रेण मनो वै यज्ञस्य ब्रह्मा तद्यदिदं मनः सोऽसौ चन्द्रः स ब्रह्मा स मुक्तिः सातिमुक्तिरित्यतिमोक्षा अथ संपदः ॥

He said,—"Yājñavalkya, this atmosphere is without foundation, as it were; by what approach (1) does (man) approach then the place of heaven?" (He replied),—"By the mind which is the moon in the shape of the priest, called the Brahman. The mind of the sacrificer is verily the Brahman; mind is the Brahman, this (moon) is the Brahman, this (Brahman) is liberation, this (liberation) absolute liberation." So far the absolute emancipation (from death). Next the means (2).

(1) In 3—5, the liberation of the sacrificer from death has been declared, but not the means by which he effects it. These means are explained in the present section.—S'.

(2) Means are either all the appliances necessary for the performance of sacred rites, or the knowledge of those means.—S'.

7. याज्ञवल्क्येति होवाच कतिभिरयमद्यर्ग्भिर्होतास्मिन्यज्ञे करिष्यतीति तिसृभिरिति कतमास्तास्तिस्र इति पुरोऽनुवाक्या च याज्या च शस्यैव तृतीया किं ताभिर्जयतीति यत्किंचेदं प्राणभृदिति ॥

He said,—" Yājñavalkya, by how many Ṛks (1) of the Ṛg-Veda does this Hotā in this sacrifice to-day perform the praise?"

(He replied),—" By three."—" By what three?"— " By those to be recited before (the sacrifice), by those to be recited for the sake of the sacrifice, and by those to be recited for the sake of praise." " What does he conquer by them?" " All that bears life " (2).

(1) A Ṛk does not mean here a single verse of the Ṛg-Veda, but it refers to certain kinds of Ṛk-verses; which may include any number of Mantras.

(2) The three worlds, according to S'., since they are the supporters of life and the three worlds, correspond with the three kinds of Ṛks.

8. याज्ञवल्क्येति होवाच कत्ययमद्याध्वर्युरस्मिन्यज्ञ आहुतीर्होष्यतीति तिस्र इति कतमास्तास्तिस्र इति या हुता उज्ज्वलन्ति या हुता अतिनेदन्ते या हुता अधिशेरते किं ताभिर्जयतीति या हुता उज्ज्वलन्ति देवलोकमेव ताभिर्जयति दीप्यत इव हि देवलोको या हुता अतिनेदन्ते पितृलोकमेव ताभिर्जयत्यतीव हि पितृलोको या हुता अधिशेरते मनुष्यलोकमेव ताभिर्जयत्यध इव हि मनुष्यलोकः ॥

He said,—" Yājñavalkya, how many oblations (1) does this Adhvaryu offer to-day in this sacrifice?" (He replied),—" Three." " Which are these three?" " The oblations which flame upwards; the oblations which make a great noise; the oblations which fall downwards " (2). What does he conquer by them? " By the oblations that flame upwards, he conquers the world of the gods; for the world of the gods (deva) shines (dīpyate) as it were; by the oblations which make a great noise, he conquers the world of the forefathers; for the world of the forefathers is very noisy (3), as it were; by the oblations which fall downwards, he conquers the world of man; for the world of man is down below, as it were."

(1) Oblations, fire offerings.

(2) In the oblations, flaming upwards, butter; in those making a great noise, meat; and in those falling downwards, milk or the Soma juice is offered.

(3) The noise refers to the lamentations of those who are punished for their crimes.—S'.

9. याज्ञवल्क्येति होवाच कतिभिरयमद्य ब्रह्मा यज्ञं दक्षिणतो देवताभि-
गोंपायतीत्येकयेति कतमा सैकेति मन एवेत्यनन्तं वै मनोऽन्ता
विश्वेदेवा अनन्तमेव स तेन लोकं जयति ॥

He said,—" Yājñavalkya, by how many deities (1) does this Brahman, (seated on the chair) to the right, protect to-day this sacrifice?" (He replied),—" By one." "Which is the one?" "The mind (2); the mind is infinite (3), infinite are the Vis'vedevas; he conquers thereby the world Infinite."

(1) The plural instead of the singular according to S'., is either used to connect this question with the former ones, or to deceive Yājñavalkya.

(2) For by the mind is Brahman meditated upon.

(3) This means, that the modifications of the mind are infinite.

10. याज्ञवल्क्येति होवाच कत्ययमद्योद्गाताऽस्मिन्यज्ञे स्तोत्रियाः स्तोष्यतीति तिस्र इति कतमास्तास्तिस्र इति पुरोऽनुवाक्या च याज्या च शस्यैव तृतीया कतमास्ता या अध्यात्ममिति प्राण एव पुरोनुवाक्याऽपानो याज्या व्यानः शस्या किं ताभिर्जयतीति पृथिवीलोकमेव पुरोनुवाक्यया जयत्यन्तरिक्षलोकं याज्यया द्युलोकꣳ शस्यया ततो ह होताश्वल उपरराम ॥

He said,—"Yājñavalkya, how many hymns of praise (1), will the Udgātā sing to-day in this sacrifice?" (He replied),—"Three." "Which are these three?" "Those to be recited before (the sacrifice), those to be recited for the sake of the sacrifice, and thirdly, those to be recited for the sake of praise." "Which are those (three) according to their relation to the soul?" "The vital air that goes forwards (respiration) is those to be recited before (2), the vital air that goes downwards those to be recited for the sake of the sacrifice (3), the vital air that equalises, those to be recited for the sake of praise." "What does he conquer by them?" "By the Mantras to be recited before, he conquers the world of man, by those to be recited for the sake of the sacrifice, the world of the atmosphere, by those to be recited for the sake of praise, the world of the heavens." Hence the Hotā As'vala became silent.

(1) Ṛks either of the Ṛk or Sāma-Veda.
(2) Both going upwards.
(3) As the wind going downwards causes a noise.

SECOND BRĀHMAṆA

1. अथ हैनं जारत्कारव आर्तभागः पप्रच्छ याज्ञवल्क्येति होवाच कति ग्रहाः कत्यतिग्रहा इत्यष्टौ ग्रहा अष्टावतिग्रहा इति ये तेऽष्टौ ग्रहा अष्टावतिग्रहाः कतमे त इति ।

Then asked (1) him Ārtabhāga (2), from the family of Jaratkāru,—" Yājñavalkya," said he, " how many fetters (3) are there, and how many auxiliaries to them ? " (He replied),—" Eight fetters and eight auxiliaries." " Which are the eight fetters and the eight auxiliaries ? "

(1) The absolute liberation from death in the relation of the latter to time and work, has been explained in the preceding Brāhmaṇa. What then is the nature of death itself ? Death is an attachment, produced from the natural ignorance of man, as to the material world and to the soul. Death is therefore a bond, and the senses and their objects by which death is characterised, are called chains and their enhancers, and it is the object of this Brāhmaṇa to show the liberation from death, as characterised by the sensual chains and their enhancers, the sensual objects.—S'.

(2) The son of Ṛtubhāga.

(3) The terms in the text are " graha " and " atigraha," graha, by which something is seized and atigraha, which aids in this seizure, by which the seizure becomes stronger.

2. प्राणो वै ग्रहः सोऽपानेनातिग्राहेण गृहीतोऽपानेन हि गन्धाञ्जिघ्रति ।

The vital air that goes forwards (1) is a fetter ; it is enhanced by the vital air going downwards (2), which is its auxiliary ; for by the vital air that goes downwards, smell is perceived.

(1) The vital air that goes forwards is here the sense of smell, from its connection with the present topic.—S'.

(2) The vital air that goes downwards is here the sensation of smell.—S'.

3. वाग्वै ग्रहः स नाम्नातिग्राहेण गृहीतो वाचा हि नामान्यभिवदति ।

Speech is a fetter; it is enhanced by the word which is its auxiliary, for by speech words are pronounced.

4. जिह्वा वै ग्रहः स रसेनातिग्राहेण गृहीतो जिह्वया हि रसान्विजानाति ।

The tongue is a fetter; it is enhanced by taste which is its auxiliary; for by the tongue various kinds of taste become manifest.

5. चक्षुर्वै ग्रहः स रूपेणातिग्राहेण गृहीतश्चक्षुषा हि रूपाणि पश्यति ।

The eye is a fetter; it is enhanced by colour which is its auxiliary; for by the eye colours are seen.

6. श्रोत्रं वै ग्रहः स शब्देनातिग्राहेण गृहीतः श्रोत्रेण हि शब्दाञ्छृणोति ।

The ear is a fetter; it is enhanced by sound which is its auxiliary; for by the ear sounds are heard.

7. मनो वै ग्रहः स कामेनातिग्राहेण गृहीतो मनसा हि कामान्कामयते ।

The mind is a fetter; it is enhanced by desire which is its auxiliary; for by mind desires are formed.

8. हस्तौ वै ग्रहः स कर्मणातिग्राहेण गृहीतो हस्ताभ्यां हि कर्म करोति ।

The hands are a fetter; it is enhanced by action which is its auxiliary: for by the hands actions are done.

9. त्वग्वै ग्रहः स स्पर्शेनातिग्राहेण गृहीतस्त्वचा हि स्पर्शान्वेद यत इत्येतेऽष्टौ ग्रहा अष्टावतिग्रहाः ।

"The skin is a fetter; it is enhanced by touch which is its auxiliary; for by the skin the various kinds of touch become known. These are the eight fetters and the eight auxiliaries." (1)

(1) The fetters above mentioned, as speech, and their auxiliaries are the impressions of words, etc.

10. याज्ञवल्क्येति होवाच यदिदꣳ सर्वं मृत्योरन्नं का स्वित्सा देवता यस्या मृत्युरन्नमित्यग्निर्वै मृत्युः सोऽपामन्नमप पुनर्मृत्युं जयति ।

He said,—"Yājñavalkya, all this is the food of death. Which then is the deity whose food is death (himself)?" (He replied)—"Fire verily is death; the same is the food of the water; (thereby) death again is conquered."

11. याज्ञवल्क्येति होवाच यत्रायं पुरुषो म्रियत उदस्मात्प्राणाः क्रामन्त्याहो ३ नेति नेति होवाच याज्ञवल्क्योऽत्रैव समवनीयन्ते स उच्छ्वयत्याध्मायत्याध्मातो मृतः शेते ।

He said,—"Yājñavalkya, when this spirit (Puruṣa) dies, do then the organs ascend from him?" (1) Yājñavalkya said;—"No, by no means; no by no means; there (2) united they are dissolved in him (3); he becomes swollen, he becomes full of wind, when blown upon: the dead sleeps" (4).

(1) From him who knows Brahman.

(2) In him who knows Brahman.

(3) In the supreme Brahman; they become of the same nature with him.

(4) There is no actual death; when the bonds are destroyed, the liberated does not proceed anywhere.

12. याज्ञवल्क्येति होवाच यत्रायं पुरुषो म्रियते किमेनं न जहातीति नामेत्यनन्तं वै नामानन्ता विश्वेदेवा अनन्तमेव स तेन लोकं जयति ।

He said,—" Yâjñavalkya, when this spirit dies, then what does not leave him?" (He replied),—" The name. The name indeed is infinite, infinite, are the Vis'vedevas; he conquers thereby the world of the infinite."

13. याज्ञवल्क्येति होवाच यत्रास्य पुरुषस्य मृतस्याग्निं वागप्येति वातं प्राणश्चक्षुरादित्यं मनश्चन्द्रं दिशः श्रोत्रं पृथिवीꣳ शरीरमाकाशमात्मौषधीर्लोमानि वनस्पतीन्केशा अप्सु लोहितं च रेतश्च निधीयते क्वायं तदा पुरुषो भवतीत्याहर सोम्य हस्तमार्तभागावामेवैतस्य वेदिष्यावो न नावेतत् सजन इति तौ होत्क्रम्य मन्त्रयांचक्राते तौ ह यदूचतुः कर्म हैव तदूचतुरथ यत्प्रशशꣳसतुः कर्म हैव तत्प्रशशꣳसतुः पुण्यो वै पुण्येन कर्मणा भवति पापः पापेनेति ततो ह जारत्कारव आर्तभाग उपरराम ।

He said,—" Yājñavalkya (1),—when the speech (2) of the spirit departed is dissolved into fire, the vital air into the wind, the eye into the sun, the mind into the moon, the ear into the quarters, the body into earth, the soul (3) into the ether, the hairs of the body into annual herbs, the hairs of the head into trees, blood and semen into the waters, where then does this spirit remain ?" —(He replied), "Take, O gentle Ārtabhāga, my hand, (and let us go to a lonely place, there) we shall know (the answer of) this question ; this our (question) cannot be (decided) in a crowded place."—Going there they deliberated. What they said there, was work (4), what they praised there, was work. By holy work verily a a person becomes holy, unholy by unholy." Hence Ārtabhāga from the family of Jaratkāru became silent.

(1) In 10 and 11, the state, which is obtained by the liberated, has been mentioned. What then does become after death of him who is not liberated ? The answer is given in the present section.

(2) By speech, the vital airs, etc., according to S'., the tutelary deities are here to be understood, and not the organs, because they do not depart.

(3) The soul (ātmā) means here the place of the soul, the ether of the heart.

(4) Work as the material cause of man again assuming a body, etc.

THIRD BRĀHMAṆA (1)

1. अथ हैनं भुज्युर्लाह्यायनिः पप्रच्छ याज्ञवल्क्येति होवाच मद्रेषु चरकाः पर्यव्रजाम ते पतञ्चलस्य काप्यस्य गृहानैम

तस्यासीद् दुहिता गन्धर्वगृहीता तमपृच्छाम कोऽसीति सोऽब्रवीत्सुधन्वाऽऽङ्गिरस इति तं यदा लोकानामन्तानपृच्छामाथैनमब्रूम क्व पारिक्षिता अभवन्निति क्व पारिक्षिता अभवन् स त्वा पृच्छामि याज्ञवल्क्य क्व पारिक्षिता अभवन्निति ।

Then asked him Bhujyu, the son of Lāhya,—"Yâjñavalkya," said he, wandering (one) in the country of the Madras for the sake of studying the Vedas, "we came to the house of Patañcala of the family of Kapi. His daughter was possessed by a Gandharva (2). We asked him,—'Who art thou?' He answered,—'I am Sudhanvā, of the family of Āṅgirasa.' When asking him about the boundaries of the world, we said to him,—'Where are the Pārikṣitas; where are the Pārikṣitas?' I (now) ask thee O Yājñavalkya, where are the Pāriksitas?"

(1) This Brāhmaṇa, according to S'., is to show, that the rites have only worldly effects, and that absolute liberation is thereby impossible. The highest among all rites is the performance of the horse-sacrifice, in its double form, either as an actual sacrifice, accompanied with knowledge, or as a symbolical sacrifice by mental representation. The effect resulting from the horse-sacrifice, is, either individual, *viz.*, the obtaining of the nature of fire and other deities, or universal, as referring to the deity of the universe, *viz.*, the obtaining of the nature of Hiraṇyagarbha, the first-born, that is to say, by neither of those effects absolute liberation from the world, or identity with Brahman is obtained.

(2) A being of superhuman power. By saying, that he has his knowledge from such a being, Bhujya means to assert, that his knowledge must be superior to that of Yājñavalkya, as not derived from such a source.—S'.

2. स होवाचोवाच वै सोऽगच्छन्वै ते तद्यत्राश्वमेधयाजिनो गच्छन्तीति क न्वश्वमेधयाजिनो गच्छन्तीति द्वात्रिꣳशतं वै देवरथाह्न्यान्ययं लोकस्तꣳसमन्तं पृथिवी द्विस्तावत्पर्येति ताꣳसमन्तं पृथिवीं द्विस्तावत्समुद्रः पर्येति तद्यावती क्षुरस्य धारा यावद्वा मक्षिकायाः पत्रं तावानन्तरेणाकाशस्तानिन्द्रः सुपर्णो भूत्वा वायवे प्रायच्छत्तान्वायुरात्मनि धित्वा तत्रागमयद्यत्राश्वमेधयाजिनोऽभवन्नित्येवमिव वै सवायुमेव प्रशशꣳस तस्माद्वायुरेव व्यष्टिर्वायुः समष्टिरप पुनर्मृत्युं जयति य एवं वेद ततो ह भुज्युर्लाह्यायनिरुपरराम ॥

He (Yājñavalkya) said,—"Verily he (the Gandharva), said—They (the Pārikṣitas) went where the performers of the As'vamedha-sacrifice go." "Where then go the performers of the As'vamedha-sacrifice?" "This world (1) extends to thirty-two days (of the journey) of the car of the sun; the earth extends twice as far everywhere; the ocean extends twice as far as the earth everywhere. There (2) as far as the edge of a razor, or the wing of a fly (extends), so far extends the ether in the midst. Indra (3) in the shape of a falcon surrendered them (the Pārikṣitas), to the wind; the wind placing them upon himself (4) carried them there, where the performers of the As'vamedha-sacrifice abide. In this manner he (the Gandharva) praised the wind; therefore the wind is indeed the individuality, the wind the totality. Whoever thus knows, conquers the second death." Hence Bhujyu, the son of Lāhya, became silent.

(1) This world is, according to S'., the space, enclosed by the mountains of the rising and the setting sun.

(2) There, according to S''s explanation, means at the aperture of the two halves of the mundane egg. To this end of the world leads a road of the length, above described, and through the aperture, which is the ether, the performers of the horse-sacrifice go, to be united with the wind that surrounds it.

(3) Parmes'vara.—S'.

(4) Making them like himself.

FOURTH BRĀHMAṆA

1. अथ हैनमुषस्तश्चाक्रायणः पप्रच्छ याज्ञवल्क्येति होवाच यत्साक्षादपरोक्षाद्ब्रह्म य आत्मा अर्वान्तरस्तं मे व्याचक्ष्व इत्येष त आत्मा सर्वान्तरः कतमो याज्ञवल्क्य सर्वान्तरो यः प्राणेन प्राणिति स त आत्मा सर्वान्तरो योऽपानेनापानिति स त आत्मा सर्वान्तरो यो व्यानेन व्यानिति स त आत्मा सर्वन्तरो य उदानेनोदानिति स त आत्मा सर्वान्तर एष त आत्मा सर्वान्तरः ।

Then asked (1) him Uṣasta, the son of Cakra,—"Yājñavalkya," said he, "do explain to me that Brahman who is a witness and present (2), that soul, which is within every (being)." (He replied),—"It is thy soul, which is within every (being)." "Which soul is within every one, O Yājñavalkya?" "That which breathes by the breath, is thy soul (3) which is within every (being); that which descends by the descending air, is thy soul which is within every (being); that which goes everywhere by the air going everywhere, in thy soul which is within every (being); that which ascends by the ascending air, is the soul which is within every (being); this thy soul is within every (being).'

(1) The connection between the present question and the two preceding ones is thus stated by S'. It has been declared that, seized by the fetters and their auxiliaries, *viz.*, the senses and their objects, which are produced by virtue and vice, man roams about in the world, again and again shaking off those fetters and again and again assuming them. The highest elevation to be gained by virtue has also been explained, that is to say, the acquirement of the same nature with the two-fold nature of Hiraṇyagarbha, *viz.*, with his nature as totality or with his nature as separated within individual existence. The present question is to enquire, whether he who, seized by the senses and their objects, assumes one body after the other, exists, or not, and if he exists what is his nature, that is to say, it shows, how to distinguish the soul from every other thing as the indispensable means of liberation; for the nature of the soul being comprehended, liberation ensues from the above described bondage.

(2) Witness and present, the first, according to S'., means "not obstructed by anything," and the second "without attributes".

(3) The soul, whose nature is knowledge.—S'.

2. स होवाचोषस्तश्चाक्रायणो यथा विब्रूयादसौ गौरसावश्व इत्येवमेवैतद्व्यपदिष्टं भवति यदेव साक्षादपरोक्षाद्ब्रह्म य आत्मा सर्वान्तरस्तं मे व्याचक्ष्वेत्येष त आत्मा सर्वान्तरः कतमो याज्ञवल्क्य सर्वान्तरो न दृष्टेर्द्रष्टारं पश्येर्न श्रुतेः श्रोतारꣳ शृणुयान्न मतेर्मन्तारं मन्वीथा न विज्ञातेर्विज्ञातारं विजानीया एष त आत्मा सर्वान्तरोऽतोऽन्यदार्तं ततो होषस्तश्चाक्रायण उपरराम ।

Uṣasta, the son of Cakra, said—"As some one may say: This is a cow, this is a horse, thus is this (Brahman) described by thee (1). Do (now) explain to me that Brahman, who is a witness and present, that soul which is within every (being)." "It is thy soul which is within every (being.)" "Which soul is within every (being), Yājñavalkya?" "Thou couldst (2) not behold the beholder of the beholding; thou couldst not hear the hearer of the hearing; thou couldst not mind the minder of the minding; thou couldst not know the knower of the knowing. This thy soul is within every (being); every thing different from it, is transient." Hence Uṣasta, the son of Cakra, became silent.

(1) To show Brahman by such signs as respiration, etc., is the same, as if some body who engages to define a cow, etc., defines it merely by signs, saying for instance, the animal which goes there is a cow; that is to say, thy definition is an improper one.

(2) Yājñavalkya declines to give a definition of Brahman in the way, as it is given of a jar, etc. And his reason for declining it, is that such a definition is contradictory to the nature of Brahman. For the nature of Brahman consists in the agency described as beholding, etc. The soul is the beholder of the beholding. The beholding, hearing, knowing, etc., is therefore two-fold, the common one and that to which it in reality applies. The common beholding, etc., is a modification of the internal organ by means of its connection with the eye, etc. This is an effect, and has therefore a commencement and an end; but the beholding, etc., of the soul, the beholding of the beholding, has, by its own nature, no beginning and no end.

FIFTH BRĀHMAṆA

1. अथ हैनं कहोलः कौषीतकेयः पप्रच्छ याज्ञवल्क्येति होवाच यदेव साक्षादपरोक्षाद्ब्रह्म य आत्मा सर्वान्तरस्तं मे व्याचक्ष्वेत्येष त आत्मा सर्वान्तरः कतमो याज्ञवल्क्य सर्वान्तरो योऽशनायापिपासे शोकं मोहं जरां मृत्युमत्येति एतं वै तमात्मानं विदित्वा ब्राह्मणाः पुत्रैषणायाश्च वित्तैषणायाश्च लोकैषणायाश्च व्युत्थायाथ भिक्षाचर्यं चरन्ति या ह्येव पुत्रैषणा सा वित्तैषणा या वित्तैषणा सा लोकैषणोभे ह्येते एषणे एव भवतस्तस्माद्ब्राह्मणः पाण्डित्यं निर्विद्य बाल्येन तिष्ठासेद्बाल्यं पाण्डित्यं च निर्विद्याथ मुनिरमौनं च मौनं च निर्विद्याऽथ ब्राह्मणः स ब्राह्मणः केन स्याद्येन स्यात्तेनेदृश एवातोऽन्यदार्तं ततो ह कहोलः कौषीतकेय उपरराम ।

Then asked him Kahola, the son of Kuṣītaka,— "Yājñavalkya," said he, "do explain to me that Brahman, who is a witness and present, that soul, which is within every (being)" (1). He replied.,—"It is thy soul, which is within every (being)." "Which (the soul), O Yājñavalkya, that is within every (being)?" "(It is the soul) which conquers hunger, thirst, grief, delusion, old age, (and) death. When Brāhmaṇas know this soul (2), then elevating themselves from the desire of obtaining a son (3), from the desire of wealth, and from the desire of gaining the worlds, they lead the life of wandering mendicants; for the desire of a son, is also the desire for wealth; the desire for wealth (4) is also the desire for the worlds; for both are even desires. Therefore knowing wisdom let the Brāhmaṇa arm himself with strength (5). Knowing wisdom and strength (6) the thinker knowing the thinking and the not thinking (7), of Brahman will become a (true) Brāhmaṇa." "By what (work) will the Brāhmaṇa live?" He will remain such an one by any (work) (8). Any (state) different from this (state of a Brāhmaṇa) is perishable. Then Kahola, the son of Kuṣītaka, became silent.

(1) In the first three Brāhmaṇas the bondage of the soul together with its cause has been declared. In the fourth the existence of the so bound soul and its independence of every other thing has been set forth. The fifth Brāhmaṇa is to show the knowledge of the soul in connection with the renunciation of the world as the cause of the liberation of the soul from bondage. In this and the preceding Brāhmaṇas the question, "Explain to me that Brahman, etc.," is the same, and it might therefore be justly asked whether the two questions refer to one and the same soul, or to two, the supreme and the individual souls. The latter case appears the correct one on the first glance for if it is one and the same soul, the second question seems useless; on a closer consideration, however, this view must be abandoned; for one and the same whole of causes and effects is possessed of soul merely by one soul. The difference between the present and the preceding questions is this, that in the latter the soul is described as far as it has existence and is independent of the body, while in the former the particular knowledge, in connection with the renunciation of the world, is described, by which the liberation from that bondage takes place.—S'.

(2) Know the soul, that is to say, their own soul as the supreme Brahman.

(3) The desire of being united with a wife for the purpose of obtaining a son, by whom they are able to conquer the world.—S'.

(4) Wealth is two fold, human, and divine wealth. Human wealth supplies the means to perform rites; by these rites, if unaccompanied with knowledge the world of the forefathers is gained. Divine wealth is knowledge; by rites, connected therewith, the world of the gods is gained, and the same also by mere knowledge. From this knowledge also an elevation is necessary to obtain perfect liberation from the world; for in reality that knowledge is ignorance.—S'.

(5) Wisdom, Pāṇḍityam, the knowledge of Brahman, strength, such as results from the knowledge of Brahman.

(6) The thinker, Muni, explained by S'. mananāt Muni, that is a Yogi.

(7) Not thinking and thinking, thus I have translated literally, different from S.'s explanation, who explains "Amaunam," the knowledge of soul and the removing a belief of non-soul, and "Maunam" the ultimate effect from removing a belief in the non-soul.

(8) The sense is, for him who has acquired the true knowledge of Brahman every work is indifferent; he is above work.

SIXTH BRĀHMAṆA

1. अथ हैनं गार्गी वाचक्नवी पप्रच्छ याज्ञवल्क्येति होवाच यदिदꣳ सर्वमप्स्वोतं च प्रोतं च कस्मिन्नु खल्वाप ओताश्च प्रोताश्चेति वायौ गार्गीति कस्मिन्नु खलु वायुरोतश्च प्रोतश्चेत्यन्तरिक्षलोकेषु गार्गीति कस्मिन्नु खल्वन्तरिक्षलोका ओताश्च प्रोताश्चेति गन्धर्वलोकेषु गार्गीति कस्मिन्नु कलु गन्धर्वलोका ओताश्च प्रोताश्चेत्यादित्यलोकेषु गार्गीति कस्मिन्नु खल्वादित्यलोका ओताश्च प्रोताश्चेति चन्द्रलोकेषु गार्गीति कस्मिन्नु खलु चन्द्रलोका ओताश्च

प्रोताश्चेति नक्षत्रलोकेषु गार्गीति कस्मिन्नु खलु नक्षत्रलोका ओताश्च प्रोताश्चेति देवलोकेषु गार्गीति कस्मिन्नु खलु देवलोका ओताश्च प्रोताश्चेतीन्द्रलोकेषु गार्गीति कस्मिन्नु खल्विन्द्रलोका ओताश्च प्रोताश्चेति प्रजापतिलोकेषु गार्गीति कस्मिन्नु खलु प्रजापतिलोका ओताश्च प्रोताश्चेति ब्रह्मलोकेषु गार्गीति कस्मिन्नु खलु ब्रह्मलोका ओताश्च प्रोताश्चेति स होवाच गार्गि मातिप्राक्षीर्मा ते मूर्धा व्यपप्तदनतिप्रश्न्यां वै देवतामतिपृच्छसि गार्गि मातिप्राक्षीरिति ततो ह गार्गी वाचक्नव्युपरराम ।

Then asked (1) him Gārgi, the daughter of Vacaknu,—"Yājñavalkya," said she, "all this (earth) is woven and rewoven on the waters (2); upon what then are the waters woven and rewoven?" (He replied), —"On the wind (3), O Gārgi." "On what then is woven and rewoven the wind?" "On the worlds of the atmosphere (4), Gārgi." "On what then are woven and rewoven the worlds of the atmosphere?" "On the worlds of the Gandharvas, O Gārgi." "On what then are woven and rewoven the worlds of the Gandharvas?" "On the worlds of Āditya, O Gārgi." "On what then are woven and rewoven the worlds of Āditya?" "On the worlds of the moon, O Gārgi." "On what then are woven and rewoven the worlds of the moon?" "On the worlds of the stars, O Gārgi." "On what then are the worlds of the stars woven and rewoven?" "On the worlds of the gods, O Gārgi." "On what then are woven and rewoven the worlds of the gods?" "On the worlds of Indra, O Gārgi." "On what then are woven and rewoven the worlds of Indra?" "On the worlds of Prajāpati, O Gārgi." "On what then are woven and rewoven the worlds of Prajāpati?" "On the worlds of Brahman, O Gārgi," "On what then are woven and rewoven the worlds of Brahman?" "Gārgi," said he, "do not ask an improper question (5), in order that thy head may not drop down. Thou askest the deity which is not to be questioned. Do not question, O Gārgi. Thence Gārgi, the daughter of Vacaknu, became silent."

(1) In the last two Brāhmaṇas it has been declared, that the soul is within all; the next three Brahmaṇas are to give a more exact definition of this.—Ā. G.

(2) This is the case, because the earth everywhere from without and within is pervaded by the water; otherwise it would be scattered everywhere like a handful of pounded rice. Here applies this argument, all that is an effect that is finite and gross, is pervaded by something, which is a cause which is infinite and subtle; and this commences from the five elements up to the soul.—S'.

(3) Instead of "on the wind," the answer "on the fire" should be here expected; but says S'., the fire has no existence of its own, independent of water and earth, and is therefore not mentioned separately.

(4) The worlds of the atmosphere are composed of the five elements.—S'.

(5) Do not ask an improper question, because it cannot be decided by argument, but only by the S'āstra.—S'.

SEVENTH BRĀHMAṆA

1. अथ हैनमुद्दालक आरुणिः पप्रच्छ याज्ञवल्क्येति होवाच
मद्रेष्ववसाम पतञ्चलस्य काप्यस्य गृहेषु यज्ञमधीयानास्तस्या-

सीद्भार्या गन्धर्वगृहीता तमपृच्छाम कोऽसीति सोऽब्रवीत्कबन्ध आथर्वण इति सोऽब्रवीत्पतञ्चलं काप्यं याज्ञिकांश्च वेत्थ नु त्वं काप्य तत्सूत्रं येनायं च लोकः परश्च लोकः सर्वाणि च भूतानि संदृब्धानि भवन्तीति सोऽब्रवीत्पतञ्चलः काप्यो नाहं तद्भगवन्वेदेति सोऽब्रवीत्पतञ्चलं काप्यं याज्ञिकांश्च वेत्थ नु त्वं काप्य तमन्तर्यामिणं य इमं च लोकं परं च लोकं सर्वाणि च भूतानि योऽन्तरो यमयतीति सोऽब्रवीत्पतञ्चलः काप्यो नाहं तं भगवन्वेदेति सोऽब्रवीत्पतञ्चलं काप्यं याज्ञिकांश्च यो वै तत्काप्य सूत्रं विद्यात्तं चान्तर्यामिणमिति स ब्रह्मवित्स लोकवित्स वेदवित्स भूतवित्स आत्मवित्स सर्वविदिति तेभ्योऽब्रवीत्तदहं वेद तच्चेत्त्वं याज्ञवल्क्य सूत्रमविद्वांस्तं चान्तर्यामिणं ब्रह्मगवीरुदजसे मूर्धा ते विपतिष्यतीति वेद वा अहं गौतम तत्सूत्रं तं चान्तर्यामिणमिति यो वा इदं कश्चिद्ब्रूयाद्वेदवेदेति यथा वेत्थ तथा ब्रूहीति ।

Then asked Uddālaka, the son of Aruṇa,—"Yājñavalkya," said he, "in the country of the Madras we (1) abode in the house of Patañcala, of the family of Kapi, for the sake of studying the science of offering. His wife was possessed by a Gandharva. We asked him (the Gandharva), 'Who art thou?' He said, 'Kabandha, the son Atharvaṇa.' He said to Patañcala, of the family of Kapi, and to (us) priests, 'O Kāpya, knowest thou that Thread by which this world, and the other world and all beings (2) are bound together?' Patañcala, of the family of Kapi, said—'I do not know it, O Venerable.' He said to Patañcala, of the family of Kapi, and to (us) priests (3), 'Knowest thou,

O Kāpya, that Inner Ruler who within rules this world and the other world, and all beings?' Patañcala, of the family, of Kapi, said, 'I do not know (this), O Venerable.' He said to Patañcala, of the family of Kapi and to (us) priests, 'O Kāpya, whoever knows the Thread and the Inner Ruler, knows Brahman, knows the worlds, knows the gods, knows the Vedas, knows the elements (4), knows the soul, knows all.' (Then the Gandharva) said (all about all Thread and the Inner Ruler) to them. Therefore do I know this. If thou, O Yājñavalkya, ignorant of the Thread and the Inner Ruler, hast taken away the Brahma-cows, (5) thy head will certainly drop down." "I know verily, Gautama, the Thread and the Inner Ruler." "Any one may say this, I know, I know; but tell the manner in which thou knowest."

(1) Patañcala's pupils.

(2) From Brahman downwards to inanimate matter.—S'.

(3) Patancala's pupils.

(4) Or the beings.

(5) The cows destined for the best knower of Brahman.

2. स होवाच वायुर्वै गौतम तत्सूत्रं वायुना वै गौतम सूत्रेणायं च लोकः परश्च लोकः सर्वाणि च भूतानि संदृब्धानि भवन्ति तस्माद्वै गौतम पुरुषं प्रेतमाहुर्व्यस्रꣳसिषतास्याङ्गानीति वायुना हि गौतम सूत्रेण संदृब्धानि भवन्तीत्येवमेवैतद्याज्ञवल्क्यान्तर्यामिणं ब्रूहीति ।

He said,—"The wind, O Gautama, is the Thread; by the wind as by a thread are this world, the other world, all beings bound together, O Gautama. Therefore, O Gautama, it is said of a dead man, that his members are relaxed; for by the wind, O Gautama, as by a thread, they are bound together." "This is so, O Yājñavalkya, (now) explain the Inner Ruler."

3. यः पृथिव्यां तिष्ठन् पृथिव्या अन्तरो यं पृथिवी न वेद यस्या पृथिवी शरीरं यः पृथिवीमन्तरो यमयत्येष त आत्मान्तर्याम्यमृतः ।

"He who dwelling in the earth is within the earth, whom the earth does not know (1), whose body is the earth, who within rules the earth, is thy soul, the Inner Ruler, immortal.

(1) The deity of the earth.

4. योऽप्सु तिष्ठन्नद्भ्योऽन्तरो यमापो न विदुर्यस्यापः शरीरं योऽपोन्तरो यमयत्येष त आत्मान्तर्याम्यमृतः ।

"He who dwelling in the waters is within the waters, whom the waters do not know, whose body are the waters, who within rules the waters, is thy soul, the Inner Ruler, immortal.

5. योऽग्नौ तिष्ठन्नग्नेरन्तरो यमग्निर्न वेद यस्याग्निः शरीरं योऽग्निमन्तरो यमयत्येष त आत्मान्तर्याम्यमृतः ।

"He who dwelling in the fire is within the fire, whom the fire does not know, whose body is the fire, who within rules the fire, is thy soul, the Inner Ruler, immortal.

6. योऽन्तरिक्षे तिष्ठन्नन्तरिक्षादन्तरो यमन्तरिक्षं न वेद यस्यान्तरिक्षꣳ शरीरं योऽन्तरिक्षमन्तरो यमयत्येष त आत्मान्तर्याम्यमृतः ।

"He who dwelling in the atmosphere is within the atmosphere, whom the atmosphere does not know, whose body is the atmosphere, who within rules the atmosphere, is thy soul, the Inner Ruler, immortal.

7. यो वायौ तिष्ठन्वायोरन्तरो यं वायुर्न वेद यस्य वायुः शरीरं यो वायुमन्तरो यमयत्येष त आत्मान्तर्याम्यमृतः ।

"He who dwelling in the wind is within the wind, whom the wind does not know, whose body is the wind, who within rules the wind, is thy soul, the Inner Ruler, immortal.

8. यो दिवि तिष्ठन्दिवोऽन्तरो यं द्यौर्न वेद यस्य द्यौः शरीरं यो दिवमन्तरो यमयत्येष त आत्मान्तर्याम्यमृतः ।

"He who dwelling in the heavens is within the heavens, whom the heavens do not know, whose body are the heavens, who from within rules the heavens, is thy soul, the Inner Ruler, immortal."

9. य आदित्ये तिष्ठन्नादित्यादन्तरो यमादित्यो न वेद यस्यादित्यः शरीरं य आदित्यमन्तरो यमयत्येष त आत्मान्तर्याम्यमृतः ।

He who dwelling in the sun, is within the sun, whom the sun does not know, whose body is the sun, who from within rules the sun, is thy soul, the Inner Ruler, immortal.

10. यो दिक्षु तिष्ठन्दिग्भ्योऽन्तरो यं दिशो न विदुर्यस्य दिशः शरीरं यो दिशोऽन्तरो यमयत्येष त आत्मान्तर्याम्यमृतः ।

He who dwelling in the quarters, is within the quarters, whom the quarters do not know, whose body are the quarters, who from within rules the quarters, is thy soul, the Inner Ruler, immortal.

11. यश्चन्द्रतारके तिष्ठꣳश्चन्द्रतारकादन्तरो यं चन्द्रतारकं न वेद यस्य चन्द्रतारकꣳ शरीरं यश्चन्द्रतारकमन्तरो यमयत्येष त आत्मान्तर्याम्यमृतः ।

He who dwelling in the moon and stars, is within the moon and stars, whom the moon and stars do not know, whose body are the moon and stars, who from within rules the moon and stars, is thy soul, the Inner Ruler, immortal.

12. य आकाशे तिष्ठन्नाकाशादन्तरो यमाकाशो न वेद यस्याकाशः शरीरं य आकाशमन्तरो यमयत्येष त आत्मान्तर्याम्यमृतः ।

He who dwelling in the ether, is within the ether, whom the ether does not know, whose body is the ether, who from within rules the ether, is thy soul, the Inner Ruler, immortal.

13. यस्तमसि तिष्ठꣳस्तमसोऽन्तरो यं तमो न वेद यस्य तमः शरीरं यस्तमोऽन्तरो यमयत्येष त आत्मान्तर्याम्यमृतः ।

He who dwelling in the darkness, is within the darkness, whom the darkness does not know, whose body is the darkness, who from within rules the darkness, is thy soul, the Inner Ruler, immortal.

14 यस्तेजसि तिष्ठꣳस्तेजसोऽन्तरो यं तेजो न वेद यस्य तेजः शरीरं यस्तेजोन्तरो यमयत्येष त आत्मान्तर्याम्यमृत इत्यधिदैवतमथाधिभूतम् ।

He who dwelling in the light, is within the light, whom the light does not know, whose body is the light, who from within rules the light, is thy soul, the Inner Ruler, immortal.

This is (his) relation to the gods. Next of (his) relation to the elements.

15. यः सर्वेषु भूतेषु तिष्ठ सर्वेभ्यो भूतेभ्योऽन्तरो यꣳ सर्वाणि भूतानि न विदुर्यस्य सर्वाणि भूतानि शरीरं यः सर्वाणि भूतान्यन्तरो यमयत्येष त आत्मान्तर्याम्यमृत इत्यधिभूतमथाध्यात्मम् ।

He who dwelling in all elements, is within the elements, whom the elements do not know, whose body are the elements, who from within rules the elements is thy soul, the Inner Ruler, immortal. This is (his) relation to the elements. Next of (his) relation to the soul.

16. यः प्राणे तिष्ठन्प्राणादन्तरो यं प्राणो न वेद यस्य प्राणः शरीरं यः प्राणमन्तरो यमयत्येष त आत्मान्तर्याम्यमृतः ।

He who dwelling in the vital air, (1) is within the vital air, whom the vital air does not know, whose body is the vital air, who from within rules the vital air, is thy soul, the Inner Ruler, immortal.

(1) In smell, accompanied by the air of respiration—Ś.

17. यो वाचि तिष्ठन्वाचोऽन्तरो यं वाङ् न वेद यस्य वाक् शरीरं यो वाचमन्तरो यमयत्येष त आत्मान्तर्याम्यमृतः ।

He who dwelling in speech, is within speech, whom speech does not know, whose body is speech, who from within rules speech, is thy soul, the Inner Ruler, immortal.

18. यश्चक्षुषि तिष्ठंश्चक्षुषोऽन्तरो यं चक्षुर्न वेद यस्य चक्षुः शरीरं यश्चक्षुरन्तरो यमयत्येष त आत्मान्तर्याम्यमृतः ।

He who dwelling in the eye, is within the eye, whom the eye does not know, whose body is the eye, who from within rules the eye, is thy soul, the Inner Ruler, immortal.

19. यः श्रोत्रे तिष्ठञ्छ्रोत्रादन्तरो यंश्रोत्रं न वेद यस्य श्रोत्रं शरीरं यः श्रोत्रमन्तरो यमयत्येष त आत्मान्तर्याम्यमृतः ।

He who dwelling in the ear, is within the ear, whom the ear does not know, whose body is the ear, who from within rules the ear, is thy soul, the Inner Ruler, immortal.

20. यो मनसि तिष्ठन्मनसोऽन्तरो यं मनो न वेद यस्य मनः शरीरं यो मनोऽन्तरो यमयत्येष त आत्मान्तर्याम्यमृतः ।

He who dwelling in the mind, is within the mind, whom the mind does not know, whose body is the mind, who from within rules the mind, is thy soul, the Inner Ruler, immortal.

21. यस्त्वचि तिष्ठ॰स्त्वचोऽन्तरो यं त्वङ् न वेद यस्य त्वक् शरीरं यस्त्वचमन्तरो यमयत्येष त आत्मान्तर्याम्यमृतः ।

He who dwelling in the skin, is within the skin, whom the skin does not know, whose body is the skin, who from within rules the skin, is thy soul, the Inner Ruler, immortal.

22. यो विज्ञाने तिष्ठन्विज्ञानादन्तरो यं विज्ञानं न वेद यस्य विज्ञान॰ शरीरं यो विज्ञानमन्तरो यमयत्येष त आत्मान्तर्याम्यमृतः ।

He who dwelling in knowledge, is within knowledge, whom knowledge does not know, whose body is knowledge, who from within rules knowledge, is thy soul the Inner Ruler, immortal.

23. यो रेतसि तिष्ठन् रेतसोऽन्तरो य॰ रेतो न वेद यस्य रेतः शरीरं यो रेतोऽन्तरो यमयत्येष त आत्मान्तर्याम्यमृतोऽदृष्टो द्रष्टाऽश्रुतः श्रोत्राऽमतो मन्ताऽविज्ञातो विज्ञाता नान्योऽतोऽस्ति द्रष्टा नान्योऽतोऽस्ति श्रोता नान्योऽतोऽस्ति मन्ता नान्योऽतोऽस्ति विज्ञातैष त आत्मान्तर्याम्यमृतोऽतोऽन्यदार्तं ततो होद्दालक आरुणिरुपरराम ।

He who dwelling in the seed (1), is within the seed, whom the seed does not know, whose body is the seed, who from within rules the seed, is the soul, the Inner Ruler, immortal. Unseen he sees, unheard he hears, unminded he minds, unknown he knows. There is none that sees, but he, there is none that hears, but he, there is none that minds, but he, there is none that knows, but he (2). He is thy soul, the Inner Ruler, immortal. Whatever is different from him, is perishable. Hence Uddālaka, the son of Aruṇa, became silent.

(1) In procreation.—S'.

(2) *Vide.* Br. Ā., 3, 4, 2, Pras'na U. 419, and Katha U. 6, 12. Muṇḍ. 3, 8 Taitt. 2. 4, Talav. U. 1, 3.

EIGHTH BRĀHMAṆA

1. अथ ह वाचक्नव्युवाच ब्राह्मणा भगवन्तो हन्ताहमिमं द्वौ प्रश्नौ प्रक्ष्यामि तौ चेन्मे वक्ष्यति न वै जातु युष्माकमिमं कश्चिद्ब्रह्मोद्यं जेतेति पृच्छ गार्गीति ।

Then (1) the daughter of Vacaknu said,—" O venerable Brāhmaṇās, I wish to ask him (further) two questions. If he answers them, then indeed none of you will ever defeat him in argument concerning Brahman." (They replied),—" Ask (him), O Gārgi."

(1) This Brāhmaṇa is to show the present, visible Brahman as independent of any attributes.—S'.

2. सा होवाचाहं वै त्वा याज्ञवल्क्य यथा काश्यो वा वैदेहो वोग्रपुत्र उज्ज्यं धनुरधिज्यं कृत्वा द्वौ बाणवन्तौ सपत्नातिव्याधिनौ हस्ते कृत्वोपोत्तिष्ठेदेवमेवाहं त्वा द्वाभ्यां प्रश्नाभ्यामुपोदस्थां तौ मे ब्रूहीति पृच्छ गार्गीति ।

She said,—" As the king of the Kās'is or of the Videhas, the offspring of heroes, when he has bound the string to the stringless bow, rises in sight with two foe-piercing arrows in his hand, so I will rise before thee with two questions. Do thou make answer to me."—"Ask, O Gārgi."

3. सा होवाच यदूर्ध्वं याज्ञवल्क्य दिवो यदवाक् पृथिव्या यदन्तरा द्यावापृथिवी इमे यद्भूतं च भवच्च भविष्यच्चेत्याचक्षते कस्मिꣳस्तदोतं च प्रोतं चेति ।

She said,—"What is above the heavens, O Yājñavalkya, what is beneath the earth, what is between, and what is these two, heavens and earth, and what is called the past, the present and the future,—upon what is all this woven and rewoven?"

4. स होवाच यदूर्ध्वं गार्गि दिवो यदवाक् पृथिव्या यदन्तरा द्यावापृथिवी इमे यद्भूतं च भवच्च भविष्यच्चेत्याचक्षत आकाशे तदोतं च प्रोतं चेति ।

He said,—"What is above the heavens, O Gārgi, what is beneath the earth, what is between, and is these two, heavens and earth, and what is called the past, the present and the future,—all this is woven and rewoven on the ether."

5. सा होवाच नमस्तेऽस्तु याज्ञवल्क्य यो म एतं व्यवोचोऽपरस्मै धारयस्वेति पृच्छ गार्गीति ।

She said,—"I bow to thee, O Yājñavalkya, who hast explained this (question) to me; be prepared for the other." "Ask, O Gārgi."

6. सा होवाच यदूर्ध्वं याज्ञवल्क्य दिवो यदवाक् पृथिव्या यदन्तरा
द्यावापृथिवी इमे यद्भूतं च भवच्च भविष्यच्चेत्याचक्षते
कस्मिँस्तदोतं च प्रोतं चेति ।

She said.—"What is above the heavens, what is beneath the earth, what is between, and what is these two, heavens and earth, and what is called past, present, and future,—upon what is all this woven and rewoven (1)!"

(1) The second question, which is same with the first, is intended firmly to establish the truth declared before.—S'.

7. स होवाच यदूर्ध्वं गार्गि दिवो यदवाक् पृथिव्या यदन्तरा द्यावा-
पृथिवी इमे यद्भूतं च भवच्च भविष्यच्चेत्याचक्षत आकाश एव
तदोतं च प्रोतं चेति कस्मिन्नु खल्वाकाश ओतश्च प्रोतश्चेति ।

He said,—"What is above the heavens, O Gārgi, what is beneath the earth, what is between, and what is these two, heavens and earth, and what is called past, present, and future—is woven and rewoven on the ether." "Upon what then is the ether woven and rewoven?"

8. स होवाचैतद्वै तदक्षरं गार्गि ब्राह्मणा अभिवदन्त्यस्थूलमनण्वह्रस्वम-
दीर्घमलोहितमस्नेहमच्छायमतमोऽवाय्वनाकाशमसङ्गमरसमगन्धम-
चक्षुष्कमश्रोत्रमवागमनोऽतेजस्कमप्राणममुखममात्रमनन्तरमबाह्यं
न तदश्नाति किंचन न तदश्नाति कश्चन ।

He said,—"It is called by the Brāhmaṇas (1) the indestructible one, O Gārgi. (This) is not of a gross body, it is not subtle (2), not long, not wide, not red (3), not viscid (4), not shadow, not darkness, not air, not ether, not adhesive (5), not taste, not smell, not eye, not ear, not speech, not mind, not light, not life, not entrance (6), not measure, not within, not without. It does not consume anything, nor does any one consume it (7).

(1) The Brāhmaṇas are here such as know Brahman.—S'.

(2) Pras'na U., 4, 9. Muṇḍ., I, 5.

(3) Like fire.—S'.

(4) Like water.—S'.

(5) Like lac.—S'.

(6) Not entrance; to whom there is no entrance, unapproachable.

(7) All these negatives are to establish the conviction, that Brahman has no attributes. *Vide* Vāj. S. U. 8, Kaṭha U., 3, 15, Muṇḍ., 1, 6.

9. एतस्य वा अक्षरस्य प्रशासने गार्गि सूर्याचन्द्रमसौ विधृते तिष्ठत एतस्य वा अक्षरस्य प्रशासने गार्गि द्यावापृथिव्यौ विधृते तिष्ठत एतस्य वा अक्षरस्य प्रशासने गार्गि निमेषा मुहूर्ता अहोरात्राण्यर्धमासा मासा ऋतवः संवत्सरा इति विधृतास्तिष्ठन्त्येतस्य वा अक्षरस्य प्रशासने गार्गि प्राच्योऽन्या नद्यः स्यन्दन्ते श्वेतेभ्यः पर्वतेभ्यः प्रतीच्योऽन्या यां यां च दिशमन्वेतस्य वा अक्षरस्य प्रशासने गार्गि ददतो मनुष्याः प्रशꣳसन्ति यजमानं देवा दर्वीं पितरोऽन्वायत्ताः ।

"By the command of this indestructible (being), O Gārgi, sun and moon are upheld in their places (1) by the command of this indestructible (being), O Gārgi, heavens and earth stay upheld in their places ; by the command of this indestructible (being), O Gārgi, minutes, hours, days and nights, the half months, the months, the seasons, the years stay upheld in their places ; by the command of this indestructible (being), O Gārgi, the eastern rivers flow from the snowy mountains (to the eastern quarter) the western (2) to the western quarter, and the others to the quarters, (ordained for them). By the command of his indestructible (being), O Gārgi, men praise the giver, gods follow the sacrificer, (and) fore-fathers the oblation.

(1) Kaṭha U., 6, 2. Taitt. U., 2, 8.

(2) The Gangā, etc. 3 The Sindhu, etc.—S'.

10. यो वा एतदक्षरं गार्ग्यविदित्वास्मिँल्लोके जुहोति यजते तपस्तप्यते बहूनि वर्षसहस्राण्यन्तवदेवास्य तद्भवति यो वा एतदक्षरं गार्ग्यविदित्वास्माल्लोकात्प्रैति स कृपणोऽथ य एतदक्षरं गार्गि विदित्वास्माल्लोकात्प्रैति स ब्राह्मणः ।

" Whoever, ignorant of this indestructible (being), O Gārgi, in this world performs offerings, adores the gods (and) practises austerities even many thousands of years, consumes at last the (fruit of his works). Whoever, ignorant of this indestructible (being), O Gārgi, departs from this world, becomes a miser (1) again ; whoever, knowing this indestructible (being), O Gārgi departs from this world, is a (true) Brāhmaṇa.

(1) Stores up the effect from works, like a miser riches.

11. तद्वा एतदक्षरं गार्ग्यदृष्टं द्रष्टृश्रुतꣳ श्रोत्रमतं मन्त्रविज्ञातं विज्ञातृ नान्यदतोऽस्ति द्रष्टृ नान्यदतोऽस्ति श्रोतृ नान्यदतोऽस्ति मन्तृ नान्यदतोऽस्ति विज्ञात्रेतस्मिन्नु खल्वक्षरे गार्ग्याकाश ओतश्च प्रोतश्चेति ।

"This indestructible (being), O Gārgi, although unseen sees, unheard hears, unminded minds, unknown knows. There is none that sees, but he, there is none that hears, but he, there is none that minds, but he, there is none that knows, but he (1). On this indestructible (being), O Gārgi, the ether is verily woven and rewoven."

(1) Prasna, 4, 8. Talavakāra U., 1, 4—8.

12. सा होवाच ब्राह्मणा भगवन्तस्तदेव बहुमन्येध्वं यदस्मान्नमस्कारेण मुच्येध्वं न वै जातु युष्माकमिमं कश्चिद्ब्रह्मोद्यं जेतेति ततो ह वाचक्नव्युपरराम ।

She said,—"O venerable Brāhmaṇas, highly respect this (my word) and acquit yourself towards him (Yājñavalkya) with salutation. None among you will ever become his conqueror in argument concerning Brahman." Hence the daughter of Vācaknu became silent.

NINTH BRĀHMAṆA

1. अथ हैनं विदग्धः शाकल्यः पप्रच्छ कति देवा याज्ञवल्क्येति
स हैतयैव निविदा प्रतिपेदे यावन्तो वैश्वदेवस्य निविद्युच्यन्ते
त्रयश्च त्री च शता त्रयश्च त्री च सहस्रेत्योमिति होवाच
कत्येव देवा याज्ञवल्क्येति त्रयस्त्रिꣳशदित्योमिति होवाच
कत्येव देवा याज्ञवल्क्येति षडित्योमिति होवाच कत्येव देवा
याज्ञवल्क्येति त्रय इत्योमिति होवाच कत्येव देवा याज्ञवल्क्येति
द्वावित्योमिति होवाच कत्येव देवा याज्ञवल्क्येत्यध्यर्ध
इत्योमिति होवाच कत्येव देवा याज्ञवल्क्येत्येक इत्योमिति
होवाच कतमे ते त्रयश्च त्री च शता त्रयश्च त्री च सहस्रेति ।

Then asked (1) him Vidagdha, the son of S'akala,—"How many gods are there, O Yājñavalkya?" He (answered),—"This can be learnt from the Nivit (2); as many (gods) as are mentioned in the Nivit of the Vais'vadeva (S'astra), (so many are there), (*viz.*,) three and three hundred, and three and three thousand (3,306)" (3) He said,—"Om! How many gods are there, O Yājñavalkya?" "Thirty-three."—He said,—"Om! How many gods are there?" "He said,—"Six." He said,—"Om! How many gods are there, O Yājñavalkya?" "Three." He said,—"Om! How many gods are there, O Yājñavalkya?" "Two." He said—"Om! How many gods are there, O Yājñavalkya?" "Adhyardha" (4). He said,—"Om! How many gods are there, O Yājñavalkya?" "One." He said,—"Om! Which are these three and three hundred, and three and three thousand."

(1) After it has been stated, that the earth, the other elements, etc., by their successively more and more subtle nature are one with regard to another in the state which has been called "woven and rewoven," Brahman has been declared to be within all (Brāhma, 4-6). It has been further stated, that Brahman has the attribute of "Ruler" in the divisions of the thread which pervade the whole manifested world, for all that is manifested requires to be understood, the Ruler as its cause. The present Brāhmaṇa undertakes now to show, how the nature of Brahman as a witness, and as present, can be comprehended by the maximum and minimum numbers of the gods.—S'.

(2) The title of a set of Mantras, defining the number of deities.—S'.

(3) This is no doubt the amount of the number of the text, according to the explanation of S'aṅkara ; the number given in the Tīkā 3,336, is probably owing to the misapprehension of a copyist who added "triṁs'at" (30).

(4) Adhyardha, which is more than half, half of two would be one ; to distinguish it from the next, this term appears to have been chosen ; see the explanation, given in 9.

2. स होवाच महिमान एवैषामेते त्रयस्त्रिꣳशत्त्वेव देवा इति कतमे ते त्रयस्त्रिꣳशदित्यष्टौ वसव एकादश रुद्रा द्वादशादित्यास्त एकत्रिꣳशदिन्द्रश्चैव प्रजापतिश्च त्रयस्त्रिꣳशाविति ।

He said,—"This is even for their glory ; there are (in reality) thirty-three gods." "Which are those thiry-three?" "Eight Vasus, eleven Rudras, twelve Ādityas. These are thirty-one ; besides Indra and Prajāpati. There are thirty-three."

3. कतमे वसव इत्यग्निश्च पृथिवी च वायुश्चान्तरिक्षं चादित्यश्च द्यौश्च चन्द्रमाश्च नक्षत्राणि चैते वसव एतेषु हीदं सर्वꣳ हितमिति तस्माद्वसव इति ।

" Which are the Vasus?" " The fire, the earth, the wind, the atmosphere, the sun, the heavens, the moon, and the stars. These are the Vasus, for upon them this all is founded; this means Vasu, therefore they are called Vasus."

4. कतमे रुद्रा इति दशेमे पुरुषे प्राणा आत्मैकादशस्ते यदास्माच्छरीरान्मर्त्यादुत्क्रामन्त्यथ रोदयन्ति तद्यद्रोदयन्ति तस्माद्रुद्रा इति ।

" Which are the Rudras?" " The ten organs (Prāṇah) in man, and the soul as the eleventh. When they leave this body after death, they weep. Therefore, because they weep (Rodayanti), they are called Rudras."

5. कतम आदित्या इति द्वादश वै मासाः संवत्सरस्यैत आदित्या एते हीदꣳ सर्वमाददाना यन्ति ते यदिदꣳ सर्वमाददाना यन्ति तस्मादादित्या इति ।

" Which are the Ādityas?" " The twelve months of the year are the Ādityas; for taking all this (1) they pass. Because taking all this they pass (ādadānā yanti), therefore they are called Ādityas."

(1) All this, the age of man and the fruit, derived from work.—S'.

6. कतम इन्द्रः कतमः प्रजापतिरिति स्तनयित्नुरेवेन्द्रो यज्ञः प्रजापतिरिति कतमः स्तनयित्नुरित्यशनिरिति कतमो यज्ञ इति पशव इति ।

"Who is Indra, who is Pajāpati?" "The cloud is Indra, the sacrifice is Prajāpati." "Which is the cloud?" "The lightning." "Which is the sacrifice?" "The animals."

7. कतमे षडित्यग्निश्च पृथिवी च वायुश्चान्तरिक्षं चादित्यश्च द्यौश्चैते षडेते हीदꣳ सर्वꣳ षडिति ।

"Which are the six?" "The fire (Agni), the earth, the wind, the atmosphere, the sun and the heavens (1); for they are six; for this all is six."

(1) In this number the moon and the stars are omitted.

8. कतमे ते त्रयो देवा इतीम एव त्रयो लोका एषु हीमे सर्वे देवा इति कतमौ तौ द्वौ देवावित्यन्नं चैव प्राणश्चेति कतमोऽध्यर्ध इति योऽयं पवत इति ।

"Which are the three gods?" "The three worlds (1), for within them all those gods are (comprehended)." "Which are the two gods?" "Food and life." "Which is the Adhyardha?" "He who purifies" (2).

(1) Earth and fire together are here considered as one god, the atmosphere and the wind as the second, and the heavens and Āditya (the sun) as the third god.—Ā. G.

(2) The wind.

9. तदाहुर्यदयमेक इवैव पवतेऽथ कथमध्यर्ध इति यदस्मिन्निदꣳ सर्वमध्यार्ध्नोत्तेनाध्यर्ध इति कतम एको देव इति प्राण इति स ब्रह्म तदित्याचक्षते ।

"Here it is objected, He who purifies, is one even; how then is he Adhyardha" (1). "Because all obtains increase in him (2) therefore is he Adhyardha." "Which is the one god?" "Life; this is called Brahman, this what is beyond" (3).

(1) The objection seems to be made from the literal meaning of Adhyardha, which is "half".

(2) Adhyārdhnodadhi ṛdhim prāpnoti.

(3) *Vid.* 2, 3, 1.

10. पृथिव्येत्र यस्यायतनमग्निर्लोको मनोज्योतिर्यो वै तं पुरुषं विद्यात्सर्वस्यात्मनः परायणꣳ स वै वेदिता स्याद्याज्ञवल्क्य वेद वा अहं तं पुरुषꣳ सर्वस्यात्मनः परायणं यमात्थ य एवायꣳ शारीरः पुरुषः स एष वदैव शाकल्य तस्य का देवतेत्यमृतमिति होवाच ।

"Whoever knows that spirit (Puruṣa), whose abode is the earth, whose place (of sight) (1) is the fire, whose light is the mind,—as the highest locality of every soul, is in truth the one who knows." "I know indeed, O Yājñavalkya, that spirit, the highest locality of every soul, of whom thou speakest. He is the spirit who abides in the body." "Say, O S'ākalya, which is the deity of the same?" He said, "Immortality."

(1) Place (of sight) lokah, lokayati aneneti.—S'.

11. काम एव यस्यायतनꣳ हृदयं लोको मनो ज्योतिर्यो वै तं पुरुषं विद्यात्सर्वस्यात्मनः परायणꣳ स वै वेदिता स्याद्याज्ञवल्क्य वेद वा अहं तं पुरुषꣳ सर्वस्यात्मनः परायणं यमात्थ य एवायं

कामभय: पुरुष: स एष वदैव शाकल्य तस्य का देवतेति स्त्रिय इति होवाच ।

"Whoever knows that spirit, whose abode is desire, whose place (of sight) is the heart (1), whose light is the mind, as the highest locality of every soul, is in truth one who knows." "I know indeed, O Yājñavalkya, that spirit, the highest locality of every soul, of whom thou speakest. He is the spirit, whose nature is desire." "Say, O S'ākalya, which is the deity of the same?" He said,—"Women."

(1) The heart, intellect.—S'.

12. रूपाण्येव यस्यायतनं चक्षुर्लोको मनो ज्योतिर्यो वै तं पुरुषं विद्यात्सर्वस्यात्मन: परायणꣳ स वै वेदिता स्याद्याज्ञवल्क्य वेद वा अहं तं पुरुषꣳ सर्वस्यात्मन: परायणं यमात्थ य एवासावादित्ये पुरुष: स एष वदैव शाकल्य तस्य का देवतेति सत्यमिति होवाच ।

"Whoever knows that spirit whose abode are colours, whose place (of sight) is the eye, whose light is the mind, as the highest locality of every soul, is in truth one who knows." "I know indeed, O Yājña-valkya, that spirit, the highest locality of the whole soul, of whom thou speakest. He is the spirit in the sun." "Say, O S'ākalya, which is the deity of the same?" He said,—"Truth."

13. आकाश एव यस्यायतनꣳ श्रोत्रं लोको मनो ज्योतिर्यो वै तं पुरुषं विद्यात्सर्वस्यात्मन: परायणꣳ स वै वेदिता स्याद्याज्ञवल्क्य वेद

वा अहं तं पुरुषꣳ सर्वस्यात्मनः परायणं यमात्थ य एवायꣳ श्रौत्रः प्रातिश्रुत्कः पुरुषः स एष वदैव शाकल्य तस्य का देवतेति दिश इति होवाच ।

"Whoever knows that spirit, whose abode is the ether, whose place (of sight) is the ear, whose light is the mind,—as the locality of the whole soul, is in truth one who knows." "I know, O Yājñavalkya, the spirit, the locality of the whole soul, of whom thou speakest. He is the spirit who abides in the ear, to whom all hearing is subject." "Say, O S'ākalya, which is the deity of the same?" He said,—"The quarters."

14. तम एव यस्यायतनꣳ हृदयं लोको मनो ज्योतिर्यो वै तं पुरुषं विद्यात्सर्वस्यात्मनः परायणꣳ स वै वेदिता स्याद्याज्ञवल्क्य वेद वा अहं तं पुरुषꣳ सर्वस्यात्मनः परायणं यमात्थ य एवायं छायामयः पुरुषः स एष वदैव शाकल्य तस्य का देवतेति मृत्युरिति होवाच ।

"Whoever knows that spirit, whose abode is darkness, whose place (of sight) is the heart, whose light is the mind,—as the highest locality of the whole soul, is in truth one who knows." "I know indeed, O Yājñavalkya, the spirit, who is the highest locality of the whole soul, of whom thou speakest. He is the spirit, whose nature is shadow." "Say, O S'ākalya, which is the deity of the same?" He said,—"Death."

15. रूपाण्येव यस्यायतनं चक्षुर्लोको मनो ज्योतिर्यो वै तं पुरुषं विद्यात्सर्वस्यात्मनः परायणꣳ स वै वेदिता स्याद्याज्ञवल्क्य वेद

वा अहं तं पुरुषꣳ सर्वस्यात्मनः परायणं यमात्थ य एवायमादर्शे पुरुषः स एष वदैव शाकल्य तस्य का देवतेत्यसुरिति होवाच ।

"Whoever knows the spirit, whose abode are the colours, whose place (of sight) is the eye, whose light is the mind,—as the highest locality of the whole soul, is in truth one who knows." "I know, O Yājñavalkya, the spirit, who is the highest locality of the whole soul, of whom thou speakest. He is the spirit who abides in the looking-glass." "Say, O S'ākalya, which is the deity of the same?" He said,—"The breath."

16. आप एव यस्यायतनꣳ हृदयं लोको मनो ज्योतिर्यो वै तं पुरुषं विद्यात्सर्वस्यात्मनः परायणꣳ स वै वेदिता स्याद्याज्ञवल्क्य वेद वा अहं तं पुरुषꣳ सर्वस्यात्मनः परायणं यमात्थ य एवायमप्सु पुरुषः स एष वदैव शाकल्य तस्य का देवतेति वरुण इति होवाच ।

"Whoever knows the spirit, whose abode are the waters, whose place (of sight) is the heart, whose light is the mind, as the locality of the whole soul, is in truth one who knows." "I know, O Yājñavalkya, the spirit, who is the highest locality of the whole soul, of whom thou speakest. He is the spirit who abides in the waters." "Say, O Sākalya, which is the deity of the same?" He said,—"Varuṇa."

17. रेत एव यस्यायतनꣳ हृदयं लोको मनो ज्योतिर्यो वै तं पुरुषं विद्यात्सर्वस्यात्मनः परायणꣳ स वै वेदिता स्याद्याज्ञवल्क्य वेद वा अहं तं पुरुषꣳ सर्वस्यात्मनः परायणं यमात्थ य एवायं

पुत्रमयः पुरुषः स एष वदैव शाकल्य तस्य का देवतेति प्रजापतिरिति होवाच ।

"Whoever knows the spirit, whose abode is in the semen, whose place (of sight) is the heart, whose light is the mind, as the highest locality of the whole soul, is in truth one who knows." "I know indeed, O Yājñavalkya, that spirit, as the highest locality of the whole soul, of whom thou speakest. He is the spirit who abides in the sun." "Tell, O S'ākalya, which is the deity of the same?" He said,—"Prajāpati."

18. शाकल्येति होवाच याज्ञवल्क्यस्त्वा३ स्विदिमे ब्राह्मणा अङ्गारावक्षयणमक्रता ३ इति ।

Yājñavalkya said,—"O S'ākalya, these Brāhmaṇās have made thee cinders."

19. याज्ञवल्क्येति होवाच शाकल्यो यदिदं कुरुपञ्चालानां ब्राह्मणानत्यवादीः किं ब्रह्म विद्वानिति दिशो वेद सदेवाः सप्रतिष्ठा इति यद्दिशो वेत्थ सदेवाः सप्रतिष्ठाः ।

S'ākalya said,—"O Yājñavalkya, (does this thy boast), that thou hast defeated these Kuru and Pancāla Brāhmaṇās in argument, (arise from a conceit that) thou knowest Brahman?" "I know the quarters with their deities and their localities." "If thou dost know the quarters with their deities and localities,

20. किंदेवतोऽस्यां प्राच्यां दिश्यसीत्यादित्यदेवत इति स आदित्यः कस्मिन् प्रतिष्ठित इति चक्षुषीति कस्मिन्नु चक्षुः प्रतिष्ठितमिति

रूपेष्विति चक्षुषा हि रूपाणि पश्यति कस्मिन्नु रूपाणि प्रतिष्ठितानीति हृदय इति होवाच हृदयेन हि रूपाणि जानाति हृदये ह्येव रूपाणि प्रतिष्ठितानि भवन्तीत्येवमेवैतद्याज्ञवल्क्य ।

Which deity art thou in the eastern quarter?" "The sun." "Where is the sun located?" "In the eye." "Where has the eye its locality?" "In colours; for by the eye colours are seen." "Where is the locality of colours?" He said,—"In the heart; for colours are produced by the heart; the heart therefore is the locality of colour." "Thus is it, Yājñavalkya.

21. किंदेवतोऽस्यां दक्षिणायां दिश्यसीति यमदेवत इति स यमः कस्मिन्प्रतिष्ठित इति यज्ञ इति कस्मिन्नु यज्ञः प्रतिष्ठित इति दक्षिणायामिति कस्मिन्नु दक्षिणा प्रतिष्ठितेति श्रद्धायामिति यदा ह्येव श्रद्धत्तेऽथ दक्षिणां ददाति श्रद्धायाᳫं ह्येव दक्षिणा प्रतिष्ठितेति कस्मिन्नु श्रद्धा प्रतिष्ठितेति हृदय इति होवाच हृदयेन हि श्रद्धां जानाति हृदये ह्येव श्रद्धा प्रतिष्ठिता भवतीत्येवमेवैतद्याज्ञवल्क्य ।

Which deity art thou in the southern quarter?" "The deity of Yama." "Where is the locality of Yama?" "In sacrifice." "Where is the locality of the sacrifice?" "In the bestowal of gifts" (1). "Where is the bestowing of gifts?" "In faith; for if a man have faith, he gives gifts; faith therefore is the locality of bestowal of gifts." "Where is the locality of faith?" "In the heart," said he; "for by the heart he knows faith; the heart therefore is the locality of faith." "Thus is it, O Yājñavalkya.

(1) To the officiating priests, from whom the sacrificer purchases the sacrifice.—Ś.

22. किंदेवतोऽस्यां प्रतीच्यां दिश्यसीति वरुणदेवत इति स वरुणः कस्मिन्प्रतिष्ठित इत्यप्स्विति कस्मिन्न्वापः प्रतिष्ठिता इति रेतसीति कस्मिन्नु रेतः प्रतिष्ठितमिति हृदय इति तस्मादपि प्रतिरूपं जातमाहुर्हृदयादिव सृप्तो हृदयादिव निर्मित इति हृदये ह्येव रेतः प्रतिष्ठितं भवतीत्येवमेवैतद्याज्ञवल्क्य ।

Which deity art thou in the western quarter?" "The deity of Varuṇa." "Where is the locality of Varuṇa?" "In the waters." "Where is the locality of the waters?" "In the semen." "Where is the locality of the semen?" "In the heart; for it is said of a son, who resembles (his father), he is dropped from (his) heart, as it were, he is made of (his) heart, as it were; the heart therefore is the locality of semen." "Thus is it, O Yājñavalkya.

23. किंदेवतोऽस्यामुदीच्यां दिश्यसीति सोमदेवत इति स सोमः कस्मिन्प्रतिष्ठित इति दीक्षायामिति कस्मिन्नु दीक्षा प्रतिष्ठितेति सत्य इति तस्मादपि दीक्षितमाहुः सत्यं वदेति सत्ये ह्येव दीक्षा प्रतिष्ठितेति कस्मिन्नु सत्यं प्रतिष्ठितमिति हृदय इति होवाच हृदयेन हि सत्यं जानाति हृदये ह्येव सत्यं प्रतिष्ठितं भवतीत्येवमेवैतद्याज्ञवल्क्य ।

Which deity art thou in the northern quarter?" "The deity of Soma." "Where is the locality of Soma?" "In the initiatory rite" (1). "Where is the locality of the initiatory rite?" "In truth; for we say concerning a person, who has performed the initiatory rite,—speak the truth; the heart therefore is the locality of the initiatory rite." "Where is the locality of truth?" "In the heart," said he; "for by the heart man knows truth; the heart therefore is the locality of truth." "Thus is it, O Yājñavalkya.

(1) A rite previous to the sacrifice. This may be also rendered, "In the initiatory Mantra," the Mantra which the sacrificer receives previous to the sacrifice.

24. किंदेवतोऽस्यां ध्रुवायां दिश्यसीत्यग्निदेवत इति सोऽग्निः कस्मिन्प्रतिष्ठित इति वाचीति कस्मिन्नु वाक् प्रतिष्ठितेति हृदय इति कस्मिन्नु हृदयं प्रतिष्ठितमिति ।

Which deity art thou in the polar quarter?" (1) "The deity of Agni." "Where is the locality of Agni?" "In speech." "Where is the locality of speech?" "In the heart." "Where is the locality of the heart?"

(1) The quarter which is above those who dwell on the mountain Meru.—Ś.

25. अहल्लिकेति होवाच याज्ञवल्क्यो यत्रैतदन्यत्रास्मन्मन्यासै यद्ध्येतदन्यत्रास्मत्स्याच्छ्वानो वैनदद्युर्वयांसि वैनद्विमथ्नीरन्निति ।

Yājñavalkya said,—"O Ahallika (1), if thou believest at any time that the heart is in any other place than in our (body), if the same is in any other place than in our (body), then why do the dogs not eat it, or the birds not tear it?"

(1) Ahallika, ahani līyate, a being who disappears in the day time, a ghost.—Ś.

26. कस्मिन्नु त्वं चात्मा च प्रतिष्ठितौ स्थ इति प्राण इति कस्मिन्नु प्राणः
प्रतिष्ठित इत्यपान इति कस्मिन्न्वपानः प्रतिष्ठित इति व्यान इति
कस्मिन्नु व्यानः प्रतिष्ठित इत्युदान इति कस्मिन्नूदानः प्रतिष्ठित
इति समान इति स एष नेतिनेत्यात्मागृह्यो नहि गृह्यतेऽशीर्यो
नहि शीर्यतेऽसङ्गो नहि सज्यतेऽसितो न व्यथते न
रिष्यत्येतान्यष्टावायतनान्यष्टौ लोका अष्टौ देवा अष्टौ पुरुषाः
स यस्तान्पुरुषान्निरुह्य प्रत्युह्यात्यक्रामत्तं त्वौपनिषदं पुरुषं
पृच्छामि तं चेन्मे न विवक्ष्यसि मूर्धा ते विपतिष्यतीति तꣳ ह
न मेने शाकल्यस्तस्य ह मूर्धा विपपातापि हास्य
परिमोषिणोऽस्थीन्यपजहुरन्यन्मन्यमानाः ।

"Where art thou and where is self (1) located?" "In the vital air that goes forwards." "Where is the location of the vital air that goes forwards?" "In the descending air." "Where is the location of the descending air?" "In the circulating air." "Where is the location of the circulating air?" "In the ascending air." "Where is the location of the ascending air?" "In the equalising air. This soul, which is neither this, nor that, nor aught else, is intangible, for it is not to be laid hold of; it is not to be dissipated, for it cannot be dissipated; it is without contact, for it does not come into contact; it is not limited; it is not subject to pain, nor to destruction.—There are eight abodes, eight places (of sight), eight deities, and eight Puruṣas. Whoever understands those Puruṣas in their division (2), and again in their union (3), has overcome (the world). I ask thee about the Puruṣas in the Upaniṣads. And thou explain not him to me, thy head will fall off." S'ākalya knew him not so his head fell off. Moreover robbers took away his bones, mistaking them for something else (4).

(1) Atma means here the body.—S'.

(2) In their eight-fold division.—S'.

(3) As they are united in the heart.—S'.

(4) While his body was being carried for the performance of the funeral rites by his disciples to his house—S'.

27. अथ होवाच ब्राह्मणा भगवन्तो यो वः कामयते स मा पृच्छतु सर्वे वा मा पृच्छत यो वः कामयते तं वः पृच्छामि सर्वान्वा वः पृच्छामीति ते ह ब्राह्मणा न दधृषुः ।

Then he said,—"O venerable Brāhmaṇas, let any one among you who wishes it, question me, or do you so all together. Or I will question any one among you who desires it; or I will question you all together." The Brāhmaṇas dared not.

28. तान् हैतैः श्लोकैः पप्रच्छ ॥ यथा वृक्षो वनस्पतिस्तथैव पुरुषोऽमृषा ॥ तस्य लोमानि पर्णानि त्वगस्योत्पाटिका बहिः ॥ त्वच एवास्य रुधिरं प्रस्यन्दि त्वच उत्पटः ॥ तस्मात्तदा तृण्णात्प्रैति रसो वृक्षादिवाहतात् ॥ मांसान्यस्य शकराणि किनाटं स्नाव तत्स्थिरम् ॥ अस्थीन्यन्तरतो दारूणि मज्जा मज्जोपमा कृता ॥ यद्वृक्षो वृक्णो रोहति मूलान्नवतरः पुनः ॥ मर्त्यः स्विन्मृत्युना वृक्णः कस्मान्मूलात्प्ररोहति ॥ रेतस इति मावोचत जीवतस्तत्प्रजायते ॥ धानारुह इव वै वृक्षोऽञ्जसा प्रेत्य संभवः ॥ यत्समूलमावृहेयुर्वृक्षं न पुनराभवेत् ॥ मर्त्यः स्विन्मृत्युना वृक्णः

कस्मान्मूलात्प्ररोहति ॥ जात एव न जायते कोन्वेवं जनयेत्पुनः ॥ विज्ञानमानन्दं ब्रह्म रातिर्दातुः परायणं तिष्ठमानस्य तद्विद इति ।

He questioned them by these S'lokas,—" As the tree is identical with the lord of the forest (1) so is the Puruṣa identical with truth. His hair are the leaves, his skin the external bark. From his skin blood flows, as sap from the bark; therefore if he be hurt, blood proceeds from him, as sap from a wounded tree. The parts of flesh are the layers (2) (of wood); the inner bark is firm like the tendons. The bones are the inner layers of wood; the pith is made like the marrow. If a tree be cut down, it springs up anew from the root. From what root rises mortal (man), if cut down by death? Do not say, from the semen, because this is produced from the living. The tree springs (also) from seed; after it has died away, it is visibly produced (again from seed). If the tree is destroyed together with its roots (3) it does not spring up afresh. If then mortal (man) be cut down by death, from what root shall he spring up? He who has (once) been born, cannot be born (any more). Who (then) produces him afterwards again?" (4)

It is Brahman, who is knowledge and bliss, the highest aim of the giver of wealth (5) (as he is) of that one who abideth (in Him) and knoweth him (6).

(1) "Vanaspati," lord of the forest, is another name for "tree".

(2) This evidently refers to the outer woody layer or alburnum.

(3) Or with its seed.—Ś.

(4) Here is the end of the narrative. The Brāhmaṇās could not answer the question of Yājñavalkya with reference to the last cause of the world, and thereby the superiority of his knowledge was established. In the next sentence the answer is given by Śruti itself—Ś.

(5) Of him who performs ceremonies, of the sacrificer.—Ś.

(6) Of him, who no longer practising rites knows Brahman in his true nature—Ś.

FOURTH CHAPTER

FIRST BRĀHMAṆA

1. जनको ह वैदेह आसांचक्रेऽथ ह याज्ञवल्क्य आवव्राज तꣳ होवाच याज्ञवल्क्य किमर्थमचारीः पशूनिच्छन्नण्वन्तानीत्युभयमेव सम्राडिति होवाच ।

Janaka (1), the king of the Videhās, sat (on his throne). Then came Yājñavalkya. He said,—" Why hast thou come, O Yājñavalkya ? Is it seeking cattle, or subtile (questions) ? " " Even both, O king of kings," said he.

(1) The connection of the two next Brāhmaṇas with the preceding chapter is thus explained by Ṣaṅkara.—It has been stated, that the eight Puruṣas (*Vide* **3**, 9, 10—**17**), are separated from each other, and again, united in the heart; that this again separates into five according to the division of the quarters (l. c. 18—24); again, that they, the heart and the body, in their mutual dependence are one, in the Sūtra or the soul of the world, Samāna by name, whose nature is present in the five vital airs (e. l. 26); and lastly, that the Puruṣa of the Upaniṣad surpasses the soul of the world or the Sūtra and is to be defined by negations, and at the same time (positively) as the present Brahman, and the substantial cause of all in the words " Knowledge and bliss, etc." (e. l. 28). In the next two Brāhmaṇas it will be explained, in what manner this Brahman may again be comprehended by the deities of speech, etc." Ānandagiri

expresses the connection briefly thus.—In the former chapter the nature of Brahman, as existence, knowledge and bliss, has been defined after the manner of wrangling dispute, in the present it is explained in the form of argument.

2. यत्ते कश्चिदब्रवीत्तच्छृणवामेत्यब्रवीन्मे जित्वा शैलिनिर्वाग्वै ब्रह्मेति यथा मातृमान्पितृमानाचार्यवान्ब्रूयात्तथा तच्छैलिनिरब्रवीद्वाग्वै ब्रह्मेत्यवदतो हि किꣳ स्यादित्यब्रवीत्तु ते तस्यायतनं प्रतिष्ठां न मेऽब्रवीदित्येकपाद्वा एतत्सम्राडिति स वै नो ब्रूहि याज्ञवल्क्य। वागेवायतनमाकाशः प्रतिष्ठा प्रज्ञेत्येनदुपासीत का प्रज्ञता याज्ञवल्क्य वागेव सम्राडिति होवाच वाचा वै सम्राड्बन्धुः प्रज्ञायत ऋग्वेदो यजुर्वेदः सामवेदोऽथर्वाङ्गिरस इतिहासः पुराणं विद्या उपनिषदः श्लोकाः सूत्राण्यनुव्याख्यानानि व्याख्यानानीष्टꣳ हुतमाशितं पायितमयं च लोकः परश्च लोकः सर्वाणि च भूतानि वाचैव सम्राट् प्रज्ञायन्ते वाग्वै सम्राट् परमं ब्रह्म नैनं वाग्जहाति सर्वाण्येनं भूतान्यभिक्षरन्ति देवो भूत्वा देवानप्येति य एवं विद्वानेतदुपास्ते हस्त्यृषभꣳ सहस्रं ददामीति होवाच जनको वैदेहः स होवाच याज्ञवल्क्यः पिता मेऽमन्यत नाननुशिष्य हरेतेति।

"Let us hear, what any has taught thee." "Jitvā, the son of S'ilina taught me, speech is Brahman." "As one having an excellent mother, father and teacher, the son of S'ilina taught, speech is Brahman—for of what use is a person who cannot speak? He, no doubt, taught thee his (Brahman's) place and site" (1). "He did not teach me that Brahman is only one-footed (2), O king of kings." "Then, O Yājñavalkya, do thou give us the explanation." "Verily, speech (3) is the place, the ether, the site, the knowledge! In this view (4) let one meditate on him (Brahman)." "What knowledge (5), O Yājñavalkya?" He said,—"Verily, speech, O king of kings. By speech, O king of kings, a friend is made known; (so are made known) the Ṛg-Veda, the Yajur Veda, the Sāma-Veda, the Atharvas and Āṅgirasa, the narratives, the doctrines of creation, the science, the Upaniṣads, the memorial verses, the aphorisms, the explanation of tenets, the explanation of Mantras (6), the fruits of sacrifices, of offerings, of bestowing food, of bestowing drink, this world and the other world and all beings. By speech, O king of kings, is Brahman known; speech, O king of kings, is the supreme Brahman. Speech does not desert him who with this knowledge meditates on that (Brahman); all beings approach him (7); having become a god, verily he goes to the gods!" "I will give thee a thousand cows, big as elephants," said Janaka, the king of the Videhās. Yājñavalkya said,—"My father admonished me—where one does not instruct, one should not take (gifts)."

(1) According to Ś., place (āyatana) means body, and site (Pratiṣṭhā) the continual existence in the past, present and future times, where body seems to denote the transient, and site, the permanent nature of Brahman with regard to time.

(2) This passage is rather obscure and admits of several explanations. The literal translation may be two-fold. First, "he did not tell me so. This Brahman is one-footed, O king of kings". And the apparent meaning is, Thou hast determined Brahman by two attributes, as having place and site. But this is not correct; for, being single in

all respects, Brahman can have only one attribute. This explanation, however, does not agree with the next passage, where speech, representing Brahman, has four attributes, *viz.*, place, ether, site, and knowledge; unless the last attribute (knowledge) be considered as the true one which defines the nature of Brahman. Or secondly,—" He did not tell me, that this (Brahman) is only one-footed,"—as thou supposest it to be, but rather four-footed. S'aṅkara adopts neither of these interpretations, but explains the passage as follows,—" The other, (Yājñavalkya) said,—' *He did not tell me* (so).' The other (the king) said,—' If this is the case, then is *Brahman one-footed*,' ' (The idea of Brahman is without effect, if he be meditated upon as having only three feet, *O king of kings)*'. ' If so, then explain the matter to me according to thy knowledge, O Yājñavalkya.' S.'s explanation agrees in sense, although not in detail, with the second version, above given."

(3) Speech, the speech of Brahman, represented by the deity of speech.—S'.

(4) By this knowledge, being the fourth foot of Brahman of the Upaniṣad.—S'.

(5) This question means, is it knowledge itself, or the cause of knowledge. Is it distinguished from Brahman, as his place and foundation are, or is it not distinguished from him? And the answer implies, that it is not distinguished—S'.

(6) *Vide* p. 179, where the above terms have been explained.

(7) With offerings and presents.

3. यदेव ते कश्चिदब्रवीत्तच्छृणवामेत्यब्रवीन्म उदङ्कः शौल्बायनः
प्राणो वै ब्रह्मेति यथा मातृमान्पितृमानाचार्यवान्ब्रूयात्तथा
तच्छौल्बायनोऽब्रवीत्प्राणो वै ब्रह्मेत्यप्राणतो हि किᳲ स्यादित्य-
ब्रवीत्तु ते तस्यायतनं प्रतिष्ठां न मेऽब्रवीदित्येकपाद्वा
एतत्सम्राडिति स वै नो ब्रूहि याज्ञवल्क्य प्राण एवायतनमाकाशः

प्रतिष्ठा प्रियमित्येनदुपासीत का प्रियता याज्ञवल्क्य प्राण एव सम्राडिति होवाच प्राणस्य वै सम्राट् कामायायाज्यं याजयत्यप्रतिगृह्यस्य प्रतिगृह्णात्यपि तत्र वधाशङ्कं भवति यां दिशमेति प्राणस्यैव सम्राट् कामाय प्राणो वै सम्राट् परमं ब्रह्म नैनं प्राणो जहाति सर्वाण्येनं भूतान्यभिक्षरन्ति देवो भूत्वा देवानप्येति य एवं विद्वानेतदुपास्ते हस्त्यृषभꣳसहस्रं ददामीति होवाच जनको वैदेहः स होवाच याज्ञवल्क्यः पिता मेऽमन्यत नाननुशिष्य हरेतेति ।

"Let us hear, what another has taught thee." "Udaṅka, the son of S'ulba, told me, life is Brahman." "As one having an excellent mother, father and teacher, the son of S'ulba taught, life is Brahman ; for of what use is a person who has no life? He, no doubt, taught thee his place and site." "He did not teach me that Brahman is only one-footed, O king of kings." "Then O Yājñavalkya, give us the explanation." "Life is even the place, the ether, the site, that which is dear to us! In this view let one meditate on him." "What dear object, O Yājñavalkya?" He said,—"Verily life is the dear object, O king of kings. For love of life, O king of kings, one desires what is not desirable, seizes on what is not to be seized ; for the desire of life, O king of kings, arises dread of being killed (1) wherever one goes. Life, O king of kings, is the supreme Brahman. Him who that knowing meditates on that (Brahman), does life not desert ; him all beings approach ; having become a god, he even goes to the gods?"

" I will give thee a thousand cows, big as elephants," said Janaka, the king of the Videhās. Yājñavalkya said,—" My father admonished me—where one does not instruct, one should not take (gifts)."

(1) **From robbers, etc.**

4. यदेव ते कश्चिदब्रवीत्तच्छृणवामेत्यब्रवीन्मे वर्कुर्वार्ष्णश्चक्षुर्वै ब्रह्मेति यथा मातृमान्पितृमानाचार्यवान्ब्रूयात्तथा तद्वार्ष्णोऽब्रवीच्चक्षुर्वै ब्रह्मेत्यपश्यतो हि किꣳ स्यादित्यब्रवीत्तु ते तस्यायतनं प्रतिष्ठां न मेऽब्रवीदित्येकपाद्वा एतत्सम्राडिति स वै नो ब्रूहि याज्ञवल्क्य चक्षुरेवायतनमाकाशः प्रतिष्ठा सत्यमित्येनदुपासीत का सत्यता याज्ञवल्क्य चक्षुरेव सम्राडिति होवाच चक्षुषा वै सम्राट् पश्यन्तमाहुरद्राक्षीरिति स आहाद्राक्षमिति तत्सत्यं भवति चक्षुर्वै सम्राट् परमं ब्रह्म नैनं चक्षुर्जहाति सर्वाण्येनं भूतान्यभिक्षरन्ति देवो भूत्वा देवानप्येति य एवं विद्वानेतदुपास्ते हस्त्यृषभꣳ सहस्रं ददामीति होवाच जनको वैदेहः स होवाच याज्ञवल्क्यः पिता मेऽमन्यत नाननुशिष्य हरेतेति ।

" Let us hear, what another has taught thee." " Varku, the son of Vṛṣṇa, taught me, the eye is Brahman." " As one having an excellent mother, father and teacher, the son of Vṛṣṇa taught, the eye is Brahman; for of what use is one who does not see? He, no doubt, taught thee his place and site." " He did not teach me that Brahman is only one-footed, O king of kings." " Then, O Yājñavalkya, give us the explanation." " Verily the eye is the place, the ether, the site, the truth! In this view let one meditate on him." " Which truth, O Yājñavalkya?" He said,—" The eye,

O king of kings. When one who sees with the eye, is asked, O king of kings, hast thou seen? (Should) he answer, I have seen, then that (which he has seen) is truth. The eye, O king of kings, is the supreme Brahman. The eye not deserts him who with this knowledge meditates on that (Brahman); all beings approach him; having become a god, verily he goes to the gods." "I will give thee a thousand cows, big as elephants," said Janaka, the king of the Videhās. Yājñavalkya said,—"My father admonished me—where one does not instruct, one should not take (gifts)."

5. यदेव ते कश्चिदब्रवीत्तच्छृणवामेत्यब्रवीन्मे गर्दभीविपीतो भारद्वाजः श्रोत्रं वै ब्रह्मेति यथा मातृमान्पितृमानाचार्यवान्ब्रूयात्तथा तद्भारद्वाजोऽब्रवीच्छ्रोत्रं वै ब्रह्मेत्यश्रृण्वतो हि किꣳ स्यादित्यब्रवीत्तु ते तस्यायतनं प्रतिष्ठां न मेऽब्रवीदित्येकपाद्वा एतत्सम्राडिति स वै नो ब्रूहि याज्ञवल्क्य श्रोत्रमेवायतनमाकाशः प्रतिष्ठानन्त इत्येनदुपासीत कानन्तता याज्ञवल्क्य दिश एव सम्राडिति होवाच तस्माद्वै सम्राडपि यां कां च दिशं गच्छति नैवास्या अन्तं गच्छत्यनन्ता हि दिशो दिशो वै सम्राट् श्रोत्रꣳ श्रोत्रं वै सम्राट् परमं ब्रह्म नैनꣳ श्रोत्रं जहाति सर्वाण्येनं भूतान्यभिक्षरन्ति देवो भूत्वा देवानप्येति य एवं विद्वानेतदुपास्ते हस्त्यृषभꣳ सहस्रं ददामीति होवाच जनको वैदेहः स होवाच याज्ञवल्क्यः पिता मेऽमन्यत नाननुशिष्य हरेतेति ।

"Let us hear what another has taught thee." "Gardabhī Vipīta, of the family of Bhāradvāja, taught me, the ear is Brahman" (1). "As one having an excellent mother, father and teacher, Bhāradvāja taught, the ear is Brahman ; for of what use is he who does not hear ? He, no doubt, taught thee his place and site." "He did not teach me that Brahman is only one-footed, O king of kings." "Then, O Yājñavalkya, give us the explanation." "Verily the ear is the place, the ether, the site, the infinite ! In this view let one meditate on him." "What infinite, O Yājñavalkya !" He said,—"Verily the quarters are infinite, O king of kings. Therefore, O king of kings, none comes to the end of any quarter whichsoever ; for the quarters are infinite. The quarters, O king of kings, are the ear ; the ear, O king of kings, the supreme Brahman. The ear not deserts him, who with this knowledge meditates on that (Brahman), all beings approach him ; having become a god, verily he goes to the gods." "I will give thee a thousand cows, big as elephants," said Janaka, the king of the Videhās. Yājñavalkya said,—"My father admonished me—where one does not instruct, one should not take (gifts)."

(1) And thus the eye differs from the other senses, for instance, from the evidence of work where doubt may arise.

6. यदेव ते कश्चिदब्रवीत्तच्छृणवामेत्यब्रवीन्मे सत्यकामो जाबालो मनो वै ब्रह्मेति यथा मातृमान्पितृमानाचार्यवान्ब्रूयात्तथा तज्जाबालोऽब्रवीन्मनो वै ब्रह्मेत्यमनसो हि किꣳस्यादित्यब्रवीत्तु ते तस्यायतनं प्रतिष्ठां न मेऽब्रवीदित्येकपाद्वा एतत्सम्राडिति स वै नो ब्रूहि याज्ञवल्क्य मन एवायतनमाकाशः प्रतिष्ठाऽऽनन्द इत्येनदुपासीत का आनन्दता याज्ञवल्क्य मन एव सम्राडिति

होवाच मनसा वै सम्राट् स्त्रियमभिहार्यते तस्यां प्रतिरूपः पुत्रो जायते स आनन्दो मनो वै सम्राट् परमं ब्रह्म नैनं मनो जहाति सर्वाण्येनं भूतान्यभिक्षरन्ति देवो भूत्वा देवानप्येति य एवं विद्वानेतदुपास्ते हस्त्यृषभꣳ सहस्रं ददामीति होवाच जनको वैदेहः स होवाच याज्ञवल्क्यः पिता मेऽमन्यत नाननुशिष्य हरेतेति ।

"Let us hear, what another has taught thee." "Satyakāma, the son of Jabālā, taught me, the mind is Brahman." "As one having an excellent mother, father and teacher, the son of Jabālā taught, the mind is Brahman; for of what use is he who has no mind? He, no doubt, taught thee his place and site." "He did not teach me that Brahman is only one-footed, O king of kings." "Then, O Yājñavalkya give us the explanation." "The mind is the place, the ether, the site, happiness! By this let one meditate on him." "Which bliss, O Yājñavalkya?" He said,—"Verily the mind, O king of kings. By the mind, O king of kings, one has a desire after a wife; through her a son similar (to one-self) is born; he the son is bliss. The mind, O king of kings, is the supreme Brahman. Mind not deserts him, who with this knowledge, meditates on that (Brahman), all beings approach him; having become a god, verily he goes to the gods." "I will give thee a thousand cows, big as elephants," said Janaka, the king of the Videhās. Yājñavalkya said,—"My father admonished me—where one does not instruct, one should not take (gifts)."

7. यदेव ते कश्चिदब्रवीत्तच्छृणवामेत्यब्रवीन्मे विदग्धः शाकल्यो हृदयं
वै ब्रह्मेति यथा मातृमान्पितृमानाचार्यवान्ब्रूयात्तथा तच्छा-
कल्योऽब्रवीद्धृदयं वै ब्रह्मेत्यहृदयस्य हि किꣳ स्यादित्यब्रवीत्तु ते
तस्यायतनं प्रतिष्ठां न मेऽब्रवीदित्येकपाद्वा एतत्सम्राडिति स
वै नो ब्रूहि याज्ञवल्क्य हृदयमेवायतनमाकाशः प्रतिष्ठा
स्थितिरित्येनदुपासीत का स्थितता याज्ञवल्क्य हृदयमेव
सम्राडिति होवाच हृदयं वै सम्राट् सर्वेषां भूतानामायतनꣳ
हृदयं वै सम्राट् सर्वेषां भूतानां प्रतिष्ठा हृदये ह्येव सम्राट्
सर्वाणि भूतानि प्रतिष्ठितानि भवन्ति हृदयं वैं सम्राट्
परमं ब्रह्म नैनꣳ हृदयं जहाति सर्वाण्येनं भूतान्यभिक्षरन्ति
देवो भूत्वा देवानप्येति य एवं विद्वानेतदुपास्ते हस्त्यृषभꣳ
सहस्त्रं ददामीति होवाच जनको वैदेहः स होवाच
याज्ञवल्क्यः पिता मेऽमन्यत नाननुशिष्य हरेतेति ।

"Let us hear, what another has taught thee." "Vidagdha, of the family of S'ākalya, taught me, the heart is Brahman." "As one, having an excellent mother, father and teacher, S'ākalya taught, the heart is Brahman; for of what use is he who has no heart. He, no doubt, taught thee his place and site." "He did not teach me that Brahman is (only) one-footed, O king of kings." "Then, O Yājñavalkya, give us the explanation." "Verily the heart is the place, the ether, the site, the locality!" "Which locality, O Yājña-valkya?" He said,—"The heart, O king of kings, is the place of all beings; the heart, O king of kings, is the site of all beings; in the heart, O king of kings, are all the beings sited. The heart, O king of kings, is the supreme Brahman. Heart not deserts him who with this knowledge meditates on that (Brahman), all beings approach him; having become a god, verily he goes to the gods." "I will give thee a thousand cows, big as elephants," said Janaka, the king of the Videhās. Yājñavalkya said,—" My father admonished me—where one does not instruct, one should not take (gifts)."

SECOND BRĀHMAṆA (1)

1. जनको ह वैदेहः कूर्चादुपावसर्पन्नुवाच नमस्तेऽस्तु याज्ञवल्क्यानु मा शाधीति स होवाच यथा वै सम्राण्महान्तमध्वानमेष्यन् रथं वा नावं वा समाददीतैवमेवैताभिरुपनिषद्भिः समाहितात्मास्येवं वृन्दारक आढ्यः सन्नधीतवेद उक्तोपनिषत्क इतो विमुच्यमानः क्व गमिष्यसीति नाहं तद्भगवन्वेद यत्र गमिष्यामीत्यथ वै तेऽहं तद्वक्ष्यामि यत्र गमिष्यसीति ब्रवीतु भगवानिति ।

Janaka, the king of the Videhās, (rising) from (his) throne, approached (Yājñavalkya) with humility, saying, —"I bow to thee, O Yājñavalkya, do thou instruct me." He said,—" As one who is going to travel a great distance (takes a chariot or a boat) so art thou prepared in mind (for the knowledge of Brahman) by those Upaniṣads (2); thus art thou venerable, wealthy; thus hast thou read the Vedas, and art instructed in the Upaniṣads (3). (I now ask thee), when liberated from this (body), where art thou to go?" "I know not, O venerable, where I am to go." "Then I will tell thee, where thou art to go." "Say, O Venerable."

(1) In the antecedent Brāhmaṇa have been mentioned some modes of meditations as conducive towards the knowledge of Brahman; the present Brāhmaṇa is to set forth the states of waking, etc., as means of attaining the knowledge of Brahman.—Ā. G.

(2) The term "Upaniṣads" means here of course not the knowledge of Brahman, but certain meditations with regard to Brahman which have been explained in the antecedent Brāhmaṇa.

(3) But though thou art furnished with all these appliances, yet thou hast not attained the highest object of man, unless thou have the knowledge of Brahman.—Ś.

2. इन्धो ह वै नामैष योऽयं दक्षिणेऽक्षन्पुरुषस्तं वा एतमिन्धꣳ सन्तमिन्द्र इत्याचक्षते परोक्षेणैव परोक्षप्रिया इव हि देवाः प्रत्यक्षद्विषः ।

Indha (1) is verily the name of that Puruṣa who dwells in the right eye. Him whose true name is Indha, they call Indra by an indirect name; for the gods like indirect names, and dislike to be named directly (2).

(1) It is intended to show the fourth (or supreme) Brahman by recapitulating what has been said before with reference to Brahman considered as Viśva (or the soul, endowed with a gross body), as Taijasa, (or the soul, endowed with a subtle body) and as Prājña (or the soul endowed with a causal body).—Ā. G.

(2) *Vide* a similar passage in the Aiter. U., 1, 3, 14.

3. अथैतद्वामेऽक्षणि पुरुषरूपमेषास्य पत्नी विराट् तयोरेष सꣳस्तावो य एषोऽन्तर्हृदय आकाशोऽथैनयोरेतदन्नं य एषोऽन्तर्हृदये लोहित-

पिण्डोऽथैनयोरेतत्प्रावरणं यदेतदन्तर्हृदये जालकमिवाथैनयोरेषा सृतिः संचरणी यैषा हृदयादूर्ध्वा नाड्युच्चरति यथा केशः सहस्रधा भिन्न एवमस्यैता हिता नाम नाड्योऽन्तर्हृदये प्रतिष्ठिता भवन्त्येव ताभिर्वा एतदास्रवदास्रवति तस्मादेष प्रविविक्ताहारतर इवैव भवत्यस्माच्छारीरादात्मनः ।

Again, that which in the shape of a Puruṣa dwells in the left eye, is his wife, the Virāṭ (1). The union of them (2) is the ether within the heart (3); again their food is the red lump within the heart; again their place of retreat is the net-work (4) within the heart; again the road to be travelled (5) on, is the artery which rises upwards from the heart. As a hair a thousand times divided thus do its (the body's) veins, called the good (6), become which are located within the heart. Proceeding by these (veins) that (food) proceeds. There is, as it were nourishment yet more subtle than that. From this corporeal soul (is nourished the higher soul) (7).

(1) Vais'vānara, although one, is, in the present sentence and in the preceding section, represented as a couple, *viz.*, Indra and Indrāṇi, for the purpose of meditating upon him—Ā. G. That Ā. is right, is evident from the term Virāṭ, another name of Vais'vānara, which refers to both Indra and Indrāṇi and points out the idea according to which they are to be comprehended as one.

(2) The union of Indra and Indrāṇi, which in the state of waking is called Vis'va (Vais'vānara, Virāṭ), bears in the state of dream the name of Taijasa.—Ā. G.

(3) The union of them (as Taijasa) takes place in the ether of the heart and the heart is here the lump of flesh on

which they subsist. To understand this it is necessary to know the different kinds of food for the different parts of the body. Food undergoes a double modification by the process of digestion, a gross and a more subtile one. The product of the former is carried off by excretion. The product of the latter is again modified by the digestive heat and converted into two juices. The one juice of mean subtlety, consisting of the five elements, nourishes the gross body by its change into blood, etc. The other juice is very subtle, and constitutes the red lump which, after it has entered the fine blood vessels of the heart, supplies the sustenance of the subtle body of Indra (as Taijasa), when united with Indrāni in the heart.—S'.

(4) It is like a net-work from the countless number of apertures between the subtle blood-vessels.—S'.

(5) The road from the place of waking to the place of dream.—S'.

(6) *Vide* Aitt. U., 1, 3, 14.

(7) Or, there is yet (a higher soul) than the one mentioned, whose food (the food of the higher soul) is more subtile. The corporeal soul is Vais'vānara, and the higher, Taijasa.

4. तस्य प्राची दिक् प्राञ्चः प्राणा दक्षिणा दिग्दक्षिणे प्राणाः प्रतीची दिक् प्रत्यञ्चः प्राणा उदीची दिगुदञ्चः प्राणा ऊर्ध्वा दिगूर्ध्वाः प्राणा अवाची दिगवाञ्चः प्राणाः सर्वा दिशः सर्वे प्राणाः स एष नेति नेत्यात्माऽगृह्यो नहि गृह्यतेऽशीर्यो नहि शीर्यतेऽसङ्गो न हि सज्जतेऽसितो न व्यथते न रिष्यत्यभयं वै जनक प्राप्तोसीति होवाच याज्ञवल्क्यः स होवाच जनको वैदेहोऽभयं त्वागच्छ-ताद्याज्ञवल्क्य यो नो भगवन्नभयं वेदयसे नमस्तेऽस्त्विमे विदेहा अयमहमस्मि ।

Its (1) eastern quarter are the vital airs that go to the east, its southern quarter the vital airs that go to the south, its western quarter the vital airs that go to the west, its northern quarter the vital airs that go to the north, his ascending quarter the ascending vital airs, his descending quarter the descending vital airs, all quarters are vital airs. This soul which is neither this, nor aught else, which is intangible (2)—for it cannot be laid hold of—, not to be dissipated—for it cannot be dissipated—, without contact—for it cannot come into contact—, not limited, not subject to pain nor to destruction ; this fearless (3) (soul), " O Janaka, is obtained by thee," thus said Yājñavalkya. Janaka, the king of the Videhās, said,—" May that fearless (Brahman) become thy own, O Yājñavalkya, which thou O Venerable, hast taught us. I bow to thee ; let this kingdom of the Videhās and this myself be thine (4).

(1) Taijasa, whose abode is in the heart, when supported by subtle life becomes life (Prāṇa), that is to say, the Prāṇa which is called Prājña (the soul of imperfect knowledge, or the third state of the individual soul, corresponding to the third state of the universal soul, which is called Īśvara, the ruler). This refers to him who knows, and who from the state of Vaiśvānara has gradually obtained the state of Taijasa and of life (Prāṇa).—Ś.

(2) One who thus knows, attains gradually the general soul. When he has identified the individual soul with the universal soul, he obtains the fourth Brahman by such negations as he is not this, he is not that..—Ś. *Vide* Br. Ā., 3, 9, 26.

(3) Fearless, because it is beyond any cause of fear, as birth, death, etc.—Ś.

(4) *Vide* Chh. U., 3, 12, 6 and Katha Up., 1, 27-29.

THIRD BRĀHMAṆA

1. जनकꣳ ह वैदेहं याज्ञवल्क्यो जगाम स मेने न वदिष्य इत्यथ ह यज्जनकश्च वैदेहो याज्ञवल्क्यश्चाग्निहोत्रे समूदाते तस्मै ह याज्ञवल्क्यो वरं ददौ स ह कामप्रश्नमेव वव्रे तꣳहास्मै ददौ तꣳ सम्राडेव पूर्वं पप्रच्छ ।

2. याज्ञवल्क्य किंज्योतिरयं पुरुष इति आदित्यज्योतिः सम्राडिति होवाचादित्येनैवायं ज्योतिषास्ते पल्ययते कर्म कुरुते विपल्येतीत्येवमेवैतद्याज्ञवल्क्य ।

Yājñavalkya (1) went to Janaka, the king of the Videhās. He bethought him, I will not say aught. (It happened that formerly), when Janaka, the king of the Videhās, and Yājñavalkya had held converse together about the fire-offering (2), that Yājñavalkya had given him (permission to ask) a boon. The boon he chose was, to question (Yājñavalkya) according to his pleasure. He granted that boon to him. The king of kings first asked him (3),—"Yājñavalkya, of what light is this Puruṣa (4)?" He said,—"Of the light of the sun, O king of kings. By the light of the sun (man) sits down, walks about, performs his work and returns (home)." "It is even so, O Yājñavalkya."

(1) In his introduction to the present Brāhmaṇa, showing its connection with the preceding section, S'. recapitulates the principal points of the third chapter. The visible and present Brahman is also the supreme Brahman whose nature is knowledge, which is evident from such passages as, "There is none that sees but he" (3, 8, 11). This (Brahman), after he has entered the body, is divided

according to the functions of speech, etc. In the Madhu-kāṇḍa, in the part relating the conversation of Ajātaśatru, Brahman is conceived by the attributes of dominion and enjoyment of life, etc. (2, 4, 17), (as something different from life, etc.). Again in the question of Uṣasta representing him under the attributes of life, etc. (3, 4), he is comprehended in a general manner by such words as, "That which breathes by breath, etc." (l. c.), and in the full power of his nature by the words, "He is the beholder of the beholding". (If it is now asked why he should enter upon a worldly state which is not his true nature, the answer is.) The worldly state of him is the attribute of the supreme one (ignorance). As it is an effect of ignorance if a rope, a desert place, a mother-of-pearl shell, the ether, etc., be respectively considered as a snake, as water, silver, impure, etc., as this is an effect of ignorance, and not their own nature (so is it an effect of ignorance, if a worldly state be attributed to the soul). (Brahman), who is without attribute and unattainable by word (or mind), must be defined by negations, as "He is not this, he is not that, etc.", and is (affirmatively) comprehended as the visible present soul (3,5), pervading all, as the indestructible Brahman (3, 8), as the Inner Ruler (3, 7), as the Puruṣa of the Upaniṣads (3, 9, 26), as the Brahman whose nature is knowledge and bliss" (4, 1). This Brahman is again conceived under the name of Indha (4, 2) as the soul, nourished by subtle food (Vaiśvānara); (again) as the soul of the subtle body (liṅgātma Taijasa), nourished by food, more subtle than that (of Vaiśvānara). Greater than this (or both, Vaiśvānara and Taijasa) is the soul of the world, having the attribute of life. From this again is distinguished by knowledge, the soul of the world, having the attribute of life by the words, —"He is not this, he is not that", as a snake, etc., (is distinguished by knowledge) from a rope, etc., and thus the visible and present Brahman (the fourth) who is within all is comprehended (4, 1). In the same manner has Janaka obtained the fearless Brahman by the succinct instruction of Yājña-valkya according to the doctrine of the Śūtri. There (4, 2), are the states of waking, dream, profound sleep and of the fourth mentioned for another purpose (for the purpose showing the gradual liberation of the soul from the attachment to the world, as the effect of those kinds of meditation.—Ā. G.), *viz.*, Indha (4, 2, 2), he whose nourishment is subtle (4, 2, 3), all life (4, 2, 4), and "He is not this, he is not that," (e. l.). In the present Brāhmaṇa Brahman is to be comprehended by means of the states of waking, dream, etc., through the operation of profound discussion, as the fearless; the existence of the soul (is to be comprehended) by removing any doubt arising from dispute, its nature (is to be comprehended) as independent, pure, similar with light, of omnipotent power as infinite bliss and as being without duality. For this purpose the present Brāhmaṇa is commenced.

(2) And Yājñavalkya was gratified by the king's knowledge.

(3) *I.e.*, On the present occasion the introductory episode of the boon and right to put questions being concluded.

(4) Puruṣa, the being, who consists of the combination of causes and effects, and has head, hands, etc. Of what light, means, by what light as cause does man discharge the business of life. S'.S'. makes here some very good reflections about the nature of this light, whether it is external or internal, separated or not separated from the body; but they are rather S'.'s reflections than those of the Upaniṣad and we will therefore omit them. The progress from one idea to another in the Upaniṣad is very clear, *viz.*, any light which is found in external nature, is incapable of being the cause of the intellectual functions of man, for it ceases to act at certain times; the light by which man acts, must therefore be something distinct from any of them.

3. अस्तमित आदित्ये याज्ञवल्क्य किंज्योतिरेवायं पुरुष इति चन्द्रमा एवास्य ज्योतिर्भवतीति चन्द्रमसैवायं ज्योतिषास्ते पल्ययते कर्म कुरुते विपल्येतीत्येवमेवैतद्याज्ञवल्क्य ।

"Of what light, O Yājñavalkya, is this Puruṣa, when the sun has set." "The moon is even his light. By the moon-light he sits down, walks about, performs his work and returns (home)." "It is even so, O Yājñavalkya."

4. अस्तमित आदित्ये याज्ञवल्क्य चन्द्रमस्यस्तमिते किंज्योतिरेवायं पुरुष इत्यग्निरेवास्य ज्योतिर्भवतीत्यग्निनैवायं ज्योतिषास्ते पल्ययते कर्म कुरुते विपल्येतीत्येवमेवैतद्याज्ञवल्क्य ।

"Of what light, O Yājñavalkya, is this Puruṣa, when the sun has set and the moon has set." "The fire is even his light. By the fire-light he sits down, walks about, performs his work and returns (home)." "It is even so, O Yājñavalkya."

5. अस्तमित आदित्ये याज्ञवल्क्य चन्द्रमस्यस्तमिते शान्तेऽग्नौ किंज्योतिरेवायं पुरुष इति वागेवास्य ज्योतिर्भवतीति वाचैवायं ज्योतिषास्ते पल्ययते कर्म कुरुते विपल्येतीति तस्माद्वै सम्राडपि यत्र स्वः पाणिर्न विनिर्ज्ञायतेऽथ यत्र वागुच्चारत्युपैव तत्र न्येतीत्येवमेवैतद्याज्ञवल्क्य ।

"Of what light, O Yājñavalkya, is this Puruṣa, when the sun has set, the moon has set, and the fire is at rest?" "Speech (1) is even his light. By the light of speech he sits down, walks about, performs his work and returns (home). Therefore, O king of kings, at a time (2), when one cannot distinguish his own hand, he resorts there, whence speech proceeds" (3). "It is even so, O Yājñavalkya."

(1) Speech means here sound, the object of the sense of hearing. When this sense is enlightened reflection is produced in the mind. By the mind effort to obtain external things is made; for by the mind one sees, one hears.—S'.

(2) When it is dark from clouds, or when every other light has ceased to shine.—S'.

(3) Where sound rises, be it the neighing of horses or the braying of donkeys, etc. Speech serves here only as an illustration and includes the other senses.—S'.

6. अस्तमित आदित्ये याज्ञवल्क्य चन्द्रमस्यस्तमिते शान्तेऽग्नौ शान्तायां वाचि किंज्योतिरेवायं पुरुष इत्यात्मैवास्य ज्योतिर्भवतीत्यात्मनैवायं ज्योतिषास्ते पल्ययते कर्म कुरुते विपल्येतीति ।

"Of what light, O Yājñavalkya, is this Puruṣa, when the sun has set, the moon has set, fire is at rest, and speech is at rest?" "Soul (1) (ātmā) is even his light. By the light of the soul he sits down, walks about, performs his work and returns (home)."

(1) Different from the whole of the causes and effects in the body and its parts, manifesting the effects and the causes, like the sun and other external lights, and not manifested by any thing else. It is light which is within and at the same time independent of effects and causes. It is not perceived by the eye or any other organs like the sun, but inferred from its effects.—S'

7. कतम आत्मेति योऽयं विज्ञानमयः प्राणेषु हृद्यन्तर्ज्योतिः पुरुषः स समानः सन्नुभौ लोकावनुसंचरति ध्यायतीव लेलायतीव स हि स्वप्नो भूत्वेमं लोकमतिक्रामति मृत्यो रूपाणि ॥

"Which soul?" (1) "That soul which among the organs has the nature of knowledge, which abides in the heart, and is the Puruṣa who is light (2). He (3), being the same (4) (with the heart) migrates (5) to both worlds (6). He, as it were, thinks; he, as it were, moves (7); for, having become dream (8), he quits this world (9), (he quits) the forms of death (10)."

(1) Although it has been proved, that the soul has an existence, independent (of the gross body), and abides within (the body), yet, seeing that (the sun, etc)., which assists the body in the operation of its functions, is of the same kind (with the body), there may proceed the delusion (that the soul which is light may also be of the same nature with the body, etc., there being no difference between the kinds of assistance), and from the want of distinction the question may arise, is the soul one of the organs, or some thing different from them? Or in other words, though it is proved, that the soul is different from the body, yet all the organs partake of the nature of knowledge, and since no distinction is apprehended between the soul and the organs, the question of the text is necessary, which soul?—S'.

(2) The whole sentence may be explained, according to S'., in a threefold manner:

1. The first part contains the question, "Which soul?" and the second the answer to it, "The Puruṣa who among the organs has the nature of knowledge and is the light of the heart."

2. Or "Which is the soul among the organs that has the nature of knowledge"? The answer in this case is, "The Puruṣa who is light alone, abiding in the heart."

3. Or "Which is the soul that among the organs has the nature of knowledge and in the Puruṣa, who is light alone, abiding in the heart"?

S'aṅkara prefers the first explanation. "Has the nature of knowledge" means, according to him, resembles knowledge or intellect (buddhi), and "heart" the intellect which has its place in the organ of the heart.

(3) He, the Puruṣa. The Puruṣa who is light alone, who manifests all and is manifested by any thing else, cannot be comprehended in the state of waking, since none of the organs is an object of perception, and since from the confusion, arising from the united action of so many causes and effects of the senses, the soul in its nature as light alone cannot be shown. The Upaniṣad, therefore, explains it by means of state of dream.—Ś.

(4) Being the same, or similar. This refers to the "heart," as is clear from the topic and from the relation which the soul has to the heart (or intellect). As light, manifesting red, green, etc., colours, becomes itself red or green, so the Puruṣa, manifesting intellect, manifests thereby the whole body, and by this intellect he becomes also like every other thing.—Ś.

(5) The cause of his migration is his similarity with intellect ; on his own accord such a migration does not take place. He migrates by leaving his present body and entering another and another in endless succession.—Ś.

(6) Both worlds, the future and the present world.

(7) He as it were thinks, that is to say, in reality he does not think or reflect for reflection does not belong to his nature Ś. (and is the effect of his being considered under the attribute of intellect).

(8) He becomes all that intellect becomes and intellect assuming the state of dream, the Puruṣa also assumes it.—Ś.

(9) This world, characterised by the functions practised during waking.—Ś.

(10) Death means, work, ignorance. etc. ; his forms, causes and effects.—Ś.

8. स वा अयं पुरुषो जायमानः शरीरमभिसंपद्यमानः पाप्मभिः
संसृज्यते स उत्क्रामन् म्रियमाणः पाप्मनो विजहाति ।

This Puruṣa (1), when born (2), when assuming a body, is allied to sin (3); when rising upwards, when dying, he lays aside the sins (4).

(1) As the Puruṣa in this body, when assuming the state of dream, quits the forms of death, and remains in his own light, so when born . . . he is allied to sins.—Ś.

(2) When born, when assuming the state of the soul within a body.—Ś.

(3) Sins means causes and effects, depending upon vice and virtue.—Ś.

(4) He lays them aside, he becomes free from them. As the Puruṣa, abiding in one and the same body, in consequence of his similarity with intellect, by assuming and laying aside causes and effects in the form of sin, continually migrates from the state of waking to that of dream and vice versa, so by assuming and laying aside those causes and effects, he continually migrates through birth and death to this and to the other world, until he is finally liberated. It is therefore evident, that the soul, which has the nature of light, is different from sins, as causes and effects, because it is joined to and separated from them.

9. तस्य वा एतस्य पुरुषस्य द्वे एव स्थाने भवत इदं च परलोकस्थानं च सन्ध्यं तृतीयꣳ स्वप्नस्थानं तस्मिन्सन्ध्ये स्थाने तिष्ठन्नेते उभे स्थाने पश्यतीदं च परलोकस्थानं च अथ यथाक्रमोऽयं परलोकस्थाने भवति तमाक्रममाक्रम्योभयान्पाप्मन आनन्दाꣳश्च पश्यति स यत्र प्रस्वपित्यस्य लोकस्य सर्वावतो मात्रामपादाय स्वयं विहत्य स्वयं निर्माय स्वेन भासा स्वेन ज्योतिषा प्रस्वपित्यत्रायं पुरुषः स्वयंज्योतिर्भवति ।

There are even two places of this Puruṣa, this place, and the place of the next world; the place of dream (1), which is between them, is the third. Abiding in the middle place, (man) sees (2) both places, this and the place of other world. In proportion to the endeavour (3) with which one is (striving to obtain) the place of the other world, does he accordingly see sin (4) or bliss. When he sleeps, (when), putting on a rudiment (only) of this world which consists of all elements (5), himself prostrating (his body), himself raising a building (6) by force of his own splendour and manifestation, he sleeps —then becomes this Puruṣa unmingled light.

(1) Dream is not a world, but only the union of two worlds, as the place between two villages is not a village itself.—Ś.

(2) How then it is proved, that there is another world, different from the place of union, or dream? The answer is, because the Puruṣa sees in dream both the present and another world.

(3) The endeavour being considered as the seed from which the tree of the body rises.

(4) Sin, the effect of sin, unhappiness. He sees them in the shape of impressions, received in a former world. What is the proof of this? Because he sees in dream many things, not to be perceived in this birth; for dream means not a perception of things seen before, which is called remembrance. Therefore, beside the places of waking and dream, there exist those two worlds.—Ś.

(5) Which consists of all elements (sarvāvan), admits of a double explanation. Sarvam avati, he preserves all, or sarvāvān=sarvavān, which contains everything. And this element is again the cause of creation.

(6) A dreamlike body.

10. न तत्र रथा न रथयोगा न पन्थानो भवन्त्यथ रथान्रथयोगान्पथः सृजते न तत्रानन्दा मुदः प्रमुदो भवन्त्यथानन्दान् मुदः प्रमुदः सृजते न तत्र वेशान्ताः पुष्करिण्य. स्रवन्त्यो भवन्त्यथ वेशान्तान् पुष्करिणीः स्रवन्तीः सृजते स हि कर्ता ।

No chariots (1) are there (2), no horses, nor roads; then he creates chariots, horses and roads. No pleasures are there, no joys, nor rejoicings; then he creates pleasures, joys and rejoicings. No tanks are there, no lakes, nor rivers; then he creates tanks, lakes and rivers; for he is the agent (3).

(1) What has been said before that the Puruṣa in dream is life alone. is here expressed in another manner.—Ā. G.

(2) There, in dream, where there are no objects of the senses as in waking.—Ś.

(3) He is the agent for the dream-land.—Ś.

11. तदेते श्लोका भवन्ति ॥ स्वप्नेन शारीरमभिप्रहत्यासुप्तः सुप्तानभिचाकशीति ॥ शुक्रमादाय पुनरेति स्थानꣳ हिरण्मयः पुरुष एकहꣳसः ॥

Here apply, these Slokas (1), "In dream, prostrating (2) the body, himself dreamless, he develops the modes of dreaming. After he has assumed the pure (form), the goldlike (3) Puruṣa, the one wanderer, proceeds (4) again to the place (of waking).

(1) Slokas means hear Mantras (memorial verses). They apply here, that is to say, to the view, that the Puruṣa is light alone.

(2) Annihilating the action.

(3) Gold-like, he whose nature is the light of consciousness.—Ś.

(4) As the consequence of his action.—Ś.

12. प्राणेन रक्षन्नवरं कुलायं बहिष्कुलायादमृतश्चरित्वा ॥ स ईयतेऽमृतो यत्र कामꣳ हिरण्मयः पुरुष एकहꣳसः ॥

By (the power of) life (1) preserving (from death) the inferior nest (2), and roaming outside (3) of it, he, the immortal one, the goldlike, Puruṣa, the one wanderer, proceeds where his desire leads him.

(1) Life in its division into the five vital airs.

(2) Nest, the body.

(3) Although the Puruṣa, while yet in the body, sees dreams, yet he is considered to be outside, because he has no connection with it.—Ś.

13. स्वप्नान्त उच्चावचमीयमानो रूपाणि देवः कुरुते बहूनि ॥ उतेव स्त्रीभिः सह मोदमानो जक्षदुतेवापि भयानि पश्यन् ॥

In his dream passing from high to low (1), he, the god, displays manifold forms, either playing with women, or laughing, or beholding fearful sights.

(1) Becoming, as fancy leads him, a good or a brute creature.—Ś.

14. आराममस्य पश्यन्ति न तं पश्यति कश्चनेति तं नायतं बोधयेदित्याहुः दुर्भिषज्यꣳहास्मै भवति यमेष न प्रतिपद्यतेऽथो खल्वाहुर्जागरितदेश एवास्यैष इति यानि ह्येव जाग्रत्पश्यति तानि सुप्त इत्यत्रायं

पुरुषः स्वयंज्योतिर्भवति सोऽहं भगवते सहस्रं ददाम्यत ऊर्ध्वं
विमोक्षाय ब्रूहीति ।

His pleasure-grounds (1) are visible; but he is visible to none; they say, none comprehends the Pervader. Difficult to be cured is the body, when the Puruṣa attains not that (door of the senses) (2). (Some) say indeed, "(his place of dream) is (the same as) his place of waking; for he sees in sleep the same (forms) which he does when awake. This is not so; (for) here the Puruṣa becomes a self-shining light." "I will give thee, O Venerable, a thousand (cows). Speak next of liberation."

(1) Pleasure-grounds in the shape of impressions.—Ś.

(2) I translated thus in accordance with Ś.'s explanation. The meaning is,—If the Puruṣa does not return to the waking state through the same door of the senses through which he entered into the state of dream, if he re-enters in any other manner, then diseases are produced, such as blindness, deafness, etc., which are difficult to cure.

15. स वा एष एतस्मिन्संप्रसादे रत्वा चरित्वा दृष्ट्वैव पुण्यं च पापं च
पुनः प्रतिन्यायं प्रतियोन्याद्रवति स्वप्नायैव स यत्तत्र
किंचित्पश्यत्यनन्वागतस्तेन भवत्यसङ्गो ह्ययं पुरुष इत्ये-
वमेवैतद्याज्ञवल्क्य सोऽहं भगवते सहस्रं ददाम्यत ऊर्ध्वं
विमोक्षायैव ब्रूहीति ।

"Having (1) in the state, where there is perfect bliss (2), enjoyed bliss, wandered about, and seen what is holy and what is sinful (3), he proceeds again in a reverse order to the place of his birth, to Dream. He is not chained by what he sees (4) there (in dream) (5); for the Puruṣa is untouched (thereby)." "This is so, O Yājñavalkya, I will give thee, O Venerable, a thousand (cows). Speak next of liberation."

(1) The proposition at the commencement of this Brāhmaṇa, that the soul is self-shining light, has been proved by the text "There that soul becomes self-shining light". But with regard to the text "Being dream, he quits this world," the meaning is doubtful; for it may be said, he may indeed quit the forms of death, but not for this reason death himself; for it is evident that, although separated from effect and cause, one may yet experience in dream joy, terror, etc., therefore he does not in truth quit death; for death being work, his effects, joy, terror, etc., are visible. And if one of his own nature be bound by death, liberation is not obtained by him, as he cannot be liberated from his own nature. Therefore we must conclude, death cannot be one's own nature, and liberation from him is possible. To show this, is the object of Yājñavalkya in his answer to the question of the king.—S'.

(2) That is to say, in the state of profound sleep; for there none experiences any grief.—S'.

(3) The effects of them.—S'.

(4) Because, in dream, he does not actually do what is holy and evil, he is not chained by either; for good or evil actions and their consequences are not imputed to the mere spectator for them. Therefore in dream he does not only overcome the forms of death, but death himself. He does not act in dream, and is therefore different in nature from death who is work, and therefore he is free from him.—S'.

(5) As is evident from common experience; for no one is blamed or praised for what he does in dream.—S'.

16. स वा एष एतस्मिन्स्वप्ने रत्वा चरित्वा दृष्ट्वैव पुण्यं च पापं च पुनः प्रतिन्यायं प्रतियोन्याद्रवति बुद्धान्तायैव स यत्तत्र किंचित्पश्यत्यनन्वागतस्तेन भवत्यसङ्गो ह्ययं पुरुष इत्येवमेवैतद्याज्ञवल्क्य सोऽहं भगवते सहस्रं ददाम्यत ऊर्ध्वं विमोक्षायैव ब्रूहीति ।

"Having in that dream enjoyed bliss, wandered about, and seen what is holy and sinful, he proceeds again in the reverse order to the place of his birth, to the waking state. He is not chained by what he sees there (1), for the Puruṣa is untouched (2)." "This is so, O Yājñavalkya. Speak next of liberation."

(1) In dream.

(2) Untouched, as being without form.—S'.

17. स वा एष एतस्मिन्बुद्धान्ते रत्वा चरित्वा दृष्ट्वैव पुण्यं च पापं च पुनः प्रतिन्यायं प्रतियोन्याद्रवति स्वप्नान्तायैव ।

Having (1) enjoyed bliss, wandered about and seen what is holy and sinful, during his waking state, he proceeds again in the reverse order to the place of his birth, to dream.

(1) But how can he be untouched in the waking state, as he does good and evil acts and sees their consequences? This is not the case, says S'., for if there is an agent, the notion of agency is admissible. It has been declared, that the soul is a self-shining light, and that, manifested by its own light as cause and effect, it is an agent. Therefore, if he be comprehended under the notion of an agent, attributes are assigned to the soul which it has not of its own nature, and this is done by means of intellect. In this passage the soul is, however, considered, as it exists

in its own nature, and not as represented by attributes taken from its connection with something else.—Ś.

18. तद्यथा महामत्स्य उभे कूलेऽनुसंचरति पूर्वं चापरं चैवमेवायं पुरुष एतावुभावन्तावनुसंचरति स्वप्नान्तं च बुद्धान्तं च ।

As a large fish (1) glides between both banks (2) the right and the left one, so glides the Puruṣa between both boundaries, the boundary of dream and the boundary of the waking state.

(1) That the Puruṣa is not touched by sin, has been shown in the three preceding sections ; this is here illustrated by a simile.—Ś.

(2) Without being seized by the current of the stream.—Ś.

19. तद्यथास्मिन्नाकाशे श्येनो वा सुपर्णो वा विपरिपत्य श्रान्तः संहत्य पक्षौ सल्लयायैव ध्रियत एवमेवायं पुरुष एतस्मा अन्ताय धावति यत्र सुप्तो न कंचन कामं कामयते न कंचन स्वप्नं पश्यति ।

As an eagle (1) or a falcon, roaming in the sky fatigued, folds his wings and is drawn (2) to his nest, so proceeds that Puruṣa to the boundary (3), where, asleep, he desires not any desire, nor sees any dream.

(1) It has been further proved before, that the soul is not in itself the cause of the worldly attributes, and that its worldly state is imputed to it through ignorance ; this, however, has only been described separately, for the soul in its three states, and the identity of the soul has not been shown comprehensively ; to set this forth, is the object of the present section.—Ś.

(2) Of his own accord.

(3) To his own self, free from every wordly attribute and from the distinctions of agent, work or fruit.—S'.

20. ता वा अस्यैता हिता नाम नाडयो यथा केशः सहस्रधा भिन्नस्तावताणिम्ना तिष्ठन्ति शुक्लस्य नीलस्य पिङ्गलस्य हरितस्य लोहितस्य पूर्णा अथ यत्रैनं घ्नन्तीव जिनन्तीव हस्तीव विच्छाययति गर्तमिव पतति यदेव जाग्रद्भयं पश्यति तदत्राविद्यया मन्यतेऽथ यत्र देव इव राजेवाहमेवेदꣳ सर्वोऽस्मीति मन्यते सोऽस्य परमो लोकः ।

His (1) vessels, which are called good, are of the fineness of a hair, a thousand-fold divided, and filled with white (2), blue, yellow, green and red juice. Therefore all the objects of terror, which a man sees when awake, are, through ignorance, fancied by him, (in dream,) when any body seems to kill him, seems to subdue him, an elephant seems to put him to flight (or when) he falls into a pit ; again (3) when he seems to be conscious I am a god, I am king, I am even all this, he has attained his highest place.

(1) It is the nature of the Puruṣa to be free from worldly attributes which are the effects of ignorance. Here the question arises, whether, ignorance belongs to his own nature, or is only accidental ? If it be accidental, liberation from it is possible. Further, is there any evidence of ignorance being accidental, and in what manner is ignorance an attribute of the non-soul ? The present section has the object to show the nature of ignorance.

(2) Food, when digested, becomes blue, if there be an abundance of the airy humour, yellow by an abundance of bile, white by an abundance of phlegm, green by a deficiency of bile, and red by an equal mixture of all the

humours ; and in this manner, the vessels also through which the humours flow, assume the same colour according to Suśruta.—Ā. G. In those very fine vessels, abides the subtle body consisting of 17 parts (the five organs of intellect, the five organs of action, the five vital airs, intellect and mind). Dependent upon the subtle body are all the impressions produced by the belief in the worldly attributes of a higher or lower state.—Ś.

(3) Again . . . I give here in substance the train of Śaṅkara's ideas on this subject. Ignorance being subdued and knowledge prevailing, what is the object of knowledge and what its character? The highest place, the highest state of the soul, is, when it exists as the soul of all in its own inherent nature. On the other hand, if the soul be considered as different from the soul of all, however little the difference may be, the state of ignorance is the consequence. The result of ignorance are the lower worlds down to the state of inanimate matter, where the nature of the soul is not comprehended. Beyond the worlds which are the objects of worldly action, the state of the universal soul, which is all-pervading, and which is without *an Other and without an Out*, is his highest state. Therefore, ignorance being subdued, and knowledge having attained its perfection, the state of the universal soul, liberation occurs. In the same manner ignorance prevailing and knowledge having disappeared, the effect is described in the passage, "When any body seems to kill him." The respective effects, then, of knowledge and ignorance are the state of the universal soul and that of the individual soul. From pure knowledge the state of the universal soul proceeds ; from ignorance, a state which is not universal. Therefore the state of ignorance consists in this, that the universal existing soul is conceived under the notion of the soul which is not universal, and that something, different from the soul, and which does not exist, is substituted for the soul. The nature of ignorance has been explained together with its effects, and the effect of knowledge, the state of the universal soul, has been shown to be opposite to ignorance. We

therefore must conclude, that ignorance is not an attribute of the soul, and that liberation from it is possible.

21. तद्वा अस्यैतदतिच्छन्दा अपहतपाप्माऽभयꣳ रूपं तद्यथा प्रियया स्त्रिया संपरिष्वक्तो न बाह्यं किंचन वेद नान्तरमेवमेवायं पुरुषः प्राज्ञेनात्मना संपरिष्वक्तो न बाह्यं किंचन वेद नान्तरं तद्वा अस्यैतदाप्तकाममात्मकाममकामꣳ रूपꣳ शोकान्तरम् ।

This is his (true) nature, which is free from desire, sin (1) and fear (2). As in the embrace of a beloved wife one is unconscious of aught, from without or within; so, embraced by the all-knowing (3) soul, this Puruṣa is unconscious of all, without or within. This is his (true) nature, when all desires are satisfied, (4) where the (only) desire is for the soul, where there is no desire, where there is no grief.

(1) Sin means here, both sin and virtue.

(2) Though the state, where no fear exists, has been already referred to at the close of the last Brāhmaṇa (p. 325), yet it has been there only enunciated while it is here established by discussion.—S'.

(3) All-knowing, Prājña, the supreme soul according to its own nature.

(4) Knowledge, its object and the agent who knows, not existing, there can be no manifestation of a special knowledge as a desire.—S'.

22. अत्र पिताऽपिता भवति माताऽमाता लोका अलोका देवा अदेवा वेदा अवेदा अत्र स्तेनोऽस्तेनो भवति भ्रूणहाऽभ्रूणहा चाण्डालोऽचाण्डालः पौल्कसोऽपौल्कसः श्रमणोऽश्रमणस्ताप-

सोऽतापसोऽनन्वागतं पुण्येनानन्वागतं पापेन तीर्णो हि तदा सर्वाञ्छोकान्हृदयस्य भवति ।

Then (1) the father is no father, the mother no mother, the worlds no worlds, the gods no gods, the Vedas no Vedas. Then the thief (2) is no thief, the murderer of a Brāhmaṇa (3) no murderer of a Brāhmaṇa, the Caṇḍāla (4) no Caṇḍāla, the Paulkasa no Paulkasa (5), the religious mendicant (S'ramaṇa) no religious mendicant, the ascetic no ascetic; he is unconnected with aught that is holy, he is unconnected with sin; for he is then beyond every grief of the heart (6).

(1) Then, when the Puruṣa has obtained the form, free from ignorance, from desire and from work, of which state profound sleep is the type. And this change takes place, because the notions of a father, mother, etc., express a relation, established by work, which relation of course ceases when work has ceased.—S'.

(2) Thief means here, according to S'., one who steals the gold of a Brāhmaṇa, as indicated by its connection with Bhrūṇaha.

(3) Bhrūṇaha means literally the murderer of an embryo; I have translated it in accordance with S'.'s and Ā. G.'s explanation.

(4) Caṇḍāla, the son of a Brāhmaṇa woman by a S'ūdra.—S'.

(5) Paulkasa, the son of a Kṣatriya woman by a S'ūdra.

(6) Intellect, abiding in the heart.

23. यद्वै तन्न पश्यति पश्यन्वै तन्न पश्यति न हि द्रष्टुर्दृष्टेर्विपरिलोपो विद्यतेऽविनाशित्वान्न तु तद्द्वितीयमस्ति ततोऽन्यद्विभक्तं यत्पश्येत् ।

It is not true, that, being thus, (in profound sleep,) seeing (1), he sees not; he does see; for there is no loss of sight to the see-er, since it is indestructible (2); and there is no second (3), no other separated from him which could see.

(1) But is it no contradiction, that the soul whose nature is perfect knowledge, should not know? It is not, from the reason assigned in the text.—S'.

(2) But here the following inference seems to apply, seeing is an action, as it is performed by the agent who sees, and every action is transient. However, the inference is not applicable; because the seeing is only seeing, and includes no agent. It is the nature of the soul to manifest, and this not through the intercession of an agent, as there is nothing else but the soul.—S'.

(3) It has been declared, that what is known in waking or in dream, is a second, and does not (really) exist, and that no difference is known in profound sleep. If this latter state be the nature of the soul, from what proceeds the difference, and if its nature is to know the difference, why does it not know this difference (in profound sleep)?—S'.

24. यद्वै तन्न जिघ्रति जिघ्रन्वै तन्न जिघ्रति न हि घ्रातुर्घ्रातेर्विपरिलोपो विद्यतेऽविनाशित्वान्न तु तद्द्वितीयमस्ति ततोऽन्यद्विभक्तं यज्जिघ्रेत् ।

It is not true, that, being thus, smelling, he smells not; he does smell; for there is no loss of smell to the smeller, since it is indestructible; and there is no second, no other, separated from him which could smell.

25. यद्वै तन्न रसयते रसयन्वै तन्न रसयते नहि रसयितू रसयतेर्विपरिलोपो विद्यतेऽविनाशित्वान्न तु तद्द्वितीयमस्ति ततोऽन्यद्विभक्तं यद्रसयेत् ।

It is not true, that, being thus, tasting, he tastes not; he does taste; for there is no loss of taste to the taster, since it is indestructible; there is no second, no other, separated from him which could taste.

26. यद्वै तन्न वदति वदन्वै तन्न वदति न हि वक्तुर्वक्तेर्विपरिलोपो विद्यतेऽविनाशित्वान्न तु तद्द्वितीयमस्ति ततोऽन्यद्विभक्तं यद्वदेत् ।

It is not true, that, being thus, speaking, he speaks not; he does speak; for there is no loss of speech to the speaker, since it is indestructible; and there is no second, no other, separated from him which could speak.

27. यद्वै तन्न शृणोति शृण्वन्वै तन्न शृणोति न हि श्रोतुः श्रुतेर्विपरिलोपो विद्यतेऽविनाशित्वान्न तु तद्द्वितीयमस्ति ततोऽन्यद्विभक्तं यच्छृणुयात् ।

It is not true, that, being thus, hearing, he hears not; he does hear; for there is no loss of hearing to the hearer, since it is indestructible; and there is no second, no other, separated from him which could hear.

28. यद्वै तन्न मनुते मन्वानो वै तन्न मनुते न हि मन्तुर्मतेर्विपरिलोपो विद्यतेऽविनाशित्वान्न तु तद्द्वितीयमस्ति ततोऽन्यद्विभक्तं यन्मन्वीत ।

It is not true, that, being thus, minding, he minds not; he does mind; for there is no loss of minding to the minder, since it is indestructible; and there is no second, no other, separated from him that could mind.

29. यद्वै तन्न स्पृशति स्पृशन्वै तन्न स्पृशति नहि स्प्रष्टुः स्पृष्टेर्विपरिलोपो विद्यतेऽविनाशित्वान्न तु तद्द्वितीयमस्ति ततोऽन्यद्विभक्तं यत्स्पृशेत् ।

It is not true, that, being thus, touching, he touches not; he does touch; for there is no loss of touching to the toucher, since it is indestructible; and there is no second, no other, separated from him that could touch.

30. यद्वै तन्न विजानाति विजानन्वै तन्न विजानाति न हि विज्ञातुर्विज्ञातेर्विपरिलोपो विद्यतेऽविनाशित्वान्न तु तद्द्वितीयमस्ति ततोऽन्यद्विभक्तं यद्विजानीयात् ।

It is not true, that, being thus, knowing, he knows not; he does know; for there is no loss of knowing to the knower, since it is indestructible; and there is no second, no other, separated from him that could know.

31. यत्र वान्यदिव स्यात्तत्रान्योऽन्यत्पश्येदन्योऽन्यज्जिघ्रेदन्योऽन्यद्रसयेदन्योऽन्यद्वदेदन्योऽन्यच्छृणुयादन्योऽन्यन्मन्वीतान्योऽन्यत्स्पृशेदन्योऽन्यद्विजानीयात् ।

Wherever some other thing, as it were, exists, there let another see another thing, another smell another thing, another taste another thing, another speak another thing, another hear another thing, another mind another thing, another touch another thing, another know another thing.

32. सलिल एको द्रष्टाऽद्वैतो भवत्येष ब्रह्मलोकः सम्राडिति हैनमनुशशास याज्ञवल्क्य एषास्य परमा गतिरेषास्य परमा संपदेषोऽस्य परमो लोक एषोऽस्य परम आनन्द एतस्यैवानन्दस्यान्यानि भूतानि मात्रामुपजीवन्ति ।

Like water (purified), the one see-er without duality, is the Brahma world (1), "O king of kings"; thus Yājñavalkya instructed him. "This is his highest aim, his highest wealth, his highest world, his highest happiness. Of this happiness, all other beings enjoy only a part."

(1) The Brahma world, the highest world. And this is the state of the soul in profound sleep—S'.

33. स यो मनुष्याणाꣳ राद्धः समृद्धो भवत्यन्येषामधिपतिः सर्वैर्मानुष्यकैर्भोगैः संपन्नतमः स मनुष्याणां परम आनन्दोऽथ ये शतं मनुष्याणामानन्दाः स एकः पितृणां जितलोकानामानन्दोऽथ ये शतं पितृणां जितलोकानामानन्दाः स एको गन्धर्वलोक आनन्दोऽथ ये शतं गंधर्वलोक आनन्दाः स एकः कर्मदेवानामानन्दो ये कर्मणा देवत्वमभिसंपद्यन्तेऽथ ये शतं कर्मदेवानामानन्दाः स एक आजानदेवानामानन्दो यश्च श्रोत्रियोऽवृजिनोऽकामहतोऽथ ये शतमाजानदेवानामानन्दाः स एकः प्रजापतिलोक आनन्दो यश्च श्रोत्रियोऽवृजिनोऽकामहतोऽथ ये शतं प्रजापतिलोक आनन्दाः स एको ब्रह्मलोक आनन्दो यश्च श्रोत्रियोऽवृजिनोऽकामहतोऽथैष एव परम आनन्द एव ब्रह्मलोकः सम्राडिति होवाच याज्ञवल्क्यः सोऽहं भगवते सहस्रं ददाम्यत ऊर्ध्वं विमोक्षायैव ब्रूहीत्यत्र ह

याज्ञवल्क्यो बिभयांचकार मेधावी राजा सर्वेभ्यो मान्तेभ्य उदरौत्सीदिति ।

(The bliss of one) (1) who among men is perfect in limb, wealthy, a sovereign lord of others, and who has the fulness of all human enjoyments, is the highest bliss of men. Further a hundredfold the bliss of men is one bliss of the forefathers who have overcome the worlds (2). Further a hundredfold the bliss of the forefathers who have overcome the worlds, is one bliss of the world of the Gandharvas. Further a hundred-fold the bliss of the world of the Gandharvas is one bliss of the ritual gods (3) who gain their divinity by rites. Further a hundredfold the bliss of the ritual gods is one bliss of those who are gods by birth, and of him who knows the Vedas, and is free from sin and desire. Further a hundredfold the bliss of those who are gods by birth is one bliss of the world of Prajāpati (4) and of him who knows the Vedas, and is free from sin and desire (5). Further a hundredfold the bliss of the world of Prajāpati, is one bliss of the world of Brahma (6) and of him who knows the Vedas and is free from sin and desire (7). Further the highest bliss (8) is even the world of Brahma (9) "O king of kings"; thus said Yājñavalkya. (He said),—"I will give thee, O Venerable, a thousand cows. Speak next of liberation." Then Yājñavalkya was afraid, that the wary king should drive him from all his last positions (10).

(1) *Vide* Taitt. Up., 2, 8, which corresponds almost liter, with this whole section.

(2) Those who by such ceremonies as the Srāddha have obtained the world of the forefathers.

(3) The ritual gods are such as have gained their divinity by the performance of Vedic rites, as the fire-offering, etc.—S'.

(4) Of Prajāpati in the body of the Virāṭ.—S'.

(5) And who at the same time knows this, that is to say, who has meditated on the soul in its form as Virāṭ.—S'.

(6) Or Hiraṇyagarbha.—S'.

(7) And who has also meditated on the nature of Hiraṇyagarbha.—S'.

(8) All the happiness up to that of the world of Brahma, compared with this happiness is like a drop of water, compared with the sea. And this state is gained by him who comprehends himself as the one identical Brahman.—S'.

(9) For the sake of comparison, I give here the scale of the degrees of happiness in the Taitt. Up.,—Man, Gandharvas, Divine Gandharvas, Forefathers, Ritual Gods, Gods by birth, Indra, Bṛhaspati, Prajāpati and Brahman.

(10) From the solutions of the questions which he had given. He was not afraid, because he was deficient in knowledge, but he was afraid that the king who by the acuteness of his understanding always observed some point not yet wholly defined, should, under the pretence of Yājñavalkya's promise to answer any question of the king, allure him to communicate to him all his knowledge.—S'.

34. स वा एष एतस्मिन्स्वप्नान्ते रत्वा चरित्वा दृष्ट्वैव पुण्यं च पापं च
पुनः प्रतिन्यायं प्रतियोन्या द्रवति बुद्धान्तायैव ।

"Having enjoyed bliss (1), wandered about and seen what is holy and sinful during his dream, he proceeds again in the reverse order to the place of his birth, the waking state.

(1) The antecedent exposition (*viz.*, of the waking state, of dream, and profound sleep) serves only as an illustration (of the soul in its bondage and liberation). The following sections undertake to describible liberation and bondage themselves, bondage being like the state of dream and waking, and liberation like profound sleep. The present section (34) seems to be an episode to recapitulate what has been said before about the nature of dream.

35. तद्यथा नः सुसमाहितमुत्सर्जद्यायादेवमेवायꣳ शारीर आत्मा प्राज्ञे नात्मनान्वारूढ उत्सर्जन्याति यत्रैतदूर्ध्वोच्छ्वासी भवति ।

As (1) a well laden cart (2) moves on noisily, so the embodied soul, directed by the omniscient soul (3), at the time, when breathing its last.

(1) Hence to the end of this Brāhmaṇa and the commencement of the next the worldly state of the soul is described. To explain the first proposition that the soul proceeds from the body, of which it is presently possessed, to another body in the same manner as proceeds from dream to the state of waking, an illustration is given,—S'.

(2) Directed by the driver.—S'.

(3) The supreme soul, which is self-shining light in its own nature.—S'.

36. स यत्रायमणिमानं न्येति जरया वोपतपता वाणिमानं निगच्छति तद्यथाम्रं वौदुम्बरं वा पिप्पलं वा बन्धनात्प्रमुच्यत एवमेवायं पुरुष एभ्योऽङ्गेभ्यः संप्रमुच्य पुनः प्रतिन्यायं प्रतियोन्याद्रवति प्राणायैव ।

When it gains its subtle state (1), when it obtains its subtle state by old age or disease, then, as the fruit of the mango tree, or of the glomerate fig-tree, or of the holy fig tree becomes free from its bond (2), becomes free this Puruṣa from those members (3) and proceeds again (4) in the reverse order (5) to its birth-place for (the obtaining of) a body.

(1) At what time does the soul attain this state, by what cause, in what manner, and for what end ? The answer is given as follows. The time is when man assumes the subtle body, the cause of it is either old age or disease, the manner is illustrated by number of similes to show the various ways in which the event may happen, and the end is the assuming of another body.—Ś.

(2) This Puruṣa who abides in subtle body.—Ś.

(3) From the eye and the other members of the body which he does not preserve as before in profound sleep (*vide*. p. 192) (12), by the agency of life.—Ś.

(4) As before, when quitting one body and assuming another.—Ś.

(5) In the order opposite to that of his entrance into the body.—Ś.

37. तद्यथा राजानमायान्तमुग्राः प्रत्येनसः सूतग्रामण्योऽन्नैः पानैरावसथैः प्रतिकल्पन्तेऽयमायात्ययमागच्छतीत्येव~ हैवंविद~ सर्वाणि भूतानि प्रतिकल्प्यन्त इदं ब्रह्मायातीदमागच्छतीति ।

As (1), on the approach of the king, men of violent deeds (2), (and) such as are addicted to every crime, charioteers and governors of villages stand prepared with food and drink and palaces, (saying,) he comes, he approaches, so on (the approach of) the conscious one (3) all beings (4) stand prepared, (saying), this Brahman comes, this Brahman approaches.

(1) But how can the Puruṣa build another body, himself having no power, in absence of any assistants? The present section gives the answer.—S'.

(2) Ugra either means people of a particular tribe or men of violent deeds.—S'.

(3) Evaṃvid, he who knows the fruit derived from work, the worldly soul.—S'.

(4) All beings, such as Āditya, upon whom the existence of body depends, and who render assistance to the organs for the performance of their work.—S'.

38. तद्यथा राजानं प्रयियासन्तमुग्राः प्रत्येनसः सूतग्रामण्योऽभिस-
मायन्त्येवमेवेममात्मानमन्तकाले सर्वे प्राणा अभिसमायन्ति
यत्रैतदूर्ध्वोच्छ्वासी भवति ॥

As, when the king is desirous of coming, men of violent deeds, (and) such as are addicted to every crime, charioteers and governors of villages go to meet him, so at the time of death all the organs (1) go to meet the soul, when breathing its last.

(1) Speech and the rest.—S'.

FOURTH BRĀHMAṆA

1. स यत्रायमात्माबल्यं न्येत्यसंमोहमिव न्येत्यथैनमेते प्राणा
अभिसमायन्ति स एतास्तेजोमात्राः समभ्याददानो हृदय-

मेवान्ववक्रामति स यत्रैष चाक्षुषः पुरुषः पराङ् पर्यावर्ततेऽथारूपज्ञो भवति ॥

When the soul (1), after having come to a state, where it has no strength (as it were) (2), comes to a state of unconsciousness, as it were (3), then the organs go to meet it. Having wholly seized those organs which are throughout resplendent with light (4), the soul enters the heart (5). When the Puruṣa dwelling in the eye (6), altogether returns, then (the soul) is unconscious of colour.

(1) It has been declared, that the Puruṣa is liberated from his bodily members ; at what time and in what manner this liberation takes place, is now more fully to be described.—S'.

(2) No strength ; the want of strength of the body is here transferred to the soul, although in reality it cannot be attributed to it.—S'.

(3) No consciousness, no power of reflection, as reflection also is the effect of the act of transferring ; for to the soul neither reflection nor its absence can be ascribed ; this sense is indicated in the text by the term "as it were".—S'.

(4) They are resplendent by their power of manifestation.—S'.

(5) The heart, the ether of the heart.—S'.

(6) The Puruṣa, dwelling in the eye, is a part of Āditya (the deity of the sun), who for the benefit of the soul in its worldly functions remains in the eye as long as life lasts. After death he quits his office, and is reunited with Āditya.—S'.

2. एकीभवति न पश्यतीत्याहुरेकीभवति न जिघ्रतीत्याहुरेकीभवति न रसयत इत्याहुरेकीभवति न वदतीत्याहुरेकीभवति न शृणोतीत्याहुरेकीभवति न मनुत इत्याहुरेकीभवति न स्पृशतीत्याहुरेकीभवति न विजानातीत्याहुस्तस्य हैतस्य हृदयस्याग्रं प्रद्योतते तेन प्रद्योतेनैष आत्मा निष्क्रामति चक्षुष्टो वा मूर्ध्नो वान्येभ्यो वा शरीरदेशेभ्यस्तमुत्क्रामन्तं प्राणोऽनूत्क्रामति प्राणमनूत्क्रामन्तꣳ सर्वे प्राणा अनूत्क्रामन्ति स विज्ञानो भवति स विज्ञातमेवान्ववक्रामति तं विद्याकर्मणी समन्वारभेते पूर्वप्रज्ञा च ॥

He is one (1); he does not see, as it is said. He is one; he does not smell, as it is said. He is one; he does not taste, as it is said. He is one; he does not speak, as it is said. He is one; he does not hear, as it is said. He is one; he does not mind, as it is said. He is one; he does not touch, as it is said. He is one; he does not know, as it is said. The entrance to the heart becomes luminous (2); through this, when thus illuminated, the soul (3) departs (4) either from the eye, or from the head, or from other parts of the body. When it departs, life departs after it; when life departs, all the organs depart after it. It is endowed with knowledge (5); endowed with knowledge it departs. Knowledge (6) and work and the knowledge of (its) former (life) pervade it wholly.

(1) With all his organs; or they become one with the subtile soul.

(2) Becomes luminous, as in dream, by the light of the soul.—S'.

(3) The soul, characterised by knowledge, and placed in the subtile body.—S'.

(4) From the eye, in order to obtain the world of Āditya, from the head to obtain that of Brahman, and so with regard to the other parts of the body according to man's good or evil actions.—S'.

(5) Endowed with knowledge, *viz.*, with such knowledge as it has in dream, which is a knowledge of impression referring to their respective objects. And this knowledge is the effect of actions, not of the soul.—S'.

(6) Knowledge, which is enjoyed, such as refers to the soul, which is prohibited, such as looking at a naked woman, which is not enjoyed and not prohibited, knowledge of different objects. The same classification applies to work.—Ā. G.

3. तद्यथा तृणजलायुका तृणस्यान्तं गत्वान्यमाक्रममाक्रम्यात्मान-
मुपसꣳहरत्येवमेवायमात्मेदꣳ शरीरं निहत्याविद्यां गमयित्वा-
न्यमाक्रममाक्रम्यात्मानमुपसꣳहरति ॥

As a leech when arrived at the top of a blade of grass, in order to gain another place of support, contracts itself; so the soul, in order to gain another place of support, contracts itself, after having thrown off this body and obtained (that state of) knowledge (1).

(1) Which is founded upon impressions as in a dream.

4. तद्यथा पेशस्कारी पेशसो मात्रामुपादायान्यन्नवतरं कल्याणतरꣳ
रूपं तनुत एवमेवायमात्मेदꣳ शरीरं निहत्याविद्यां गमयित्वा-
न्यन्नवतरं कल्याणतरꣳ रूपं कुरुते पित्र्यं वा गान्धर्वं वा दैवं
वा प्राजापत्यं वा ब्राह्मं वान्येषां वा भूतानाम् ॥

As a goldsmith, taking a piece of gold, forms another shape, which is more new and agreeable, so throwing off this body and obtaining (that state of) knowledge, the soul forms a shape which is more new and agreeable, either suited to the world of the forefathers, or of the Gandharvas, or of the gods, or of Prajāpati, or of Brahma, or of the other beings.

5. स वा अयमात्मा ब्रह्म विज्ञानमयो मनोमयः प्राणमयश्चक्षुर्मयः श्रोत्रमयः पृथिवीमय आपोमयो वायुमय आकाशमयस्तेजोमयोऽतेजोमयः काममयोऽकाममयः क्रोधमयोऽक्रोधमयो धर्ममयोऽधर्ममयः सर्वमयस्तद्यदेतदिदंमयोऽदोमय इति यथाकारी यथाचारी तथा भवति साधुकारी साधुर्भवति पापकारी पापो भवति पुण्यः पुण्येन कर्मणा भवति पापः पापेन। अथो खल्वाहुः काममय एवायं पुरुष इति स यथाकामो भवति तत्क्रतुर्भवति यत्क्रतुर्भवति तत्कर्म कुरुते यत्कर्म कुरुते तदभिसंपद्यते ॥

This soul (1),—which is Brahman (2), which resembles knowledge (3), mind, life (4), eye (5), ear, earth (6), water, air, ether, light, not light (7), desire, not desire (8), wrath, not wrath, virtue, not virtue (9), which resembles all, which is this, which is not this,—becomes as are its work (10), and conduct. He whose works are good becomes good; he whose works are evil becomes evil. By holy works one becomes holy, by evil works, evil. Likewise (others) say (11), this Puruṣa has the nature of desire. As his desire so is his resolve, as his resolve, so is his work, as his work, so is his reward (12).

(1) The soul, which proceeds from the bodily state to another.—S'.

(2) Brahman in his true nature.

(3) Intellect.

(4) The five vital functions.

(5) By the perception of colour, and thus it resembles the other organs by the perception of their objects.

(6) By the assuming of an earthly body.—S'.

(7) Light, by assuming the body of a god, not light, by assuming the body of a brute, etc.—S'.

(8) When discovering, that a desire is wrong.—S'.

(9) Through desire and wrath, etc., man becomes vicious or virtuous, no action being possible without previous desire; by the performance of good or bad actions he becomes all, as the world in its manifested state is the effect of virtue and vice.—S'.

(10) Works, which are expressly enjoined or prohibited, conduct which is not expressly enjoined, or prohibited.

(11) It is true, that vice and virtue are the causes of worldly existence, provided they are preceded by desire, etc. —S'.

(12) Therefore is desire the root of the whole world.—S'.

6. तदेष श्लोको भवति। तदेव सक्तः सह कर्मणैति लिङ्गं मनो यत्र निषक्तमस्य। प्राप्यान्तं कर्मणस्तस्य यत्किंचेह करोत्ययम्। तस्माल्लोकात्पुनरैत्यस्मै लोकाय कर्मण इति नु कामयमानोऽथाकामयमानो योऽकामो निष्काम आप्तकाम आत्मकामो न तस्य प्राणा उत्क्रामन्ति ब्रह्मैव सन्ब्रह्माप्येति ॥

Here applies this memorial verse,—He who is attached (1) (to worldly objects), obtains by means of work the object to which his mind is the cause is attached. Having arrived at the last (effect) of the work which he here performs, he comes from that world again to this world in consequence of (his) work. Thus he who desires (wanders from world to world). But the organs of him who does not desire (2), who has no desires, who is beyond desires, whose desires are satisfied, whose desire is the soul, do not depart (from the body) (3). Being even Brāhman (4), he obtains Brahman (5).

(1) Has a desire to obtain any object.

(2) For he who does not desire, does not act.—S'.

(3) There being no cause for it.—S'.

(4) In this world, although yet remaining in the body.—S'.

(5) After his death.—S'.

7. तदेष श्लोको भवति। यदा सर्वे प्रमुच्यन्ते कामा येऽस्य हृदि श्रिताः। अथ मर्त्योऽमृतो भवत्यत्र ब्रह्म समश्नुत इति। तद्यथाहिनिर्ल्वयनी वल्मीके मृता प्रत्यस्ता शयीतैवमेवेदꣳ शरीरꣳ शेतेऽथायमशरीरोऽमृतः प्राणो ब्रह्मैव तेज एव सोऽहं भगवते सहस्रं ददामीति होवाच जनको वैदेहः॥

Here applies this memorial verse,—"When all desires dwelling in the heart (1) have been quitted, then the mortal becomes immortal (2); (then) he enjoys here (3) Brahman." "As the slough of a snake as (something) dead is abandoned on an ant-hill, so is this body (by the soul). Then this uncorporeal, immortal life (4) is even Brahman, even light" (5). "I will give thee, O Venerable, a thousand (cows)," said Janaka, the king of the Videhās.

(1) In intellect.

(2) The desires which refer to what is not the soul, characterised by ignorance, are death ; by separation from death, immortality ensues.—S'.

(3) In this body.—S'.

(4) Life means here Brahman, the supreme soul.

(5) The self-shining light of the soul, by which the world is manifested.

8. तदेते श्लोका भवन्ति । अणुः पन्था विततः पुराणो माᳲ स्पृष्टोऽनुवित्तो मयैव । तेन धीरा अपि यन्ति ब्रह्मविदः स्वर्गं लोकमित ऊर्ध्वं विमुक्ताः ॥

"Here apply these memorial verses (1),—"The narrow (2), wide-extended (3), ancient (4) road is touched by me, fully obtained by me. On this (road) proceed (5) also the (other) sages who know Brahman, to heaven (6), to (their) place, when liberated from this body.

(1) The following S'lokas are intended to explain more fully the view, obtained in the Mantra Brāhmaṇa, that liberation ensues for him whose only object of desire is the soul and who has the knowledge of Brahman.—S'.

(2) Narrow from the difficulty in discovering it.—S'.

(3) Instead of vitata (wide extended) another reading, mentioned by S'., is vitara (which causes man to turn from the common road to Brahman).

(4) Because it is taught by the eternal S'ruti.—S'.

(5) Proceed to obtain liberation, the effect resulting from the knowledge of Brahman.—S'.

(6) Heaven means here the supreme Brahman.—S'.

9. तस्मिञ्छुक्लमुत नीलमाहुः पिङ्गलꣳ हरितं लोहितं च । एष पन्था ब्रह्मणा हानुवित्तस्तेनैति ब्रह्मवित्पुण्यकृत्तैजसश्च ॥

Here (in this dissent) (1), (Some) call it white, some blue, some yellow, or green, or red (2). The road is fully penetrated by Brahman. On this (road) proceeds he who knows Brahman, who has been a doer of good (3), whose nature is like light.

(1) Among those who are desirous of liberation.—S'.

(2) They consider the road either to be those vessels, like S'uṣumnā, which from the juice they contain (*vide* p. 227 and Chh. U., 8, 6, 1) are white, etc., or to be the same with the path that leads to Āditya. But Brahman is different from any of those colours, the road which leads to him, bears no relation to the world; those, therefore, who proceed by any particular road, as by the eye, the head, or any other part of the body, gain the world of Brahman, etc., but not liberation which is only gained by knowledge of Brahman.—S'.

(3) Who has been a doer of good, thus I translated in accordance with S'.'s correct remark, that he has been so in a former time, before he attained perfect knowledge, as on its attainment, every desire has ceased to exist.

10. अन्धं तमः प्रविशन्ति येऽविद्यामुपासते । ततो भूय इव ते तमो य उ विद्यायाꣳ रताः ॥

Those who worship ignorance (1) enter into gloomy darkness (2), into still greater darkness those who are devoted to knowledge (3).

(1) Those who worship any objects different from the object of knowledge, that is to say, are those who are engaged in action.—S'.

(2) Darkness means any place where the nature of the soul is unknown.—S'.

(3) Knowledge, which has reference to the objects of ignorance, even the knowledge of the three Vedas as they are intended for the performance of work.—S'. *Vide* Vāj S. U. 9 (B. I. vol. 15, p. 73 note), where the same S'loka occurs.

11. अनन्दा नाम ते लोका अन्धेन तमसावृताः । तांस्ते प्रेत्याभि-
गच्छन्त्यविद्वांसोऽबुधो जनाः ॥

To the so-named blissless (1) worlds, covered with gloomy darkness, go all the people, when departing (from this world) who are ignorant, unintelligent (2).

(1) This passage is similar to that in Vāj S., 3, where instead of "blissless" the term "godless" occurs.

(2) Who are incapable of comprehending the soul.—S'.

12. आत्मानं चेद्विजानीयादयमस्मीति पूरुषः । किमिच्छन्कस्य कामाय
शरीरमनुसंज्वरेत् ॥

If one knows (1) the soul (2) so as to comprehend it as his own self, then for what desire or for whose wish should he suffer the ills of the body ?

(1) To extol the knowledge of the soul, the text declares that he who has this knowledge is exempt from bodily ills.—Ā. G.

(2) The supreme soul as his own self.

13. यस्यानुवित्तः प्रतिबुद्ध आत्मास्मिन्संदेह्ये गहने प्रविष्टः । स विश्व-
कृत्स हि सर्वस्य कर्ता तस्य लोकः स उ लोक एव ॥

He whose soul, penetrated (and) illumined by the supreme (Brahman), has entered this (body) which abounds with doubts and perplexities, is the creator of the universe; for he is the lord of all; he is the place of it; he is even the place (1).

(1) One soul of all.—S'.

14. इहैव सन्तोऽथ विद्मस्तद्वयं न चेदवेदीर्महती विनष्टिः । ये तद्विदुरमृ-
तास्ते भवन्त्यथेतरे दुःखमेवापि यन्ति ॥

Being here (1) we know perhaps, (Brahman); if we do not know him, if there be ignorance (of him), then great calamity (2) (ensues). Those who know him become immortal; again (all) others undergo even unhappiness.

(1) That one who knows Brahman has obtained highest object of life, is not only proved by the S'ruti, but also by his own experience.—Ā. G.

(2) Calamity, by being subject to endless transmigrations from one body to another.—S'., *Vide* a similar passage in Kena. U. 2, 5.

15. यदैतमनुपश्यत्यात्मानं देवमञ्जसा । ईशानं भूतभव्यस्य न ततो विजु-
गुप्सते ॥

When a person beholds (his own) soul as god, as the true Ruler of what was and what is to be, then he does not wish to conceal (his self) from him (1).

(1) From the Ruler; for all persons who perceive themselves different from him wish to conceal themselves from God.—S'.

16. यस्मादर्वाक्संवत्सरोऽहोभिः परिवर्तते। तद्देवा ज्योतिषां ज्योति-
रायुर्होपासतेऽमृतम् ॥

Adore him, ye gods, after whom (1) the year by rolling days is completed, the light of lights, as the immortal life.

(1) Ruler, *Vide* Kaṭh. U., 6, 3 and Taitt. U., 2, 8.

17. यस्मिन्पञ्च पञ्चजना आकाशश्च प्रतिष्ठितः। तमेव मन्य आत्मानं
विद्वान्ब्रह्मामृतोऽमृतम् ॥

I, the wise, immortal comprehend as the immortal Brahman, the soul upon which the five (kinds of) beings (1) and the ether (2) are founded.

(1) *Viz.*, the Gandharvas, the fore-fathers, the gods, the Asuras and the Rākṣasas, or the five castes, including the Niṣādas.—S'.

(2) The ether upon which every thing is woven and rewoven.—S'.

18. प्राणस्य प्राणमुत चक्षुषश्चक्षुरुत श्रोत्रस्य श्रोत्रं मनसो ये मनो विदुः।
ते निचिक्युर्ब्रह्म पुराणमग्र्यम् ॥

Those who know him as the life of life, the eye of the eye, the ear of the ear (1), (and) the mind of the mind, have comprehended the old, before existing Brahman.

(1) For by themselves, without the light of Brahman, or all these organs inanimate like a tree or a clod of earth. —S'. *Vide* a similar passage in Kena U., 1, 2, Kaṭha U., 6, 2, and Taitt. U., 2, 8.

19. मनसैवानुद्रष्टव्यं नेह नानास्ति किंचन । मृत्योः स मृत्युमाप्नोति य इह नानेव पश्यति ॥

By the mind is he to be seen (1), in him there is no variety. Whoever sees variety in him, proceeds from death to death (2).

(1) Kaṭha U., 4, 11. S'vet., 4, 17.

(2) *Vide*, a similar passage in Kaṭha U., 4, 10 and 11.

20. एकधैवानुद्रष्टव्यमेतदप्रमेयं ध्रुवम् । विरजः पर आकाशादज आत्मा महान्ध्रुवः ॥

In one manner (only) (1) is to be seen (the being) which cannot be proved (2), which is eternal, without spot (3), higher than the ether (4), unborn, (5) the great eternal soul.

(1) That is to say, in an uniform manner, without any distinction.

(2) It cannot be proved, because it is without difference, uniform; for proof is only possible by means of another thing, but Brahman is one, and there is nothing, beside him. Here appears to be a contradiction,—it cannot be proved, and yet it is known, that is to say, it cannot be comprehended by proof. This objection, however, has here no force, because the prohibition refers to the relation between proof and object of proof concerning common things, but has no authority respecting the S'ruti.—S'.

(3) Without virtue or vice.—S'.

(4) The ether signifies unmanifested state of the world, and "higher" either more subtle or more pervading.—S'.

(5) Unborn, by this epithet all other modifications are excluded, because every thing must have first an origin before it can have any relation.—S'.

21. तमेव धीरो विज्ञाय प्रज्ञां कुर्वीत ब्राह्मणः । नानुध्यायाद्बहूञ्छब्दान्वाचो
विग्लापनꣳ हि तदिति ॥

Knowing (1) him let the wise Brāhmaṇa form his notion after him; let him not meditate on many sounds (2); for words are embarrassing.

(1) Knowing, according to the instruction of the teacher and the S'āstra.

(2) Because plurality is forbidden, and it is said "By Om" meditate on the soul.—S'.

22. स वा एष महाजन आत्मा योयं विज्ञानमयः प्राणेषु य एषोऽन्तर्हृदय आकाशस्तस्मिञ्छेते सर्वस्य वशी सर्वस्येशानः सर्वस्याधिपतिः स न साधुना कर्मणा भूयान्नो एवासाधुना कनीयानेष सर्वेश्वर एष भूताधिपतिरेष भूतपाल एष सेतुर्विधरण एषां लोकानामसंभेदाय तमेतं वेदानुवचनेन ब्राह्मणा विविदिषन्ति यज्ञेन दानेन तपसानाशकेनैतमेव विदित्वा मुनिर्भवति एतमेव प्रव्राजिनो लोकमिच्छन्तः प्रव्रजन्ति एतद्ध स्म वैतत्पूर्वे विद्वाꣳसः प्रजां न कामयन्ते किं प्रजया करिष्यामो येषां नोऽयमात्माऽयं लोक इति ते ह स्म पुत्रैषणायाश्च वित्तैषणायाश्च लोकैषणायाश्च व्युत्थायाथ भिक्षाचर्यं चरन्ति या ह्येव पुत्रैषणा सा वित्तैषणा या वित्तैषणा सा लोकैषणोभे ह्येते एषणे एव भवतः । स एष नेति नेत्यात्मागृह्यो नहि

गृह्यतेऽशीर्यो नहि शीर्यतेऽसङ्गो नहि सज्यतेऽसितो न व्यथते न रिष्यत्येतमुहैवैते न तरत इत्यतः पापमकरवमित्यतः कल्याणमकरवमित्युभे उ हैवैष एते तरति नैनं कृताकृते तपतः ॥

This great (1), unborn soul is the same which abides as the intelligent (soul) in all living creatures, the same which abides as ether (2) in the heart ; in him it sleeps ; it is the subduer of all, the (3) Ruler of all, the sovereign lord of all ; it does not become greater by good works, nor less by evil work. It is the Ruler of all, the sovereign lord of all beings (4) the Preserver (5) of all beings, the bridge (6), the Upholder of the worlds (7) so that they fall not to ruin. In accordance with the word of the Vedas (8) the Brāhmaṇas (9) desire to comprehend him by sacrifice (10), gift, ascetic work (11) and subduing of desires (12). One who knows him thus, becomes a Muni (13). Desiring him as (their) place, the waṇdering mendicants wander about (14). This is indeed the cause of the state of wandering (mendicant), that the ancient sages did not desire offspring (15) (thinking by themselves),—What shall we do by means of offspring. Those to whom, (like) us (16), the soul (17) is the (supreme) place. lead the life of a religious mendicant, after they have abandoned the desire for a son, the desire for wealth and the desire for (heavenly) places ; for the desire for a son is the same as the desire for wealth ; the desire for wealth is the same as the desire for (heavenly) places ; for both are even desires. The soul (18), which is not this, nor that, nor aught else, is intangible ; for it cannot be laid hold of, it is not to be dissipated ; for it cannot be dissipated ; it is without contact, for it does not come into contact ; it is not limited ; it is not subject to pain nor to destruction ; those (19) two do verily not subdue him ; therefore (he does not say,)—I have done evil, or I have done good. He subdues them both ; neither good nor evil deeds agitate him.

(1) Bondage and liberation, together with their causes, have been described in the Mantras, Brāhmaṇas, and S'lokas ; again, the nature of liberation has been fully explained. The present section has the object to show the relation which the whole Veda bears to the knowledge of the supreme Brahman.—S'.

(2) Ether, the abode of intellect and knowledge, or it may be, according to S'., the ether, abiding in the internal organ at the time of profound sleep, that is to say, the supreme soul without attributes, whose nature is knowledge, his own nature. In this his own nature, or in the supreme soul which is called ether, he sleeps.

(3) Of Brahmā, Indra, etc.—S'.

(4) From Brahman down to inanimate matter.—S'.

(5) Of the rules of the castes and orders, etc.—S'.

(6) *Vide* Chh. U., 8, 4.

(7) From the earth up to the Brahma world.--S'.

(8) That is to say, Mantras and Brāhmaṇas.—S'.

(9) The Brāhmaṇas indicate here the three first castes ; for there is no difference between them with regard to knowledge.—S'.

(10) Sacrifice, or ceremonial work in general, although not a direct means of producing the knowledge of Brahman,

is necessary to purify the mind; when the mind is so purified, knowledge is possible, no obstacle opposing it.—S'.

(11) Ascetic work, as the Cāndrāyaṇa, says S'., which is a kind of fasting for the expiation of sin.

(12) Literally, abstaining from food. The three first obligations (sacrifice, gift and ascetic work) include all the permanent works, enjoined by the Vedas, and the last (fasting) on abstaining from desires. By those means, a desire to comprehend the soul is produced.—S'.

(13) Muni, mananāt muni, a Yogi, who, while yet alive, has obtained liberation.—S'.

(14) That is to say, they have abandoned all works.—S'.

(15) Offspring indicates work and the knowledge of the inferior Brahman as the cause of obtaining the three external worlds.—S'.

(16) Like us who have the true knowledge of the soul.—S'.

(17) In its own nature.

(18) If it be admitted, that the soul is the place, why is there a means required for obtaining it, and for what reason is the state of wandering mendicant necessary, since it is said, work should not be entered upon? The answer is, the soul, for whose desire one should enter the state of wandering mendicant has no connection with works. Why? It evidently follows from such negations as, it cannot be seized. Because the soul thus comprehended, *viz.*, independent of work, cause and effect, free from every worldly attribute, beyond every desire, not possessed of grossness and the like attributes, unborn, undecaying, immortal, beyond fear, like a lump of rock-salt, of one uniform nature which is knowledge, a self-shining light, one alone, without duality, without beginning, without end, not within, not without, because this is established by the S'ruti and by discussion, especially by the conversation between Janaka

and Yājñavalkya, therefore, it is also established, that no work is entered into, if the soul be thus comprehended.—Ś.

(19) Sin and virtue.

23. तदेतदृचाभ्युक्तम्। एष नित्यो महिमा ब्राह्मणस्य न वर्धते कर्मणा नो कनीयान्। तस्यैव स्यात्पदवित्तं विदित्वा न लिप्यते कर्मणा पापकेनेति तस्मादेवंविच्छान्तो दान्त उपरतस्तितिक्षुः समाहितो भूत्वात्मन्येवात्मानं पश्यति सर्वमात्मानं पश्यति नैनं पाप्मा तरति सर्वं पाप्मानं तरति नैनं पाप्मा तपति सर्वं पाप्मानं तपति विपापो विरजोऽविचिकित्सो ब्राह्मणो भवत्येष ब्रह्मलोकः सम्राडेनं प्रापितोऽसीति होवाच याज्ञवल्क्यः सोऽहं भगवते विदेहान् ददामि मां चापि सह दास्यायेति ॥

The same (1) is said in the following Ṛk,—"The eternal greatness of the Brāhmaṇa is neither increased by work (2), nor diminished (3). Let him even know the nature of that (greatness); knowing that (greatness), he is not stained by evil work (4). Therefore one who thus knows, who has subdued his senses (5), who is calm (6), free from all desires, enduring (7), and composed in mind (8), beholds the soul in the soul alone, beholds the whole soul; sin does not subdue him; he subdues sin; sin does not consume him; he consumes sin (9). He is free from sin, free from doubt, he is pure, he is the (true) Brāhmaṇa; this is the (true) world of Brahman, O king of kings," thus spoke Yājñavalkya. "I will give thee, O Venerable, the kingdom of the Videhās, and my own self, to become thy slave."

(1) The same which has been said in the Brāhmaṇa, is also declared in a Mantra.—S'.

(2) By good work.

(3) By evil work.

(4) Or exalted by good work.

(5) The external senses.—S'.

(6) Who has overcome the desires of the internal organ.—S'.

(7) Capable of bearing such opposite agents, as hunger and thirst, heat and cold, etc.—S'.

(8) Having fixed his attention upon one point only.—S'.

(9) He consumes sin by the fire of the knowledge of the soul.—S'.

24. स वा एष महानज आत्मान्नादो वसुदानो विन्दते वसु य एवं वेद ॥

This soul (1) is great, unborn, the consumer of food (2), the giver of wealth. Whoever thus knows, obtains wealth.

(1) That is to say, the soul whose nature has been explained in the conversation between Janaka and Yājña-valkya.—S'.

(2) Abiding in all beings, consuming every food.

25 स वा एष महानज आत्माजरोऽमरोऽमृतोऽभयो ब्रह्माभयं वै ब्रह्मा-
भयꣳ हि वै ब्रह्मा भवति य एवं वेद ॥

This (1) great, unborn, undecaying, immortal, fearless soul is Brahman; Brahman is verily fearless;

he who thus knows becomes verily the fearless Brahman.

(1) The meaning of the whole Āraṇyaka is expressed in the present section.—S'.

FIFTH BRĀHMAṆA (1)

1. अथ ह याज्ञवल्क्यस्य द्वे भार्ये बभूवतुर्मैत्रेयी च कात्यायनी च तयोर्ह मैत्रेयी ब्रह्मवादिनी बभूव स्त्रीप्रज्ञैव तर्हि कात्यायन्यथ ह याज्ञवल्क्योऽन्यद्वृत्तमुपाकरिष्यन् ॥

Yājñavalkya then had two wives, Maitreyī and Kātyāyanī. Among them, Maitreyī was fond of discussing the nature of Brahman, Kātyāyani wise in the duties of a house-wife. Yājñavalkya was desirous of attaining another order superior (to that of householder).

(1) The present Brāhmaṇa, with the exception of the first section and part of the fourteenth and fifteenth sections, is a literal repetition of the fourth Brāhmaṇa in the second chapter, *vide* pp. 235-244. S'aṅkara's explanation of this circumstance is ingenious, although somewhat strained. We give it here in order that the reader may judge for himself. The nature of Brahman has been determined in the Madhukāṇḍa, the principal part of the S'āstra, and also in the Brahmakāṇḍa. Again it has been thoroughly sifted by discussion in the Yājñavalkyakāṇḍa, which is the principal part as to the method by which that knowledge is acquired. And lastly, it has been declared after full discussion by means of the relation between disciple and teacher in the fourth chapter. The Maitreyī Brāhmaṇa

serves there to show the conclusion after the manner of the logicians, who define a conclusion to be "the repetition of the proposition, because the reason has been stated". (Nyāya Sūtras, 1, 38.) The proposition, here referred to, is that the knowledge of Brahman, when accompanied with the renunciation of the world is the means by which immortality is attained.

2. मैत्रेयीति होवाच याज्ञवल्क्यः प्रव्रजिष्यन्वा अरेऽयमस्मात्स्थानादस्मि हन्त तेऽनया कात्यायन्यान्तं करवाणीति ॥

"Maitreyī," said Yājñavalkya, "Behold, I am desirous of quitting this order for that of a wandering mendicant; therefore, let me divide (my property) amongst thee and Kātyāyanī there."

3. सा होवाच मैत्रेयी यन्नु म इयं भगोः सर्वा पृथिवी वित्तेन पूर्णा स्यात्स्यां न्वहं तेनामृताहो३ नेति नेति होवाच याज्ञवल्क्यो यथैवोपकरणवतां जीवितं तथैव ते जीवितꣳ स्यादमृतत्वस्य तु नाशास्ति वित्तेनेति ॥

Maitreyī said,—"If, O Venerable, this whole world with all its wealth were mine, could I become immortal thereby?" Yājñavalkya said, "By no means. Like the life of the wealthy thy life might become; by wealth, however, there is no hope of (obtaining) immortality."

4. सा होवाच मैत्रेयी येनाहं नामृता स्यां किमहं तेन कुर्यां यदेव भगवान्वेद तदेव मे विब्रूहीति ॥

Maitreyī said,—"Of what use would be wealth to me, if I did not become thereby immortal. Tell me, O

Venerable, any (means of obtaining immortality) which thou knowest."

5. स होवाच याज्ञवल्क्यः प्रिया वै खलु नो भवती सती प्रियमवृधद्धन्त तर्हि भवत्येतद्व्याख्यास्यामि ते व्याचक्षाणस्य ते मे निदिध्यासस्वेति ॥

Yājñavalkya said,—"Behold, (thou wast) dear to us before (and now) sayest thou what is dear. Come, sit down; I will explain to thee (the means of obtaining immortality); endeavour to comprehend my explanation."

6. स होवाच न वा अरे पत्युः कामाय पतिः प्रियो भवत्यात्मनस्तु कामाय पतिः प्रियो भवति न वा अरे जायायै कामाय जाया प्रिया भवत्यात्मनस्तु कामाय जाया प्रिया भवति न वा अरे पुत्राणां कामाय पुत्राः प्रिया भवन्त्यात्मनस्तु कामाय पुत्राः प्रिया भवन्ति न वा अरे वित्तस्य कामाय वित्तं प्रियं भवत्यात्मनस्तु कामाय वित्तं प्रियं भवति न वा अरे पशूनां कामाय पशवः प्रिया भवन्त्यात्मनस्तु कामाय पशवः प्रिया भवन्ति न वा अरे ब्रह्मणः कामाय ब्रह्म प्रियं भवत्यात्मनस्तु कामाय ब्रह्म प्रियं भवति न वा अरे क्षत्रस्य कामाय क्षत्रं प्रियं भवत्यात्मनस्तु कामाय क्षत्रं प्रियं भवति न वा अरे लोकानां कामाय लोकाः प्रिया भवन्त्यात्मनस्तु कामाय लोकाः प्रिया भवन्ति न वा अरे देवानां कामाय देवाः प्रिया भवन्त्यात्मनस्तु कामाय देवाः प्रिया भवन्ति न वा अरे वेदानां कामाय वेदाः प्रिया भवन्त्यात्मनस्तु कामाय वेदाः प्रिया भवन्ति न वा अरे भूतानां कामाय भूतानि प्रियाणि भवन्त्यात्मनस्तु कामाय भूतानि प्रियाणि भवन्ति न वा अरे सर्वस्य कामाय सर्वं प्रियं भवत्यात्म-

नस्तु कामाय सर्वं प्रियं भवति आत्मा वा अरे द्रष्टव्यः श्रोतव्यो मन्तव्यो निदिध्यासितव्यो मैत्रेय्यात्मनि खल्वरे दृष्टे श्रुते मते विज्ञात इदꣳ सर्वं विदितम् ॥

He said,—"Behold, not indeed for the husband's sake the husband is dear (to the wife), but for the sake of the self is dear the husband. Behold, not indeed for the wife's sake the wife is dear (to the husband), but for the sake of the self is dear the wife. Behold, not for the sons' sake the sons are dear (to the parents), but for the sake of the self are dear the sons. Behold, not for the property's sake, property is dear (to one), but for the sake of self is property dear, Behold, not for the Brāhman's sake the Brāhman is dear, but for the sake of self is dear the Brāhman. Behold, not for the Kṣattra's sake is the Kṣattra dear, but for the sake of the self is dear the Kṣattra. Behold, not for the worlds' sake the worlds are dear, but for the sake of the self are dear the worlds. Behold, not for the gods' sake the gods are dear, but for the sake of the self are dear the gods. Behold, not for the Vedas' sake are the Vedas dear, but for the sake of the self are dear the Vedas. Behold, not for the elements' sake the elements are dear, but for the sake of the self are dear the elements. Behold, not for the sake of the universe the universe is dear but for the sake of the self is dear the universe. Behold, the self is verily to be seen, heard, minded (and) meditated upon. Behold, O Maitreyī, by seeing, hearing, minding, knowing the self all this universe is comprehended.

7. ब्रह्म तं परादाद्योऽन्यत्रात्मनो ब्रह्म वेद क्षत्रं तं परादाद्योऽन्यत्रात्मनः क्षत्रं वेद लोकास्तं परादुर्योऽन्यत्रात्मनो लोकान्वेद देवास्तं परादुर्योऽन्यत्रात्मनो देवान्वेद वेदास्तं परादुर्योऽन्यत्रात्मनो वेदान्वेद भूतानि तं परादुर्योऽन्यत्रात्मनो भूतानि वेद सर्वं तं परादाद्योऽन्यत्रात्मनः सर्वं वेदेदं ब्रह्मेदं क्षत्रमिमे लोका इमे देवा इमे वेदा इमानि भूतानीदꣳ सर्वं यदयमात्मा ॥

"The Brahman should disown a person, who considers the Brahman caste as something different from his self; the Kṣattra should disown a person, who considers the Kṣattra caste as something different from his self: the world should disown a person, who considers the world as something different from his self; the gods should disown a person, who considers the gods as something different from (his) self; the elements should disown a person who considers the elements as something different from (his) self; the universe should disown a person, who considers the universe as something different from (his) self. This (own) self is this Brahman, this Kṣattra, these worlds, these gods, these elements, is this universe.

8. स यथा दुन्दुभेर्हन्यमानस्य न बाह्याञ्छब्दाञ्छक्नुयाद्ग्रहणाय दुन्दुभेस्तु ग्रहणेन दुन्दुभ्याघातस्य वा शब्दो गृहीतः ॥

"As a person, when a drum (unseen by him) is beaten, is unable to perceive the sounds proceeding from it (as sounds of a drum), but on the perception of the drum the sound of a drum beaten is perceived.

9. स यथा शङ्खस्य ध्मायमानस्य न बाह्याञ्छब्दाञ्छक्नुयाद्ग्रहणाय
शङ्खस्य तु ग्रहणेन शङ्खध्मस्य वा शब्दो गृहीतः ॥

"As a person, when, a shell (unseen by him) is blown, is unable to perceive the sounds proceeding from it (as sounds of a shell), but on the perception of the shell the sound of a shell blown is perceived.

10. स यथा वीणायै वाद्यमानायै न बाह्याञ्छब्दाञ्छक्नुयाद्ग्रहणाय वीणायै
तु ग्रहणेन वीणावादस्य वा शब्दो गृहीतः ॥

"As a person, when a flute unseen to him is played, is unable to perceive the sounds proceeding from it, but on the perception of the flute the sound of a flute played is perceived.

11. स यथार्द्रैधाग्नेरभ्याहितस्य पृथग्धूमा विनिश्चरन्त्येवं वा अरेऽस्य महतो
भूतस्य निःश्वसितमेतद्यदृग्वेदो यजुर्वेदः सामवेदोऽथर्वाङ्गिरस
इतिहासः पुराणं विद्या उपनिषदः श्लोकाः सूत्राण्यनुव्याख्यानानि
व्याख्यानानीष्टꣳ हुतमाशितं पायितमयं च लोकः परश्च लोकः
सर्वाणि च भूतान्यस्यैवैतानि सर्वाणि निःश्वसितानि ॥

"As from fire, made of damp wood, proceed smoke, sparks, etc., of various kind, thus, behold, the breathing of this great being is the Ṛg-Veda, the Yajur Veda, the Sāma Veda, the Atharva and Āngirasa, the narratives, the doctrines on creation, the science, the Upaniṣads, the memorial verses, the aphorisms, the explanation of tenets, the explanation of mantras,—all these are his breathing.

12. स यथा सर्वासामपाꣳ समुद्र एकायनमेवꣳ सर्वेषाꣳ स्पर्शानां त्वगेकायनमेवꣳ सर्वेषां गन्धानां नासिके एकायनमेवꣳ सर्वेषाꣳ रसानां जिह्वैकायनमेवꣳ सर्वेषाꣳ रूपाणां चक्षुरेकायनमेवꣳ सर्वेषाꣳ शब्दानाꣳ श्रोत्रमेकायनमेवꣳ सर्वेषा संकल्पानां मन एकायनमेवꣳ सर्वासां विद्यानाꣳ हृदयमेकायनमेवꣳ सर्वेषां कर्मणाꣳ हस्तावेकायनमेवꣳ सर्वेषामानन्दानामुपस्थ एकायनमेवꣳ सर्वेषां विसर्गाणां पायुरेकायनमेवꣳ सर्वेषामध्वनां पादावेकायनमेवꣳ सर्वेषां वेदानां वागेकायनम् ॥

" As the only site of the waters is the sea, thus the only site of every touch is the skin, thus the only site of every taste the tongue, thus the only site of every smell the nose, thus the only site of every colour the eye, thus the only site of every sound the ear, thus the only site of every determination the mind, thus the only site of every knowledge the heart, thus the only site of every act the hands, thus the only site of every pleasure the organ of generation, thus the only site of every evacuation the anus, thus the only site of every motion the feet, thus the only site of every Veda, speech.

13. स यथा सैन्धवघनोऽनन्तरोऽबाह्यः कृत्स्नो रसघन एवैवं वा अरेऽयमात्माऽनन्तरोऽबाह्यः कृत्स्नः प्रज्ञानघन एवैतेभ्यो भूतेभ्यः समुत्थाय तान्येवानुविनश्यति न प्रेत्य संज्ञास्तीत्यरे ब्रवीमीति होवाच याज्ञवल्क्यः ॥

" As a piece of salt, when thrown into water, is dissolved into mere water, and none is capable of perceiving it, because, from whatever place a person might take (water), it would have the taste of salt, (but be no piece of salt), thus, behold, this great being, which is infinite, independent and mere knowledge. Springing forth together with those elements, (the individual soul) is destroyed, when they are destroyed. After death, no conscience remains; thus, O Maitreyī, I hold." Thus said Yājñavalkya.

14. सा होवाच मैत्रेय्यत्रैव मा भगवान्मोहान्तमापीपिपन्न वा अहमिमं विजानामीति स होवाच न वा अरेऽहं मोहं ब्रवीम्यविनाशी वा अरेऽयमात्मानुच्छित्तिधर्मा ॥

Maitreyī said,—" With regard to the soul thou hast bewildered me, O Venerable, (by the saying,—After death no conscience remains.) I do not comprehend that (soul)." Yājñavalkya said,—" Behold, I verily do not create bewilderment; behold this soul is indestructible; its nature is without variance.

15. यत्र हि द्वैतमिव भवति तदितर इतरं पश्यति तदितर इतरं जिघ्रति तदितर इतरꣳ रसयते तदितर इतरमभिवदति तदितर इतरꣳ शृणोति तदितर इतरं मनुते तदितर इतरꣳ स्पृशति तदितर इतरं विजानाति यत्र त्वस्य सर्वमात्मैवाभूत्तत्केन कं पश्येत्तत्केन कं जिघ्रेत्तत्केन कꣳ रसयेत्तत्केन कमभिवदेत्तत्केन कꣳ शृणुयात्तत्केन कं मन्वीत तत्केन कꣳ स्पृशेत्तत्केन कं विजानीयाद्येनेदꣳ सर्वं विजानाति तं केन विजानीयात्स एष नेति नेत्यात्माऽगृह्यो न हि गृह्यतेऽशीर्यो न हि शीर्यतेऽसङ्गो न हि सज्जतेऽसितो न व्यथते न रिष्यति विज्ञातारमरे केन विजानीयादित्युक्तानु-

शासनासि मैत्रेय्येतावदरे खल्वमृतत्वमिति होक्त्वा याज्ञवल्क्यो विजहार ॥

" For where there is, as it were, duality, there sees another another thing, there smells another another thing, there tastes another another thing, there speaks another another thing, there hears another another thing, there minds another another thing, there touches another another thing, there knows another another thing; but how does one, to whom all has become mere soul, see any thing, how smell any thing, how taste any thing, how speak any thing, how hear any thing, how mind any thing, how touch any thing, how know any thing? How should he know him by whom he knows this all? This soul is not this, nor aught else; it is unseizable; for it cannot be seized; it is not scattered; for it cannot be scattered; it is without contact; for it comes not into contact; it is without colour; it is not subject to pain or destruction. How should one know the knower? In this manner art thou instructed. So far, O beloved Maitreyī, extends in truth immortality." Having said thus, Yājñavalkya went to the forest.

SIXTH BRĀHMAṆA

1. अथ वꣳशः पौतिमाष्यात्पौतिमाष्यो गौपवनाद्गौपवनः पौतिमाष्यात्पौतिमाष्यो गौपवनाद्गौपवनः कौशिकात्कौशिकः कौण्डि-

न्यात्कौण्डिन्यः शाण्डिल्याच्छाण्डिल्यः कौशिकाच्च गौतमाच्च गौतमः ॥

Next follows the school commencing from Pautimāshya (1). Pautimāshya succeeded Gaupavana,—Gaupavana, Pautimāshya,—Pautimāshya, Gaupavana,—Gaupavana, Kaus'ika,—Kaus'ika, Kauṇḍinya,—Kauṇḍinya, S'āṇḍilya,—S'āṇḍilya, Kausika and Gautama—Gautama.

(1) Two more lists of teachers are given in this Upanishad, *viz.*, 4, 6, and 6, 5.

2. आग्निवेश्यादाग्निवेश्यो गार्ग्याद्गार्ग्यो गार्ग्याद्गार्ग्यो गौतमाद्गौतमः सैतवात्सैतवः पाराशर्यायणात्पाराशर्यायणो गार्ग्यायणाद्गार्ग्यायण उद्दालकायनादुद्दालकायनो जाबालायनाज्जाबालायनो माध्यन्दिनायनान्माध्यन्दिनायनः सौकरायणात्सौकरायणः काषायणात्काषायणः सायकायनात्सायकायनः कौशिकायनेः कौशिकायनिः ॥

Āgnives'ya—Āgnives'ya (1), Gārgya,—Gārgya, Gārgya—Gārgya, Gautama,—Gautama, Saitava,—Saitava Pārās'aryāyaṇa,—Pārās'aryāyaṇa, Gārgyāyaṇa,—Gārgyāyaṇa, Uddālakāyana,—Uddālakāyana, Jābālāyana,—Jābālāyana, Mādhyandināyana,—Mādhyandināyana, Saukarāyana,—Saukarāyana, Kāṣāyaṇa,—Kāṣāyaṇa, Sāyakāyana,—Sāyakāyana, Kaus'ikāyani,—Kausikāyani.

(1) From Āgnives'ya to Kausikāyani the names of teachers differ from those given in 4, 6, 2.

3. घृतकौशिकाद्घृतकौशिकः पाराशर्यायणात्पाराशर्यायणः पाराशर्यात्पाराशर्यो जातूकर्ण्याज्जातूकर्ण्य आसुरायणाच्च यास्काच्चासुरायणस्त्रैवणेस्त्रैवणिरौपजङ्घनेरौपजङ्घनिरासुरेरासुरिर्भारद्वाजाद्भारद्वाज आत्रेयादात्रेयो माण्टेर्माण्टिर्गौतमाद्गौतमो गौतमाद्गौतमो वात्स्याद्वात्स्यः शाण्डिल्याच्छाण्डिल्यः कैशोर्यात्काप्यात्कैशोर्यः काप्यः कुमारहारितात्कुमारहारितो गालवाद्गालवो विदर्भीकौण्डिन्याद्विदर्भीकौण्डिन्यो वत्सनपातो बाभ्रवाद्वत्सनपाद्बभ्रवः पथः सौभरात्पन्थाः सौभरोऽयास्यादाङ्गिरसादयास्य आङ्गिरस आभूतेस्त्वाष्ट्रादाभूतिस्त्वाष्ट्रो विश्वरूपात्त्वाष्ट्राद्विश्वरूपस्त्वाष्ट्रोऽश्विभ्यामश्विनौ दधीच आथर्वणाद्दध्यङ्ङाथर्वणो दैवादथर्वा दैवो मृत्योः प्राध्वंसनान्मृत्युः प्राध्वंसनः प्रध्वंसनात्प्रध्वंसन एकर्षेरेकर्षिर्विप्रचित्तेर्विप्रचित्तिर्व्यष्टेर्व्यष्टिः सनारोः सनारुः सनातनात्सनातनः सनगात्सनगः परमेष्ठिनः परमेष्ठी ब्रह्मणो ब्रह्म स्वयंभुब्रह्मणे नमः ॥

Ghṛtakaus'ika,—Ghṛtakaus'ika, Pārās'aryāyaṇa,—Pārās'aryāyaṇa, Pārās'arya,—Pārās'arya, Jātūkarṇya,—Jātūkarṇya, Āsurāyaṇa and Yāska,—Āsurāyana Straivani,—Straivani, Aupajanghani,—Aupajanghani, Ās'uri,—Ās'uri, Bhāradvāja,—Bhāradvāja, Ātreya,—Ātreya, Māṇṭi, Māṇṭi,—Gautama,—Gautama, Gautama,—Gautama, Vātsya,—Vātsya, S'āṇḍilya,—S'aṇḍilya, Kaisorya Kāpya,—Kaisorya Kāpya, Kumārahārita,—Kumā, rahārita, Gālava—Gālava, Vidarbhī Kauṇḍinya,—Vidarbhī Kauṇḍinya, Vatsanapāt Bābhrava,—Vatsanapāt Bābhrava, Pathāh Saubhara,—Panthāh Saubhara-Ayāsya Āṅgirasa,—Ayāsya Āṅgirasa, Ābhuti Tvāṣṭra,—Ābhuti Tvāṣṭra, Visvarūpa Tvāṣṭra,—Visvarūpa Tvāṣṭra, the two As'vins,—the two As'vins, Ḍadhīṅ Atharvana,—Dadhyaṅṅ—Atharvana, Atharva Daiva,—Atharva Daiva, Mṛtyu Prādhvaṁsana,—Mṛtyu Prādhvaṁsana, Pradhvaṁsana,—Pradhvaṁsana, Ekarṣi,—Ekarṣi, Vipracitti,—Vipracitti, Vyaṣṭi,—Vyaṣṭi, Sānaru,—Sanāru, Sanātana,—Sanātana, Sanaga,—Sanaga, Parameṣṭhi,—Parameṣṭhi, Brahman (1),—Brahman, is the self-existent ; salutation to Brahman.

(1) Parameṣṭhī denotes Virāt, and Brahman, Hiraṇyagrabha.—S'.

FIFTH CHAPTER

FIRST BRĀHMAṆA

1. ॐ पूर्णमदः पूर्णमिदं पूर्णात्पूर्णमुदच्यते ॥ पूर्णस्य पूर्णमादाय पूर्णमेवावशिष्यते ॥ ॐ ३ खं ब्रह्म खं पुराणं वायुरं खमिति ह स्माह कौरव्यायणीपुत्रो वेदोऽयं ब्राह्मणा विदुर्वेदैनेन यद्वेदितव्यम् ॥

Infinite (1) is that (2), infinite is this. From the infinite one proceeds the infinite one. On taking the infinity (3) of the infinite one, there is left infinity.

Om is the ether (4), is Brahman. The ether (5) exists of old, the ether is the source of the wind, thus said the son of Kauravyāyaṇi. That (Oṅkāra) is the Veda. The Brāhmaṇas know (vidur) that by this (name) one knows (Veda) all that is to be known (Veditavya).

(1) In the preceding four chapters the knowledge of Brahman in his independent nature has been explained; in the present chapter the modes of meditation on the soul in its various relations are set forth. These modes not at variance with the performance of work, lead to a higher and higher state of existence, and effect the gradual liberation of the soul from the world. The first of them is the Omkāra, as being the most eminent, after which follow the commands of restraint, liberality, and compassion.—Ś.

(2) *That* (adaḥ) refers to the imperceptible Brahman, who is all-pervading and independent of any relation, *this* (idam) to Brahman as conceived under relations. "Infinite," Pūrṇa; the literal meaning of which is full and which S'., explains by not finite, all-pervading. It is finite, (or full), he continues, as pervaded by the supreme soul, not by the individual soul, since the latter is involved in relations. "The infinite,"—considered as effect "proceeds from the infinite,"—considered as cause.—S'.

(3) Taking the infinite, literally the infinite one, and the sense is, comprehending the one identical nature of Brahman, by the omission of all relative attributes.

(4) According to S'., Brahman is the subject, and Kha (the ether) the predicate of the sentence.

(5) The ether (Kha) contains two meanings, as ancient it represents the supreme soul, and as the source of the wind, it represents the inferior Brahman. The same applies to the sound Om, the representative of Kha.—S'.

SECOND BRĀHMAṆA

1. त्रयाः प्राजापत्याः प्रजापतौ पितरि ब्रह्मचर्यमूषुर्देवा मनुष्या असुरा उषित्वा ब्रह्मचर्यं देवा ऊचुर्ब्रवीतु नो भवानिति तेभ्यो हैतदक्षरमुवाच द इति व्यज्ञासिष्टा ३ इति व्यज्ञासिष्मेति होचुर्दाम्यतेति न आत्थेत्योमिति होवाच व्यज्ञासिष्टेति ॥

The three-fold offspring of Prajāpati, gods, men and Asuras followed as religious students their father Prajāpati. The gods, having finished their time of learning, said (to Prajāpati),—"Tell us, O Venerable, (our duty)." He proclaimed to them the syllable *Da*,

"Do you comprehend?" They answered,—"We do comprehend. Restrain your desires, hast thou said to us." He said,—"Om! you have fully comprehended."

2. अथ हैनं मनुष्या ऊचुर्ब्रवीतु नो भवानिति तेभ्यो हैतदेवाक्षरमुवाच द इति व्यज्ञासिष्टा ३ इति व्यज्ञासिष्मेति होचुर्दत्तेति न आत्थेत्योमिति होवाच व्यज्ञासिष्टेति ॥

Then the men said to him,—"Tell us, O Venerable, (our duty)." He proclaimed to them the letter *Da*. "Do you comprehend?" They answered,—"We do comprehend. Be liberal, hast thou said to us." He said,—"Om! you have fully comprehended."

3. अथ हैनमसुरा ऊचुर्ब्रवीतु नो भवानिति तेभ्यो हैतदेवाक्षरमुवाच द इति व्यज्ञासिष्टा ३ इति व्यज्ञासिष्मेति होचुर्दयध्वमिति न आत्थेत्योमिति होवाच व्यज्ञासिष्टेति तदेतदेवैषा दैवी वागनुवदति स्तनयित्नुर्द द द इति दाम्यत दत्त दयध्वमिति तदेतत्त्रयꣳ शिक्षेद्दमं दानं दयामिति ॥

Then the Asuras said to him, "Tell us, O Venerable, (our duty)." He proclaimed to them the letter *Da*. "Do you comprehend?" They answered,—"We do comprehend. Be clement, hast thou said to us." He said—"Om! you have fully comprehended." The same is repeated by a divine voice with the force of thunder, *viz.*, the syllables *Da*, *Da*, *Da*, meaning, Be restrained (*dā*myata), be liberal (*da*tta), and be clement (*day*adhvam). Therefore let one learn the triad of restraint, liberality and clemency.

THIRD BRĀHMAṆA (1)

1. एष प्रजापतिर्यद्धृदयमेतद्ब्रह्मैतत्सर्वं तदेतत्त्र्यक्षरꣳहृदयमिति हृ इत्येकमक्षरमभिहरन्त्यस्मै स्वाश्चान्ये च य एवं वेद द इत्येकमक्षरं ददत्यस्मै स्वाश्चान्ये च य एवं वेद यमित्येकमक्षरमेति स्वर्गं लोकं य एवं वेद ॥

This Prajāpati (2) is the heart (hṛdaya) (3), this Brahman (4), this all. "Hṛdaya" consists of three syllables. The first syllable is *Hṛ*. To him who thus knows, the senses and the rest (5) perform (abhi*har*anti), (their work). The second syllable is *Da*. The senses and the rest bestow (da*da*ti) (power) on him who thus knows. The third syllable is *Ya*. He who thus knows, proceeds, (*e*ti) to heaven, (his) place.

(1) Restraint, liberality and clemency are the highest of all modes of adoration; for he, whose passions are subdued, who is not desirous of gain, and who is merciful, is in possession of all those modes. In the preceding two Brāhmaṇas the meditation on Brahman without attributes has been explained, the present show the elevated places, obtained from meditating on Brahman as endowed with attributes.

(2) The creator, of all beings.—Ś.

(3) The intellect, abiding in the heart.—Ś.

(4) Brahman, from his growing (bṛhattvāt) and from his being the soul of all.—Ś.

(5) The rest, according to Ś., means the object of the senses, as sound, etc.

FOURTH BRĀHMAṆA

1. तद्वै तदेतदेव तदास सत्यमेव स यो हैतं महद्यक्षं प्रथमजं वेद सत्यं ब्रह्मेति जयतीमाँल्लोकान् जित इन्वसावसद्य एवमेतं महद्यक्षं प्रथमजं वेद सत्यं ब्रह्मेति सत्यꣳ ह्येव ब्रह्म ॥

This (1) (Brahman) was even truth (2). Whoever knows that he, the great, the venerable, the first-born, (3), is the true Brahman, conquers (his enemy), as (the true Brahman conquers the worlds), and destroys him (also); for Brahman is truth.

(1) In the text the demonstrative pronoun "tat" is three times repeated. According to S'. the first refers to Brahman, described by the name of the heart in the preceding Brāhmaṇa, the second connects it with "etat" which is to enunciate some other predicate of Brahman, and the third "tat" indicates the new predicate.

(2) Truth, Sachcha tyachcha mūrtancāmurtanca satyam Brahma pancabhūtatmakam, S'.

(3) Born before every other being which has a worldly existence.—S'.

FIFTH BRĀHMAṆA (1)

1. आप एवेदमग्र आसुस्ता आपः सत्यमसृजन्त सत्यं ब्रह्म ब्रह्म प्रजापतिं प्रजापतिर्देवाꣳस्ते देवाः सत्यमेवोपासते तदेतत्त्र्यक्षरꣳ सत्यमिति स इत्येकमक्षरं तीत्येकमक्षरं यमित्येकमक्षरं प्रथमोत्तमे अक्षरे सत्यं मध्यतोऽनृतं तदेतदनृतमुभयतः सत्येन परिगृहीतꣳ सत्यभूयमेव भवति नैनं विद्वाꣳसमनृतꣳ हिनस्ति ॥

Water (2) was at first this (world) (3). Water created truth. Truth is Brahman (4), Brahman (created) Prajāpati (5), Prajāpati the gods. The gods adore even truth. The name of satya (truth) consists of three syllables. The first syllable is "*Sa*," the second syllable "*Ti*" and the third syllable "*Ya*". The first and the last syllables (Sa and Ya) are truth (6), the middle is falsehood (anṛta), falsehood is on either side encompassed by truth; there is, (therefore), a preponderance of truth. Falsehood does not hurt him who (thus) knows.

(1) This Brāhmaṇa has the object of extolling the truth Brahman.—S'.

(2) Water indicates here the unmanifested state of the world, before its creation, together with the creator, therefore the seeds of all creation.—S'.

(3) The world in its manifestation.—S'.

(4) The first born, Hiraṇyagarbha, or the S'ūtrātmā.—S'.

(5) Or the Virāṭ.—S'.

(6) Because these two syllables occur neither in the word "mṛtyu" (death) nor in the word "anṛta," while the middle syllable "ta" is found as well in "mṛtyu" as in "anṛta".—S'.

2. तद्यत्तत्सत्यमसौ स आदित्यो य एष एतस्मिन्मण्डले पुरुषो यश्चायं दक्षिणेऽक्षन्पुरुषस्तावेतावन्योन्यस्मिन्प्रतिष्ठितौ रश्मिभिरेषोऽस्मिन् प्रतिष्ठितः प्राणैरयममुष्मिन्स यदोत्क्रमिष्यन्भवति शुद्धमेवैतन्मण्डलं पश्यति नैनमेते रश्मयः प्रत्यायन्ति ॥

That truth (1) is Āditya, the Puruṣa, (dwelling) in that orb, and also the Puruṣa, (dwelling) in the right eye. They abide in each other. The former abides through his rays in the latter (2), and the latter in the former through his senses. When he quits the body, he beholds that pure orb (3); the rays do return to him.

(1) This section exhibits the meditation on the true Brahman in the several localities.—S'.

(2) The sun assists man by the manifestation of objects, and man the sun by perception.—S'.

(3) The moon.—S'.

3. य एष एतस्मिन्मण्डले पुरुषस्तस्य भूरिति शिर एकꣳ शिर एकमेतदक्षरं भुव इति बाहू द्वौ बाहू द्वे एते अक्षरे स्वरिति प्रतिष्ठा द्वे प्रतिष्ठे द्वे एते अक्षरे तस्योपनिषदहरिति हन्ति पाप्मानं जहाति च य एवं वेद ॥

Bhū (the earth) (1) is the head (2) of the Puruṣa, dwelling in that orb, there being one head and also one syllable,—Bhuvaḥ (the atmosphere) the arms,—there being two arms, and also two syllables,—Svaḥ (the heavens) the foundation (3),—there being two foundations and also two syllables. His representative name is Ahar (4) (day); for whoever thus knows, destroys (hanti) and relinquishes (jahāti) sin.

(1) This section replies to the question, which are the sacred names and the corresponding parts of the body of the Puruṣa whose name is "Satya," in that orb.—S'.

(2) The head from its excellence.—S'.

(3) Denoting "foot".

(4) Ahar is here derived from the root "Hā" meaning either to destroy, or to relinquish.

4. योऽयं दक्षिणेऽक्षन्पुरुषस्तस्य भूरिति शिर एकꣳ शिर एकमेतदक्षरं
भुव इति बाहू द्वौ बाहू द्वे एते अक्षरे स्वरिति प्रतिष्ठा प्रतिष्ठे
द्वे द्वे एते अक्षरे तस्योपनिषदहमिति हन्ति पाप्मानं जहाति च
य एवं वेद ॥

Bhū is the head of the Puruṣa, dwelling in the right eye,—there being one head and also one syllable,—Bhuvaḥ, the arms,—there being two arms and also two syllables.—Svaḥ the foundation,—there being two foundations and also two syllables. His representative name is Aham (1), for whoever thus knows, destroys and relinquishes sin.

(1) The derivation of Aham is here the same as that of Ahar.

SIXTH BRĀHMAṆA

1. मनोमयोऽयं पुरुषो भाः सत्यस्तस्मिन्नन्तर्हृदये यथा व्रीहिर्वा यवो वा
स एष सर्वस्येशानः सर्वस्याधिपतिः सर्वमिदं प्रशास्ति यदिदं
किंच ॥

The Puruṣa, who resembles (1) mind, is the true light (2); (he abides) within the heart, (in size) like a grain of rice or barley (3) He is the Ruler of all, the sovereign lord of all; he overrules whatever exists in this universe.

(1) S' explains the affix "maya" in "manomaya," not by "Svarūpa" (of the same nature with the mind), but

by "object of the mind," because comprehended either *in* or *by* the mind.

(2) Because the mind manifests all, and everything is an object of the mind. Ś.

(3) *Vide* Kaṭha, U., 3, 11, and Svetāśvatara U., 3, 13.

SEVENTH BRĀHMAṆA

1. विद्युद्ब्रह्मेत्याहुर्विदानाद्विद्युद्विद्यत्येनं पाप्मनो य एवं वेद विद्युद्ब्रह्मेति विद्युद्ध्येव ब्रह्म ॥

It is said, that "vidyut" (lightning) is Brahman, for vidyut is derived from vidānāt, (tearing asunder) (1). Whosoever thus knows, that Brahman is vidyut, tears asunder the sins of that (soul); for vidyut is even Brahman.

(1) From tearing asunder the darkness; for by destroying the darkness of the clouds, lightning is manifested.—Ś.

EIGHTH BRĀHMAṆA

1. वाचं धेनुमुपासीत तस्याश्चत्वारः स्तनाः स्वाहाकारो वषट्कारो हन्तकारः स्वधाकारस्तस्य द्वौ स्तनौ देवा उपजीवन्ति स्वाहाकारं च वषट्कारं च हन्तकारं मनुष्याः स्वधाकारं पितरस्तस्याः प्राण ऋषभो मनो वत्सः ॥

Let one meditate on speech (under the semblance of) a milch-cow. Her four udders are the words Svāhā, Vaṣaṭ, Hanta and Svādhā (1), Two udders, the words Svāhā and Vaṣaṭ, feed the gods, the word Hanta (feeds) men, and the word Svadhā the forefathers. Her bull is life, her young one the mind.

(1) Ghee is offered to the gods by pronouncing "Svāhā and vaṣaṭ," rice to men by saying "Hanta," and "Svadhā" to the forefathers by saying "Svadhā".

NINTH BRĀHMAṆA

1. अयमग्निर्वैश्वानरो योऽयमन्तः पुरुषे येनेदमन्नं पच्यते यदिदमद्यते
तस्यैष घोषो भवति यमेतत्कर्णावपिधाय श्रृणोति स
यदोत्क्रमिष्यन्भवति नैनं घोषꣳ श्रृणोति ॥

The fire whose name is Vais'vānara is that fire in the midst of the body, by which all the food that is eaten is digested. From this (fire) arises a noise which one hears on closing his ears. When he (1) quits the body, he does not hear the noise.

(1) The individual who experiences pain or pleasure in the body.—S'.

TENTH BRĀHMAṆA (1)

1. यदा वै पुरुषोऽस्माल्लोकात्प्रैति स वायुमागच्छति तस्मै स तत्र
विजिहीते यथा रथचक्रस्य खं तेन स ऊर्ध्व आक्रमते स

आदित्यमागच्छति तस्मै स तत्र विजिहीते यथा लम्बरस्य खं तेन स ऊर्ध्व आक्रमते स चन्द्रमसमागच्छति तस्मै स तत्र विजिहीते यथा दुन्दुभेः खं तेन स ऊर्ध्व आक्रमते स लोकमागच्छत्यशोकमहिमं तस्मिन्वसति शाश्वतीः समाः ॥

When the Puruṣa (2) proceeds from this world (to another), he comes to the air. The air opens there as wide for him as the aperture of a chariot-wheel. By this (aperture) he ascends, (and) comes to the sun. The same opens there for him as wide as the aperture of a Lambara (3). By this he ascends, and comes to the moon. The same opens there for him as wide as the aperture of a small drum. By this he ascends, and comes to the world (4), where there is no grief, where there is no snow (5); there he dwells endless years (6).

(1) In this Brāhmaṇa, the fruits, consequent upon the abovementioned kinds of meditation, are stated.—S'.

(2) The Puruṣa who has the knowledge before described.—S'.

(3) A kind of musical instrument, probably a large drum.

(4) To the world of Prajāpati.—S'.

(5) Grief denotes mental pain, and snow pain, arising from the body.—S'.

(6) Many Kalpas of Brahmā.—S'.

ELEVENTH BRĀHMAṆA

1. एतद्वै परमं तपो यद्व्याहितस्तप्यते परमꣳ हैव लोकं जयति य एवं वेदैतद्वै परमं तपो यं प्रेतमरण्यꣳ हरन्ति परमꣳ हैव लोकं जयति य एवं वेदैतद्वै परमं तपो यं प्रेतमग्नावभ्यादधति परमꣳ हैव लोकं जयति य एवं वेद ॥

The greatest pain surely is that, which one endures from sickness. Whoever thus knows, gains the highest world. The greatest pain surely is (to think) that they carry one after death to the forest. Whoever thus knows, gains the highest world. The greatest pain surely is (to think) that they lay the (body of the) deceased in the fire. Whoever thus knows, gains the highest world.

TWELFTH BRĀHMAṆA

1. अन्नं ब्रह्मेत्येक आहुस्तन्न तथा पूयति वा अन्नमृते प्राणात्प्राणो ब्रह्मेत्येक आहुस्तन्न तथा शुष्यति वै प्राण ऋतेऽन्नादेते ह त्वेव देवते एकधाभूयं भूत्वा परमतां गच्छतस्तद्ध स्माह प्रातृदः पितरं किꣳस्विदेवैवं विदुषे साधु कुर्यां किमेवास्मा असाधु कुर्यामिति स ह स्माह पाणिना मा प्रातृद कस्त्वेनयोरेकधाभूयं भूत्वा परमतां गच्छतीति तस्मा उ हैतदुवाच वीत्यन्नं वै वि अन्ने हीमानि सर्वाणि भूतानि विष्टानि रमिति प्राणो वै रं प्राणे हीमानि सर्वाणि भूतानि रमन्ते सर्वाणि ह वा अस्मिन्भूतानि विशन्ति सर्वाणि भूतानि रमन्ते य एवं वेद ॥

Some say, "Food is Brahman." This is not so; food decays (1), without (the support of) life. Others say, "Life is Brahman." This is not so; life dries up without (the support of) food. Those deities (2) verily, when becoming one, attain the highest state (3). Thus (reflecting) Prātṛda said to his father,—"Can I do any good or evil to one who thus knows?" He answered (checking him) with his hand,—"Do not (speak thus), O Prātṛda; for who, that is, the unity of them, can ever obtain the highest state?" He (4) said to him "Vi"; food is verily "Vi"; for all these beings enter (5) food. (Again he said to him) "Ram"; life verily is "Ram"; for all these beings sport in life. Into him who thus knows, enter all beings; in him sport all beings.

(1) While Brahman is without decay.—Ś.
(2) Food and life.
(3) The state of Brahman.
(4) The father.
(5) Are dependent upon food.

THIRTEENTH BRĀHMAṆA

1. उक्थं प्राणो वा उक्थं प्राणो हीदꣳ सर्वमुत्थापयत्युद्धास्मादुक्थवि-
द्वीरस्तिष्ठत्युक्थस्य सायुज्यꣳ सलोकतां जयति य एवं वेद ॥

The Uktha (1) is verily life; therefore (let one meditate on) the Uktha; for life causes this all to spring up, (utthāpayati). From him who thus knows, springs up a son who knows the Uktha, and is firm. Whoever thus knows, gains the same nature (2) and the same place with the Uktha.

(1) Uktha is the principal mantra in the rite called Mahāvrata. The Uktha is the principal rite, and life is also first among the other functions.—S'.

(2) S'. explains Sāyujya by identity of body, organs and consciousness. The Sāyujya and Salokatā are two of the five kinds of liberation which are specified in the S'rī-Bhāgavata, 3, 29, *viz.*, Sālokya, Sarṣti, Sāmīpya, Sārūpya and Ekatva. *Vide*, S'abda K. D.

2. यजुः प्राणो वै यजुः प्राणे हीमानि सर्वाणि भूतानि युज्यन्ते युज्यन्ते हास्मै सर्वाणि भूतानि श्रैष्ठ्याय यजुषः सायुज्यꣳ सलोकतां जयति य एवं वेद ॥

The Yajus is verily life; therefore (let one meditate on) the Yajus; for in life are all these beings united (yujyante). With him who thus knows are all beings united for the sake of his superiority. Whoever thus knows, obtains the same nature and the same place with the Yajus.

3. साम प्राणो वै साम प्राणे हीमानि सर्वाणि भूतानि सम्यञ्चि सम्यञ्चि हास्मै सर्वाणि भूतानि श्रैष्ठ्याय कल्पन्ते साम्नः सायुज्यꣳ सलोकतां जयति य एवं वेद ॥

The Sāma is verily life; therefore (let one meditate on) the Sāma; for in life meet all these beings together (Samyañci). For him who thus knows meet all these beings together for the sake of his superiority, Whoever thus knows, obtains the same nature and the same place with the Sāma.

4. क्षत्रं प्राणो वै क्षत्रं प्राणो वै क्षत्रं हि त्रायते हैनं प्राणः क्षणितोः प्र-
क्षत्रमत्रमाप्नोति क्षत्रस्य सायुज्यꣳ सलोकतां जयति य एवं वेद ॥

The Kṣattra is verily life; (therefore let one meditate on) the Kṣattra; for life saves (trāyate) this (body), when it is wounded (Kṣanitoḥ). Whoever thus knows, gains the Kṣattra which is Attra (1), and obtains the same nature and the same place with the Kṣattra.

(1) Attra means, according to Ś., what is not preserved by another (na trāyate anyena kenacit, iti attram). Kṣattra which is Attra seems to denote one who is not preserved by any body else, that is to say, who preserves himself.

FOURTEENTH BRĀHMAṆA (1)

1. भूमिरन्तरिक्षं द्यौरित्यष्टावक्षराण्यष्टाक्षरꣳ ह वा एकं गायत्र्यै
पदमेतदु हैवास्या एतत्स यावदेषु त्रिषु लोकेषु तावद्ध जयति
योऽस्या एतदेवं पदं वेद ॥

Bhūmi (earth), Antarikṣa (the atmosphere), Dyau (the heavens) are eight syllables (2); the first foot of the Gāyatrī consists of eight syllables; this (foot) of the Gāyatrī is that (nature of the earth, of the atmosphere and of the heavens). Whoever thus knows the (first) foot of the Gāyatrī, conquers all that is in the three worlds.

(1) S'. gives the following introduction to the fourteenth Brāhmaṇa. The meditation upon Brahman, as endowed with many fictitious attributes such as the heart, etc., has been explained; the present Brāhmaṇa is to set forth the meditation upon him, represented by the Gāyatrī.

(2) See a similar play with letters Chh. U., 1, 3, 6—7.

2. ऋचो यजूꣳषि सामानीत्यष्टावक्षराण्यष्टाक्षरꣳ ह वा एकं गायत्र्यै पदमेतदु हैवास्या एतत्स यावतीयं त्रयी विद्या तावद्ध जयति योऽस्या एतदेवं पदं वेद ॥

The Ṛcaḥ, Yajūṁṣi (and) Sāmāni are eight syllables; the second foot of the Gāyatrī consists of eight syllables; this (foot) of the Gāyatrī is that (nature of the three Vedas). Whoever thus knows, conquers all that is conquerable by the knowledge of three Vedas.

3. प्राणोऽपानो व्यान इत्यष्टावक्षराण्यष्टाक्षरꣳ ह वा एकं गायत्र्यै पदमेतदु हैवास्या एतत्स यावदिदं प्राणि तावद्ध जयति योऽस्या एतदेवं पदं वेदाथास्या एतदेवं तुरीयं दर्शतं पदं परो रजा य एष तपति यद्वै चतुर्थं तत्तुरीयं दर्शतं पदमिति ददृश इव ह्येष परोरजा इति सर्वमुह्येवैष रज उपर्युपरि तपत्येवꣳ हैव श्रिया यशसा तपति योऽस्य एतदेवं पदं वेद ॥

Prāṇa (the vital air which goes forward), Apāna (the vital air which descends), (and) Vyāna (the vital air which equalises), these are eight syllables; the third foot of the Gāyatrī consists of eight syllables; this (foot) of the Gāyatrī is that (nature of the three vital airs). Whoever thus knows the third foot of the (Gāyatrī) conquers all that has life. Again, the turiya (the fourth), the Dars'ata foot of the Gāyatrī, is the Paro Rajā (1), which sheds rays. What is (commonly called) Caturtha (the fourth), is (the same as) the " turīya ". It is, as it were, beheld (dadṛs'a) ; hence it is called the Dars'ata foot. (It is called) Paro Rajā, because it sheds rays upon all the dust-born creatures of the universe. Whoever thus knows that (foot of the Gāyatrī), is radiant with power and glory.

(1) Paro Rajā, Āditya or the sun, the representative of Brahman.

4. सैषा गायत्र्यैतस्मिꣳस्तुरीये दर्शते पदे परोरजसि प्रतिष्ठिता तद्वैतत्सत्ये प्रतिष्ठितं चक्षुर्वै सत्यं चक्षुर्हि वै सत्यं तस्माद्यदिदानीं द्वौ विवदमानावेयातामहमदर्शमहमश्रौषमिति य एवं ब्रूयादहमदर्शमिति तस्मा एव श्रद्दध्याम तद्वै तत्सत्यं बले प्रतिष्ठितं प्राणो वै बलं तत्प्राणे प्रतिष्ठितं तस्मादाहुर्बलꣳ सत्यादोजीय इत्येवं वैषा गायत्र्यध्यात्मं प्रतिष्ठिता सा हैषा गयाꣳस्तत्रे प्राणा वै गयास्तत्प्राणाꣳस्तत्रे तद्यद्गयाꣳस्तत्रे तस्माद्गायत्री नाम स यामेवामूꣳ सावित्रीमन्वाहैषैव स यस्मा अन्वाह तस्य प्राणाꣳस्त्रायते ॥

This Gāyatrī (1) is founded upon the fourth, the Dars'ata foot, the Paro Rajā. This (fourth foot) is founded upon truth. The eye is verily truth ; for (that) the eye is truth (is evident). Hence, if at present two have entered upon a dispute (one saying),—I have seen, the other,—I have heard, then we believe him, who has said, I have seen. Truth is founded upon power ; life is verily power. Upon this life (truth) is founded.

Therefore it is said, power is stronger than truth (2). In the same manner the Gāyatrī is founded upon that which bears a relation to the soul for this (Gāyatrī) preserves (tattre) the Gayas; the vital organs (Prāṇās) are the Gayas; therefore, because it preserves the Gayas (gayāṁstattre), it is called Gāyatrī. The Sāvitrī which he (3) teaches, is this (Gāyatrī); it preserves the life of him to whom he has taught it.

(1) This Gāyatrī with its three feet representing the world in its twofold state, as being endowed with form, and as being without form.—S'.

(2) *Vide* Chha. U., 7, 8.

(3) The teacher.

5. ताꣳहैतामेके सावित्रीमनुष्टुभमन्वाहुर्वागनुष्टुबेतद्वाचमनुब्रूम इति न
तथा कुर्याद्गायत्रीमेव सावित्रीमनुब्रूयाद्यदिह वा अप्येवंविद्बह्विव
प्रतिगृह्णाति न हैव तद्गायत्र्या एकं च न पदं प्रति ॥

Some (1) call this Sāvitrī Anuṣṭup, (saying), "Speech is Anuṣṭup; we repeat that speech is Anuṣṭup." Let none do so, let him call the Gāyatrī Sāvitrī. If one who thus knows, receive even many (gifts) (2), yet he would not receive so much as is equal to one foot of the Gāyatrī.

(1) Some followers of Veda schools.

(2) Many gifts, at the time of investiture, when the pupil begs for presents.

6. स य इमाꣳस्त्रींल्लोकान्पूर्णान्प्रतिगृह्णीयात्सोऽस्या एतत्प्रथमं पद-
माप्नुयादथ यावतीयं त्रयी विद्या यस्तावत्प्रतिगृह्णीयात्सोऽस्या

एतद्द्वितीयं पदमाप्नुयादथ यावदिदं प्राणि यस्तावत्प्रतिगृह्णीयात्सोऽस्या एतत्तृतीयं पदमाप्नुयादथास्या एतदेव तुरीयं दर्शतं पदं परोरजा य एष तपति नैव केनचनाप्यं कुत उ एतावत्प्रतिगृह्णीयात् ॥

If one receive the three worlds, full (of all their riches), he would obtain (no more than is equal to) the first foot. Again if one receive as much as the science or the three Vedas extends, he would obtain (no more than what is equal to) the second foot. Again, if one receive as much as all that has life extends, he would obtain (no more than what is equal to) its third foot. Again, the fourth Dars'ata Paro Rajā foot of the Gāyatrī is never by any one obtainable (1). Hence how could he receive (an equivalent) which extends so far?

(1) Obtainable by any wealth which may be given.

7. तस्या उपस्थानं गायत्र्यस्येकपदी द्विपदी त्रिपदी चतुष्पद्यपदसि नहि पद्यसे नमस्ते तुरीयाय दर्शताय पदाय परोरजसेऽसावदो मा प्रापदिति यं द्विष्यादसावस्मै कामो मा समृद्धीति वा न हैवास्मै स कामः समृद्ध्यते यस्मा एवमुपतिष्ठतेऽहमदः प्रापमिति वा ॥

This praise of this Gāyatrī is given in the following Mantra :—Thou art of one foot (1), of two feet, of three feet, and of four feet; for thou art not obtained. Salutation to thy fourth Dars'ata Paro Rajā foot. May this (enemy of thine) (2) not accomplish this (work) (3).

If (one who thus knows) hates any body (and makes against him this invocation), " this (man is my enemy); may his wish not be accomplished," then the wish of the latter will verily not be accomplished, if he make against him the invocation, "I have obtained his wish".

(1) The first foot, representing the three worlds, the second representing the knowledge of the three Vedas, the third representing all living creatures.

(2) Enemy, sin. The sentence is elliptical, but the above sense appears to be intended; which is corroborated by the explanation given by the Upaniṣad itself.

(3) By which he seeks to harm thee.

8. एतद्ध वै तज्जनको वैदेहो बुडिलमाश्वतराश्विमुवाच यन्नु हो तद्गायत्रीविदब्रूथा अथ कथꣳ हस्तीभूतो वहसीति मुखꣳ ह्यस्याः सम्राण्न विदांचकारेति होवाच तस्या अग्निरेव मुखं यदिह वा अपि बह्विवाग्नावभ्यादधति सर्वमेव तत्संदहत्येव हैवैवंविद्यद्यपि बह्विव पापं कुरुते सर्वमेव तत्संप्साय शुद्धः पूतोऽजरोऽमृतः संभवति ॥

Janaka, the king of the Videhās, thus addressed Buḍila, the son of As'vatarāsva,—" (If) thy saying that thou knowest the Gāyatrī (be true) then why hast thou become an elephant to carry (me)?" He said,—" I did not know the mouth of the Gāyatrī, O king of kings." Its mouth is fire. Even much wood, thrown into fire, is consumed by the same; in like manner, one who thus knows, although committing many sins, consumes them all, becomes clean and pure, and is without decay and immortal.

FIFTEENTH BRĀHMAṆA

1. हिरण्मयेन पात्रेण सत्यस्यापिहितं मुखं। तत्त्वं पूषन्नपावृणु सत्यधर्माय दृष्टये। पूषन्नेकर्षे यमसूर्यप्राजापत्य व्यूहरश्मीन्समूह तेजो यत्ते रूपं कल्याणतमं तत्ते पश्यामि योऽसावसौ पुरुषः सोऽहमस्मि। वायुरनिलममृतमथेदं भस्मान्तꣳ शरीरम्। ॐ ३ क्रतो स्मर कृतꣳ स्मर क्रतो स्मर कृतꣳ स्मर। अग्ने नय सुपथा राये अस्मान्विश्वानि देव वयुनानि विद्वान्। युयोध्यस्मज्जुहुराणमेनो भूयिष्ठां ते नमउक्तिं विधेम॥

Open, O Pūṣan, the mouth of truth, concealed in the golden vessel (1), to (me who have been) devoted to true piety, for the sake of beholding (the truth). O Pūṣan (2), thou sole Ṛṣi (3), Yama, Sūrya, son of Prajāpati, do withhold thy rays, diminish thy splendour, that I may behold thy most auspicious form. I, that Puruṣa, am immortal. (Let) my vital air (join) the wind: then (let) my body, when reduced to ashes, (join) the earth. Om! Kratu, remember (my) acts; Remember, O Kratu, remember my acts, remember! Guide (me), O Agni, by the road of bliss to enjoyment; O god, who knowest all dispositions, deliver (me from) crooked sin. Let us offer thee our best salutation (4).

(1) S'aṅkara thus explains this passage: He who has performed both acts of knowledge and rites, prays to the

sun at the time of his death, holding a golden vessel in his hands. As a valuable thing is concealed in a vessel, so Brahman, who is denoted as truth (*vide* 5, 4), and who abides in the resplendent orb of the sun, is concealed from him whose mind is not concentrated.

(2) Pūṣan from Poṣaṇāt, because he upholds the world.

(3) Ṛṣi from Darśanāt, the sole beholder, or from ṛ to go. Sūrya, ekāki caratīti ; Yama, jagataḥ saṁyamanam tvatkṛtam.—Ś.

(4) The whole passage is nearly identical with Vājasaneya S. U., 15—18.

SIXTH CHAPTER

FIRST BRĀHMAṆA

1. यो ह वै ज्येष्ठं च श्रेष्ठं च वेद ज्येष्ठश्च श्रेष्ठश्च स्वानां भवति प्राणो वै ज्येष्ठश्च श्रेष्ठश्च ज्येष्ठश्च श्रेष्ठश्च स्वानां भवत्यपि च येषां बुभूषति य एवं वेद ॥

Whoever (1) knows what is oldest and best (2), becomes the oldest and best among his own. Life is verily what is oldest and best. Whoever thus knows, becomes the oldest and best amongst his own and also amongst others, should he wish so.

(1) It has been declared that life is the Gāyatrī. For what reason again is the Gāyatrī respresented by life, and not by speech or other functions ? The answer is, because life is the oldest and best, not so speech, etc. The present chapter has the object to determine, how life has those attributes. Or the connection of this with the preceding chapter may also thus be stated,—The meditation upon life in preference to the other organs has been declared, life being the Uktha, Yajus, Sāma, etc. The meditation upon life which in the former chapter has been enunciated merely as to its principal qualities, is here continued, although it is not meant to conclude this meditation. This chapter, as is evident even from the name of "compilation" which it bears has rather the object to enumerate the special fruits, not mentioned before, which result from a meditation on

life.—S'. This introduction of S'. is thus prefaced by Ā. G. The Omkāra, the triad of restraint, liberality and clemency, the meditation upon what is Brahman and what is not Brahman, the fruit of such a meditation, the place gained thereby, and the adoration of Āditya and the other deities, have been set forth in the fifth chapter. The sixth chapter has the object to explain especially the meditation on that which is not Brahman together with the fruit, resulting from it, and also certain ceremonies, of which the Srimantha is the first.

(2) *Vide* Chhand. U., 5, 2., 4. Br. Ā. U., 4, 1, 3.

2. यो ह वै वसिष्ठां वेद वसिष्ठः स्वानां भवति वाग्वै वसिष्ठा वसिष्ठः
स्वानां भवत्यपि च येषां बुभूषति य एवं वेद ॥

Whoever knows the best foundation (1), becomes best founded among his own. Speech is verily best founded. Whoever thus knows, becomes best founded amongst his own, and also amongst others, should he wish so.

(1) Vasiṣṭha means either best founded, or best clothed, of which is the effect from a superior power of speech. S'. *Vide*. Ch. 5, 2, 4. Br. Ā., 4, 1, 2.

3. यो ह वै प्रतिष्ठां वेद प्रतितिष्ठति समे प्रतितिष्ठति दुर्गे चक्षुर्वै प्रतिष्ठा
चक्षुषा हि समे च दुर्गे च प्रतितिष्ठति प्रतितिष्ठति समे प्रतिति-
ष्ठति दुर्गे य एवं वेद ॥

Whoever knows the best standing place, is best placed ; he stands firmly on what is even and uneven. The eye (1) is verily a firm standing place ; for by the eye he stands firmly on what is even and uneven.

Whoever thus knows, stands firmly upon what is even and uneven.

(1) Br. Ā., 4, 1, 4.

4. यो ह वै संपदं वेद सꣳ हास्मै पद्यते यं कामं कामयते श्रोत्रं वै संपच्छ्रोत्रे हीमे सर्वे वेदा अभिसंपन्नाः सꣳहास्मै पद्यते यं कामं कामयते य एवं वेद ॥

Whoever knows what is treasure, obtains whatever he desires. The ear (1) is treasure; for in the ear all the Vedas are treasured. Whoever thus knows, obtains whatever he desires.

(1) Br. Ā. 4, 1, 5.

5. यो ह वा आयतनं वेदायतनꣳ स्वानां भवत्यायतनं जनानां मनो वा आयतनमायतनꣳ स्वानां भवत्यायतनं जनानां य एवं वेद ॥

Whoever knows the place of refuge (1) becomes a place of refuge amongst his own. Mind (2) is verily the place of refuge. Whoever thus knows becomes a place of refuge amongst his own.

(1) For the mind is the place, upon which the organs and their objects are dependent, the objects of the senses being enjoyed by the soul through the mind.—Ś.

(2) *Vide* Br. Ā., 4, 1, 6.

6. यो ह वै प्रजापतिं वेद प्रजायते ह प्रजया पशुभी रेतो वै प्रजापतिः प्रजायते ह प्रजया पशुभिर्य एवं वेद ॥

Whoever knows Prajāpati (the lord of creation), becomes rich in offspring and in cattle. The seed is the source of creation. Whoever thus knows, creates offspring, and becomes rich in cattle.

7. ते हेमे प्राणा अहꣳ श्रेयसे विवदमाना ब्रह्म जग्मुस्तद्धोचुः को नो
वसिष्ठ इति तद्धोवाच यस्मिन्व उत्क्रान्त इदꣳ शरीरं पापीयो
मन्यते स वो वसिष्ठ इति ॥

The vital organs (1), disputing about their superiority, went to Brahman (2), and spoke to him,—"Who amongst us is best founded." He said,—"He amongst you is best founded, by whose departure the body is thought to suffer most."

(1) Speech and the rest *S*. *Vide* Chh. U., 5—15, Praśna U., 2, 2—4, where the dispute among the organs is also described.

(2) Brahman means here Prajāpati.

8. वाग्घोच्चक्राम सा संवत्सरं प्रोष्यागत्योवाच कथमशकत मदृते जीवितु-
मिति ते होचुर्यथा कला अवदन्तो वाचा प्राणन्तः प्राणेन पश्य-
न्तश्चक्षुषा शृण्वन्तः श्रोत्रेण विद्वाꣳसो मनसा प्रजायमाना
रेतसैवमजीविष्मेति प्रविवेश ह वाक् ॥

Speech departed. Returning after the absence of a year, it said, "How could you live without me?" They said,—"As dumb people who do not speak by speech, breathing by the vital breath, seeing by the eye, hearing by the ear, thinking by the mind, and begetting children, so have we lived." Then speech re-entered (the body).

9. चक्षुर्होच्चक्राम तत्संवत्सरं प्रोष्यागत्योवाच कथमशकत मदृते जीवितु-
मिति ते होचुर्यथा अन्धा अपश्यन्तश्चक्षुषा प्राणन्तः प्राणेन

वदन्तो वाचा शृण्वन्तः श्रोत्रेण विद्वाꣳसो मनसा प्रजायमाना रेतसैवमजीविष्मेति प्रविवेश ह चक्षुः ॥

The eye departed. Returning after the absence of a year, it said,—"How could you live without me?" They said—"As blind people, who do not see by the eye (live), breathing by the vital breath, speaking by the organ of speech, hearing by the ear, thinking by the mind, and begetting children, so have we lived." Then the eye re-entered (the body).

10. श्रोत्रꣳ होच्चक्राम तत्संवत्सरं प्रोष्यागत्योवाच कथमशकत मदृते जीवितुमिति ते होचुर्यथा बधिरा अशृण्वन्तः श्रोत्रेण प्राणन्तः प्राणेन वदन्तो वाचा पश्यन्तश्चक्षुषा विद्वाꣳसो मनसा प्रजायमाना रेतसैवमजीविष्मेति प्रविवेश ह श्रोत्रम् ॥

The ear departed. Returning after the absence of a year, it said,—"How could you live without me?" They said,—"As deaf people, who do not hear by the ear (live), breathing by the vital breath, speaking by the organ of speech, seeing by the eye, thinking by the mind, and begetting children, so have we lived." Then the ear re-entered (the body).

11. मनो होच्चक्राम तत्संवत्सरं प्रोष्यागत्योवाच कथमशकत मदृते जीवितुमिति ते होचुर्यथा मुग्धा अविद्वाꣳसो मनसा प्राणन्तः प्राणेन वदन्तो वाचा पश्यन्तश्चक्षुषा शृण्वन्तः श्रोत्रेण प्रजायमाना रेतसैवमजीविष्मेति प्रविवेश ह मनः ॥

The mind departed. Returning after the absence of a year, it said,—"How could you live without me?"

They said,—"As idiots who do not think by the mind (live), breathing by the vital breath, speaking by the organ of speech, seeing by the eye, hearing by the ear, and begetting children, so have we lived." Then the mind re-entered (the body).

12. रेतो होच्चक्राम तत्संवत्सरं प्रोष्यागत्योवाच कथमशकत मदृते जीवि-
तुमिति ते होचुर्यथा क्लीबा अप्रजायमाना रेतसा प्राणन्तः प्राणेन
वदन्तो वाचा पश्यन्तश्चक्षुषा शृण्वन्तः श्रोत्रेण विद्वाꣳसो मन-
सैवमजीविष्मेति प्रविवेश ह रेतः ॥

The organ of generation departed. Returning after the absence of a year, it said,—"How could you live without me?" They said,—"As impotent people who do not beget children (live), breathing by the vital breath, speaking by the organ of speech, seeing by the eye, hearing by the ear, and thinking by the mind, so have we lived." Then the organ of generation re-entered (the body).

13. अथ ह प्राण उत्क्रमिष्यन्यथा महासुहयः सैन्धवः पड्वीशशङ्कून्सं-
वृहेदेवꣳ हैवेमान्प्राणान्संववर्ह ते होचुर्मा भगव उत्क्रमीर्न वै
शक्ष्यामस्त्वदृते जीवितुमिति तस्यो मे बलिं कुरुतेति तथेति ॥

Then, the vital breath being about to depart, as a great, noble horse, born in the Sindhu country, raises its hoofs, so it shook those vital organs (from their places). They said,—"Do not depart, O venerable. We cannot live without thee." "If I am such, then offer sacrifice (1) to me." (They answered),—"Be it so."

(1) Or, as S'. explains it, "tribute".

14. सा ह वागुवाच यद्वा अहं वसिष्ठास्मि त्वं तद्वसिष्ठोऽसीति यद्वा अहं प्रतिष्ठास्मि त्वं तत्प्रतिष्ठोऽसीति चक्षुर्यद्वा अहꣳ संपदस्मि त्वं तत्संपदसीति श्रोत्रं यद्वा अहमायतनमस्मि त्वं तदायतनमसीति मनो यद्वा अहं प्रजातिरस्मि त्वं तत्प्रजातिरसीति रेतस्तस्यो मे किमन्नं किं वास इति यदिदं किंचाश्वभ्य आकृमिभ्य आकीट-पतङ्गेभ्यस्तत्तेऽन्नमापो वास इति न ह वा अस्यानन्नं जग्धं भवति नान्नं परिगृहीतं य एवमेतदन्नस्यान्नं वेद तद्विद्वाꣳसः श्रोत्रिया अशिष्यन्त आचामन्त्यशित्वाचामन्त्येतमेव तदनमनग्नं कुर्वन्तो मन्यन्ते ॥

Speech said,—" That I am founded, is, because thou art founded." The eye said, " That I am a standing place, is, because thou art a standing place." The ear said,—" That I am a treasure, is, because thou art a treasure." The mind said,—" That I am a place of refuge, is, because thou art a place of refuge." The organ of generation said,—" That I am a source of procreation, is, because thou art a source of procreation." (Life said),—" If I am such, what then is my food, what then is my foundation ? " (They said),—" All this whatsoever, horses, worms, small insects, locusts, and so on, is thy food ; the waters are thy dwelling place " (1). He who thus knows, does not eat (any food) which is not to be eaten (2), nor does he take (any gift) which is not to be taken (3). Therefore those acquainted with the Vedas who thus know, sip water when commencing to eat, and sip water (again) after they have eaten, thinking, that (thereby) they have clothed the naked (life).

(1) Or thy garment.

(2) He is not guilty of any fault by eating food which is prohibited.

(3) Thus I rendered "anannam" in accordance with S'aṅkara's explanation. It is the same term which in the first half of the sentence is translated by "not to be eaten".

SECOND BRĀHMAṆA

1. श्वेतकेतुर्ह वा आरुणेयः पञ्चालानां परिषदमाजगाम स आजगाम जैवलिं प्रवाहणं परिचारयमाणं तमुदीक्ष्याभ्युवाद कुमार ३ इति स भो ३ इति प्रतिशुश्रावानुशिष्टोन्वसि पित्रेत्योमिति होवाच ॥

S'vetaketu (1), Āruṇeya (2), came to the assembly of the Pañcālas. He came to Pravāhaṇa, the son of Jīvala, who was attended by his courtiers. Seeing him, he saluted him by the words,—"Is it thou, O youth (3)?" He answered, "Ah, yes, O friend" (4). "Art thou instructed by thy father?" He said, "Om (I am)."

(1) All that has been omitted in the former chapters of this Upaniṣad, is to be mentioned in this part, the "Khilakāṇda". At the end of the seventh chapter he who has been addicted during his life to both, to knowledge and to the performance of rites, asks on the approach of death for the road of Agni with the words "Agni lead me on the good path". By the qualification of "good" the existence of many paths is indicated, and the roads themselves are paths towards the acquirement of the effects, resulting from works. They succinctly show the whole result of worldly endeavours, be they works flowing from mere natural

knowledge or from scriptural knowledge. Although, therefore, natural sin has been explained in the words "threefold is the offspring of Prajāpati," and also its effects in the words: "He has not to perform this work," and although the consequences of scriptural knowledge have been set forth at the end of the topic on "the obtaining of the nature of the three-fold food" and at the commencement of the knowledge of Brahman, as implied in the injunction to abstain from those consequences, yet it has merely been said, that by work alone the world of the forefathers and by knowledge and by work, accompanied with knowledge, the world of the gods is gained, but by what means either is to be obtained has not been stated. To exhibit them and to give finally a succinct view of the whole meaning of the Śāstra, is the object of the present Khilakāṇḍa. Ś.—The present narrative, with the modification of some words, is essentially the same with Chh. U., 5, 3—10.

(2) Āruṇeya, the son of Āruṇi, who is the son of Aruṇa.—Ś.

(3) The address of the king is merely Kumāra, of which the last syllable is Pluta (three times the length of a short vowel), to indicate contempt, says—Ś.

(4) Śvetaketu returns the salutation of the king by the simple syllable, Bho' with Pluta, which, according to Ś., is not a particle suited in addressing a king.

2. वेत्थ यथेमाः प्रजाः प्रयत्यो विप्रतिपद्यन्ता ३ इति नेति होवाच वेत्थो यथेमं लोकं पुनरापद्यन्ता ३ इति नेति हैवोवाच वेत्थो यथासौ लोक एवं बहुभिः पुनः पुनः प्रयद्भिर्न संपूर्यता ३ इति नेति हैवोवाच वेत्थो यतिथ्यामाहुत्याꣳ हुतायामापः पुरुषवाचो भूत्वा समुत्थाय वदन्ती ३ इति नेति हैवोवाच वेत्थो देवयानस्य वा पथः प्रतिपदं पितृयाणस्य वा यत्कृत्वा देवयानं वा पन्थानं प्रतिपद्यन्ते पितृयाणं वापि हि न ऋषेर्वचः श्रुतं । द्वे सृती अश्रृणवं पितृणामहं देवानामुत मर्त्यानां । ताभ्यामिदं विश्वमेज-

त्समेति यदन्तरा पितरं मातरं चेति नाहमत एकंच न वेदेति होवाच ॥

"Dost thou know, how the creatures who depart this life, proceed on different roads?" "He said,—" I do not know." "Dost thou know, how they return to this world?" He said,—" I do not know." "Dost thou know, how many, who have quitted again and again this world, no more return to it?" He said,—" I do not know." "Dost thou know at which sacrifice the waters become the words of man, and rise to speak?" He said,—" I do not know." "Dost thou know the means of obtaining the road, which is called Devayāna, or the road, called Pitṛyāna, (that is to say, dost thou know) by which work the road to the world of the gods or of the forefathers is obtained? It is heard (also) the words of the Ṛṣi (1), I heard of two roads, the one (2) of the forefathers; and the other of the gods (either of which must be proceeded on) by mortals. As distant as is the father from the mother (3), (distant is the one road from the other)." "I do not know anything of all this," said he.

(1) Of the Mantra.—S'.

(2) Leading to the world of the forefathers.

(3) Father and mother denote heaven and earth, the two halves of the mundane egg.—S'.

3. अथैनं वसत्योपमन्त्रयांचक्रेऽनादृत्य वसतिं कुमारः प्रदुद्राव स आजगाम पितरं तꣳ होवाचेति वाव किल नो भवान्पुरानुशिष्टा-

नवोचदिति कथꣳ सुमेध इति पञ्च मा प्रश्नान् राजन्यबन्धुर-
प्राक्षीत्ततो नैकंचन वेदेति कतमे त इतीम इति ह प्रतीकान्युदा-
जहार ॥

Then he invited him to sit. Not heeding the proffered seat the youth hastened away. He went to his father and said to him, "Hast thou not before declared us to be instructed (in all science)?" "What then, O youth of subtile mind?" "The man whose companions are kings, asked me five questions, of which I did not know one." "Which are they?" "These," and he mentioned them one after another.

4. स होवाच तथा नस्त्वं तात जानीथा यथा यदहं किंच वेद सर्वमहं
तत्तुभ्यमवोचं प्रेहि तु तत्र प्रतीत्य ब्रह्मचर्यं वत्स्याव इति भवानेव
गच्छत्विति स आजगाम गौतमो यत्र प्रवाहणस्य जैवलेरास
तस्मा आसनमाहृत्योदकमाहारयांचकाराथ हास्मा अर्घ्यं चकार
तꣳ होवाच वरं भगवते गौतमाय दद्म इति ॥

He said, "Thou must know, O beloved one, that I told thee all which I know myself. Up then. Going there, let us perform the service of a Brahma student (to the king)." "Do thou go, O Venerable." Gautama went, where Pravāhaṇa, the son of Jīvala held his residence. (The king) bringing a seat for him, had (also) water brought; then he made the oblation according to rite. He said to him, "We grant thee a boon (1) O respected Gautama."

(1) By which is meant a gift of cows, horses, etc.—Ś.

5. स होवाच प्रतिज्ञातो म एष वरो यां तु कुमारस्यान्ते वाचमभाषथास्तां मे ब्रूहीति ॥

He said,—"(I accept) the boon which thou hast promised me. Explain to me the word which thou hast said before to the youth."

6. स होवाच दैवेषु वै गौतम तद्वरेषु मानुषाणां ब्रूहीति ॥

He said, "That is a boon concerning gods; name one concerning men."

7. स होवाच विज्ञायते हास्ति हिरण्यस्यापात्तं गोअश्वानां दासीनां प्रवाराणां परिधानस्य मा नो भवान्बहोरनन्तस्यापर्यन्तस्याभ्यवदान्योऽभूदिति स वै गौतम तीर्थेनेच्छासा इत्युपैम्यहं भवन्तमिति वाचाह स्मैव पूर्व उपयन्ति स होपायनकीर्त्योवास ॥

He said, "Thou knowest well, I have enough of gold, of cows and horses, female slaves, dependants and garments. Do thou not withhold from us the gift which is great, permanent, and extends (to many generations)." He said, "Verily according to rite thou desirest, O Gautama (to obtain knowledge from me)." He said, "I approach thee as pupil according to the rite" (1). With words others also approached of old (2) (their teachers). He resided there through the mere name of a respectful gift.

(1) Enjoined by the Sāstra.—S'.

(2) Brāhmans went to Kṣatriyas, or Kṣatriyas to Vaiśyas for acquiring knowledge, only with words, and not with presents.

8. स होवाच यथा नस्त्वं गौतम मापराधास्तव च पितामहा यथेयं विद्येतः पूर्वं न कस्मिंश्चन ब्राह्मण उवास तां त्वहं तुभ्यं वक्ष्यामि को हि त्वैवं ब्रुवन्तमर्हति प्रत्याख्यातुमिति ॥

He said, "Do not hold us guilty, O Gautama, as thy forefathers (held not guilty my forefathers). That this knowledge in former times was not possessed by a Brāhmaṇa thou knowest thyself. But I will explain it to thee; for whoever could refuse it to one who thus speaks.

9. असौ वै लोकोऽग्निर्गौतम तस्यादित्य एव समिद्रश्मयो धूमोऽहरर्चिर्दिशोऽङ्गारा अवान्तरदिशो विस्फुलिङ्गास्तस्मिन्नेतस्मिन्नग्नौ देवाः श्रद्धां जुह्वति तस्या आहुत्यै सोमो राजा संभवति ॥

That world (1) is the fire, O Gautama. The sun Āditya is its fuel; his rays the smoke (2); the day the flame (3); the quarters the coals (4); the within lying quarters (5) the sparks. The gods (6) offer faith to this fire. From this offering king Soma springs forth (7).

(1) The king answers first the fourth question, because, says Ś., on its solution also the other questions are solved. That world, *viz.*, the heavens.

(2) As likewise rising from the fuel.—Ś.

(3) Being alike through manifestation.—Ś.

(4) Resembling them by their bringing to rest.—Ś.

(5) Flying off from the other quarters like the sparks from fire.—S'.

(6) Indra, and the rest.—S'.

(7) He is king of the forefathers and of the Brāhmaṇas.—S'.

10. पर्जन्यो वाग्निर्गौतम तस्य संवत्सर एव समिदभ्राणि धूमो विद्युदर्चिरशनिरङ्गारा ह्रादुनयो विस्फुलिङ्गास्तस्मिन्नेतस्मिन्नग्नौ देवाः सोमꣳ राजानं जुह्वति तस्या आहुत्यै वृष्टिः संभवति ॥

Or Parjanya (1) is fire,—O Gautama ; the year (2) is its fuel ; the clouds the smoke (3) ; the lightning the flame (4) ; the thunderbolt the coals (5) ; the thunder claps the spark (6). The gods offer king Soma to this fire. From this offering rain springs forth.

(1) Parjanya, the second locality of the offerings, is the tutelary deity of rain.—S'.

(2) The two offerings of the fire sacrifice, *viz.*, the offerings in the morning and in the evening, exist in this world in a manifested form, as do also the necessary appliances of the sacrifice, *viz.*, the sacrificial fire, the wood, the coals and the sparks of the fire, the things which are offered as milk, ghee, etc. When they rise to the other world, to heaven or their unmanifested state, they exist according to their subtile nature as do also those appliances. Again, at the time of manifestation, or at the creation of the world the ceremonial work is changed by assuming the state of the fire of the atmosphere, etc. The same changes undergo also at present the work, called fire-sacrifice. In this manner the whole world is the effect of the invisible changes of the two offerings of the fire-sacrifice. Those six necessary appliances will be mentioned afterwards for the sake of extolling the two offerings ; but here, where the consequences, resulting from the work of the sacrifices are

to be explained, the object is to set forth the doctrine of the five fires as the cause of obtaining the northern path for the enjoyment of the fruit derived from special work. The organs of the body in their relation to the soul are here the offering priests of the fire-sacrifice. Considered in their relation to the gods, they are Indra and the other gods who are the offering priests for the fire of heaven, etc. They offer the fire-sacrifice for the sake of the fruit, derived from it. When they have enjoyed the whole fruit, they perform the same sacrifice again. • In this manner the organs are called gods. In this our present state, also, any offering, as milk, etc., dependent on the rite of the fire sacrifice, which has been thrown in the sacrificial fire and consumed by it, enters in its invisible, subtile form, together with the sacrificer, this world further in the form of smoke, the atmosphere, and from the atmospheres the heavens. These are the subtile waters, the effect of offerings, the part of the fire-sacrifice, bearing the name of faith, which at the world of the moon create another body for the sacrificer, and when entering the heavens, are offered. Therefore the waters which are parts of the fire-sacrifice and the cause that the sacrifice obtains another body in the world of the moon are called faith. They bear the name of waters, because the greater part of their composition is water. The fire-sacrifice however, is merely a representative of all the other Vedic rites, and what has been said about the former, applies also to the latter.—S'.

(3) They are smoke, either from their being produced from smoke or from their similar appearance.—S'.

(4) Both having the power of manifestation.—S'.

(5) Both being alike extinguishable and hard.—S'.

(6) Both flying off and being alike frequent.—S'.

11. अयं वै लोकोऽग्निर्गौतम तस्य पृथिव्येव समिदग्निर्धूमो रात्रिरर्चिश्चन्द्रमा
अङ्गारा नक्षत्राणि विस्फुलिङ्गास्तस्मिन्नेतस्मिन्नग्नौ देवा वृष्टिं
जुह्वति तस्या आहुत्या अन्नꣳ संभवति ॥

This world (1) is fire, O Gautama. The earth is its fuel (2); fire the smoke (3); night the flame (4); the moon the coals (5): the stars the sparks. The gods offer rain to this fire. From this offering food springs forth.

(1) This world, the place where living creatures are born, and have their enjoyment.—S'.

(2) For by the earth, furnished with the means of enjoyment for innumerable living creatures, this world is nourished.—S'.

(3) It is fire, as rising from the earth in the same manner as smoke from fire.—S'.

(4) The night is the flame, because as the flame has its origin from the connection of fuel with fire, so the night from the connection with its fuel; *viz.*, the earth, the darkness of the night being called the shadow of the earth, S'. To which Ā. G. adds; for darkness is the place of Rāhu, and this is the shadow of the earth.

(5) The moon is the coals, from similarity of origin; for as from the name, coals are produced, so the moon is produced in the night. Or because both are alike extinguishable.—S'.

12. पुरुषो वाग्निर्गौतम तस्य व्यात्तमेव समित्प्राणो धूमो वागर्चि-
श्चक्षुरङ्गाराः श्रोत्रं विस्फुलिङ्गास्तस्मिन्नेतस्मिन्नग्नौ देवा अन्नं
जुह्वति तस्या आहुत्यै रेतः संभवति ॥

Man is fire, O Gautama. His open mouth is the fuel (1); breath the smoke (2); speech, the flame (3); the eye the coals; the ear the sparks. The gods offer food in this fire. From this offering seed springs forth.

(1) For through the mouth man is lighted up, *i.e.*, enlightened with regard to speech, study of the Vedas, etc.—S'.

(2) Both rising equally upwards.—S'.

(3) From their like power of manifestation.—S'.

13. योषा वा अग्निर्गौतम तस्या उपस्थ एव समिल्लोमानि धूमो यो-
निरर्चिर्यदन्तः करोति तेऽङ्गारा अभिनन्दा विस्फुलिङ्गा-
स्तस्मिन्नेतस्मिन्नग्नौ देवा रेतो जुह्वति तस्या आहुत्यै पुरुषः
संभवति स जीवति यावज्जीवत्यथ यदाम्रियते ॥

Woman is fire, O Gautama, her haunch the fuel; the hairs on the body the smoke (1); the organ of generation the flame (2); cohabitation the coals (3); the fits of enjoyment the sparks. The gods offer seed in this fire. From this offering man springs forth (4). He lives as long as he lives (5). When he dies.

(1) Both rising equally upwards.—S'.

(2) From likeness of colour.—S'.

(3) Both equally extinguishing—S'.

(4) In this manner the waters, bearing the name of faith, are gradually offered in the fires of heaven, of Parjanya, of this world, of man, and of woman, and having assumed gradually a grosser and grosser shape, they are the cause of the creation of man. And thereby the fourth question, *viz.*, "Dost thou know, at the offering of which sacrifice, the waters becoming the worlds of man, rise to speak?" is decided, *viz.*, they become so, on the performance of the fifth offering in the fire which is woman, when the waters become seed.—S'.

(5) As long as the fruit of the work continues, which had been the cause of his having assumed his present body.—S'.

14. अथैनमग्नये हरन्ति तस्याग्निरेवाग्निर्भवति समित्समिद्धूमो धूमोऽर्चिरर्चिरङ्गारा अङ्गारा विस्फुलिङ्गा विस्फुलिङ्गास्तस्मिन्नेतस्मिन्नग्नौ देवाः पुरुषं जुह्वति तस्या आहुत्यै पुरुषो भास्वरवर्णः संभवति ॥

Then they (1) take him (2) to the fire; his fire becomes fire: his fuel, fuel; his smoke, smoke; his flame, flame; his coals, coals; his sparks, sparks. The gods offer man in this fire. From this offering, man in radiant splendour springs forth.

(1) The Ṛtviks or priests, performing the last rites.—Ś.

(2) The deceased who in this case is himself the offering.—Ś.

15. ते य एवमेतद्विदुर्ये चामी अरण्ये श्रद्धाꣳ सत्यमुपासते तेऽर्चिरभिसंभवन्त्यर्चिषोऽहरह्न आपूर्यमाणपक्षमापूर्यमाणपक्षाद्यान्षण्मासानुदङ्ङादित्य एति मासेभ्यो देवलोकं देवलोकादादित्यमादित्याद्वैद्युतं तान्वैद्युतान्पुरुषो मानस एत्य ब्रह्मलोकान् गमयति तेषु ब्रह्मलोकेषु पराः परावतो वसन्ति तेषां न पुनरावृत्तिः ॥

Those (1) who have this knowledge (2), and those who in the forest (3) meditate with faith on truth (4), obtain the flame (5), from the flame the day; from the day the light half of the moon; from the light half of the moon the six months when the sun moves to the north; from those months the world of the gods; from the world of the gods the sun; from the sun the world of the lightning. Those who have obtained the world of the lightning, are removed by the Puruṣa created by the mind (6) to the Brahma worlds (7). In those Brahma worlds exalted they live infinite years. For them, there is no return (to this world) (8).

(1) The present section replies to the first question and to part of the fifth, *viz.*, "Dost thou know, in what way the creatures, departing this life proceed on different roads ?" and "Dost thou know the means of obtaining the road which is called Devayāna" ?

(2) Those who thus know. The knowledge does not refer to one of those fires only, but to the five fires together, as is evident from the Chha. U., where (5, 10, 10) the knowledge of the five first is expressly mentioned with reference to the same topic. The knowledge concerns the nature of those first and not the comparisons, which are only made for the sake of extolling the fire-sacrifice. But how are those who thus know ? not the householders in general ; for those among them who have not the knowledge of the five fires, are to gain the worlds of smoke as the fruit, etc., resulting from sacrifice, gifts and austerity, (16). Not those who have retired to the forest, nor religious mendicants ; for they are mentioned in the passage of the text immediately following, "those who in the forest," and the knowledge of the five fires has connection with the work of the householders, and not with that of hermits, or religious mendicants. Nor lastly the Brahmacāris, because their entering upon the northern path is proved by the Smṛti. Therefore the words "those who know," refer to the house-holders who have a knowledge of the five fires.—S'.

(3) Those who in the forest, *viz.*, those who have retired from the world to the forest (the vanaprasthās,) and also the religious mendicants (Parivrājakas).

(4) Who meditate on truth, that is to say on truth, that is to say on Brahman in the form of Hiraṇyagarbha,

not such as meditate with faith simply. As long as the householders have not the knowledge of the five fires, or of Brahman, so long, after the fifth offering in the gradual order of those offerings has been performed, they are again born from the fire of woman, and on their return to this world they perform again ceremonial work. By means of this work they go again in the gradual procession from one world to another up to the world of the forefathers, and from there backwards in the reverse order to this world. Here, being again born from the fire of woman, the same circle is to be described like the continual rotation of a water-wheel.—S′.

(5) Flame means here the tutelary deity of the fire, and so the terms "the day," "the light half of the moon," the tutelary deities of the day, etc.

(6) By Brahman.—S′.

(7) The Brahma worlds, the plural refers either to different regions in the Brahma world, which is only one, or to the difference of the rewards, derived from different modes of meditation.—S′.

(8) That to say, there is no return for them during the present duration of the world, but they return of course on a new creation, as absolute liberation from transmigration, is only the effect from the knowledge of Brahman, while the knowledge here in question is merely a knowledge of the five fires, or of Brahman in the form of Hiraṇyagarbha. This view is clear from the whole doctrine of this Upaniṣad, and does not require any further proof; but S′. wastes much ingenuity to prove it from the form of language of another passage, where the "not return" has the addition "to this world".

16. अथ ये यज्ञेन दानेन तपसा लोकाञ्जयन्ति ते धूममभिसंभवन्ति धूमाद्रात्रिꣳ रात्रेरपक्षीयमाणपक्षमपक्षीयमाणपक्षाद्यान्षण्मासान्द-क्षिणादित्य एति मासेभ्यः पितृलोकं पितृलोकाच्चन्द्रं ते चन्द्रं

प्राप्यान्नं भवन्ति तांस्तत्र देवा यथा सोमं राजानमाप्यायस्वापक्षीयस्वेत्येवमेनांस्तत्र भक्षयन्ति तेषां यदा तत्पर्यवैत्यथेममेवाकाशमभिनिष्पद्यन्त आकाशाद्वायुं वायोर्वृष्टिं वृष्टेः पृथिवीं ते पृथिवीं प्राप्यान्नं भवन्ति ते पुनः पुरुषाग्नौ हूयन्ते ततो योषाग्नौ जायन्ते लोकान्प्रत्युत्थायिनस्त एवमेवानुपरिवर्तन्तेऽथ य एतौ पन्थानौ न विदुस्ते कीटाः पतङ्गा यदिदं दन्दशूकम् ॥

Again (1), those who conquer the worlds by sacrifice, gifts and austerity (2), obtain smoke (3), from smoke night; from night the dark half of the moon; from the dark half of the moon the six months when the sun moves to the south; from those months the world of the forefathers; from the world of the forefathers the moon. Having obtained the moon, they become food. As (the offering priests) consume (again and again) king Soma, saying, do increase, and do decrease, so the gods consume them there (4). When that (fruit of their works) ceases, then they obtain the ether, from the ether the air, from the air rain, from rain the earth. Having obtained the earth, they become food (5). Again they are offered in the fire of man; hence they are born in the fire of woman. Proceeding from world to world, they return in this way again and again. Again, those who do not know those roads, become worms, locusts and gnats (6).

(1) Those householders, who have not the knowledge of the five fires.

(2) Ś. says that "gifts and austerity" do not refer to such as are enjoined by the Vedas, as they would be included in "sacrifice".

(3) The deities of smoke, etc.

(4) As the offering priests consume again and again the Soma juice, so the performers of rites who are the supporters of the gods by sacrifices, etc., on their obtaining new bodies in the Soma world, are turned back again and again to this world for the performance of troublesome work by the gods, from whom they receive such rewards as are in correspondence with their work.—Ś. And thereby is answered the second-half of the fifth question.

(5) This is the reply to the second question.

(6) The answer to the third question.

THIRD BRĀHMAṆA

1. स यः कामयेत महत्प्राप्नुयामित्युदगयन आपूर्यमाणपक्षस्य पुण्याहे द्वादशाहमुपसद्व्रती भूत्वौदुम्बरे कꣳसे चमसे वा सर्वौषधं फलानीति संभृत्य परिसमुह्य परिलिप्याग्निमुपसमाधाय परिस्तीर्यावृताज्यꣳ सꣳस्कृत्य पुꣳसा नक्षत्रेण मन्थꣳ संनीय जुहोति—यावन्तो देवास्त्वयि जातवेदस्तिर्यञ्चो घ्नन्ति पुरुषस्य कामान् । तेभ्योऽहं भागधेयं जुहोमि ते मा तृप्ताः सर्वैः कामैस्तर्पयन्तु स्वाहा । या तिरश्ची निपद्यतेऽहं विधरणी इति । तां त्वा घृतस्य धारया यजे सꣳराधनीमहꣳ स्वाहा ॥

Whoever desires (1) to obtain greatness, (has to perform the following rite). At the time when the sun moves to the north on an auspicious day of the light half of the moon, the twelfth day of his performing the vow named Upasad (2), after he has gathered and mixed together all kinds of herbs and fruits in a shell-shaped vessel or in a spoon, either made of the wood of the conglomerate fig-tree; after he has sprinkled with water (the place of offering), placed the cow-dung, lightened the fire spread (the kus'a grass), cleaned the covered ghee, and taken the mixture at the time of a male star, he performs the offering (3), (saying),—"To all the gods of crooked mind who under thy control, O Jātaveda (4), obstruct man's desire, do I offer a share (of the sacrifice). Satisfied, let them satisfy me with all desires. Svāhā to the goddess of crooked mind who under the thought that she is the upholder (of all) has taken refuge to thee; to this deity who is the accomplisher of all, I offer a part of the ghee, Svāhā!

(1) The ultimate effect, derived from knowledge and work, has been declared. Knowledge is independent of any other thing, but work depends both upon the wealth of gods and upon that of man. For the sake of work, therefore, wealth must be acquired, and this by means unaccompanied with sin. For the acquirement of wealth the ceremony, called Mantha, is ordained, in order that greatness be obtained; for wealth is the consequence of greatness.—S'.

(2) The vow which is called Upasad is part of the Votiṣṭoma rites, and consists in limiting the food for a period of twelve days taking the first day as much milk as is contained in one udder of a cow, the second as is contained in two, the third in three, and the fourth in four, then on the fifth again taking three, and so down to one, when again one is added on each successive day.—S'.

(3) Then while offering ghee, he speaks the following Mantras.—S'.

(4) Fire.

2. ज्येष्ठाय स्वाहा श्रेष्ठाय स्वाहेत्यग्नौ हुत्वा मन्थे स॰स्रवमवनयति प्राणाय स्वाहा वसिष्ठायै स्वाहेत्यग्नौ हुत्वा मन्थे स॰स्रवमवनयति वाचे स्वाहा प्रतिष्ठायै स्वाहेत्यग्नौ हुत्वा मन्थे स॰स्रवमवनयति चक्षुषे स्वाहा संपदे स्वाहेत्यग्नौ हुत्वा मन्थे स॰स्रवमवनयति श्रोत्राय स्वाहाऽयतनाय स्वाहेत्यग्नौ हुत्वा मन्थे स॰स्रवमवनयति मनसे स्वाहा प्रजात्यै स्वाहेत्यग्नौ हुत्वा मन्थे स॰स्रवमवनयति रेतसे स्वाहेत्यग्नौ हुत्वा मन्थे स॰स्रवमवनयति ॥

"Svāhā to the eldest, Svāhā to the best!" (1) with these words offering to the fire, he drops the remainder (of the ghee) into the churning vessel. "Svāhā to life, Svāhā to what is firmly founded!" with these words offering to the fire, he drops the remainder (of the ghee) into the churning vessel. "Svāhā to speech, Svāhā to the standing place!" with these words offering to the fire, he drops the remainder (of the ghee) into the churning vessel. "Svāhā to the eye, Svāhā to the treasure!" with these words offering to the fire, he drops the remainder of the ghee into the churning vessel. "Svāhā to the ear, S'vāhā to the place of refuge!" with these words offering to the fire, he drops the remainder (of the ghee) into the churning vessel. "Svāhā to the mind, Svāhā to the source of procreation!" with these words offering to the fire, he drops the remainder (of the ghee) into the churning vessel "Svāhā to the seed!" with these words offering to the fire, he drops the remainder (of the ghee) into the churning vessel.

(1) The eldest and the best is life. Compare this passage with 6, 1, 1—6.

3. अग्नये स्वाहेत्यग्नौ हुत्वा मन्थे संस्रवमवनयति सोमाय स्वाहेत्यग्नौ हुत्वा मन्थे संस्रवमवनयति भूः स्वाहेत्यग्नौ हुत्वा मन्थे संस्रवमवनयति भुवः स्वाहेत्यग्नौ हुत्वा मन्थे संस्रवमवनयति स्वः स्वाहेत्यग्नौ हुत्वा मन्थे संस्रवमवनयति भूर्भुवः स्वः स्वाहेत्यग्नौ हुत्वा मन्थे संस्रवमवनयति ब्रह्मणे स्वाहेत्यग्नौ हुत्वा मन्थे संस्रवमवनयति क्षत्राय स्वाहेत्यग्नौ हुत्वा मन्थे संस्रवमवनयति भूताय स्वाहेत्यग्नौ हुत्वा मन्थे संस्रवमवनयति भविष्यते स्वाहेत्यग्नौ हुत्वा मन्थे संस्रवमवनयति विश्वाय स्वाहेत्यग्नौ हुत्वा मन्थे संस्रवमवनयति सर्वाय स्वाहेत्यग्नौ हुत्वा मन्थे संस्रवमवनयति प्रजापतये स्वाहेत्यग्नौ हुत्वा मन्थे संस्रवमवनयति ॥

"Svāhā to the fire!" with these words offering to the fire, he drops the remainder (of the ghee) into the churning vessel. "Svāhā to Soma!" with these words offering to the fire, he drops the remainder (of the ghee) into the churning vessel. "Svāhā to the earth!" with these words offering to the fire, he drops the remainder (of the ghee) into the churning vessel. "Svāhā to the atmosphere!" with these words offering to the fire, he drops the remainder (of the ghee) into the churning vessel. "Svāhā to the heavens!" with these words offering to the fire, he drops the remainder (of the ghee) into the churning vessel. "Svāhā to the earth, to the atmosphere and to the heavens!" with these words offering to the fire, he drops the remainder (of the ghee) into the churning vessel. "Svāhā to the Brahman!" with these words offering to the fire, he drops the remainder (of the ghee) into the churning vessel. "Svāhā to the Kṣattra," with these words offering to the fire, he drops the remainder (of the ghee) into the churning vessel. "Svâhā to the past!" with these words offering to the fire, he drops the remainder (of the ghee) into the churning vessel. "Svāhā to the future!" with these words offering to the fire, he drops the remainder (of the ghee) into the churning vessel. "Svāhā to the universe!" with these words offering to the fire he drops the remainder (of the ghee) into the churning vessel. "Svāhā to all!" with these words offering to the fire, he drops the remainder (of the ghee) into the churning vessel. "Swāhā to Prajāpati" with these words offering to the fire, he drops the remainder (of the ghee) into the charning vessel.

4. अथैनमभिमृशति भ्रमदसि ज्वलदसि पूर्णमसि प्रस्तब्धमस्येकसभमसि हिंकृतमसि हिंक्रियमाणमस्युद्गीथमस्युद्गीयमानमसि श्रावितमसि प्रत्याश्रावितमस्यार्द्रे संदीप्तमसि विभूरसि प्रभूरस्यन्नमसि ज्योतिरसि निधनमसि संवर्गोऽसीति ॥

Then he touches that (mixture saying), "Thou art moveable (1); thou art resplendent (2), thou art full (3);

thou art unshaken (4); thou art the one pervader of this (universe); thou art proclaimed (5); thou art proclaimed again (6); thou art sung (7); thou art sung again (8); thou art sounded (9); thou art resounded (10); thou shinest in the cloud (11); thou art pervading; thou art powerful; thou art food (12); thou art splendour (13); thou art destruction (14); thou art identity."

(1) Moveable, because life is moveable, and thou art of the same nature as life.—Ā. G.

(2) Because fire, the same as thou, is so.—Ā. G.

(3) In thy nature as Brahman.—Ā. G.

(4) In thy likeness of the sky.—Ā. G.

(5) By the Prastotā at the commencement of the sacrifice.—Ā. G.

(6) By the same in its middle.—Ā. G.

(7) By the Udgāta at the commencement of the sacrifice.—Ā. G.

(8) By the same in its middle.—Ā. G.

(9) By the Adhvaryu.—Ā. G.

(10) By the Agnīdhra.—Ā. G.

(11) According to Ā. G.'s explanation; Literally, in what is moist.

(12) Food, represented by Soma, all things to be enjoyed.—Ā. G.

(13) Splendour as represented by fire, in its nature as consumer.—Ā. G.

(14) Destroyer, being the cause of destruction of all things according to their relation to the soul and to the deities.—Ā. G.

5. अथैनमुद्यच्छत्यामꣳ स्यामꣳ हि ते महि स हि राजेशानोऽधिपतिः स माꣳ राजेशानोऽधिपतिं करोत्विति ।

Then he raises that (mixture, saying),—"Thou thinkest (of all); we think of thy greatness; for he is king, lord and sovereign. Let him, the king and lord, make me a sovereign."

6. अथैनमाचामति तत्सवितुर्वरेण्यं मधुवाता ऋतायते मधु क्षरन्ति सिन्धवः माध्वीर्नः सन्त्वोषधीर्भूः स्वाहा भर्गो देवस्य धीमहि मधु नक्तमुतोषसो मधुमत्पार्थिवꣳ रजः मधु द्यौरस्तु नः पिता भुवः स्वाहा धियो यो नः प्रचोदयान्मधुमान्नो वनस्पतिर्मधुमाँ ३ अस्तु सूर्यः माध्वीर्गावो भवन्तु नः स्वः स्वाहेति सर्वां च सावित्रीमन्वाह सर्वाश्च मधुमतीरहमेवेदꣳ सर्वं भूयासं भूर्भुवः स्वः स्वाहेत्यन्तत आचम्य पाणी प्रक्षाल्य जघनेनाग्निं प्राक्शिराः संविशति प्रातरादित्यमुपतिष्ठते दिशामेकपुण्डरीकमस्यहं मनुष्याणामेकपुण्डरीकं भूयासमिति यथेतमेत्य जघनेनाग्निमासीनो वꣳशं जपति ।

Then he eats (1) that (mixture, and with the words),—"Let us reflect on the adorable light of Savitā," (*viz.*) May the winds convey happiness; may the rivers drop happiness; may the herbs be of sweet juice to us. "Svāhā to the earth!" let him take the first morsel. (With the words),—"Let us reflect on the adorable light of savitā," (*viz.*). May the night, yea even the morning-dawns (bring us) happiness, (may be fraught with happiness) the dust of the earth. May the heavens, our father, (bring us) happiness. "Svāhā to the atmosphere!" (let him take the second morsel). With the words,—" (Let us reflect on the adorable light of Savitā) who quickens our understanding, (*viz.*) May Vanaspati (bring) us happiness; may the sun (bring) us happiness; may his rays (bring) us happiness. Svāhā to the heavens!" let him take the third morsel. And having repeated the whole Sāvitri and all the benedictions (2), he says at the close (of the rite), "May I become this all, Svāhā to the earth, the atmosphere and the heavens!" Then having sipped (water) and cleaned his hands, he touches the fire with his thigh, his head turned towards the east. (Then) in the morning dawn he adores Āditya (with the Mantra),—" Thou art the one lotus of the quarters; may I become the one lotus of men." As he (before) approached the fire, so he (again) approaches it with the thigh, and after being seated, he mutters the school (3).

(1) He shall gradually take three morsels. With the first morsel he shall recite the first foot of the Gāyatrī and the first sacred word (Bhū), with the second the second foot and the second sacred word (Bhuvaḥ), and with the third the third foot and the third sacred (Svaḥ). After he has muttered the three sacred words, he should clean the vessel, in which he has dropped the remainder of the ghee, and drink this in silence.—S'.

(2) He eats the fourth morsel.—Ā. G.

(3) The succession of teachers and disciples.

7. तꣳहैतमुद्दालक आरुणिर्वाजसनेयाय याज्ञवल्क्यायान्तेवासिन
उक्त्वोवाचापि य एनꣳ शुष्के स्थाणौ निषिञ्चेज्जायेरञ्छाखाः
प्ररोहेयुः पलाशानीति ।

Uddālaka Āruṇi having explained this (mixture) to his disciple, Yājñavalkya, of the Vājasaneya school, said,—" Whoever pours it on a dry trunk, (will see) its branches rise and its leaves spring forth."

8. एतमुहैव वाजसनेयो याज्ञवल्क्यो मधुकाय पैङ्ग्यायान्तेवासिन उक्त्वोवाचापि य एनꣳ शुष्के स्थाणौ निषिञ्चेज्जायेरञ्छाखाः प्ररोहेयुः पलाशानीति ।

Yājñavalkya of the Vājasaṇeya school, having explained this (mixture) to his disciple, Madhuka Paiṅgya, said,—" Whoever pours it on a dry trunk, (will see) its branches rise and its leaves spring forth."

9. एतमुहैव मधुकः पैङ्ग्यश्चूलाय भागवित्तयेऽन्तेवासिन उक्त्वोवाचापि य एनꣳ शुष्के स्थाणौ निषिञ्चेज्जायेरञ्छाखाः प्ररोहेयुः पलाशानीति ।

Madhuka Paiṅgya having explained this (mixture) to his disciple, Cūla Bhāgavitti, said,—" Whoever pours it on a dry trunk, (will see) its branches rise and its leaves spring forth."

10. एतमुहैव चूलो भागवित्तिर्जानकय आयस्थूणायान्तेवासिन उक्त्वोवाचापि य एनꣳ शुष्के स्थाणौ निषिञ्चेज्जायेरञ्छाखाः प्ररोहेयुः पलाशानीति ।

Cūla Bhāgavitti, having taught this (mixture) to his disciple, Jānaki Āyasthūṇa, said,—" Whoever pours it on a dry trunk, (will see) its branches rise and its leaves spring forth."

11. एतमुहैव जानकिरायस्थूणः सत्यकामाय जाबालायान्तेवासिन उक्त्वोवाचापि य एनꣳ शुष्के स्थाणौ निषिञ्चेज्जायेरञ्छाखाः प्ररोहेयुः पलाशानीति ।

Jānaki Āyasthūṇa having explained this (mixture) to his disciple, Satyakāma Jābāla, said,—" Whoever pours it on a dry trunk, (will see) its branches rise and its leaves spring forth."

12. एतमु हैव सत्यकामो जाबालोऽन्तेवासिभ्य उक्त्वोवाचापि य एनꣳ शुष्के स्थाणौ निषिञ्चेज्जायेरञ्छाखाः प्ररोहेयुः पलाशानीति तमेतन्नापुत्राय वानन्तेवासिने वा ब्रूयात् ।

Satyakāma Jābāla having explained this (mixture) to his disciples, said,—" Whoever places it on a dry trunk, (will see) its branches rise, and its leaves spring forth. Let none teach it to one who is not a son, or a disciple."

13. चतुरौदुम्बरो भवत्यौदुम्बरः स्रुव औदुम्बरश्चमस औदुम्बर इध्म औदुम्बर्या उपमन्थन्यौ दश ग्राम्याणि धान्यनि भवन्ति व्रीहियवास्तिलमाषा अणुप्रियङ्गवो गोधूमाश्च मसूराश्च खल्वाश्च खलकुलाश्च तान् पिष्टान्दधनि मधुनि घृत उपषिञ्चत्याज्यस्य जुहोति ।

There should be four things made of the wood of the conglomerate fig-tree, the Sruva (1), the Camasa (2), the sacrificial wood, and the two churning vessels; there should be ten kinds of cultivated seeds, *viz.*, rice, barley, sesamum—seed, kidney beans, millet (3), panick seed, wheat, lentil, pulse and vetch. When they are ground down, and sprinkled with curdled milk, honey and ghee, he shall offer the clarified butter.

(1) A kind of ladle with which the ghee is taken when offered to the fire.

(2) Another kind of ladle, to be put in the water used for the sacrifice.

(3) Anu, a sort of corn of very small seed, which is called China in Bengali.

FOURTH BRĀHMAṆA

1. एषां वै भूतानां पृथिवी रसः पृथिव्या आपोऽपामोषधय ओषधीनां पुष्पाणि पुष्पाणां फलानि फलानां पुरुषः पुरुषस्य रेतः ।

Verily, of created things here earth is the essence; of earth, water; of water, plants; of plants, flowers; of flowers, fruits; of fruits, man (Puruṣa); of man, semen.

2. स ह प्रजापतिरीक्षांचक्रे हन्तास्मै प्रतिष्ठां कल्पयानीति स स्त्रियꣳ ससृजे ताꣳ सृष्ट्वाऽध उपास्त तस्मात्स्त्रियमध उपासीत स एतं प्राञ्चं ग्रावाणमात्मन एव समुदपारयत्तेनैनामभ्यसृजत् ।

Prajāpati ('Lord of creatures') bethought himself: 'Come, let me provide him a firm basis!' So he created woman. When he had created her, he revered her below.—Therefore one should revere woman below.—He stretched out for himself that stone which projects. With that he impregnated her.

3. तस्या वेदिरुपस्थो लोमानि बर्हिश्चर्माधिषवणे समिद्धो मध्यतस्तौ मुष्कौ स यावान् ह वै वाजपेयेन यजमानस्य लोको भवति तावानस्य लोको भवति य एवं विद्वानधोपहासं चरत्यासाꣳ स्त्रीणाꣳ सुकृतं वृङ्क्तेऽथ य इदमविद्वानधोपहासं चरत्यस्य स्त्रियः सुकृतं वृञ्जते ।

Her lap is a sacrificial altar; her hairs, the sacrificial grass; her skin, the soma-press. The two lips of the vulva are the fire in the middle. Verily, indeed, as great as is the world of him who sacrifices with the Vajapeya ('Strength-libation') sacrifice, so great is the world of him who practises sexual intercourse, knowing this; he turns the good deeds of women to himself. But he who practises sexual intercourse without knowing this—women turn his good deeds unto themselves.

4. एतद्ध स्म वै तद्विद्वानुद्दालक आरुणिराहैतद्ध स्म वै तद्विद्वान्नाको मौद्गल्य आहैतद्ध स्म वै तद्विद्वान्कुमारहारित आह बहवो मर्या ब्राह्मणायना निरिन्द्रिया विसुकृतोऽस्माल्लोकात्प्रयन्ति य इदमविद्वाꣳसोऽधोपहासंचरन्तीति बहु वा इदꣳ सुप्तस्य वा जाग्रतो वा रेतः स्कन्दति ।

5. तदभिमृशेदनु वा मन्त्रयेत यन्मेऽद्य रेतः पृथिवीमस्कान्त्सीद्यदोष धीरप्यसरद्यदप इदमहं तद्रेत आददे पुनर्मामैत्विन्द्रियं पुनस्तेजः

पुनर्भगः पुनरग्निर्धिष्ण्या यथास्थानं कल्पन्तामित्यनामिकाङ्गुष्ठाभ्यामादायान्तरेण स्तनौ वा भ्रुवौ वा निमृज्यात् ।

This, verily, indeed, it was that Uddalaka Āruṇi knew when he said:

This, verily, indeed, it was that Naka Maudgalya knew when he said:

This, verily, indeed, it was that Kumaraharita knew when he said: 'Many mortal men, Brahmans by descent, go forth from this world, impotent and devoid of merit, namely those who practise sexual intercourse without knowing this.'

(If) even this much semen is spilled, whether of one asleep or of one awake, 5. then he should touch it, or (without touching) repeat:

What semen has of mine to earth been spilt now,
Whate'er to herb has flowed, whate'er to water—

This very semen I reclaim!
Again to me let vigor come!
Again, my strength; again, my glow!
Again the altars and the fire
Be found in their accustomed place!

Having spoken thus, he should take it with ring-finger and thumb, and rub it on between his breasts or his eye brows.

6. अथ यद्युदक आत्मानं पश्येत्तदभिमन्त्रयेत मयि तेज इन्द्रियं यशो द्रविणꣳ सुकृतमिति श्रीर्ह वा एषां स्त्रीणां यन्मलोद्वासास्तस्मान्मलोद्वाससं यशस्विनीमभिक्रम्योपमन्त्रयेत ।

Now, if one should see himself in water, he should recite over it the formula: 'In me be vigor, power, beauty, wealth, merit!'

This, verily, indeed, is loveliness among women: when (a woman) has removed the (soiled) clothes of her impurity. Therefore when she has removed the (soiled) clothes of her impurity and is beautiful, one should approach and invite her.

7. सा चेदस्मै न दद्यात्काममेनामवक्रीणीयात् सा चेदस्मै नैव दद्यात्काममेनां यष्ट्या वा पाणिना वोपहत्यातिक्रामेदिन्द्रियेण ते यशसा यश आदद इत्ययशा एव भवति ।

If she should not grant him his desire, he should bribe her. If she still does not grant him his desire, he should hit her with a stick or with his hand, and overcome her, saying: 'With power, with glory I take away your glory!' Thus she becomes inglorious.

8. सा चेदस्मै दद्यादिन्द्रियेण ते यशसा यश आदधामीति यशस्विनावेव भवतः ।

If she should yield to him, he says: 'With power, with glory I give you glory!' Thus they two become glorious.

9. स यामिच्छेत्कामयेत मेति तस्यामर्थं निष्ठाय मुखेन मुखꣳ संधायोपस्थमस्या अभिमृश्य जपेदङ्गादङ्गात्संभवसि हृदयादधि जायसे । स त्वमङ्गकषायोऽसि दिग्धविद्धामिव मादयेमाममूं मयीति ।

The woman whom one may desire with the thought, 'May she enjoy love with me!'—after coming together with her, joining mouth with mouth, and stroking her lap, he should mutter :

> Thou that from every limb art come,
> That from the heart art generate,
> Thou art the essence of the limbs !
> Distract this woman here in me,
> As if by poisoned arrow pierced !

10. अथ यामिच्छेन्न गर्भं दधीतेति तस्यामर्थं निष्ठाय मुखेन मुखꣳ संधायाभिप्राण्यापान्यादिन्द्रियेण ते रेतसा रेत आदद इत्यरेता एव भवति ।

Now, the woman whom one may desire with the thought, 'May she not conceive offspring!'—after coming together with her and joining mouth with mouth, he should first inhale, then exhale, and say : 'With power, with semen, I reclaim the semen from you!' Thus she comes to be without seed.

11. अथ यामिच्छेद्दधीतेति तस्यामर्थं निष्ठाय मुखेन मुखꣳ संधायापान्याभिप्राण्यादिन्द्रियेण ते रेतसा रेत आदधामीति गर्भिण्येव भवति ।

Now, the woman whom one may desire with the thought, 'May she conceive!'—after coming together with her and joining mouth with mouth, he should first exhale, then inhale, and say : 'With power, with semen, I deposit semen in you!' Thus she becomes pregnant.

12. अथ यस्य जायायै जारः स्यात्तं चेद्द्विष्यादामपात्रेऽग्निमुपसमाधाय प्रतिलोमꣳ शरबर्हिस्तीर्त्वा तस्मिन्नेताः शरभृष्टीः प्रतिलोमाः सर्पिषाक्ता जुहुयान्मम समिद्धेऽहौषीः प्राणापानौ त आददेऽसाविति मम समिद्धेऽहौषीः पुत्रपशूꣳस्त आददेऽसाविति मम समिद्धेऽहौषीरिष्टासुकृते त आददेऽसाविति मम समिद्धेऽहौषीराशापराकाशौ त आददेऽसाविति स वा एष निरिन्द्रियो विसुकृतोऽस्माल्लोकात्प्रैति यमेवं विद्वान्ब्राह्मणः शपति तस्मादेवंविच्छ्रोत्रियस्य दारेण नोपहासमिच्छेदुत ह्येवंवित्परो भवति ।

Now, if one's wife have a paramour, and he hate him, let him put fire in an unannealed vessel, spread out a row of reed arrows in inverse order, and therein sacrifice in inverse order those reed arrows, their heads smeared with ghee, saying:

'You have made a libation in my fire! I take away your inbreath and out-breath (prāṇāpānau)—you, so-and-so!

You have made a libation in my fire! I take away your sons and cattle—you, so-and-so!

You have made a libation in my fire! I take away your sacrifices and meritorious deeds—you, so-and-so!

You have made a libation in my fire! I take away your hope and expectation—you, so-and-so!'

Verily, he whom a Brahman who knows this curses—he departs from this world impotent and devoid of merit. Therefore one should not desire sport with the spouse of a person learned in sacred lore (śrotriya) who knows this, for indeed he who knows this becomes superior.

13. अथ यस्य जायामार्तवं विन्देत्त्र्यहं कंसेन पिबेदहतवासा नैनां
वृषलो न वृषल्युपहन्यात्त्रिरात्रान्त आप्लुत्य व्रीहीनवघातयेत् ।

Now, when the monthly sickness comes upon any one's wife, for three days she should not drink from a metal cup, nor put on fresh clothes. Neither a low-caste man nor a low-caste woman should touch her. At the end of the three nights she should bathe and should have rice threshed.

14. स य इच्छेत्पुत्रो मे शुक्लो जायेत वेदमनुब्रुवीत सर्वमायुरियादिति
क्षीरौदनं पाचयित्वा सर्पिष्मन्तमश्नीयातामीश्वरौ जनयितवै ।

In case one wishes, 'That a white son be born to me! that he may be able to repeat a Veda! that he may attain the full length of life!'—they two should have rice cooked with milk and should eat it prepared with ghee. They two are likely to beget (him).

15. अथ य इच्छेत्पुत्रो मे कपिलः पिङ्गलो जायेत द्वौ वेदावनुब्रुवीत
सर्वमायुरियादिति दध्योदनं पाचयित्वा सर्पिष्मन्तमश्नीयातामी-
श्वरौ जनयितवै ।

Now, in case one wishes, 'That a tawny son with reddish-brown eyes be born to me! that he may be able to recite two Vedas! that he may attain the full length of life!'—they two should have rice cooked with sour milk and should eat it prepared with ghee. They two are likely to beget (him).

16. अथ य इच्छेत्पुत्रो मे श्यामो लोहिताक्षो जायेत त्रीन्वेदाननुब्रुवीत सर्वमायुरियादित्युदौदनं पाचयित्वा सर्पिष्मन्तमश्नीयातामीश्वरौ जनयितवै ।

Now, in case one wishes, 'That a swarthy son with red eyes be born to me! that he may be able to repeat three Vedas! that he may attain the full length of life!'—they two should have rice boiled with water and should eat it prepared with ghee. They two are likely to beget (him).

17. अथ य इच्छेद्दुहिता मे पण्डिता जायेत सर्वमायुरियादिति तिलौदनं पाचयित्वा सर्पिष्मन्तमश्नीयातामीश्वरौ जनयितवै ।

Now, in case one wishes, 'That a learned (*paṇḍitā*) daughter be born to me! that she may attain the full length of life!'—they two should have rice boiled with sesame and should eat it prepared with ghee. They two are likely to beget (her).

18, अथ य इच्छेत्पुत्रो मे पण्डितो विगीतः समितिंगमः शुश्रूषितां वाचं भाषिता जायेत सर्वान्वेदाननुब्रुवीत सर्वमायुरियादिति मांसौदनं पाचयित्वा सर्पिष्मन्तमश्नीयातामीश्वरौ जनयित वा औक्षेण वार्षभेण वा ।

Now, in case one wishes 'That a son, learned, famed, a frequenter of council-asemblies, a speaker of discourse desired to be heard, be born to me! that he be able to repeat all the Vedas! that he attain the full length of life!'—they two should have rice boiled with meat and should eat it prepared with ghee. They two are likely to beget (him), with meat, either veal or beef.

19. अथाभिप्रातरेव स्थालीपाकावृताज्यं चेष्टित्वा स्थालीपाकस्योपघातं जुहोत्यग्नये स्वाहानुमतये स्वाहा देवाय सवित्रे सत्यप्रसवाय स्वाहेति हुत्वोद्धृत्य प्राश्नाति प्राश्येतरस्याः प्रयच्छति प्रक्षाल्य पाणी उदपात्रं पूरयित्वा तेनैनां त्रिरभ्युक्षत्युत्तिष्ठातो विश्वावसोऽन्यामिच्छ प्रपूर्व्यां सं जायां पत्या सहेति ।

Now, toward morning, having prepared melted butter in the manner of the Sthālīpāka,[1] he takes of the Sthālīpāka and makes a libation, saying: "To Agni, hail! To Anumati, hail! To the god Sāvitri ('Enlivener!' the sun), whose is true procreation (*satya-prasava*), hail!" Having made the libation, he takes and eats. Having eaten, he offers to the other (*i.e.*, to her). Having washed his hands, he fills a vessel with water and therewith sprinkles her thrice, saying:

Arise from hence, Viśvāvasu!
Some other choicer maiden seek!
This wife together with her lord—

20. अथैनामभिपद्यतेऽमोऽहमस्मि सा त्वꣳ सा त्वमस्यमोऽहं सामाहमस्मि ऋक्त्वं द्यौरहं पृथिवी त्वं तावेहि सꣳरभावहै सह रेतो दधावहै पुꣳसे पुत्राय वित्तय इति ।

Then he comes to her and says:

This man (*ama*) am I; that woman (*sā*), thou!
That woman, thou; this man am I!

[1] 'Pot-of-cooked-food.'

I am the Sāman ; thou, the Ṛg !
I am the heaven ; thou, the earth !

Come, let us two together clasp !
Together let us semen mix,
A male, a son for to procure !

21. अथास्य ऊरू विहापयति विजिहीथां द्यावापृथिवी इति तस्यामर्थं
निष्ठाय मुखेन मुखꣳ संधाय त्रिरेनामनुलोमामनुमार्ष्टि ।
विष्णुर्योनिं कल्पयतु त्वष्टा रूपाणि पिꣳशतु । आसिञ्चतु
प्रजापतिर्धाता गर्भं दधातु ते । गर्भं धेहि सिनीवालि गर्भं धेहि
पृथुष्टुके । गर्भं ते अश्विनौ देवावाधत्तां पुष्करस्रजौ ।

Then he spreads apart her thighs, saying : 'Spread yourselves apart, heaven and earth !' Coming together with her and joining mouth with mouth, he strokes her three times as the hair lies, saying :

Let Viṣṇu make the womb prepared !
Let Tvaṣṭṛ shape the various forms !
Prajāpati—let him pour in !
Let Dhātṛ place the germ for thee !

O Sinīvāli, give the germ ;
O give the germ, thou broad-tressed dame !
Let the Twin Gods implace thy germ—
The Aśvins, crowned with lotus-wreaths !

22. हिरण्मयी अरणी याभ्यां निर्मन्थतामश्विनौ । तं ते गर्भं हवामहे
दशमे मासि सूतवे । यथाऽग्निगर्भा पृथिवी यथा द्यौरिन्द्रेण
गर्भिणी । वायुर्दिशां यथा गर्भ एवं गर्भं दधामि तेऽसाविति ।

With twain attrition-sticks of gold,
The Aśvin Twins twirl forth a flame ;
'Tis such a germ we beg for thee,
In the tenth month to be brought forth.

As earth contains the germ of Fire (*agni*),
As heaven is pregnant with the Storm (*indra*),
As of the points the Wind (*vayu*) is germ,
E'en so a germ I place in thee,
So-and-so!

23. सोष्यन्तीमद्भिरभ्युक्षति यथा वायुः पुष्करिणीꣳसमिङ्गयति सर्वतः ।
एवा ते गर्भ एजतु सहावैतु जरायुणा । इन्द्रस्यायं व्रजः कृतः
सार्गलः सपरिश्रयः । तमिन्द्र निर्जहि गर्भेण सावराꣳसहेति ।

When she is about to bring forth, he sprinkles her with water, saying:

Like as the wind doth agitate
A lotus pond on every side,
So also let thy fetus stir.
Let it come with its chorion.

This fold of Indra's has been made
With barricade, enclosed around.
O Indra, cause him to come forth—
The after-birth along with babe!

24. जातेऽग्निमुपसमाधायाङ्क आधाय कꣳसे पृषदाज्यꣳ संनीय
पृषदाज्यस्योपघातं जुहोत्यस्मिन्सहस्रं पुष्यासमेधमानः स्वे
गृहे । अस्योपसंद्यां मा च्छैत्सीत् प्रजया च पशुभिश्च स्वाहा ।
मयि प्राणाꣳस्त्वयि मनसा जुहोमि स्वाहा । यत्कर्मणात्यरीरिचं
यद्वा न्यूनमिहाकरम् । अग्निष्टत्स्विष्टकृद्विद्वान्स्विष्टꣳ सुहुतं करोतु
नः स्वाहेति ।

(When the child is born) let him light a fire, and placing it on his lap, and taking curdled milk mixed with clarified butter in a goblet, he offers repeatedly of the curdled milk and clarified butter, (saying),—" May

I, magnified (by this son) in this house, support a thousand (men). When he has obtained offspring, let there be no loss of, prosperities in offspring and in cattle. Svāhā! I offer with my mind to thee my vital airs. Svāhā! May the wise Agni who fulfils all desires right for us any work which ought not to have been done, or any work which ought to have been done in this rite."

25. अथास्य दक्षिणं कर्णमभिनिधाय वाग्वागिति त्रिरथ दधिमधुघृतꣳ संनीयानन्तर्हितेन जातरूपेण प्राशयति भूस्ते दधामि भुवस्ते दधामि स्वस्ते दधामि भूर्भुवः स्वः सर्वं त्वयि दधामीति ।

Then, putting (his mouth) near the child's rignt ear, he mutters three times, "Speech, speech!" Then, taking curdled milk, honey and clarified butter together with unmixed gold, he feeds it (saying),—"I give thee the earth, I give thee the atmosphere, I give thee the heavens. I give thee all, earth, atmosphere and heavens."

26. अथास्य नाम करोति वेदोऽसीति तदस्य तद्गुह्यमेव नाम भवति ।

Then he gives him the name "Veda," which is his secret name.

27. अथैनं मात्रे प्रदाय स्तनं प्रयच्छति यस्ते स्तनः शशयो यो मयोभूर्येन विश्वा पुष्यसि वार्याणि यो रत्नधा वसुविद्यः सुदत्रः सरस्वति तमिह धातवेऽकरिति ।

Then giving him to his mother, he makes him take the breast (saying),—"O Sarasvati, enter for the suckling (of the child) into this (breast of the mother) thy breast, which is fruitful, the support (of all creatures), the giver of jewels, the knower of wealth, and the liberal donor, by which thou causeth to grow all that is desirable."

28. अथास्य मातरमभिमन्त्रयते इलासि मैत्रावरुणी वीरे वीरमजीजनत् ।
सा त्वं वीरवती भव यास्मान् वीरवतोऽकरदिति तं वा
एतमाहुरतिपिता बताभूरतिपितामहो बताभूः परमां बत काष्ठां
प्रापच्छ्रिया यशसा ब्रह्मवर्चसेन य एवंविदो ब्राह्मणस्य पुत्रो
जायत इति ।

Then he addresses the child's mother with this Mantra,—" Thou art worthy of praise, thou art like Maittrāvaruṇī. Thou, who hast born to the strong a strong (son), be strong, thou who giveth us a strong (son)." Of him people may say,—" Thou indeed excellest thy father, thou indeed excellest thy grand-father." The son born to a Brāhmaṇa who has this knowledge, obtains the highest goal by prosperity, fame and the glory of a Brāhmaṇa.

FIFTH BRĀHMAṆA

1. अथ वंशः पौतिमाषीपुत्रः कात्यायनीपुत्रात्कात्यायनीपुत्रो
गौतमीपुत्राद्गौतमीपुत्रो भारद्वाजीपुत्राद्भारद्वाजीपुत्रः पाराशरी-
पुत्रात्पाराशरीपुत्र औपस्वस्तीपुत्रादौपस्वस्तीपुत्रः पाराशरी-
पुत्रात्पाराशरीपुत्रः कात्यायनीपुत्रात्कात्यायनीपुत्रः कौशिकी-

पुत्रात्कौशिकीपुत्र आलम्बीपुत्राच्च वैयाघ्रपदीपुत्राच्च वैयाघ्रपदीपुत्रः काण्वीपुत्राच्च कापीपुत्राच्च कापीपुत्रः ।

Now the school. The son of Pautimāṣī succeeded the son of Kātyāyanī,—the son of Kātyāyanī the son of Gautamī,—the son of Gautamī the son of Bhāradvājī,—the son of Bhāradvājī the son of Pārās'arī,—the son of Pārās'arī the son of Aupasvastī,—the son of Aupasvastī the son of Pārās'arī,—the son of Pārās'arī the son of Kātyāyanī,—the son of Kātyāyanī the son of Kaus'ikī,—the son of Kaus'ikī the son of Ālambī and the son of Vaiyāghrapadī,—the son of Vaiyāghrapadī the son of Kāṇvī and the son of Kāpī—the son of Kāpī,

2. आत्रेयीपुत्रादात्रेयीपुत्रो गौतमीपुत्राद्गौतमीपुत्रो भारद्वाजीपुत्राद्भारद्वाजीपुत्रः पाराशरीपुत्रात्पाराशरीपुत्रो वात्सीपुत्राद्वात्सीपुत्रः पाराशरीपुत्रात्पाराशरीपुत्रो वार्कारुणीपुत्राद्वार्कारुणीपुत्रो वार्कारुणीपुत्राद्वार्कार्णीपुत्र आर्तभागीपुत्रादार्तभागीपुत्रः शौङ्गीपुत्राच्छौङ्गीपुत्रः सांकृतीपुत्रात्सांकृतीपुत्र आलम्बायनीपुत्रादालम्बायनीपुत्र आलम्बीपुत्रादालम्बीपुत्रो जायन्तीपुत्राज्जायन्तीपुत्रो माण्डूकायनीपुत्रान्माण्डूकायनीपुत्रो माण्डूकीपुत्रान्माण्डूकीपुत्रः शाण्डिलीपुत्राच्छाण्डिलीपुत्रो राथीतरीपुत्रा-द्राथीतरीपुत्रो भालुकीपुंत्राद्भालुकीपुत्रः क्रौञ्चिकीपुत्राभ्यां क्रौञ्चिकीपुत्रौ वैदभृतीपुत्राद्वैदभृतीपुत्रः कार्शकेयीपुत्रात्कार्शकेयी पुत्रः प्राचीनयोगीपुत्रात्प्राचीनयोगीपुत्रः सांजीवीपुत्रात्सांजीवीपुत्रः प्राश्नीपुत्रादासुरिवासिनः प्राश्नीपत्र आसुरायणादासुरायण आसुरेरासुरिः ।

The son of Ātreyī,—the son of Ātreyī the son of Gautamī,—the son of Gautamī the son of Bhāradvājī,—

the son of Bhāradvājī the son of Pārās'arī—the son of Pārās'arī the son of Vātsī,—the son of Vātsī, the son of Pārās'arī,—the son of Pārās'arī the son of Vārkāruṇī—the son of Vārkāruṇī the son of Vārkāruṇī—the son of Vārkāruṇī the son of Ārtabhāgi,—the son of Artabhāgī the son of S'aungi,—the son of S'aungī the son of Sānkṛtī,—the son of Sānkṛtī the son of Ālambāyanī,—the son of Ālambāyanī the son of Ālambī,—the son of Ālambī the son of Jāyantī,—the son of Jāyantī the son of Māṇḍūkāyanī,—the son of Māṇḍūkāyanī the son of Māṇḍūkī,—the son of Māṇḍūkī the son of S'āṇḍilī,—the son of Sāṇḍilī the son of Rāthītarī,—the son of Rāthītarī the son of Bhālukī,—the son of Bhālukī the two sons of Krauncikī,—the two sons of Krauncikī the son of Vaidabhṛtī,—the son of Vaidabhṛtī the son of Kārs'akeyī,—the son of Kārs'akeyī the son of Prācinayogī,—the son of Prācinayogī the son of Sāñjīvī,—the son of Sāñjīvī the son of Prās'nī,—the son of Prās'nī Āsurayaṇa,—Āsurāyaṇa Āsuri,—Āsuri,

3. याज्ञवल्क्याद्याज्ञवल्क्य उद्दालकादुद्दालकोऽरुणादरुण उपवेशेरुपवेशिः कुश्रेः कुश्रिर्वाजश्रवसो वाजश्रवा जिह्वावतो बाध्योगाज्जिह्वावान्बाध्योगोऽसिताद्वार्षगणादसितो वार्षगणो हरितात्कश्यपाद्धरितः कश्यपः शिल्पात्कश्यपाच्छिल्पः कश्यपः कश्यपान्नैध्रुवेः कश्यपो नैध्रुविर्वाचो वागम्भिण्या आम्भिण्यादित्यादित्यानीमानि शुक्लानि यजूꣳषि वाजसनेयेन याज्ञवल्क्येनाख्यायन्ते ।

Yājñavalkya,—Yājñavalkya Uddālaka,—Uddālaka Aruṇa,—Aruṇa Upaves'i,—Upaves'i Kus'ri,—Kus'ri

Vājas'ravas,—Vājas'ravas Jihvāvān Bādhyoga Jihvāvān Bādhyoga Asita Vārṣagaṇa,—Asita Vārṣagaṇa Harita Kas'yapa,—Harita Kas'yapa S'ilpa Kas'yapa,—S'ilpa Kas'yapa Kas'yapa-Naidhruvi,—Kas'yapa Naidhruvi, Vāk—Vāk Ambhiṇī,—Ambhiṇī Āditya. These Mantras of the white Yajur, which are derived from Āditya, have been declared by Yājñavalkya of the Vājasaneya school.

4. समानमा सांजीवीपुत्रात्सांजीवीपुत्रो माण्डूकायनेर्माण्डूकायनिर्माण्डव्यान्माण्डव्यः कौत्सात्कौत्सो माहित्थेर्माहित्थिर्वामकक्षायणाद्वामकक्षायणः शाण्डिल्याच्छाण्डिल्यो वात्साद्वात्स्यः कुश्रेः कुश्रिर्यज्ञवचसो राजस्तम्बायनाद्यज्ञवचा राजस्तम्बायनस्तुरात्कावषेयात्तुरः कावषेयः प्रजापतेः प्रजापतिर्ब्रह्मणो ब्रह्म स्वयंभुब्रह्मणे नमः ।

From (Prajāpati until the son of S'āñjīvī is the same (succession to teachers) (1). The son of S'āñjīvī succeeded Māṇḍūkāyani,—Māṇḍūkāyani Māṇḍavya,—Māṇḍavya Kautsa,—Kautsa Māhitthi,—Māhitthi Vāmakakṣāyaṇa,—Vāmakakṣāyaṇa S'āṇḍilya,—S'āṇḍilya Vātsya—Vātsya Kus'ri,—Kus'ri Yajñavacas Rājastambāyana,—Yajñavacas Rājastambāyana Tura Kāvaṣeya,—Tura Kāvaṣeya Prajāpati,—Prajāpati Brahman. Brahman is the self-existent. Salutation to Brahman !

(1) In all the Vājasaneyi schools.